THE LANGUAGE ARTS

in the elementary school

RUTH G.
STRICKLAND

THE LANGUAGE ARTS

in the elementary school

Third Edition

D. C. HEATH AND COMPANY
A Division of Raytheon Education Company
Lexington, Massachusetts

Chalk art by Gisela Héau

The photographs on pages 29, 95, 114, 178, 247, 379, and 437 are by Odyssey Studios. Those on pages 91, 121, 160, and 275 are by Anna Kaufman. The photograph on page 449 is by Patricia Hollander Gross.

Printed in the United States of America

Library of Congress Catalog Card No: 69-19924

ACKNOWLEDGMENTS

Grateful acknowledgment is made to the following publishers and authors for permission to reprint copyright material:

The Bobbs-Merrill Company, Inc., for excerpts from *They All Want to Write,* by June Ferebee, Doris Jackson, Dorothy Saunders, and Alvina Treut.

Harcourt, Brace & World, Inc., for an excerpt from the preface to *Complete Poems,* by Carl Sandburg.

Initial Teaching Alphabet (i/t/a) Publications, Inc., for a chart of the Initial Teaching Alphabet and a selection from a reader in the Early-to-Read series. Reproduced with the permission of Initial Teaching Alphabet Publications, Inc., 20 East 46th Street, New York City, N.Y.

The Macmillan Company, for a portion of a table from Henry D. Rinsland, *A Basic Vocabulary of Elementary School Children,* copyright 1945 by The University of Oklahoma and used with The Macmillan Company's permission.

The National Society for the Study of Education, for excerpts from "Growth in Language Power as Related to Child Development," by Dora V. Smith, in *Teaching Language in the Elementary School,* the Forty-third Yearbook, Part II, of The National Society for the Study of Education. Quoted by permission of the Society.

The New Republic, for excerpts from "The Primary School Revolution in England," in *The New Republic,* the issue of August 10, 1967. Reprinted by Permission of The New Republic, © Harrison-Blaine of New Jersey, Inc.

Fannie J. Ragland and the National Council of Teachers of English, for the list of working goals for the growth of children as individuals and for the list of goals suggested for teachers, from "Helping Children to Write," by Fannie J. Ragland, in Ragland, Fannie J. (Comp.), *Children Learn to Write.* Pamphlet Publication No. 7. Chicago: National Council of Teachers of English, 1944.

The University of Iowa, for the table on increase in size of vocabulary in relation to age, from *An Investigation of the Development of the Sentence and the Extent of Vocabulary in Young Children,* by Madorah E. Smith.

To the Memory of My Father,
from whom I gained my first interest in language

PREFACE

English teaching from kindergarten through college has been brought to the attention of the American public during the last few years as never before. Four scholarly organizations cooperated in 1959 to produce the report, *Basic Issues in the Teaching of English.* In 1961 the National Council of Teachers of English and the Modern Language Association brought out *The National Interest and the Teaching of English,* a report which was put into the hands of all members of the Congress and of educational leaders throughout the country. Both reports called public attention to some of the problems the schools face in the teaching of English. The United States Office of Education has set aside a portion of the research funds appropriated by the Congress to be used for Project English to encourage individual research projects and the establishment of curriculum centers in universities and colleges to help the schools improve the teaching of English. The 88th Congress expanded the National Defense Education Act to include English and reading along with the mathematics, science, and foreign languages provided for in the original act. This evidence of national concern for the teaching of the English language arts should challenge all schools to reevaluate their programs and search for ways to improve them.

Any quest for ways to improve the work of our schools turns sooner or later to the field of English. It is not only a subject with content of its own but the medium through which all teaching takes place. Consequently, to improve the teaching of English in our schools, particularly in our elementary schools where the basic skills are learned, is to make possible higher academic attainment at all educational levels. Elementary teachers are eager for all the help they can obtain to enable them to develop in children the basic attitudes, knowledge, and skills on which they can build a lifetime of learning.

The first edition of this book was in a very real sense a pioneer—one of the first books to treat the language arts as an interrelated whole. Since that book was published, a great deal has been written about the language arts and about each of the separate components. Significant research has been accomplished and more is in progress. Scholars in the fields of linguistics, psychology, and English are eager to join with teachers and leaders in elementary education to find ways to improve all aspects of English teaching. They are convinced that the more teachers know about language in general, and the English language in particular, the better they will teach. Teachers have long known that the more they know about the development of children and the way children learn, the better they can teach.

This third edition of *The Language Arts in the Elementary School* has been expanded to include additional help for teachers on both points. New material has been added on the English language itself, and linguists have been drawn upon for guidance to improve the teaching of reading, spelling and grammar. New emphases and experimental programs have been given attention in several chapters. The space given to reading has been doubled to recognize new approaches being proposed and tested for the teaching of beginning reading. A chapter has been added on foreign language in the elementary school and also one on evaluation.

It was difficult to decide what to do about Chapters II and III on general aspects of language growth and learning. While in some schools prospective teachers learn much of what is in these chapters in their courses in child psychology and child development, it was found that in other schools teachers rely on these chapters for general background for their students, so the chapters have been retained.

Many professional friends and co-workers, as well as great numbers of children, have left their imprint on the thinking that shaped this book. To all of them the author is grateful.

Special recognition must be given to my colleague Dr. James D. Walden who helped with the chapters on reading and added new materials to the chapters on writing. To him the author is especially grateful.

R. G. S.

TABLE of CONTENTS

□ I — AN INTRODUCTION TO THE ENGLISH LANGUAGE 1

Language as a System of Symbols
English Today
The Language and How It Came To Be
American English
English in Our Schools
What Children Can Learn About Language
The Language Arts in the Elementary School

□ 2 — SOME ASPECTS OF LANGUAGE AND MENTAL DEVELOPMENT 17

The Functions of Language and Speech
The Language of Gesture and Facial Expression
Communication Through Behavior, Attitudes, and Feeling
Language and Experience
Language and Thinking
From the Concrete to the Abstract in Language
Self-centered Outlook on all Experience
Awareness of others and Interaction
Dispute an Early Form of Socialized Speech
Conversation and Communication
Some Social Aspects of Language
Orientation in the World of Things
Developing Concepts of Space and Time
Cause and Effect Thinking
Language in Human Relationships
The Development of Appreciations, Attitudes, and Ideals
The Place and Function of Language in the Elementary School

☐ 3—FACTORS THAT INFLUENCE LANGUAGE GROWTH 47

The Child's Equipment for Language Learning
Home and Family Influences
Language of Twins, Singletons with Siblings, and only Children
Sex Differences in Language Development
The Relation of Socioeconomic Status
Home Atmosphere
Bilingualism
Language and Personality Development
School Influences on Language Development
Community Influences on Language Development
Mass Media

☐ 4—LANGUAGE DEVELOPMENT IN THE PRESCHOOL YEARS 71

A Child's First Use of His Vocal Apparatus
Early Forms of Communications
The Babbling Period
Association, Conditioning, and Motivation
The First Words
The Vocabulary of the Preschool Child
Talkativeness as an Index of Growth
Length and Structure of Remarks as a Measure of Growth
Experience and Language
Social Development
Handicaps to Normal Speech Development
Speech and Personality Development

☐ 5—LANGUAGE DEVELOPMENT IN THE NURSERY SCHOOL AND KINDERGARTEN 103

Guidance Through Language
Stimulation of Language Growth
Learning From the Teacher's Example
The Two-Year-Old in Nursery School
The Three-Year-Old
The Four-Year-Old in School
The Five-Year-Old in Kindergarten

Learning Through Experience with Things
Learning Through Experience with Children
Language Opportunities in the Nursery School
Language in the Kindergarten
Caring for Individual Differences
Head Start Programs

□ 6—LEARNING TO LISTEN 127

Kinds and Stages of Listening
Listenability
Preschool Experiences in Listening
Listening Problems of the Primary School Child
Helping Children Grow in Ability to Listen
Improving Listening at the Intermediate Grade Level
Evaluating Children's Listening
Television and Children

□ 7—SPEAKING AND LISTENING IN THE PRIMARY SCHOOL 143

Freeing the Child to Talk
Following Up the Head Start Program
Listening, Speaking, Reading, and Writing
The Goal of Easy Use of Language
Language at Work in Free and Disciplined Situations
The Goal of Clear, Intelligible Language
The Goal of Language that Suits Occasion and Need
The Goal of Originality in the Use of Language

□ 8—SPOKEN LANGUAGE IN THE INTERMEDIATE SCHOOL 167

The Need for Oral Language in the Intermediate Grades
Communication Through Spoken Language
Listening is Important
Keen Interest in Communications
Slang and Other Unauthorized Language
Characteristic Language Abilities and Interests

A Suitable Environment for Language Growth
Language in the Period Before School Begins
Interrelated Work in Social Studies and Language
Utilizing Opportunities to Teach About Language
Social Studies and Language Skills
Language Values in the Science Program
Mathematical Thinking
Language an All-Day Program
Essential Skills for Speaking and Listening
Oral Language Comes First

□ 9—INDIVIDUAL DIFFERENCES IN LANGUAGE NEEDS 203

Speech Improvement for all Children
The Speech of the Teacher
Children Whose Language Development Will Deviate
The Linguistically Gifted Child
The Child Who is a Slow Starter
The Handicap of Poor Environment and Experience
Our Latest Concern—The Culturally Deprived
Our Migrant Children
The Mentally Retarded Child
The Child with Defective Speech
Other Physical Handicaps and their Effect Upon Language Development
The Problem of a Foreign Language

□ 10—VOCABULARY 229

Various Types of Vocabularies
Studies of Size of Vocabulary at Different Ages
Studies of the Vocabulary of Preschool Children
Studies of the Vocabulary of School Children
Word Lists Useful to Elementary Teachers
Semantics
A Language Grows and Changes
The Development of Vocabulary in Children

□ 11—TEACHING CHILDREN TO READ 255

When Shall Reading be Taught?
The Background for Success in Learning to Read

Children Who Read Early
Shall the Kindergarten Teach Reading?
How to Teach Beginning Reading: An Unending Debate
Basal Reading Programs
Phonics—When and How Much?
A Linguistic Approach
The Alphabet Problem and ITA
Language Experience Approach to Reading
Developing Word Recognition Skills
Oral Reading in the Primary Grades
Grouping and Care for Individual Differences
Learning to Read by Reading
Lack of Conclusive Research
An Eclectic Method
Follow-up Programs and Help for the Culturally Disadvantaged
Reading in English Primary Schools

□ 12—MAKING READERS OF CHILDREN 281

The Transition Period in Learning to Read
Sharpening the Reading Tool
Individualized Reading
Books of all Sorts
The Need for Wide Reading
Later Stages of Reading
Utilizing Resources for Learning
Guidance Through Reading
Primary Grade Methods and Intermediate Grade Achievement
Diagnosis of Special Reading Problems

□ 13—LEARNING TO WRITE 299

First Experiences with Written Language
Steps in Growth in Written Language
Dictation: The Teacher Serving as Scribe
Dictation with Copying
Writing with All the Help He Needs
The Beginning of Independent Writing
Creative Expression Through Language
The Climate for Creative Expression

Motivation for Imaginative Writing
Forms of Creative Expression
Examples of Experiences that Stimulate Expression
Some Typical Primary Grade Stories
Goals for Written Expression in the Primary School

☐ 14—WRITING IN THE INTERMEDIATE GRADES 325

Situations Calling for Writing
Range in Ability in the Intermediate Grades
Setting Standards that Are Realistic
The Writing of Letters
Other Forms of Practical Writing
Teaching and Evaluation
Evaluation
Creative Writing
Poetic Expression
Interest, Experience, and Growth
Evaluation
Goals for Written Expression in the Intermediate School

☐ 15—GRAMMAR AND USAGE 357

Grammar Versus Usage
Helping Children Improve Usage
Grammar—What Do We Mean?
A New Approach to Grammar: Why?
An Application of Generative Grammar
Utilizing an Inherent Interest of Children
Learning to Expand Sentences
The Terminology of Grammar
Transforming Sentences
Summarizing a Point of View
American English Dialects
Handwriting
Punctuation
Choice of Words

□ 16—SPELLING 387

English Spelling
Patterns in English Spelling
Two Important Objectives for Teachers
Preparation for Spelling
Spelling in the School Program
A Basic Spelling Vocabulary
Methods of Teaching Spelling
Utilizing Symbols-Sound Correspondences
A New Development
Using the Dictionary
Evaluation in Spelling

□ 17—STORIES, POETRY, AND BOOKS 419

Storytelling
Reading Aloud
The Nebraska Literature Project
Enjoying Poetry
Choral Reading
Books and More Books
Libraries for Children
Individualized Reading
The Ever-Present Comics

□ 18—DRAMATIC INTERPRETATION 447

Dramatic Play of School Age Children
Dramatization in the Primary School
Playmaking for Older Children
Meeting the Needs of Individuals
Practice in Democratic Procedures
Understanding Human Behavior and Motivation
Puppets and Marionettes
Pantomine and Shadow Plays
The Children's Theater
The Child as Doer, Not Absorber

□ 19—FOREIGN LANGUAGES IN THE ELEMENTARY SCHOOL 465

Foreign Language in the Elementary School
Variations in Plans and Curriculum

Enthusiasm Tempered with Caution
Choice of Language
Teaching English to Speakers of Other Languages
Generally Accepted Principles of Language Learning

☐ 20—EVALUATION, INTERPRETATION, AND A FINAL WORD 475

The Responsibility of the Elementary School
Desirable Outcomes of a Language Arts Program
Evaluating Individual Growth
Language and Intelligent Behavior
Evaluating the Language Arts Program
Interpreting the School's Efforts to Parents

Index 493

THE LANGUAGE ARTS

in the elementary school

AN INTRODUCTION TO THE ENGLISH LANGUAGE

Language increases in significance in the world today as enlightened people strive to find ways to solve the problems of human relationships through speech and the marks that represent speech rather than through missiles made of metals and chemicals. It is impossible to know when communication through language became important in the lives of human beings but from the beginning of recorded history it has played an important part in the lives of groups and of nations. The closer the relationships of people become, the more significant is the matter of language. The people of the world are alike in their basic human needs regardless of where they live or how they manage their affairs, but the languages in which they communicate those needs are numerous and they divide people as truly as did the Biblical Tower of Babel.

Language is a concern of governments as well as people. It is a serious problem of many of the newly emerging nations. India is striving to weld into a nation people who speak well over eight hundred different languages and dialects. The Philippines have three major languages among the more than sixty used in the islands, and the tribes which make up the still newer nations of Africa each speak a separate language. The problems created by this diversity are incredible to people in the United States because everyone who has come here since the earliest migrations has accepted the fact that English is the language of the country and has learned it as rapidly as possible in order to become a part of the life of his adopted home. But their mother language is dear to people, and when they remain in the old environment and try to merge their interests to form a new nation, they tend to cling tenaciously to their own language and the history and culture it represents.

The lives of people in the United States are more and more closely tied up with the lives and destinies of people all around the globe. There are few places in the world where there are not Americans who have come under the auspices of government, business and industry, or religious, social welfare or other American or world organizations. The Peace Corps is a recent example. Many boys and girls now in our elementary and secondary schools will, in the course of their lifetimes, be called on to go to parts of the world where people speak languages not taught in our schools. The success with which they meet their responsibilities and utilize their opportunities will depend in large measure on the speed and ease with which they acquire the language of the people among whom they must live and work.

Americans are by no means the only people visiting foreign countries for purposes of business or pleasure. Delegates from many nations attend conferences in various places to work on international problems. Governments send farmers, industrialists, scientists, and people representing the arts abroad to make contributions to other countries and to learn from them. Thousands of students are studying in foreign universities all around the world. A single class conducted by the author in a midwestern university included students from Nigeria, Liberia, Sierra Leone, Egypt and Ethiopia in Africa; Brazil and British Guiana in South America; Irak, Thailand and Pakistan in Asia; and from the Philippine Islands, Mexico, and Puerto Rico. As people learn new languages and interact with the people who commonly use them, they learn something of the culture—the ways of thinking and the value systems—represented by those languages.

□ LANGUAGE AS A SYSTEM OF SYMBOLS

Through the ages, man has developed a vast and intricate system of symbols in order to communicate with his fellows and to preserve his experience and his codes of values to make them available to succeeding generations. Language is the basic element in the system but included also are traffic signs, uniforms, badges and insignia, religious emblems and the like. Materialistic status symbols have always existed; currently they cover the range from food, clothing and housing to beatnik attire, rugs on the office floor, foreign automobiles and private swimming pools. Symbols and their meaning change from time to time; few of them are stationary. Yet it is this mass of shifting symbols that a child must learn to understand and apply if he is to interact with his world of people, ideas and things.

Learning a language, whether it is the mother language or a foreign one, is learning a system of sounds and their arrangements in words and patterns of organization together with the concepts the words and patterns represent. Becoming literate in the language calls for mastery of the graphic symbols and orthography that stand for the sounds and patterns of the language and therefore for the meanings these symbolize.

Means of verbal communication have moved a long way since the days when man could communicate with man only when each saw the other's face and heard the sound of his voice. But communication through television and other sound pictures, radio, telephone, and intercommunication systems of all sorts is still basically speaking and listening. What man communicates and the patterns of sound he uses have changed enormously through the centuries as man has amassed knowledge in countless fields and coined new words in which to express his new meanings.

Communication through visual signs and symbols developed later than speaking and listening but it has changed in equally spectacular manner. From blazed trails, smoke signals, signal drums, and picture writing, man has progressed to written language which appears in teletype and in millions of leaflets, bulletins, newspapers, magazines, and books which flow from the presses of many countries each year, as well as in innumerable neon and other types of signs.

Modern libraries have become so overcrowded with the material which needs to be stored for historical purposes and current material which is needed for circulation and reference that they are experimenting with a variety of mechanical devices for recording bulky material in small space. Microfilm and microfiche are being used in major libraries to meet this problem and other devices are in the making. Certainly they will be needed as the mass of recorded material in many languages grows.

Listening and speaking, reading and writing are the means of communicating through language, though the sounds and symbol patterns used differ from language to language. All languages have interesting histories and language history is being made daily, the world over. A language grows and changes as the needs, the experiences, and the thinking of its users change.

A language, then, is a body of sounds and meanings held in common by the members of a linguistic group. The French understand their sounds and symbols and the Japanese theirs. It is a social matter and each individual accepts it as he finds it. The major portion of a language becomes fixed and can be recorded in dictionaries and grammars. "Everybody in a speech community accepts the common words as completely as he accepts earth and sky." When there is no word for a new object, event, or idea, one is invented or borrowed. Slang and other innovations creep in, and if they are useful they stay. "But for the great body of the mother tongue," says Stuart Chase, "we agree to keep it as we learned it lest we suffer the fate of Babel. Of all the unconscious agreements which hold a society together, this is the strongest" (4, p. 99). Every language has a growing edge but the bulk of it remains constant.

☐ ENGLISH TODAY

Through the centuries, some languages expand and flourish and others die, depending in large measure on the economic and social significance of the users of the language. Latin, which was forced on the leaders of much of Europe by the Roman conquests, died as a spoken language when the Romans withdrew and their empire disintegrated, though much of the influence of Latin and a great deal of its vocabulary remained. French gained the ascendancy among the world's languages in the 18th and 19th centuries. But today, English is the leading language of the entire world. To be sure, Chinese in its various dialects is spoken by a larger number of people but its influence and geographic spread is far less than that of English.

This English language is "frustrating, wonderful, irrational, logical, simple and now the universal tongue." [1] So says the introduction to an article in LIFE Magazine about this amazing and often little-appreciated language of ours.

Within this century, English has become the most widely spoken of any language on earth. It comes closer to being a world language than has any language in the history of man. It is the primary language of well over 250 million people—approximately one in ten—and is used in some measure by fully 600 million—one in four of the people of the world. It is spoken, written, broadcast and understood by at least some people on every continent (1, p. 76).

Look at the map of the world and locate the English-speaking countries. The British Isles, Canada, Australia, and the United States are the main ones, of course. In India, Pakistan, and the Philippines, where there are many languages, English is the language of government. In parts of Africa which were for many years under British rule, the same is true. In some of these countries with their competing regional languages,

[1] Lincoln Barnett. "The English Language," LIFE Magazine, pp. 78-83, March 2, 1962.

English is the only language known in common by all the educated people, and it can be used impartially because it avoids favoritism toward any one of the local languages. Because of the vast resources of scientific and technical knowledge as well as literature available in English, the language is for many people what Nehru said it is for India, "the major window for us to the outside world." English is a window to the world for people in parts of Europe as well as in Asia and Africa.

It is interesting to note some of the areas in which English reigns supreme. It is the language of pilots and control tower operators on all the airways of the world. It is accepted everywhere as the language of sports and of jazz. It is widely used in Japan, Korea, and other countries whose economy and security are tied up with the English-speaking peoples of the world. The trade names of American and British commercial products have found their way into many countries, though the pronunciation of the names varies with the sound structure of the language they invade.

□ THE LANGUAGE AND HOW IT CAME TO BE

The English language was made in Britain, though the raw materials out of which it was fashioned were imported from the continent of Europe. Americans have, since the days of the earliest colonists, put their own American stamp on it here and there, but it is still a British product.

English has been the language of England for a comparatively short period. It began when Germanic tribes overran and occupied the lowlands of Britain, not long after the Roman conquerors withdrew in 410 A.D. The English language covers a time span of little more than fifteen hundred years, though the island had been inhabited by man for at least 50,000 years, possibly as long as 250,000 years, and each race of earlier inhabitants had a language (2, p. 47).

The Angles, Saxons and Jutes who migrated from the region of Denmark and the Low Countries brought with them dialects which belonged to the great Germanic branch of the most important of all linguistic families, the Indo-European. The English language of today is derived from the language of the Angles, which gained the ascendancy among the invaders, and the influence of the later Danish invasions, the Norman conquest, and the revival of learning. Modern scholars would add to this list of influences the spreading of English to America,

Australia and South Africa during the last century and its growth in significance throughout the world in this century.

The invading Teutonic tribes found the island natives speaking their own Celtic language, little influenced by the language of their Roman conquerors. The people of the towns may have learned Latin during the centuries of the Roman occupation, but it appears that little was left when the new waves of invaders crossed the channel. The Celts were largely absorbed or expelled by their Teutonic conquerors and their language was forced into the remote corners of the islands. The conversion of the English to Christianity in about 600 A.D. ushered in new ideas pertaining to the new religion. But while people accepted some Latin words connected with the new faith, they expressed most of their new-found meanings in their own language, modifying native words to meet new needs (7, p. 38).

The Danish invasions of King Alfred's time followed four hundred years of intermittent internal strife but of freedom from outside aggression. Like the Angles, Saxons and Jutes, the Danes were a Germanic or Teutonic tribe, enterprising, restless, and eager to better themselves through conquest. While their relationships with the English were fraught with fighting and bitterness, language was no serious problem. Danish and Anglo-Saxon were not separate languages but varying dialects of the same language. An enormous number of words were identical in the two languages so that an Englishman would have had no great difficulty in understanding a Viking even though pronunciation and word endings might vary slightly (5, 7). The Danish invasion added more words of Teutonic origin to the expanding English language but had relatively little influence on the grammar.

The next invasion, that of the Normans in 1066, was a very different affair. Although the Normans were also of Teutonic extraction, they had lived in France so long that their language was French and their vocabulary and grammar derived from Latin, as was true of all Romance languages. They were a race of foreign conquerors, alien to the English in both speech and manner of life. They became an upper class of rulers in both Church and State, quite remote from the lives of the common people. The languages they knew were Norman-French and Latin and they forced these on the English, along with the institutions and customs they inaugurated. Since the conquerors demanded obedience and their orders were given in Norman, the English were forced to learn enough Norman to understand them (5, p. 45).

Great numbers of words dealing with important aspects of life were added to the English language during this period. A large proportion of the words dealing with government were established in the language at this time: *power, minister, authority, parliament, sovereign, country, council, people, nation,* and the word *government* itself (5, p. 44; 7, p. 79). Words denoting rank in the feudal hierarchy: *peer, prince, duke, duchess, count* and the code of moral and social behavior they were to exemplify: *courteous, noble, fine, honor* and *glory* were among the additions to vocabulary. The administration of justice added other words: *justice, judge, court, jury, crime, attorney, property, real estate* and *privilege* among them. Norman influence on the Church resulted in such words as: *religion, service, saint, sermon, pray, conscience, discipline* and *mercy* (5, 7). The list is far from complete but it suggests the extent of the vocabulary additions which were clearly French or French derived from Latin.

But while vast changes were taking place at the upper levels of society, the English language was left in the possession of the common people, free from the influences of writing and pedagogy, those two major forces which hold a language stationary. During this period the "lowly" folk, who were almost its sole users, modified the English language to suit their own purposes, simplifying its grammar and in a variety of ways making of it the language it is today. Perhaps, if these "lowly" people had had English in their sole charge for another century, all verbs might form their past tenses by the adding of "ed" to the present and all comparatives and superlatives might end in "er" and "est." Great strides were made in this direction before scholars began again to write in English, to check it against a yardstick of Latin, and to crystallize its irregularities in dictionaries and grammar books.

The Renaissance began to be felt in England as early as the fourteenth century, and since that time the invasion of classical terms and of new words built of Latin or Greek parts has never ceased. Any page in an unabridged dictionary provides a list of them. More and more new ideas have had to be expressed and new words coined to serve them. In our own time, scientists continuously coin new words to name or describe new processes and products. People in all realms of life are assiduously adding new forms to old words through the addition of "ism" or "ist" to make such words as *absenteeism* and *determinist,* or turning nouns and adjectives into verbs through adding "ize" as in *circularize* or *nationalize.* The English language is subject to constant change and addition as more and more people use it in varying situations all around the world.

In 1582 Richard Mulcaster wrote, "The English tongue is of small reach, stretching no farther than this island of ours, nay not there over all." But in succeeding centuries the forging of the British empire carried it to the four corners of the earth. Bismarck is said to have remarked that the most important single event of the eighteenth century was the establishment of English as the language of North America. There is significance in this half century in the fact that the armies which crossed the Channel into France under General Eisenhower at the end of World War II all knew English. The Canadian, American, British, Indian, Australian and South African troops needed no interpreters. They had a working solidarity that grew out of a common language. English is now one of the major languages for the transaction of business throughout the world (Russian exports are labeled in English, "Made in U.S.S.R."). It has gained tremendous power in world diplomacy. When Egypt and Indonesia, both Moslem countries, drew up a cultural treaty, it was specified that the offical document be the English language copy. Today, less than four hundred years after Mulcaster's remark, the English language is the most far-reaching and widely used of any language and promises to become of even greater significance.

The proportion of the world's population that can read and write is rapidly growing. People in the underdeveloped countries of the world are reaching out hungrily for education so that they can learn to govern themselves and improve their standard of living. Perhaps, as time goes on, English-speaking peoples can find more and better ways of helping them achieve their aspirations.

□ AMERICAN ENGLISH

The history of English in America is a record of growth, change and spread. The colonists who came in the seventeenth century all spoke and wrote the English of their time. Captain John Smith's Jamestown settlers, Calvert's Marylanders, the Plymouth Fathers, the Bostonians of Massachusetts Bay Colony,

Roger Williams' Rhode Islanders and William Penn's Quakers all used Elizabethan English – the English used by Shakespeare and Ben Jonson. Most of them had learned their English before the year 1600, Miles Standish while Shakespeare was beginning to write and twenty-one-year-old John Alden at the height of Shakespeare's career (11, pp. 151-152). It was not the English of the aristocrat but that of the middle classes, and it was the same on both sides of the Atlantic until time and other forces brought about change.

A language changes as the people who use it have new experiences and meet new needs – in other words, as things happen to them. The early settlers were busy people with new conditions to meet and critical problems to solve. They found new flora and fauna and adopted the names used for them by the local Indians. Words were borrowed from the Spanish settlers of the Caribbean, the French of the Mississippi and St. Lawrence valleys, the Germans of Pennsylvania, the Dutch of New Amsterdam, and the African Negroes who were brought to the South. The loan words tell a good deal about the early history of America (5, 7, 11).

The languages which various groups of settlers brought from Europe influenced the English of the areas where they were concentrated. The structure of the language remained distinctly English, though the vocabulary was expanded by the addition of new words and new meanings for old words.

The Westward Movement carried eastern speech into the midwest, from New York to Michigan, from Pennsylvania to Ohio and on to California. Students of American dialects recognize specific regional characteristics and can trace the movements of dialects from one area to another (12, pp. 500-543; 9, pp. 37-51). In fact some who have made a special study of dialects can guess, within even a hundred miles, the area in which a speaker grew up.

☐ ENGLISH IN OUR SCHOOLS

Every child in every school in the United States studies and uses the English language. The family name he must learn to write and spell may be Sokolsky, Francescatti, Liberopolous, Chen or Koyama, or it may be Murphy, McRae, Llewellyn, Stirling, Mueller or Peterson. The family may proudly trace its American ancestry to the Mayflower or it may have come to the United States hopefully and gratefully from the camps of the dispossessed in Europe, the Near East or Southeast Asia. The roster of any school contains names of many origins, but in school all children operate in the English language. The point at which the school must start its teaching depends on the quality of English each child has learned in his home environment, whether that is a culturally deprived neighborhood or the home of a college teacher of English.

The schools have always assumed the responsibility for teaching children the basic skills that are essential to literacy, though the methods and materials they have utilized have changed greatly through the years. Reading, spelling and writing, together with arithmetic were the curriculum of such schools as existed in pioneer days. Gradually, other content has been added, all of it dependent upon the basic language skills.

However, the field of English has also a content, much of which has been overlooked or neglected in many schools. Children are interested in the language for its own sake and would be deeply interested in learning how it came to be what it is, how it operates, and what is happening to it at home and around the world. They are interested in their own language and work intensively at the task of expanding and sharpening their use of it. They would be interested also in refining their use of language if teachers could find ways to appeal to their inherent interest in self-building.

Children love language, but they have not always liked the way it is taught in the schools. Asked what subjects they like best in school, many of them put English at the bottom of the list. Yet, if teachers could teach English as a dynamic, living language and help children to understand it, the motivation would be the children's own.

□ WHAT CHILDREN CAN LEARN ABOUT LANGUAGE

Children learn the basic sound structure of their language in the preschool years; they can speak it and comprehend it through listening. Throughout the world, Henry Lee Smith, Jr. tells us,

> about ninety eight per cent of all children attain full control of the *structure* of their group's communication system at about the same age. This is of extreme importance both as a demonstration of what has been termed "the psychic unity of mankind" and as a clear indication that all languages as structured systems must be of about the same order of difficulty, simplicity or complexity. It

> helps point out the fact that all languages do the job that languages must do just about as well—or as badly—as all others. It makes us realize that the underlying patterns that compose language are the important part of this marvelous system and that once these are internalized, vocabulary items are easy to add, and are added rapidly, as the individual's experience in his culture increases (14, p. 9).

Certain concepts about language can begin to germinate as early as kindergarten or first grade if teachers will plant the seeds. Bruner, in the significant book *The Process of Education*,[2] states the conviction of a group of scholars that any important concept which children need to learn can be taught in some form to all ages. By the end of elementary school, children can be well on the way toward the following concepts:

1. Language is a system of sounds.
2. The sounds convey meaning only when put together in patterns of words and sentences.
3. The patterns of sound convey meaning to the initiated—those who know the language.
4. Pitch, stress, and juncture are a part of the sound system of the language and help to convey meaning.
5. The sounds and their connection with the things they represent is purely arbitrary.
6. The sounds are put together in characteristic designs; these designs can be composed of a great variety of appropriate fillers.
7. A language changes; old words may be given new meanings and new uses.
8. Likewise, old words are dropped and new words are coined of old parts to represent new meanings or modifications of old ones.

The fact that language is a system of sounds and that the sounds put together in characteristic patterns carry meaning is something that children can understand. Researchers have found young children, ages two to five, working intensively at a number of tasks in their attempt to understand how their language operates. "They were working on preciseness of expression; on discovering the possibilities of the language for humor and pleasure; and on the creative use of language" (16, pp. 85-86). Children are impressed to learn the arbitrary nature of

[2] Bruner, Jerome S., *The Process of Education*, Harvard University Press, Cambridge, Mass., 1960.

language when they discover that a dog may be called "le chien," "el perro" or "der Hund" as well as "the dog," depending on the language being spoken – or that children in their own group may call the stream near the school a "run," a "creek" or a "brook," depending on family usage.

All children are intrigued to have their attention called to the use of pitch, stress and juncture as conveyors of meaning. To test the shades of meaning that can be portrayed through the simple question, "What are you doing?" would fascinate any group.

Teachers at all grade levels can add greatly to children's zest for learning English through taking note of newly coined words as they are used on television and in the daily newspapers and also noting the unusual, obsolete or outmoded expressions which are found in the literature of earlier periods or of other geographic areas. Learning English can be an exciting experience for both teachers and children if they will work together to make it so.

☐ THE LANGUAGE ARTS IN THE ELEMENTARY SCHOOL

Any study of the teaching of the language arts must draw upon the knowledge amassed by the linguists for help with understanding the language and what to teach about it and upon the work of the psychologists and other students of child development for help with when and how to teach the various aspects of the skills and content that elementary school children need. Attention is given throughout this book to what is known about how children learn and how best to teach them. This emphasis is fairly familiar to all teachers of children. There are, however, some aspects of language which are new to the curriculum of the elementary school and some ways of utilizing linguistic knowledge which are relatively new to the elementary teacher.

The tremendous expansion of knowledge which is taking place in this quarter century reaches into every field of the curriculum. It has caused the public as well as the schools to reevaluate all aspects of curriculum for their basic values, their harmony with present knowledge, and the effectiveness with which children are taught. Some aspects of change at the elementary school level have received more public attention than others, but each field is expanding and undergoing basic changes. Certainly this is true of the language arts. Articles have appeared in magazines and newspapers under the title

"The New English" and new approaches to the teaching of reading have created wide public interest.

As the relationships of men and nations become closer, communication takes on added significance. Because so much of the work of the world is being done through oral language, there is renewed emphasis in the schools on speaking and listening. Because the ability to communicate effectively plays such a vital role in the lives of individuals, there is major concern that each child, the physically, mentally, and environmentally handicapped as well as the more favored, be helped to develop language skills to the extent of his ability. The significance of language in human relationships has brought about greater interest in language as a phenomenon – what it is and how it operates – than ever before.

The studies of linguists have amassed more knowledge of language in general and of specific languages than has been available at any time. The English language has come in for its share of study as well as have hundreds of the other 3,000 or more languages in use in the world. Linguists are students of language – scholars who study languages as other scientists study other kinds of phenomena. The field of linguistic study is a broad one subsuming a number of specialized interests, each of which has values for the elementary school program in the language arts if what is selected from it fits the needs of boys and girls.

The linguistic historians study the historical backgrounds of languages and how language has throughout the centuries influenced the history of people and of nations. No study of Canada, Switzerland, or Belgium in social studies classes could be complete without attention to their language history and its problems. Somewhat in contrast and even more important, it is impossible to study life in the countries of Asia or the newly emerged countries of Africa without giving attention to their problems which grow out of diverse languages and dialects. Children in the primary grades study their own communities and middle grade children study American history. No such study would be complete without attention to the languages brought by the earliest settlers and what remains in place names, local expressions, and the like – French, German, Spanish, Slavic, Scandinavian, whatever it may be. Children would find it interesting and some of them who bear family names not of English origin might find new pride in their origins.

The linguistic geographer and dialectologist can be drawn

upon to help children recognize and savor the dialects of New England, the Pennsylvania Dutch, the hill people of Kentucky and Tennessee, the people of Georgia, and the Negro dialects of the much-loved Spirituals and Uncle Remus. And there is literature from India, Australia, Ireland and other parts of the English-speaking world—folk tales, modern stories, and poetry—which either originated in English or has been translated into English. Children who learned in their homes a dialect which deviates from that taught in the school especially appreciate evidence that English does not sound the same wherever it is spoken. They can be helped to understand, though, that the dialect the school utilizes and strives to help each child acquire is one that will be good anywhere in the English-speaking world.

The lexicographer and the semanticist also make contributions the children should increasingly understand. The lexicographer is the scholar who gathers the material for the dictionaries, and the semanticist studies word meanings as they have occurred in the past and as they are found in the present. Elementary school children should learn what a dictionary is and what it is not, what it does and does not do, and why. They should learn to think of a language as a man-made product—one which man expands and modifies to meet his changing and expanding interests and needs—and a dictionary as a record of that language and what man does with it. Children begin to be aware of changes in the meaning and use of words as they learn the Mother Goose rhymes and expand that awareness throughout their study of literature culminating, perhaps, in their study of Shakespeare in high school and college.

The grammarian is the linguist whose work and ideas teachers are increasingly aware of at this time. He studies the structure of a language, its sound structure and particularly its syntactic structure. Present-day grammarians who are concerned with generative or transformational grammar are interested in studying the rules which are used to generate the infinite sentences that are possible in the language but which exclude those that do not fit the language.

The work of the linguists is of increasing importance to the teaching of reading, spelling, grammar, and composition in the schools. Some of the contributions of linguists are discussed in the chapters which deal with these topics.

The language arts are an interwoven fabric. No single skill can be taught in isolation. The interrelationships among the language arts are manifest in every chapter of this book.

☐ SELECTED REFERENCES ☐

1. Barnett, Lincoln, *The Treasure of Our Tongue.* (New York: Alfred A. Knopf, 1964).
2. Baugh, Albert C., *A History of the English Language.* New York: Appleton-Century-Crofts, Inc., Second Edition, 1957.
3. Bodmer, Frederick, *The Loom of Language.* (Lancelot Hogben, Ed.) New York: W. W. Norton and Co., Inc., 1944.
4. Chase, Stuart, *Power of Words.* New York: Harcourt, Brace and Company, 1953.
5. Davies, Hugh Sykes, *Grammar Without Tears.* New York: The John Day Company, 1953.
6. Hook, N. N. and Mathews, E. G., "Changes in the English Language," in *Essays on Language and Usage.* Edited by Leonard F. Dean and Kenneth G. Wilson. New York: Oxford University Press, 1963.
7. Jesperson, Otto, *Growth and Structure of the English Language.* Oxford: Basil Blackwell, 1962.
8. Laird, Charlton, *The Miracle of Language.* New York: The World Publishing Company, 1953.
9. Malmstrom, Jean and Ashley, Annabel, *Dialects USA.* Champaign, Illinois: National Council of Teachers of English, 1963.
10. Marckwardt, Albert H., *American English.* New York: Oxford University Press, 1958.
11. Marckwardt, Albert H., "The Language of the Colonists," in *Essays on Language and Usage.* Edited by Leonard F. Dean and Kenneth G. Wilson. New York: Oxford University Press, 1963.
12. McDavid, Raven I., Jr., "The Dialects of American English." Chapter in *The Structure of American English* by W. Nelson Francis. New York: Ronald Press, 1958.
13. Mencken, H. L., *The American Language.* New York: Alfred A. Knopf, Inc., 1936 (4th Ed., Rev. & Enl.) Supplement One, 1945.
14. Smith, Henry Lee, Jr., *Linguistic Science and the Teaching of English.* Inglis Lecture. Cambridge: Harvard University Press, 1958.
15. Strickland, Ruth G., *The Contribution of Structural Linguistics to the Teaching of Reading, Writing, and Grammar in the Elementary School.* Bulletin of the School of Education. Bloomington: Indiana University, January 1964.
16. Wann, Kenneth D.; Dorn, Miriam Selchen; and Liddle, Elizabeth Ann, *Fostering Intellectual Development in Young Children.* New York: Bureau of Publications, Teachers College, Columbia University, 1962.

SOME ASPECTS OF LANGUAGE AND MENTAL DEVELOPMENT.

It is of the utmost consequence in the life of an individual that he learn to use the forms of communication. The skill he develops in the use of these tools influences his choice of vocation, the friends he draws about him, and the pattern of personal living he builds for himself. A young person who expresses himself clearly and with confidence and who enjoys books and reading tends to select academic work in the high school, to go to college, and to enter the professions or to become a business, industrial, social, or political leader. A person who lacks linguistic skill, who has a less extensive vocabulary and less facility in self-expression or reading, tends to turn for his vocation to types of work with people and things in which the linguistic demands are of a different sort and other competencies are more important than facility in the use of language. People who talk well and read widely tend to choose others of similar interests for their friends and associates and to spend some of their leisure time in reading, discussion, or perhaps creative writing. Those of less linguistic skill may turn to athletics, to doing things with their hands, to watching television, or to attendance at movies, and may prefer association with people of like interests. One type of life may be fully as satisfying as another but the pattern is often determined by skill in the use of language.

The work of selective service boards has for a number of years brought to light an astonishing number of illiterates for a country which has prided itself for generations on its free public schools. All of these men were leading types of lives in which a high level of linguistic skill was not a prerequisite. They were laborers, small farmers, unemployed drifters for the most part, and came from homes of low cultural and economic level. Many of them were eager to take advantage of the literacy program of the armed services because they saw in it opportunity to prepare for life on a higher social and economic level when the war was over.

Scholars and teachers have always been interested in language. Urban, of Yale, in a philosophic treatise on language, has called interest in language "one of the oldest and most constant preoccupations of men." Scholars in the field of linguistics are concerned with the science of language and with comparisons between languages. Teachers and parents are interested chiefly in the functions of language, its development by children, and its effect upon their lives and personalities.

Precisely the same problem exists in the penal institutions of the country. A high proportion of the inmates cannot read or write at fourth grade level. Some states are attacking the problem through adult education in the institutions as part of an over-all program of rehabilitation and are finding that, with proper help, young people of relatively low intelligence can learn far more than the schools have succeeded in teaching, and do so eagerly.

The national concern for today's school drop-outs shows the magnitude of the current problem. Young people who cannot achieve in school because of lack of language skills become discouraged or rebellious and leave the school because their needs are not being met. The growing public relief costs and juvenile delinquency problems are closely related to the school's inability to help each of its students acquire the ability to read and write. There are few jobs left for people who cannot acquire these skills. A part of the program of the federally supported Job Corps is planned to help these young people with reading and other language skills as well as job training.

☐ THE FUNCTIONS OF LANGUAGE AND SPEECH

Language is used to serve many purposes. A child learns to use language to express meaning, though he later may use it on occasions to camouflage or to conceal meaning or intention. He learns to use it to express feeling, though he may also use it to cover up and hide his feelings. He begins very early to employ it to influence or control the feelings and actions of others. Through it, he expresses purpose or intention and enjoys experiences vicariously. He thinks aloud, as a little child, until he has gained enough experience with language to think silently, but he uses language all his life to facilitate thought and memory. Before the child has passed through the elementary school, he has learned to use language to gain attention and information, to describe objects and experiences, to give directions, to reason through simple problems, to explain, to criticize and dispute, to express or to produce feelings, and to enjoy rhythm, tone, word pictures, and humor.

The social side of language is important to a child as well as to an adult. One of the baby's first expressions may be "Hi," because he discovers early that it arrests attention and brings a response. Such expressions as "Hello" and "How are you?" are means of making a pleasant connection. Telling an incident from the child's own experience may serve the same purpose. Language is a part of the response which people make in many practical situations.

□ THE LANGUAGE OF GESTURE AND FACIAL EXPRESSION

Adult influence over children takes place through the language of words and also through the language of gesture, facial expression, bodily contact, and action. An approving nod, an understanding smile, or a comforting pat on the shoulder tells a child that he is on the right track and gives him the emotional support to go on in the direction in which he is going. A frown of doubt, irritation, or disapproval; a warning or disapproving headshake; a pointed nod or wave of the hand in a different direction tells the child that he is on the wrong course and that he must change it to win adult approval. Families that are closely bound together by affection and understanding express the attitudes that exist within the group in ways that are not dependent upon words. Even a tiny infant with no awareness of words senses his mother's love through the feel of her hands, the sound of her voice, and the expressions of her face. The comforting ministrations of firm, gentle hands give the child a secure sense of well-being. A teacher who loves children and is deeply interested in each of them builds bonds of understanding and appreciation within her group that are not dependent upon words for realization or expression. Her relaxed, friendly ways of working with the children, her awareness of each child's needs, and her genuine appreciation of his efforts and his achievement tell the children of the warmth and sincerity of her interest. Children expand and grow under such conditions just as plants respond to good conditions for growth.

The language of action and facial expression operates on the adult level as well. There are a number of adages that bear out the point. We say, "Actions speak louder than words," or of a person, "What you are speaks so loudly that I cannot hear what you say." The story is told of Abraham Lincoln that when a certain man was urgently recommended for a cabinet post, Lincoln declined to appoint him, saying, "I don't like the man's face." When the advocate insisted, "But the poor man is not responsible for his face," Lincoln answered, "Every man over forty is responsible for his face." Facial expressions, quality of manner, graciousness, considerateness, and fondness for people all show on brief contact with adults. Intellectual quality and attainment are indicated also. We say after acquaintance that a person is interesting, well-read, a keen thinker, or a person of discernment. We arrive at these generalizations from his expressions and behavior fully as much as from his verbal responses. Two widely read books call attention, on the international as well as the personal level, to problems of human relations which grow out of the failure of people to recognize and heed what their author calls *The Silent Language* and *The Hidden Dimension* of human communication (9, 10).

□ COMMUNICATION THROUGH BEHAVIOR, ATTITUDES, AND FEELING

Communication is commonly recognized as having many aspects on the adult level, but there are times when that fact tends to be forgotten in dealing with children. All adults who guide and teach children are aware of the direct teaching which they do through the planned use of words and materials. Lessons and experiences which adults provide and precepts which they teach are a part of the child's learning experience, but so are the adult's own attitudes, responses, and behavior. A group of six-year-old children were soon vying with one another to anticipate the needs of a crippled child who was brought to school in a wheel chair, because they saw the teacher quietly providing ways for the child to participate in group activities without calling attention to the child's handicap. The satisfaction and pride the children showed in quiet, unobtrusive consideration for this less fortunate member of the group grew from example rather than from direct teaching.

It is one of the eternal verities of teaching that we teach by means of what we are as well as by means of what we say and do. Indirect teaching may counteract direct teaching, as when a child becomes afraid of lightning and thunder because he senses his mother's fear, regardless of her painstaking care to tell him that the storm is beautiful and that it will not hurt him. In a schoolroom the children found it difficult to accept a child whose physical defect made him unattractive, because the teacher was obviously repelled by him even though she insisted that the children include him in all their activities. A child absorbs interests, ideals, and prejudices, not so much from direct teaching as from contact, just as he acquires the speech patterns and habits of those about him.

The story is told of the experience of a noisy, boisterous little boy whose behavior was out of bounds. He ran ahead of his adult guide and dashed through the open doorway of a beautiful church. The adult hurried after him to keep him from disturbing worshipers who might be in the church. As she sped to catch him, she saw the little boy slow his pace to a quiet walk as he started down the aisle. When the adult approached, he held out his hand and whispered, "Let's sit down." After a period of feeling the quiet and beauty of the place and looking at the light which came through the stained glass windows, he whispered, "Let's go now." And with quiet composure, he walked from the church with his companion.

Direct teaching is not always the best method of communication. Listening to beautiful music, watching the changing colors of a sunset, feeling the rhythm and beauty of words, reconstructing in one's own mind a clear picture, or catching the meaning and significance of color and line in picture and sculpture are all forms of communication. Feeling the awe and sense of proportion that come with gazing into the star-illuminated sky on a clear, moonless night and sensing the smallness of oneself in the midst of such vastness, or watching the purposeful busyness of ants and honeybees, may develop in a child far more understanding and appreciation than any amount of direct teaching.

The child is not only the recipient of adult communication, but he is also a communicator. His facial expressions and behavior, as well as his words, communicate his interest or his boredom, his understanding or his vagueness and bewilderment, his acceptance or his skepticism or rebellion. The adult who studies children's responses will know what a child is really learning, when he is ready for an experience, and how to make the experience most fruitful for him.

☐ LANGUAGE AND EXPERIENCE

Language and experience are closely interrelated throughout the lifetime of all individuals. The relationship is clearly evident in the responses of the little child. He learns the language of his parents, not because he has inherited the predisposition toward that language, but because it is the one he hears about him constantly and the one which becomes associated with the other elements that make up his living. He says "mommy" because his mother calls herself by that name and "bottle" because she uses that word as she helps him with his feeding. For the little child who has begun to acquire language, each new experience adds new words or new and deeper meanings for old words. It is a challenge to parents to realize the child's dependence on their speech for the quality of his speech and vocabulary and upon the experiences they provide for the extent and richness of that vocabulary.

Many of the words that make up a language can be understood only through experience. Such words as "big," "little," "which," "was," "what," and countless others can be understood only in relationship to experience and to other words. Even a noun such as the word "dog" has to be learned through experience. The child first associates it only with the dog in his own home, and later he learns that dogs can be of many sorts and sizes from a Great Dane to a toy terrier; have long hair like a Pekinese or short hair like a Dalmatian; be brown, white, black, or spotted. He may call all four-legged creatures "dog" at first, but gradually he learns other names for other classifications. Even when he has learned about the animal *dog*, he still has other meanings for the word to learn as they are used in colloquial and vulgar expressions such as "tired as a dog," "dog-eared," or the various slang expressions which include the word "dog."

Experiences with words can be confusing to a child. When he cries to go with his father, his mother says, "You are too little to go with Daddy. You must wait until you are big." But when he falls down and cries, she says, "Pick yourself up. You are too big to cry!" Bigness and littleness as they relate to people and things require a great deal of experience for understanding.

The words the child learns in his early years are mainly words that are associated with direct, firsthand experience. As the child grows older, he learns also through the vicarious experience of stories, books, illustrations, the conversation and related experiences of others, the radio, television, and motion pictures. He can begin to experience vicariously when his own background of knowledge and understanding gained from direct experience makes it possible for him to relate new, unfamiliar material to similar material within his own experience and comprehend the new through the old. For example, the child who knows the water of lakes and rivers and has traveled on boats can identify and comprehend the canals of Holland and her water transportation when he sees it pictured, far more clearly than can the child who lacks such an experience background. The older the child grows the more he can learn through the vicarious experience of books if he has first been well grounded in firsthand experience with his own environment and its many interrelationships. Vicarious experiences play a larger part than firsthand experience in the expansion of thinking and knowledge as adults read from books the accumulated wisdom and experience of the ages and participate in its application to modern problems. Credit for much of the growth man has attained must be given to his acquired ability to learn through vicarious experience.

□ LANGUAGE AND THINKING

The relationship which exists between language and thought needs to be understood if parents and teachers are to appreciate the difficulties which children encounter in mastering the language.

The point at which real thinking begins in the life of a child is uncertain. He sees his mother put on her coat and pick up her purse to go to the market and runs for his sweater and cap to go with her. He sees Daddy leaving for work and runs to the window to wave good-bye. A dog will bring his leash when he wants to go out if leash and going out are clearly associated in his mind, and a kitten will learn early to run to the kitchen when she hears the refrigerator door open. These are responses of association which may involve rudimentary thinking. Some authorities hold that a little child is incapable of much that can be called thinking until he learns to talk or at least until he senses the meaning of words. The three-year-old who accompanies his play with a running account of what he is doing is thinking aloud. In the process of acquiring speech he must at many points use it orally if he is to use it at all.

As a child grows in his mastery of speech, it becomes possible for him to think in areas in which he is thoroughly familiar. He can think of a farm after he has visited one and has used the terms that are necessary for this thinking. Even here he can think only so far as his experience with words has taken him.

Many people have always conceived of thought as taking shape in the mind of the thinker and then being expressed, yet all people at times do some of what has come to be called "thinking aloud." Jespersen, the Danish philologist, mentions a girl who said, "I talk so as to find out what I think, don't you?" People who have problems to solve and little time to spend on them often find, when they come to express themselves on a problem, that thinking has been taking place but it is not recognized until it is expressed. Thinking and speaking or writing take place simultaneously in most self-expression.

Both the immature child and the uneducated adult have to utter their thoughts aloud in order to know what they are. Teachers, especially, need to recognize this fact in order to avoid calling upon children to work "in the inner world of the mind" before they are capable of doing so. Children need many opportunities during each school day to bring thought into being through expressing it.

There is a difference between creative thought and reproductive thought of which one needs to be aware in guiding children. Creative thought is new to the thinker. It breaks fresh ground, makes new trails in the mind, and must be expressed in order to be recognized. A new idea is vague and nebulous in a thinker's mind until he has expressed it in words, either to himself or to others. Thoughts that are deeply familiar, that deal with things the thinker has come to know, he can keep to himself. An educated person has a great many thoughts he can identify without expressing them. Reproductive thought deals with material the thinker knows and recognizes.

Content and ideas that are new to children call for a great deal of opportunity for oral expression. Watts, who has studied the language of English children, calls attention to the fact that teachers should distinguish between the sort of knowledge they can reasonably expect children to be able to put into words and the sort that will be a source of trouble to them. Subject matter that is new and unfamiliar will be difficult for children to discuss, or to report on from their reading, but as they continue to work with the subject and the ideas become more thoroughly assimilated, they can discuss it with ease and confidence. Relatively unfamiliar ideas reside "in the twilight between clear knowledge and blank ignorance" (21, p. 21). Thus, it is easier for a child to read a story suited to his age level than it is to read a textbook, because the story deals in expressions with which the child is familiar, while the formal, factual presentation of the textbook utilizes sentence structure and vocabulary less familiar to him.

☐ FROM THE CONCRETE TO THE ABSTRACT IN LANGUAGE

The first words the young child learns deal entirely with the concrete things and activities of his environment. He becomes interested first in the fact that things have names and acquires a number of nouns which he supplements with verbs expressing common activities of things, and he begins to generalize. Gradually he builds a fund of general terms like "what," "become," "how," which he cannot picture concretely, and common class names such as "girl," "boy," "dog," "people," and "food." The story is told of a toddler waiting in a well-baby clinic who went from one to another of the waiting children each sitting on his mother's lap and inquired regarding each, "Baby?", "Mommy?" Then he went from chair to chair saying inquiringly to his mother as he pointed to each, "Chair?" On being assured by his mother that he was in each instance right, he climbed into her lap and settled down contentedly to wait his turn. Recognition of all types, colors, and sizes of birds as "birds" comes long before the child thinks of them as members of the larger classification, "animals."

Common descriptive adjectives such as "big" and "little" are used by the child at an early age, but Watts found through tests that the power to think clearly about shapes and sizes begins to be acquired between the ages of nine and eleven. The concepts "alike" and "different" are achieved by the child long before he can think "opposite."

Most children can conceive of generalizations only in concrete and specific terms. "Being good" means doing just what the adult wishes him to do; "punctuality" means coming to school on time; "truth" means telling exactly what happened; "fairness" to a young child means sharing and taking turns. Smith tells of a two-year-old child who was promised a treat which should be a "secret." He had recently become acquainted with a cricket and demanded to see the "seacrick" (17). A child requires many experiences with a non-picturable abstraction such as "secret" before he can comprehend its meaning.

Adults need to avoid with care the assumption that because

a child uses a word, he understands its meaning. Teachers are sadly prone to accept the ability to verbalize as evidence of knowledge. Countless amusing tales are told of children's efforts to make sense of words adults expect them to understand. The child whose version of the first stanza of "America," which he was learning at school, was "My country 'tis a bee, sweet land of liver tree," was doing his best with unfamiliar words. The little girl who came home from Sunday School insisting upon carrots for dinner had interpreted the memory verse for the day, "He careth for me," in the only manner her experience with words permitted; she learned them, "Eat carrots for me."

Word forms such as "what," "was," "once," and "although" are far more difficult for the child to recognize in learning to read than are such words as "boy," "mother," and "car," partly because the child can neither form an emotional association with them nor can he picture their meaning in his mind. The concreteness of nouns and action words that can be pictured makes them far easier for the child to learn to recognize.

The abstractions of ideals, attitudes, and descriptive qualities are learned over a long period, and the child's ideas may have to be revised many times. "Good people" to the little child may be the ones who are kind to him and "bad people" those who are less to his liking. Gradually goodness and badness become relative concepts which are modified in form and meaning according to the way in which they are applied.

☐ SELF-CENTERED OUTLOOK ON ALL EXPERIENCE

Each person is the center of his own universe and sees, comprehends, and interprets all that touches him in the light and within the perspective of his own experience. This is true of all human beings of all ages. The young child can learn the properties, conditions, and behaviors of things only as he experiences them himself, and can comprehend them only with reference to himself. "I," "my," "mine," and "me" are his most frequently used words during this stage of development because he needs them constantly in his thinking. Later he may speak and act with less obvious attention to self, but the self always is the point of reference in learning situations. Every individual, adult or child, can see only with his own eyes, hear only with his own ears, and build meaning only with the funds available in his own mind and through his own experience.

Each individual is quite literally the center of his own universe and must interpret and react to all of the experience that comes his way from that center of focus.

The child first acquires facility in handling language in the common experiences of everyday life. He learns first the vocabulary that deals with his food, rest, play, and social contacts with his family. Words and meanings are acquired through association and imitation.

☐ AWARENESS OF OTHERS AND INTERACTION

A child shows his awareness of others through addressing his remarks to them even though the remarks may deal entirely with the child himself and his own interests and concerns. A relatively large percentage of the remarks made by preschool children are of the self-assertive variety. "I want to do it," "It's my turn now," and "Mine is bigger than yours" are characteristic remarks of this age period.

Piaget (15), who studied the language of French-speaking children in Geneva, Switzerland, found little ability to carry on conversation or use language for a real meeting of minds below the age of seven or eight years. He found children's speech previous to this age to be largely of the egocentric type. He uses the term "egocentric" to mean lacking in understanding of the thoughts and concerns of others, rather than to mean selfishness as it is usually conceived. Egocentric speech may be of the collective monologue type in which children in a group make remarks and assertions without any real interchange of ideas or consideration of the point of view expressed by others.

Observation of children of kindergarten age in this country yields some examples of what Piaget calls "collective monologue." Children drawing pictures at a table may each be talking about his own picture with little attention to what others are saying. This does not appear to be the predominant form of speech among five-year-olds in our schools. Many examples can be observed in which speech is definitely of the sharing and interaction type.

Teachers of English children have found evidence of conversation between children a year or two younger than the age of seven or eight found by Piaget (15), and studies of American children have arrived at similar conclusions. Socialized speech begins when the child talks to influence others and to gain response from them, and when he listens to learn the meaning of the response so that he can react to it. McCarthy (14) found not more than four per cent of egocentric responses in the groups which she studied utilizing Piaget's methods as contrasted with the thirty-eight per cent in Piaget's own analysis. In a free play situation studied (5), the percentage of egocentric remarks was found to be 6.3 per cent, well under the figure given by Piaget. The difference appears to be one of rate of development at different ages, though the sequence of development is the same.

□ DISPUTE AN EARLY FORM OF SOCIALIZED SPEECH

Real interaction begins when one child's interests conflict with and overlap those of another child. Such interaction occurs frequently as young children learn to share materials and work and play together. Remarks made by one child which hurt or annoy another may be ignored at first or responded to with tears, angry shrieks, or even blows. Children quarrel in this manner because they have not learned how to argue. Argument calls for reasoning and for expression of thinking, which children have to learn as they gain maturity. Quarreling with words appears to begin when the child is about five years of age. Learning to disagree and to work through their disagreements politely comes much later. Disputes are often of the "'tis not!" "'tis so!" type and end only when one child tires of the dispute and turns to something else. Watts (21) found that arguments in which children cite reasons in support of their contentions rarely appear before the age of seven. Adults are most helpful to children when they cause them to feel a need for making themselves clearly understood through what they say.

□ CONVERSATION AND COMMUNICATION

In social speech a child talks, not at random but to specified persons, with the object of making them listen and understand. Real social interaction calls for listening as well as speaking. The child must learn to give attention to responses, to take in and comprehend them, and to react to them. This aspect of communication, as well as the expression aspect, has to be learned. It is frequently easier for a child to express his point of view than it is to attend to and comprehend the point of view

of others, especially if it differs from his own. A real meeting of minds is evidence of mature interaction.

Other types of communication include commands, expressions of criticism or derision, and assertions, many of which may be assertions of personal superiority. These are frequent when the child is learning to participate in conversation.

Questions, for the young child, are both a source of information and a means of getting and holding attention. The child who asks questions one after another in rapid succession may be gaining far more satisfaction from the attention the adult is giving him than from the information that is forthcoming in answer to his questions. The story is told of a three-year-old whose mother counted the questions she asked her father during an automobile trip. They averaged seven to a mile. Also, the parents of a four-year-old alternated in keeping track of his questions throughout the day. They totaled three hundred and fifty. One's interest is aroused not only by the purpose of the questions but by the tremendous energy expended in asking them.

When the question asked by a child is an information-seeking one, he wants a simple, direct answer. Accuracy is important, but an adult need not tell all that he knows. The story is told of a child whose mother responded to a question with, "Wait and ask Daddy tonight. He knows lots more about it than I do." The child thought a minute, then protested, "But I don't want to know that much." His father's wealth of knowledge and detailed explanations were overwhelming at his age. An accurate answer but a simple, brief one was more satisfying.

The ability to carry on a conversation is evidence of language power. Disputes, as was said earlier, may be the first form of social interaction between children and may appear whenever their areas of interest overlap. Children may reach the point where they can converse with an adult before they are able to do so with children. They grow in ability gradually, and growth is discernible from year to year, but there are great differences between individuals at any age.

By the time a child has reached the age of ten or twelve he may be able to carry on detailed conversations or discussions over a fairly long period if the subject matter of the conversation or discussion interests him. He asks penetrating questions and responds intelligently and thoughtfully to answers.

☐ SOME SOCIAL ASPECTS OF LANGUAGE

Social interaction begins slowly with the young child and passes through many developmental stages as he progresses from complete self-absorption to understanding of the feelings, needs, and attitudes of others. The child of eighteen months who calls all men and women "daddy" and "mommy" has made a beginning, but he has a long way to go in social awareness and understanding before he senses the unique differences which make each person the individual that he is.

The learning of social behavior and acquisition of forms of courtesy parallel the child's growth in awareness of others and consideration for them. While the two- and three-year-old child may absorb words which are forms of courtesy, such as "please" and "thank you," from their use in his environment, these forms should not be considered mastered until the child can at least partially understand the attitudes and feelings they engender in others. Real courtesy is not the mere saying of words, but the emotional and social understanding and appreciation of the reactions of others which come only when one has had enough experience to be able to think of himself in the situation of the others. This requires both maturity and many social experiences.

Children of elementary school age need help many times to appreciate the fact that human relationships are highly dependent upon language. They have to be helped to realize that a thoughtless, critical, or derisive remark may result in hurt feelings and anger, which is expressed in withdrawal or tears on the part of some and aggressive fighting reactions on the part of others. Children's verbal disagreements, name-calling, and sometimes actual physical combats may grow out of misunderstanding of words or failure to sense the emotional response those words stimulate in others. Children learn very early that words are not only means of expressing thinking and reactions but also weapons for aggression.

It is important for children to learn that words may have different connotations for different people, depending upon their background of experience. They find that the tone of voice and the manner in which a remark is made may determine favorable or unfavorable response. Occasional analysis of crudely or discourteously worded remarks serves to make children aware of the psychological effects of language. Talking over problems, explaining word meaning, and explaining the effect of those meanings upon others resolve many conflicts. Older children can find in the current periodicals an abundance of material dealing with the psychological effects of language in economic and political life on the local, national, and international levels. Such momentous problems as those which exist between the United States and Russia in the postwar period are colored and in some cases created by the utilization of language.

Families as well as larger cultural groups develop modes of expression that are peculiarly their own and that serve as a social index to the level of culture within the group. Children absorb the family linguistic system with its peculiarities and private meanings and pronunciations. The school must permit and respect home language but gradually bring about the use of socially accepted standards of informal language. The English have this problem in the "cockney" forms children bring to school, and in many countries children speak a dialect in the home and community rather than the standard form of the language. In the United States there are some regional differences in pronunciation and usage as well as some problems of racial and cultural groups within the population which have developed their own adapted language forms. These must be respected in the school but supplemented by experience with standard usage.

American pronunciations and grammatical forms have come to differ at some points from English forms, and many words carry different meanings. These forms may gain recognition and acceptance in the national family and may eventually attain official recognition and incorporation into the national language and be recorded in dictionaries and grammars, whereas the forms used by the individual family tend to be modified by the culture outside the home. Group understanding takes place when the language is clear.

☐ ORIENTATION IN THE WORLD OF THINGS

The first major step in the child's orientation in the world of objects is his recognition of what is self and what is not self. An infant a few weeks old will watch his own hand in motion for minutes at a time and later will play with a foot, perhaps getting it into his mouth. He may even pull his own hair so hard that it hurts without being aware that he is producing the pain. In time he becomes aware of objects through perceiving them with his senses and comes to recognize their behavior traits. During his second year he learns that things have names, and his question, "What's 'at?" is persistent until he can attach names to most of the objects of his environment. Need for generalization follows almost immediately, because words like *doll* and *chair* are applied to objects which differ in size, coloring, and contour.

Learning the properties of common objects takes a long time and involves many and varied experiences. Adults speak of one ball as *big*, another one as *little;* one block as *heavy* and another as *light;* one toy is *soft*, and another is *hard.* Cream is *thick*, and so is the child's coat, the dog's fur, and the fog. Progress in mental development depends upon numerous experiences of a great variety of types and upon the association of descriptive words with these contrasting experiences. The general ideas the child is evolving are not abstractions in the fullest sense, because they remain attached to the objects which represent them in his thinking.

Concepts of comparison come considerably later in the child's development and are the result of many experiences. He learns comparisons such as *shorter, heavier, slower*, or *sooner* before he can recognize opposites. The notion of what is meant by doing a thing *quietly, quickly*, or *carefully* also evolves very gradually and as the result of firsthand experiences with objects and events.

Color naming takes on great interest between the ages of four and six. Naming and classifying things according to their colors was a consuming interest with one group of three-and-a half and four-year-old children at the nursery school lunch table. They identified the pastel colors of everyone's dishes and counted the number of pink, blue, green, and yellow plates at the table before they would set about the task of eating. The naming of primary colors usually comes first, but children soon become able to distinguish some tints and shades.

Most children express interest very early in what things are and what can be done with them. Many questions deal with the use to which things are put, what they are made of, how they are made, who made them, and with four-year-olds the ever recurring question of "why?" The child wants to know what makes the egg beater turn, how the telephone rings, and what makes the radio or television operate. He is interested in the source of toys, flowers, stars, and babies. Manipulative exploration and verbal exploration proceed hand in hand and lead to the more mature experimentation of later childhood and the adult years. Without such insatiable intellectual curiosity, man could not succeed in laying hold on even a small share of the mass of accumulated knowledge in one life span. Such curiosity and thirst for knowledge drive man on to explore atomic energy, discover new drugs for the benefit of mankind, and add to the sum total of knowledge and understanding available to each generation.

Children's ability to distinguish between living and non-living things grows during this period also. A very young child will talk to a toy as if it were a person like himself, and he may pat his chair and talk to it as he rocks in it but kick it angrily if it tips over. Even after children learn to distinguish between living and non-living things they delight in make-believe stories that invest inanimate things with life and give animals powers of human speech. Hans Andersen's "The Steadfast Tin Soldier," the *Wizard of Oz, Winnie-the-Pooh,* and Kipling's *Jungle Books* are perennial favorites with older primary school children.

Tests show that a primary grade child defines or describes an object in terms of its use: a chair is to sit on; an orange is to eat; a cap is what you wear on your head. A delightful collection of such definitions is found in a charming little book, *A Hole is to Dig.*[1] At a later age children learn to classify objects on the basis of like factors, even though they may differ on other factors. Dogs and cats are classified as animals, apples and grapes as fruits. Still later, children learn such relatively difficult classifications as liquid, solid, chemical, and instrument. A twelve-year-old child can be expected to define a hammer as a *tool* used to drive nails.

All children will tend to use "omnibus" words which will carry many types of meanings until they are encouraged to find exact and colorful words to express their meaning. Asked to make the sentence, "The boy went down the street," tell more about the situation, they find many words to paint a clearer picture of the boy and to indicate his method of going.

Concepts of number, size, quantity, weight, and distance grow slowly, along with the growth of other descriptive terms and meanings. The young child learns from experience what is

[1] Ruth Krauss, *A Hole is to Dig*, Harper and Brothers, 1952.

meant by *here, there; these, those; near, far; a few, many; in, on, under;* and all the other common words which express quantitative and spatial relationships. Concepts of number begin to develop early so that, according to Gesell (6), a child of two understands the concept *two* and three-year-olds can understand and recognize *three*. Five-year-olds in kindergarten can count by ones up to twenty but become confused in going from decade to decade beyond twenty. They can count and indicate a small number of objects by pointing to each one, though at four years of age they were unable to manage words and objects simultaneously. From the age of six upward, growth in number concepts and manipulation of numbers proceeds rapidly when the child is given sufficient concrete experience to make the necessary abstractions take on meaning.

☐ DEVELOPING CONCEPTS OF SPACE AND TIME

Events take place in time and place settings, and it is through experience with events and the words used in connection with them that the child develops his concepts of time and space. Both native ability and the quality of the child's language environment influence his rate of growth.

Young children can think only in terms of present time and things immediately at hand. The growth of time sense is an interesting one to trace. A two-year-old lives chiefly in the present, but he may use such expressions as "gonna" and "in a minute." He has several words which indicate present time: *now, today, "aw" day, "dis" day,* but he has no words for the past. Gesell has found that he does attempt to use the past tense of verbs but often inaccurately (6). Mothers and nursery school teachers help the child understand time sequence by calling attention to familiar routines in such sentences as "We can go out to play after nap," or "Time for dinner now. Let's wash our hands." Six months later, at two and a half years, the child has more words for the present and a few denoting future time: *some day, tomorrow, pretty soon.* Past tense for some children is all lumped into the expression *last night*.

A three-year-old child uses most of the basic time words. He has added more of them to his vocabulary during the past six months than in any other equal period of time (6). He has words for past and present and a number denoting future. He uses the word *time* very freely, in expressions such as "It's time" or "lunch time," and before the year is over, may add more complicated expressions, such as "a whole week," "a nice long time." By the age of four he has fairly clear concepts of when the events of the day take place in relation to one another.

A child of five or six years still lives in the here and now. His dramatic play involves time sequences such as daily routines. He can discriminate time intervals roughly. He thinks of seasons in terms of the activities of each. If told his birthday is next week, he may still ask tomorrow morning, "Is it next week now? Is it my birthday?" A seven- or eight-year-old may be able to tell time, season, month, and year.

An eight-year-old is beginning to be interested in primitive peoples and in the past, though he has little or no concept of the sequence of past happenings. A child of nine is becoming interested in biography and likes some history stories. Gesell's studies indicated an interest in history at age nine, but a study of English children brought to light very little interest or insight that pertains to history. Watts concluded that history is scarcely a study for children and suggests that it would be well to confine the teaching of history during the elementary school years to simple biography in order to enlarge children's experience with human behavior (21, p. 180).

☐ CAUSE AND EFFECT THINKING

The development of cause and effect thinking has been studied by a number of researchists and is significant as an indication of growth and maturity. Watts calls attention to the necessity of encouraging children to observe and understand the natural behavior of objects in the physical world as soon as they are mature enough (43). He believes that it is possible to introduce a superior child to the idea of natural cause and effect as early as four or five, and that every child needs help to distinguish between reality and illusion. Chisholm, a psychiatrist and the former leader of the World Health Organization, not only concurs in this but believes it essential that such thinking begin to develop in the preschool years.

The pioneer work in this difficult field was done by Piaget, the Swiss researchist, who studied children's explanations of various events, using an individual-interview method (15). He used experiments, demonstrations, and questions to investigate their ideas about the movement of clouds, the nature of air, the origin of wind, the floating of boats, and similar phenomena. He concluded that certain types of reasoning are characteristic of certain levels of development and that children think consistently at that level until they mature to the next stage. His findings have not been borne out in their entirety in research done in this country.

Deutsche, in a study of the thinking of American children based on techniques similar to those of Piaget, found that causal explanations vary from one level to another, depending on the problem being attacked and the child's experience in this realm (8). She found that girls tend to give more explanations which show no concept of relations than do boys. Boys give a higher percentage of logical-deduction answers involving reasoning from a principle. The quality of reasoning a child does with regard to cause and effect shows some relationship to the age, grade, and sex of the child but seems not to be related to his socioeconomic level. Deutsche's study suggests that training, such as is given in the public schools, is an important factor in determining the kind and quality of thinking children do with regard to cause and effect.

Logical reasoning and scientific thinking begin during the elementary school years. The parent who guides his child through helping him to see how unwise behavior can lead to natural penalty and wise behavior can lead to natural reward, both of which are inherent in the behavior itself, is starting his child on the right track. Good teaching helps children to pull out a problem, think it through carefully, analyze possible solutions, select the one they think best suited to the need, and follow the solution with evaluation of its effectiveness. Judgment and reasoning develop through guided experience which helps a child to face up to reality and work through real situations which involve thinking, reasoning, making choices, and accepting the consequences of one's choices.

□ LANGUAGE IN HUMAN RELATIONSHIPS

The expansion of the child's social sense can be observed through observing his language. A number of researchists have studied the use the child makes of pronouns to learn his growth in self-awareness and awareness of others. Several tabulations of early uses of pronouns indicate that, as Jersild says, "The I's have it" (12). *I, mine, my,* and *me* are hard-worked words between the ages of two and five. The child is the center of his own expanding universe and can comprehend other phenomena only with relation to himself. Pronouns of the first person singular were used more frequently in play with other children than when talking to an adult (8). The three-year-old, in spite of his strong sense of self, can combine self with another and use *we*.

The child of four has an expanded sense of self which is expressed in bragging, boasting, and what Gesell calls "out of bounds" behavior. His feeling for home and family is strong and he boasts extravagantly about them. Five is a somewhat impersonal age, when the child takes himself and others for granted, but six is a rather difficult age. He knows everything, wants everything, and wants to do everything in his own way. He wants to be first in everything, the best loved, the most praised, the winner. He is self-centered but expansive and not very discriminating (6).

Seven is an age when the child appears self-conscious and withdrawn; he seems to live in "another world" and does not hear requests made of him. He wants his own place in the school and family group and fears that he may lose his identity. His world is expanding rapidly and he is trying to find his place in it.

As the child adds maturity, he becomes more confident and shows great interest in relationships with others, both adults and children. He is becoming a distinct personality, better oriented toward his contemporaries than toward his parents. His relationships with mother, father, siblings, other children, and teachers are shown through both attitude and speech. These relationships change in intensity and expand or contract as his understanding of the world and life expands and takes on meaning. He is forever seeking orientation in his enlarging universe of things, people, ideas, and relationships. Orientation, understanding, and language grow in related manner from year to year, a network of growth in which each strand is dependent upon the others.

Children show very little ability to analyze personality until they are seven or older. Watts found that from seven to eleven they make rapid progress in mastering the language needed to describe the more striking characteristics of the people they meet (21). At first people are labeled *nice, good, hateful,* or *mean.* In their reaction to stories and especially to comic books many children appear to recognize two basic kinds of people–good people and bad people. A six-year-old boy playing with tin soldiers lined up all those in United States uniform on one side, all those in the uniforms of other countries on the other side–"the good guys" and "the bad guys," he called them. With experience and knowledge children learn to refine their concepts and terms so that their descriptions and evaluations become clearer and more specific. Experience in discussing characters in the books they read helps them to clarify and refine their thinking. Dramatic play and interpretation also aid in this learning process.

□ THE DEVELOPMENT OF APPRECIATIONS, ATTITUDES, AND IDEALS

Attitudes and ideals grow in the social and cultural setting in which the children live, and acquiring them is part of the process of growing up, of becoming socialized and civilized. The feelings and emotions which children experience are closely tied up with attitudes and ideals and influence their development. Individuals whose childhood experiences are so unfortunate as to cause them to have feelings and emotions which do not permit them to develop the attitudes and ideals of their culture are considered neurotic or criminal in their tendencies. Both the neurotic and the criminal lack the social feeling which evolves under normal conditions in early childhood and is progressively developed by years of contact with the realities of life. The neurotic tends to evade social responsibility by developing symptoms which prevent him from taking his part in real life, while the criminal tends to fight social standards and conventions to gain his personal ends.

Feelings are of many sorts. There are those which are associated with health and a sense of well-being, a secure sense that all is going well in the life of the individual, and there are feelings which are unpleasantly associated with physical deficiency or physical ill-health or with experiences which result in unhappy moods or tensions. There are also feelings related to sense impressions of sights, sounds, tastes, smells, and tactile feelings. The colors of a sunset, the soft feel of a kitten's fur, the fragrance of flowers, or the restfulness of soft music may result in pleasant feelings; while harsh sounds, blatant colors, and offensive tastes and odors result in feelings of unpleasantness. These feelings are frequently expressed in exclamations of pleasure or displeasure. Feeling or emotion may be related also to desires and impulses to do things the child wants to do. These desires and impulses result in pleasure if afforded outlet and in fear or anger if frustrated.

Studies of anger responses illustrate the development of response to feeling as it takes place between infancy and maturity. In her study of anger in young children, Goodenough found that as children grew older primitive bodily responses were replaced by reactions of a less violent and more symbolic nature (8). Children up to the age of two and a half or three express themselves through crying, screaming, and angry noises. The five- and six-year-old may resort to verbal aggressiveness with the threat, "I'll hit you" or "I hate you." He calls names and asserts angrily that he is "mad." The seven-year-old expresses his anger with "That isn't fair," "It's a gyp," or he threatens with "I'll beat you up" (7). As children grow older, if they are maturing normally they learn to suit their anger responses to the accepted behavior patterns of the culture.

Sentiments develop early in the life of the child and are the outgrowth of experiences. The sense of protection and well-being which the infant feels as he is ministered to by firm, gentle, loving hands is probably the beginning of the sentiment of love. The child absorbs the attitudes about him as he grows. Affectionate, considerate attitudes beget affection, while inconsiderate, unreasonable, and neglectful attitudes result in insecurity and may form the beginnings of sentiments of hatred. The child absorbs also the enthusiasms, interests, and aspirations of the people about him and these influence the development of sentiments and values for his own later life. Emotionalized habits of thought and standards of conduct are shaped in this manner during childhood and color and influence all future experience. (12)

The growth gradient charts presented by Gesell sketch the development of sentiments and attitudes up to sixteen years (6, pp. 287-294; 7, pp. 277-287). The child of two shows real affection toward his mother and possibly toward other adults; but by two and a half, when he is thrusting forward rapidly in his first surge of independence, he tends to be "domineering, imperious, selfish, possessive, demanding—verbally asserting domination over members of the family." Three is a period of consolidation of gains and the child is more friendly, conforming, and desirous of pleasing. By four he is thrusting forward again and his behavior may be out of bounds, quarrelsome, argumentative, boastful, and he is often a tattler, but he is affectionate again at bedtime. At five he is more businesslike, serious, realistic, and loves to talk. At six he tends again to lack stability and equilibrium; he may use language aggressively and be explosive, rebellious, rude, and stubborn. Seven is another period of seriousness and the child is more thoughtful, absorbed, and inhibited. His goals for himself may go beyond his ability and make him moody and unhappy. He may complain that nobody likes him and that he is unfairly treated. Eight is a period of disequilibrium when the child may be affectionate or rude, gay and cheerful or moody. The nine-year-old is more independent and in better equilibrium. He can use language to express more subtle and refined emotions such as pity, envy, and self-criticism. The Gesell charts of growth gradients should be helpful and comforting to both parents and teachers.

The preadolescent period is a period of rapid growth in independence and in social awareness. Abstract words are becoming more meaningful, though the exact meaning of such words as *justice, beauty,* or *goodness* is dependent upon the individual's experience with those qualities in his own personal contacts with people and things.

A child's relationships with his peers affect him deeply. Studies which locate the isolated and the socially inept children in a group make it possible for the teacher to concentrate on helping these children to develop social skills and find social satisfactions in the group. Such social satisfaction and status influence personality development as well as academic achievement.

Secret languages such as "pig Latin" may appear during the preadolescent period. They represent the efforts of a pair or a group of children to communicate so that close social contact may be maintained without communicating with those on the "outside." This interest in language might be directed into interests in a foreign language if it were taught so that the learners could enjoy and utilize it in daily contacts.

Interest in slang also develops during the preadolescent period. Mothers are made unhappy because their children who previously spoke acceptable English now sound like the children from "across the tracks." The boy or girl at this age prefers the language of the gang to that of school and parents, at least for his street and playground contacts. The only comfort the schools can offer parents at this time is the assurance that, when boys and girls reach an age at which sophistication becomes important to them, they will reduce the proportion of slang and adapt their language more appropriately to the situations they encounter. Slang is not necessarily bad. Vivid, colorful, forceful slang may make a real contribution to the language and be accepted in time as an integral part of it. Cheap and vulgar slang tends to disappear or become revamped by succeeding generations of young people.

The adolescent period is a hero-worshipping period. Both boys and girls are prone to attach their affections to anyone who excites their admiration. With boys, admiration may be focused on physical prowess or vocational skill, as well as social leadership and personal magnetism; while with girls, personal magnetism and social leadership may be most important.

Attitudes and appreciations grow out of the child's individual experiences and are colored by the attitudes and interests of his immediate associates, particularly by the members of his family. Generosity, tolerance, and appreciation for people grow in happy homes and school groups where each member appreciates and respects the personality of the others. Intolerance and other negative attitudes are learned from others also; they are not innate characteristics or tendencies to be overcome. The child's ideals are at first those set for him by the standards and ideals of his home. During and after the period of adolescence they gradually emerge as the individual's own ideals, modified, adapted, or left unchanged by experience and the individuality of the young person attaining them.

□ THE PLACE AND FUNCTION OF LANGUAGE IN THE ELEMENTARY SCHOOL

Speech and writing are the expression or outgoing aspects of language and communication. They serve the purposes of social contact and enlightenment and are used to bring about a meeting of minds. Listening and reading are the means by which one enriches himself through enjoyment and through adding to his accumulated store of knowledge, insight, and understanding.

The school has always accepted the responsibility for the language arts, oral and written language, writing, spelling, and reading; though the subject matter, methods, and emphases have changed many times. Educators have come to realize that the language arts are a single pattern of interrelated skills which cannot be learned separately, and that the child's learning of the language arts is closely related to his individual growth patterns and to his experience. They also recognize that the ease with which a child masters the language arts and his facility in the use of them have direct influence upon his personality and behavior as well as upon his later social and economic efficiency.

The development of the language arts occupies almost the entire school day; in reality, language is taught from the time the first child enters the classroom in the morning until the last child goes home. It is the medium of operation in nearly everything that is done throughout the day. The teacher teaches both directly, through the activities and experiences she plans and carries through with the children, and indirectly, through her own speech, language, and behavior.

Language is therefore both an academic subject and a constantly used medium which can be enlarged and refined on the child's level only through experience in using it. The teacher must of necessity take each child where he is, and must learn through study and observation of his use of language and his responses to language the level of development he has reached and his points of strength and weakness. Then she can meet his needs through the utilization of carefully planned combinations of language and experience.

Progress in the mastery of language is a matter of planned instruction and thoughtful learning, as well as a process of natural development and maturation in an environment which provides stimulation and guidance. There are levels of mental development following one another in natural sequence which represent new powers and which are portrayed in the language used to express them. Language and thought develop together as an integrated whole. Language is of little value without ideas to express, and ideas are themselves dependent upon language.

Education cannot be a hurried process of forced development. It must proceed in a leisurely manner, providing an abundance of rich and varied experiences and time to talk them through to real understanding and clear expression. Each concept built should be as well formed and accurate as the mind of the child can conceive at his level of maturity, because each concept and each step in language development form part of the foundation for the thinking and learning yet to come and influence its quality.

SELECTED REFERENCES

1. Almy, Millie, *Young Children's Thinking.* New York: Teachers College Press, 1966.
2. Bruner, Jerome S., *The Process of Education.* Cambridge: Harvard University Press, 1960.
3. Chukovsky, Kornei, *From Two to Five.* Berkeley: University of California Press, 1963.
4. Church, Joseph, *Language and the Discovery of Reality.* New York: Random House, 1961.
5. Deutsche, Jean Marquis, "The Development of Children's Concepts of Causal Relationships." Minneapolis: The University of Minnesota Press, 1937.
6. Gesell, Arnold, and Ilg, Frances L., *The Child from Five to Ten.* New York: Harper and Brothers, 1946.
7. Gesell, Arnold; Ilg, Frances L.; and Ames, Louise B., *Youth: The Years from Ten to Sixteen.* New York: Harper and Brothers, 1956.
8. ———, "The Use of Pronouns by Young Children: A Note on the Development of Self-Awareness." *Journal of Genetic Psychology* 52:333-346, June, 1938.
9. Hall, Edward T., *The Hidden Dimension.* Doubleday, 1966.
10. ———, *The Silent Language.* Doubleday, 1959.
11. Hughes, Marie M., and Sanchez, George I., *Learning a New Language.* Washington, D.C.: Association for Childhood Education International, 1958.
12. Jersild, Arthur T., and Ritzman, Ruth, "Aspects of Language Development: The Growth of Loquacity and Vocabulary." *Child Development* 9:243-259. September, 1938.
13. Loban, Walter D., *The Language of Elementary School Children.* Research Report No. 1, Champaign, Ill.: National Council of Teachers of English, 1963.
14. McCarthy, Dorothea A., "Language Development in Children." *Manual of Child Psychology.* (Leonard Carmichael, Ed.), Rev. Ed., New York: John Wiley and Sons, Inc., 1954, pp. 492-630.
15. Piaget, Jean, *The Language and Thought of the Child.* (Tr. Marjorie Warden.) New York: Harcourt, Brace and Company, 1926.

16. Russell, David H., *Children's Thinking.* Boston: Ginn and Company, 1956.
17. Smith, Dora V., "Growth in Language Power as Related to Child Development." *Teaching Language in the Elementary School.* The Forty-third Yearbook, Part II, of the National Society for the Study of Education, Chap. IV, pp. 52-97. Chicago: University of Chicago Press, 1944.
18. Strickland, Ruth G., *The Language and Mental Development of Children.* Bulletin of the School of Education, Vol. 23, No. 2. Bloomington: Indiana University, 1947.
19. Templin, Mildred C., *Certain Language Skills in Children.* Minneapolis: The University of Minnesota Press, 1957.
20. Vygotsky, Lev Semenovich, *Thought and Language.* Cambridge: Massachusetts Institute of Technology, The M.I.T. Press, 1962.
21. Watts, A. F., *The Language and Mental Development of Children.* London: George G. Harrap & Co., Ltd., 1944. Boston: D. C. Heath and Co., 1947.

FACTORS THAT IN-FLUENCE LAN-GUAGE GROWTH

Language development is closely related to other aspects of the child's growth. Developing language in its various forms is one of the most difficult developmental tasks the child must perform. Adults can motivate and guide as the child learns to listen, talk, read, write, spell, and use the many forms of oral and written language, but the child carries on the learning process himself and achieves the result.

□ THE CHILD'S EQUIPMENT FOR LANGUAGE LEARNING

A child's ability to respond to his learning environment depends to a large extent on his own basic equipment for the task of learning language. He must be able to see, hear, feel, move, understand, make associations, coordinate his activities, and adjust to the people and things in his environment if he is to achieve language and to do so at a normal rate (35). The equipment he needs is both physical and mental.

■ *Physical equipment* – In order to learn language a child must have, first of all, the power to make associations. He must have the power to build neural pathways, to receive impressions and to respond to them. He must have the ability to see so that associations can be made through visual experience. He must have the ability to hear so that he can receive and learn to comprehend the auditory stimuli that bombard him. He needs a respiratory system that operates well enough to provide the air stream for the production of vocal tone. He must master the actual movements of sound production and articulation that are necessary for the production of speech. To achieve words, the child needs all of the physical equipment that will enable him to form the sounds of which the words in his language are composed. He needs tongue, lips, palate, throat passages, nasal cavities, and teeth that are properly formed or within normal limits and can be used to shape the sounds of which words are made (41, p. 3).

During the process of mastering speech sounds, the child learns to coordinate his activities. He receives cues – sounds, gestures, and facial expression – selects a word or words for response, and produces the response in spoken form. He does these things simultaneously or in sequence in a short space of time while he sits or stands or moves about. How well he coordinates his activities depends somewhat on his physical and emotional state at the moment. If he is rested, well, and happy, he will probably respond easily and well. If he is tired or upset, his responses will be less mature and less adequate.

■ *Intellectual equipment*—A number of studies have dealt with the relationship between language and intelligence. Since most intelligence tests are highly dependent on the use of language, it is difficult to know how accurate a measure they may be. Certainly a child with a good command of language should score better than a child with a poor command of language, but to what extent his intelligence is responsible for that command of language is difficult to ascertain. Again, environment and school or home experience enter into the problem.

An example serves to illustrate this point. Harry, the son of feeble-minded parents, was brought to school at the age of seven. The child appeared as low in intelligence as his parents, but, knowing the meagerness of his preschool life, the school sought to build both vocabulary and background of knowledge and experience through stories, pictures, books, and excursions out into the environment. At the end of six months of such intensive enrichment of experience, the child tested low average on an individual standardized intelligence test. The ability to learn was present but his preschool experience had afforded little opportunity for exercise of that ability.

Terman's study of gifted children (38) indicated that they tended to begin talking at an earlier age than normal children. Studies of mentally defective children, on the other hand, have indicated that with such children, the beginning of talking may be delayed for two years or more. There seems to be some relationship between the age at which talking begins and the quality of mental ability, though this is not always true. Slow starters may be slow for lack of motivation or other reasons and may achieve satisfactorily once they set to work on the task of learning to talk. A child who talks early is at least normal, and probably superior, but a child who begins to talk at the average age may prove to be bright and so may a child who delays talking for a few months. Jersild (20) calls attention to the fact that though a mentally defective child is likely to be late in learning to talk it does not follow that all slow starters are defective.

■ *Aptitude for language*—Children vary greatly in the speed and ease with which they develop the forms of language. Some children learn to talk at an early age and make rapid progress in all language skills. Adults provide sympathetic interest in the child's progress and a normal amount of motivation, and the child carries on his task with interest and a high degree of success. Children who learn to talk at an early age and progress without difficulty tend to make similar progress in the development of reading and other language skills.

Some children are late starters in learning to talk, though they show evidence of understanding language and take an interest in it. Some of the slow starters listen carefully and absorb a great deal before they try to talk. They are similar to the little girl from an Italian-speaking home who remained silent for several months in kindergarten. However, when the desire to help decorate the Christmas tree overcame timidity and lack of confidence, she began her use of English speech with a complete sentence, "Please, I want some paste." The slow starters may make rapid progress when they reach the point of motivation at which they try to talk, because they have learned a great deal through listening and observation.

Many of these children ultimately talk as well and as much as those who started earlier. They may be slow in learning to read as they were in learning to speak, but achieve up to their mental capacity when they are ready to read if they are safeguarded from discouragement and frustration during the intervening period of development.

There are some children who never become adept in the handling of language and who are linguistically handicapped all of their lives. Culturally deprived children who are given little stimulation or help with language in their early years at home may be unable to overcome their handicap without a great deal of individual stimulation and guidance at school. The Head Start programs being initiated in many communities may succeed in salvaging some of these children and preparing them for success in school rather than for failure. It is undoubtedly true that teachers can do relatively little for the language of a student unless the student is sufficiently interested to put forth some effort for his own improvement, but there are many methods of motivating interest in self-improvement which should be tried before the school accepts the handicap as irremediable.

Children who, because of mental deficiency or neurological problems, find the acquisition of language skills especially difficult should be given expert motivation and guidance so that they achieve to the limit of their capacity. What they are able to do should be accepted and utilized for their upbuilding while every effort is made to help each child build up all his resources and avenues of strength to compensate for his lack of linguistic aptitude. The child is truly the master of his own learning but parents and teachers must clear the way and assist at every possible point.

□ HOME AND FAMILY INFLUENCES

The child's first language lessons are in the home and his mother is the first teacher. Her smile and her voice stimulate his first responses and his first echoing vocalizations (22). The more contact the child has with his mother's friendly voice and the more opportunity he has to hear her speech, the more rapidly he grows in the acquisition of language. An only child who has his mother's undivided attention learns to speak and to use language earlier and more readily than the child who has only a portion of his mother's attention and interest.

■ *Mother-child relationships*—Psychologists have called attention to the importance of the kind of relationship that exists between mother and child in this early period (22). If the child is babied and pampered his speech tends to remain immature. If the mother attempts to hold him to standards that are too high for him to achieve comfortably, his speech development may be retarded. If such mothers as these can be helped to release their children emotionally and enjoy them as they grow and develop, the children make more satisfactory progress in correcting their speech difficulties (41).

Babies who are brought up in a normal family situation tend to vocalize more and to show more interest in speech than children brought up in an institutional environment (22, 33). The differences show even during the first six months of life. Children who have been separated from their families and who have spent much of their babyhood in a hospital or foundling home tend to manifest serious and permanent retardation in language. The lack of individual attention and mothering in early years is deprivation from which children do not easily recover even when more attention is showered on them later on in their development (22).

■ *Motivation and growth in language*—The age of the people with whom a child associates appears to influence his growth in language. The child who associates largely with adults may develop more rapidly than the child who associates mainly with children and may develop a more mature vocabulary, use longer sentences, and more complex ones. One researchist found that only children tend to surpass in language development children who have siblings, probably for this reason (10). The child who associates mainly with children not only has a less mature pattern to copy but may be able to communicate with other children with whom he plays without much effort to use language.

Deliberate efforts of adults to motivate a child to talk appear to produce little result unless they fit into the child's own growth needs. It is true that a child learns to talk by being talked to because he must learn through association, example, and experience. A normal amount of attention to the child is essential to his success, but anxious parents who devote extra time and attention to efforts to encourage a child to talk are often disappointed. Children talk when they are ready to talk, in their own good time, given a reasonable amount of motivation. Once a child has become interested in talking, the motivation of adult contact and adult help may spur him on to more rapid achievement than he could attain without such individual attention. What constitutes the most satisfactory amount and kind of motivation to talk is not accurately known. It is probably true that the stimulation of other types of experience than direct language motivation enters in, though normal maturation is undoubtedly the most important factor.

Experience in a home situation in which parents or older children talk "baby talk" or talk down to a child is almost certain to provide a stumbling block to learning. If the child's own mispronunciations and inaccurate grammatical constructions are given back to him through the talk of others in the home, he lacks correct patterns and stimulation to effort and gradually irons in his own incorrect forms instead of acquiring better ones. He will probably outgrow these patterns ultimately, but he is handicapped upon entrance to school, and unless he is helped to improve immediately, he may be ridiculed into self-consciousness, which makes the necessary relearning doubly difficult. "Scout" Finch in Harper Lee's *To Kill a Mockingbird,* spoke the dialect of her small Alabama community, although through her father's interest in reading to and with her, she had become an able reader before entering the first grade. She and children like her learn more than one dialect in home, community, and school and are soon using each one in the setting in which it is appropriate.[1]

□ LANGUAGE OF TWINS, SINGLETONS WITH SIBLINGS, AND ONLY CHILDREN

A number of researchists have studied the development of twins. It has been found that children of multiple birth tend to progress less rapidly in language development than do children of single birth. Children of the same age in a family tend to be brought up in close association with one another. They appear to understand each other and to carry on their contacts with less need for speech than children who differ in age. Facial expressions, gestures, grunts, single words and jargon seem to take the place of words and sentences quite satisfactorily. Day (11), in a study of eighty pairs of twins, twenty pairs each at 2, 3, 4, and 5 years of age, found several significant points with regard to language development. The twins studied were slightly below average in intelligence quotients as well as in language development. They began to talk one month later than their older siblings, though they were not retarded in age of learning to walk or appearance of the first tooth. A comparison of the length of verbal responses given by twins and singletons showed the responses of twins to be slightly shorter at all ages. The average length of the responses of twins at five was about the same as that of singletons at three. Twins showed a smaller percentage of verbs at two, a smaller percentage of adjectives, pronouns, and conjunctions at all ages, and a greater percentage of interjections at all ages. As was the case with children of single birth, girls used more words and more advanced sentence structure than boys. In agreement with other studies, the older twins showed the same resemblance in language traits as the younger twins.

A study by Davis (10) included twins, singletons with siblings, and only children. Only children were found to be def-

[1] Harper Lee, *To Kill a Mockingbird*, J. B. Lippincott Co., 1960.

initely superior to children with siblings in every phase of linguistic skill. Singletons with siblings were found to be somewhat superior to twins. Twins of the ages studied were especially retarded in perfection of articulation. This inferiority was marked during the kindergarten period, particularly in twins of lower occupational groups. Twins from the upper occupational groups by nine and one-half years had practically overcome their language handicap, but twins from lower occupational groups had made relatively little progress. Twins of unlike sex appear to progress more rapidly than twins of like sex.

☐ SEX DIFFERENCES IN LANGUAGE DEVELOPMENT

Girls have been found to surpass boys in a number of aspects of language development, although the amount of difference has varied in different studies. Day (11) found that girls use more words than boys and that they show all forms of the complete sentence earlier and in larger proportion than boys, though she found the difference less marked in twins than in singletons. Davis (10) found the articulation of girls superior to that of boys and the length of remarks made by girls up to nine and one-half years to be slightly greater than the length of remarks made by boys. She found, however, that the performance of twin boys compared more favorably with the performance of only children and of singletons with siblings than did that of twin girls. Boys were found likely to be less shy than girls and to ask more questions. They made more spontaneous remarks and also made more errors and used more slang.

☐ THE RELATION OF SOCIOECONOMIC STATUS

Studies carried on at the preschool level indicate a relationship between the socioeconomic status of the home and the language children develop in the home (10, 11, 12, 23). Children whose socioeconomic status is higher tend to use longer sentences and a larger vocabulary, to ask more questions, and to use more remarks involving adapted information. A more recent study by Templin (37) of children 3 to 8 years of age showed that children of upper socioeconomic level exceeded children of lower socioeconomic level in articulation of speech sounds, speech sound discrimination, sentence structure, and vocabulary. Living in a superior environment appears to give these children additional advantage, though the difference may be partly one of intelligence. Children of higher socioeconomic status tend to rate higher on intelligence tests than children of lower status. They also tend to have the advantage of parents of a higher level of education and to hear a larger vocabulary in daily use. Also, the child in the home of higher status is provided with books, play materials, and enriching experiences, in most instances, which facilitate the development of language.

A study of the vocabulary of several thousands of children in Birmingham, England, showed that at ten years of age, children from well-to-do districts scored on an average 50 per cent higher than children from poor districts. As the age rose, the difference between the two groups narrowed and at the age of fourteen, there was little difference between the children in vocabulary scores (40, pp. 25-26). Watts concludes that judgments as to relative amounts of intelligence of children being studied may be dangerous unless the children have been brought up in similar environments and have had the same kind of school training. Similar conclusions have been arrived at by Alison Davis and others in this country.

☐ HOME ATMOSPHERE

Differences in home atmosphere and parental behavior are reflected in children's language attainment in school as well as at home. Milner investigated the home experience of children who were in the lowest third and the highest third of their first grade class in language scores and found interesting and significant differences (26). Those in the lowest third of the class did not eat breakfast with their parents and participated in no two-way conversation with adults before leaving for school. Some of them were given orders and instructions but had no give-and-take conversation or stimulation to talk either before or after school or while carrying through the usual routines of the home. There was little evidence of acceptance of the children on the part of the parents and no outward show of affection. The children whose language scores were in the upper third of the class did have breakfast with their families and engaged in considerable two-way conversation both before and after school. They also received considerable show of affection which helped to make them feel secure and wanted in the family group. Disciplinary methods differed in the homes of the two groups. Those in the lowest language group received a good deal of direct physical punishment, while those in the upper group had discipline of the preventing, prohibiting, and controlling type involving oral communication rather than physical punishment.

These differences in methods of controlling and guiding children appear to be differences of socioeconomic levels. Also, the differences in opportunity for verbal interaction may be characteristic of socioeconomic differences in large measure. Socioeconomic differences may also be responsible in part for the affection shown children in their homes. The effect of these on children's language growth helps to explain the differences so often noted between the language development of the various socioeconomic groups. (22).

☐ BILINGUALISM

Whether learning two languages at home in the child's early years is more of an asset than a liability in ultimate language development is a question that has been long discussed. This problem is again coming into prominence in American schools with the tremendous influx of Spanish-speaking families and people of other origins and a good many displaced families.

Parents in foreign-speaking homes differ in their attitudes toward children's language learning and in what they expect of children. Some parents who have inherited a foreign language fear that their children will not learn this language unless they do so before they learn English, and consequently they use only the foreign language in the home. Thoughtful German parents who speak English with a Germanic accent brought their child to a nursery school to learn English. The child had learned only German in the home and the parents had been careful not to speak English before her. They wanted her to learn English at a good school so that she would speak it with proper English accent. Other parents, who spoke both English and French in their home, brought a child to nursery school complaining that the child was doing poorly with language. Their older children, the parents said, had always responded in French when spoken to in French and in English when spoken to in English. This child was mixing the two languages, much to her parents' disapproval. Still other parents who have grown up with a language other than English as their native tongue continue to use it in their homes, though they give their children opportunity to learn the out-of-home language as well. The children are not expected to learn to speak the home language but merely to understand it. In this case the children learn their patterns of English speech largely from playground and street experiences, and come to school with poor quality of speech and meager vocabulary.

Occasionally, parents who have painstakingly learned a second language feel that early childhood, with its apparent facility in learning oral language, is the ideal time for a child to learn a language other than the one common to the environment. These English-speaking parents who know also another language may decide that there is value in teaching the child the second language first and adding the English at a later time, probably when the child enters school. Such a decision almost inevitably isolates the child from other children during this period, but it has the advantage of giving the child only the stimulus and pattern of adult speech. These parents know that the language of the environment is sure to be learned sooner or later. They are convinced that to start a child with what will later become his second language insures a good start in learning that language and the development of correct articulation and pronunciation patterns.

Learning two languages during his early years forms a complex problem for a child—and one fraught with many social and emotional hazards. This is true whether he encounters one language almost exclusively until he reaches school age, and then is called upon to learn another, or is confronted with two languages from the start. If he is learning in his home exclusively a language other than that of his environment, he may encounter isolation, ridicule, and neighborhood prejudices which result in feelings of inferiority and emotional and social tensions. These may stay with the child long after he enters school and may complicate, not only his learning of the language used by the other children, but also all other aspects of his learning. In some neighborhoods a child encounters prejudices which lead to severe persecution by other children when he enters school and call for sympathetic protection and guidance from the teacher. A teacher needs to be alert for these underlying hostilities, for such prejudices are not always apparent on the surface.

It is commonly assumed that the child who is learning two

languages will progress more slowly in each than he would if he were learning only one language. Three studies by Smith, two of them made with a limited number of children, indicate the truth of this assumption. She concludes that a bilingual environment may not delay the beginnings of speech but is likely to handicap the child later. The most extensive of the three studies dealt with mastery of English by preschool children of non-American ancestry in Hawaii. The survey was made with a representative sampling of a thousand children who were either below school age or in their first school year, all between eighteen and seventy-eight months of age. She found children in the group retarded to a degree so marked that at the time of entrance to school they were at about the level of three-year-olds in a less polyglot environment (32). The retardation was due to the prevalent use of pidgin English and to the bilingualism of many homes. Kindergarten and nursery school attendance was found to be a definite advantage for the bilingual child in Hawaii as it is in the United States.

Manuel, in 1950, summarized the studies on bilingualism and pointed out that children who come from foreign-speaking homes do appear to be at a disadvantage in English-speaking schools (25). He called attention also to the difficulty of measuring the ability and achievement of these children of foreign background because of the socioeconomic and cultural differences that exist.

Arsenian (1) compared the mental growth of monolingual children matched on the basis of age, race, sex, and socioeconomic status. The group included more than a thousand American-born Jewish children, more than a thousand American-born children of Italian parentage, and samplings of foreign-born Italian and Jewish children as well as children of mixed parentages. The age range of the children studied was from nine to fourteen years. He found no reliable differences in mental growth and achievement in school between children from homes in which the foreign language was used a great deal and homes in which the foreign language was used relatively little.

Barham,[2] in a recent study of bilingual Maori children in Auckland, New Zealand, found that the main difference between six-year-old children who live during their out-of-school

[2] Lan H. Barham. *The English Sentence Patterns and Vocabulary of Some Maori and Pakeha Children*. Unpublished study. New Zealand Council for Educational Research.

hours mainly in a Maori environment and children who live in an English-speaking environment was in the number of English words and meanings they knew. Maori children were nearly two years behind the others in vocabulary, though when they spoke English they used the same sentence patterns as did the children from English-speaking homes.

Evidence of the effect of bilingualism on language development is not entirely clear and results in conflicting opinions. It does appear true that it presents complex learning problems for children which have many social and emotional facets as well as linguistic and intellectual ones. New evidence may come from the work being done in Florida by Pauline Rojas and others with large numbers of refugee Cuban children.

The present interest in teaching foreign languages in the elementary school will be considered in Chapter 9.

☐ LANGUAGE AND PERSONALITY DEVELOPMENT

Language and personality development are closely related in children, as are language and mental development. The child who acquires language easily appears to find it easy to make social contacts, to be outgoing in his reactions and interests. The child for whom language skills present problems may feel inadequate and ineffective; he may respond in a variety of ways. This shows very clearly in the case of the child who comes to school using infantile expressions which other children either have never used or have long outgrown. His awareness of other children's reactions toward him may cause him to become withdrawn and silent, if he fears their ridicule and criticism, or highly aggressive if he feels frustrated or rebels against the treatment he receives.

Children with hearing handicaps are very apt to develop personality traits which are direct outgrowths of inability to communicate. Teddy, a five-year-old boy in kindergarten, handicapped by poor vision and serious loss of hearing, responded like an enraged animal when other children's interests conflicted with his use of toys and building materials. His violently aggressive reactions grew out of his inability to make his needs and desires known, and thus to protect what he conceived to be his rights and interests. With the help of speech specialists and finally a hearing aid, he learned to express his thoughts in words and to read the thoughts of others from their lips. As a result, his violent reactions disappeared. Evidence of understanding and sympathy for the interests and needs of others grew as he learned to communicate and became more acceptable to other children.

Negativism and rebellion against adult pressures and demands may show themselves in the child's language behavior. Silence may become a means of protection from excessive demands or criticism. Jersild (20) tells the story of a little girl of three and a half years who became known in neighborhood and nursery school as "the girl who won't talk." Overwhelming and constant attention from her mother and the anticipation of every need and desire had resulted in the child's use of silence as a form of passive resistance to the excessive domination. In a situation in which her curiosity was aroused and her behavior ignored she proved able to talk in a very satisfactory manner. She became herself because she felt no need for self-protection.

Learning to read has become a necessity and a point of extreme pressure in many schools and homes and the child who finds difficulty in mastering the process is often sadly warped by his failure. A child who has shown no personality problems during his preschool years may develop serious problems of behavior and attitude if his efforts to learn to read bring only defeat and frustration instead of the satisfaction and commendation he sees other children receiving. If the teacher does not recognize his problem, diagnose it, and offer the necessary guidance to achieve success, he develops a sense of inadequacy and inability which makes him feel he is different from other children and which forms a stumbling block to success in other areas as well. A school in which children are helped to grow into reading rather than being forcibly pushed into it, creates fewer learning problems. Nothing is more devastating to the child's personality than inability to do what he wants and tries to do and what is expected of him. Unfavorable habits and attitudes grow rapidly and may follow the child through life because of his linguistic failures. Success in mastering linguistic skills opens the way to many types of satisfying experiences, and makes possible wholesome social, emotional, and mental development.

□ SCHOOL INFLUENCES ON LANGUAGE DEVELOPMENT

Children have had several years of language learning and have traveled a long way by the time they reach the elementary school. Whether a child is bright or dull, the quality of language and the amount of vocabulary he brings to school are the products of the experiences that have been provided for him by his home and neighborhood. His patterns of language behavior are pretty well set and will not be easily changed, whether they are good or bad.

■ *The influence of the teacher*—The teacher is, herself, an important part of each child's language curriculum. Her voice, vocabulary, enunciation, pronunciation, choice of words, and sentence structure serve as an ever-present model for the children. How much each of them is influenced by her speech and language depends on several factors. If the feeling a child has toward his teacher is one of admiration and affection and if he feels comfortable and secure with her he will tend to imitate her unconsciously. The similarity between the child's home language and the language he hears at school has an important bearing on his attitude. If the language is similar or if differences are respected, he will find it easier to grow in language power at school. Children sense the teacher's attitudes, ideals, standards, and reactions even though they are never expressed in words. The emotional tone of the teacher's speech and the uses to which speech is put, determine the feelings the speech engenders in the child. Young children in the early grades tend to be influenced by the teacher's speech quite unconsciously while children in the middle grades are often more strongly influenced by the language standards of the peer group (34). Children react to the personality of the teacher as much as to her language.

Sometimes the teacher's use of language results in reactions quite different from those she intends. Teachers mean to use language to stimulate thinking but sometimes the way they use it cuts off thinking. Teachers mean to use language to help children think and reason independently but at times what they say encourages children to accept dogmatic statements without question or protest. Teachers mean to build up each child's self-respect and sense of the worth of his own thinking but sometimes what is said tears down a child and makes him feel inadequate or unworthy because of voiced or implied criticism, impatience, or intolerance. It takes keen insight and real skill to devalue a child's unacceptable idea or behavior without devaluing the child himself. Teachers teach children to be sincere and outgoing or to be cautious and hypercritical, to express their thoughts and feelings or to conceal them behind silence or pretense.

Positive and constructive language produces integrative behavior on the part of children, while ineffective or divisive language may produce resistance or aggression (29, p. 307). Integrative language improves the child's mental and emotional states or at least keeps them in equilibrium, while destructive language causes them to deteriorate progressively. A study of language used by teachers to control children's behavior yielded some interesting generalizations (21). Suggestions and encouraging remarks impelled children to accept or to continue tasks, whereas if they were given no guidance or approval they abandoned the tasks. Pleasant requests were more effective than scolding and hopeful remarks were more valuable than depriving ones. Encouragement caused children to work promptly, whereas verbal hurrying tended to delay rather than expedite. Simple requests were found more effective than threats.

The values a teacher holds shine forth in all that she does. Children need as their teacher an emotionally mature person who looks at life in a straightforward and wholesome manner and who can help them to do likewise.

■ *The peer group and its influence*—Young children are influenced by the quality of the teacher's language far more than are older children—at least they appear to copy it more unconsciously. They need help to give attention and consideration to other children's ideas and contributions in sharing, reporting, planning, and evaluating experiences. From the ego-centered speech behavior of the young child to a mature meeting of minds is a long process of growth which requires guidance all along the way.

At eight years of age and even more strongly at nine and ten there is interest in breaking away from adult domination and developing closer ties with the peer group. Authorities who have studied children of this age consider this group life before puberty an important step in the growth of independence for the individual (3, 29, 44). It serves as a haven from parental authority and an opportunity for social contacts that make fewer demands than do adult ones. This is the period in which children disregard adult standards in matters of grooming and manners. They develop secret signs and secret language to prevent adults from checking on their activities.

Disregard for the speech standards of both home and school is characteristic of this period, also. Interest is keen in new, colorful, vigorous vocabulary. Some children reach out eagerly for all new bits of slang and even a little of completely unauthorized language. Strang (34) suggests that some of this interest in language might possibly be directed into acquisition of a foreign language if it were taught so that it could be enjoyed and utilized in daily contacts.

The preadolescent period is one of rapid growth in vocabulary if children's interests are encouraged and fed. It is a period of tremendous intellectual curiosity and wide and vital interests together with the manifestation of a good deal of initiative and industry in the pursuit of those interests.

■ *The school environment and atmosphere*—Movable furniture, stimulating work centers, a good classroom library, and quantities of raw material for work are advocated by the child development specialists who study children's language development. The equipment in the classroom is such that it can be arranged and rearranged to fit all types of activities and needs. There are centers of interest (art, science, arithmetic, social studies, library, etc.) so that children do not need to wait for the teacher's next assignment in order to use their time purposefully. The furniture lends itself to both individual and group work. Grouping for various activities encourages thoughtful and helpful interaction so that children learn to work cooperatively as well as independently.

Oral language is used to meet natural classroom needs. There is time for sharing personal and intellectual interests; for planning, discussing, reporting, and evaluating the interests and work of the group. Written language and reading are means to practical ends and also sources of personal pleasure and means of personal expansion.

First-hand and vicarious experience are both essential to language development. Field trips, experimentation, and various types of individual exploration are used where they prove valuable. Reading and audio-visual materials supply vicarious experience. Language skills are worked on in situations in which their value is apparent so that interest in improvement is kept at the highest possible level and children are encouraged to discipline their use of language and strive for increasingly higher levels of attainment.

The school's influence on children through books, reading, and literature has four major parts; the provision of adequate quantity and variety of books and materials to interest all children and the provision of plenty of time and motivation for the use of them; help with developing and refining skill in reading; guidance in the selection and use of materials; and any individual encouragement as therapy that may be needed. Building interest in reading comes first, then help with the development of reading skill. Classroom and school libraries are made as attractive and comfortable as possible so that children are encouraged to use them. Skillful guidance on the part of teacher and librarian helps each child to find material he can enjoy and profit from and helps him to gain satisfaction from it.

■ *Interrelationships among the language arts*—One conviction has grown as educators have studied children's growth in the language arts in the schools: that the various elements cannot be taught separately with satisfactory results because of the inherent interrelationships which exist among the uses and functions of language (2, 19). The child comes to school able to talk and to listen, though each of these skills needs further building. The school teaches him to read, write, spell, and use written language for many purposes. One cannot read reading nor write writing. One must read and write something; there must be content of some kind if children are to learn skills in such form that they are ready for use.

British writers reiterate again and again that if what children write is poor the teacher must work on oral language (6, 31). American writers are saying increasingly that elementary school children cannot read with understanding sentences that are much more mature and involved than those they use in talking. Research evidence indicates clear and important relationships between the various facets of the language arts program. All of this means that teachers cannot successfully teach the parts in isolation but must increasingly find ways to relate the various elements of language learning to one another and to the uses to which they are put in life. Methods of teaching are as important as what is taught.

□ COMMUNITY INFLUENCES ON LANGUAGE DEVELOPMENT

The community serves as a laboratory for the growth of language and its use (5). The contacts and first-hand experiences a child has in the community add to his vocabulary of words and meanings and help to set the standard for his language. Ethel Waters' description of her childhood in the slums of Philadelphia in her book, *His Eye Is on the Sparrow,* makes clear the effect of her experience on her language. She had a long, long way to climb, mainly unaided but partly with the help of the school, before she could operate satisfactorily in an entirely different language environment and at an entirely different language level. Francie, in *A Tree Grows in Brooklyn*, had inner drives which took her to the library for books through which she could live in a different world; her eagerness for something better caused her to list a false address so that she could attend a school outside her district. Lovejoy, in the English story *An Episode of Sparrows* by Rumer Godden, was forever searching for something better. She was a poor reader because reading mattered so little in her sordid and unhappy world. Billie Davis, who grew up in a jalopy and in the camps of migrant workers, recalls being slapped for using her school-learned English because in the eyes of her mother she was "putting on airs."

■ *Community as laboratory*—As children are helped to see the possibilities in community participation which call for the use of language—talking, writing, reading—their inner drive to achieve is strengthened. Trips into the environment, learning about the work of various community groups, and participation in community enterprises frequently prove sources of motivation. In the English film *Near Home,* the children used all forms of the language arts in realistic and vital manner in carrying on their study of their community. In the French film *Passion for Life,* the boys in the school turned from formal grammar, in which they had little interest, to keen interest in improving their school and used language of increasingly high quality in the doing. The community project for slow learners, described in *Language Arts for Today's Children,* showed how children improved all of their language skills as they performed the very real service of rehabilitating the home of an elderly couple under the inspiration of the local community chest (27, pp. 312-315). A fourth grade in a Philadelphia private school enriched and sharpened their oral and written language skills and found vital motivation for reading in a study of the history of their city.

■ *Community agencies*—Boy and Girl Scout programs, Boys' Clubs, and 4-H Clubs provide children with many opportunities to enrich their background and vitalize their learning of the language arts. Community provision for camp experiences for boys and girls is growing rapidly throughout the country. Some school systems have purchased or built camps so that all children may have camping experience at public expense. All camp programs include story telling, dramatics, letter writing, and creative activities as well as talk and discussion (17).

All churches carry on programs for children and youth. Increasingly, these programs include planning, discussion, creative and practical writing of various types, and dramatics. Church school workers are studying child development and methods for teaching and guidance in order to help boys and girls understand themselves and their behavior and understand the teachings and aspirations of the church. Children are guided into reading books which are designed to change attitudes and to build and strengthen character.

The library in any community is a resource for the language arts program. Extensive library collections are loaned to the schools, even transported to them by bookmobile in rural areas, to enrich children's reading experience. Libraries are adding collections of films and recordings of music, great speeches, and great events so that these may be borrowed by schools or homes or used in the library.

Many libraries hold story hours for children on Saturday mornings to interest children in books and reading. A rapidly expanding service is the summer reading program for boys and girls. Usually it is announced in the schools in the spring and children are encouraged to participate. Recognition is provided for quantity and quality of vacation-time reading.

□ MASS MEDIA

Television viewing still occupies about three hours a day of the time of many children, according to studies that have been made (42). Some parents guide children's selection of programs and some permit children to see what they wish whenever they wish. In a study of the television interests of five groups of kindergarten children in Cincinnati, it was found that children in homes of higher socioeconomic level knew and followed the good programs for children, while children of the lowest socioeconomic level appeared not to know these programs but listed unsuitable programs they saw, apparently because the older members of the family chose the programs (28).

Comic books are a community influence which has come under critical surveillance in recent years. Parents' groups in some communities have found ways to discourage or stop the sale of harmful comics, while in other communities adults have given the matter of their children's diet of comics little or no attention. Libraries and schools have worked to limit the reading of comics through making better books readily available to children and encouraging children to raise their sights. Community groups concerned with the rising rate of juvenile delinquency have turned some of their attention to comics, television, radio, and movies and their effect on children.

Since one's language is an intimate part of him, all influences that help to build the self affect the growth and the use of language. Recognition is growing rapidly that the language arts cannot be separated one from the other nor can any of them for any individual be separated from the personality and the life experience of the user.

□ SELECTED REFERENCES □

1. Arsenian, S., *Bilingualism and Mental Development.* Teachers College Contributions to Education, No. 712. New York: Bureau of Publications, Teachers College, Columbia University, 1937.
2. Artley, A. Sterl, "Research Concerning Interrelationships Among the Language Arts." *Elementary English.* XXVII:527-37, 1950.
3. Blair, Arthur W., and Burton, William H., *Growth and Development of the Pre-Adolescent.* New York: Appleton-Century-Crofts, Inc., 1951.

4. Church, Joseph, *Language and the Discovery of Reality.* New York: Random House, 1961.
5. Crosby, Muriel, "Factors that Influence Language Growth: Community Influences." *Elementary English,* 30:34-41, Jan. 1953.
6. Cutforth, John A., *English in the Primary School.* Oxford: Basil Blackwell, 1954.
7. Darcy, Natalie T., "The Performance of Bilingual Puerto Rican Children on Verbal and Non-language Tests of Intelligence." *Journal of Educational Research* XLV:499-506, March, 1952.
8. Davis, Allison, *Social Class Influences Upon Learning.* Cambridge: Harvard University Press, 1952.
9. Davis, A. E., *English in the Modern School.* London: Methuen and Co., Ltd., 1954.
10. Davis, Edith A., *The Development of Linguistic Skills in Twins, Singletons with Siblings, and Only Children from Age Five to Ten Years.* Institute of Child Welfare Monograph Series, No. 14. Minneapolis: University of Minnesota Press, 1937.
11. Day, Ella J., "The Development of Language in Twins: A Comparison of Twins and Single Children." *Child Development* 3:179-199, September, 1932.
12. Fisher, Mary S., *Language Patterns of Preschool Children.* Child Development Monographs, No. 15. New York: Bureau of Publications, Teachers College, Columbia University, 1934.
13. Gesell, Arnold, and Ilg, Frances L., *The Child From Five to Ten.* New York: Harper and Brothers, 1946.
14. ——, *Infant and Child in the Culture of Today.* New York: Harper and Brothers, 1943.
15. Gesell, Arnold; Ilg, Frances L.; and Ames, Louise B., *Youth: The Years from Ten to Sixteen.* New York: Harper and Brothers, 1956.
16. Hammett, Catherine T., and Musselman, Virginia, *The Camp Program Book.* New York: National Recreation Association, 1951.
17. Henry, George H., "Can Your Child Really Read?" *Harper's Magazine* 192:72-76, January, 1946.
18. Hughes, Marie M., and Sanchez, George I., *Learning a New Language.* Washington, D. C.: Association for Childhood Education International, 1958.
19. Hughes, Virgil H., "A Study of the Relationships Among Selected Language Abilities." *Journal of Educational Research* 49:97-106, October, 1953.
20. Jersild, Arthur T., *Child Psychology.* (Rev. & Enl.) Englewood Cliffs, N. J.: Prentice-Hall, Inc., 1961.

21. Johnson, Marguerite W., *Verbal Influences on Children's Behavior.* Ann Arbor: University of Michigan Press, 1938.
22. McCarthy, Dorothea, "Factors that Influence Language Growth: Home Influences." *Elementary English* 29:421-428, November, 1952.
23. ——, *The Language Development of the Pre-School Child.* Institute of Child Welfare Monograph Series, No. 4. Minneapolis: University of Minnesota Press, 1930.
24. ——, "Personality and Learning" in American Council on Education Studies, 1949, Series I, No. 35, pp. 93-96.
25. Manuel, Herschel T., "Bilingualism" *Encyclopedia of Educational Research.* (Ed. Walter S. Monroe, Rev. ed.) New York: The Macmillan Co., 1950.
26. Milner, Esther, "A Study of the Relationships Between Reading Readiness in Grade One School Children and Patterns of Parent-Child Interaction." *Child Development* XXII:95-112, 1951.
27. National Council of Teachers of English, Commission on the English Curriculum, *Language Arts for Today's Children.* N.C.T.E. Curriculum Series, Vol. II. New York: Appleton-Century-Crofts, Inc., 1954.
28. Nunnally, Nancy, "Primary Films as a Factor in Promoting Conceptual and Factual Learning in Kindergarten Children." *Thesis Abstract Series,* No. 7, Studies in Education. Bloomington: Bureau of Cooperative Research and Field Service, School of Education, Indiana University, 1955.
29. Olson, Willard, *Child Development.* Boston: D. C. Heath and Co., Revised Edition, 1959.
30. Redl, Fritz, "Preadolescents: What Makes Them Tick?" *Child Study* XXI:44-48, 1944.
31. Smith, A. E., *English in the Modern School.* London: Methuen and Co., Ltd., 1954.
32. Smith, Madorah E., "Some Light on the Problem of Bilingualism as Found from a Study of the Progress in Mastery of English among Preschool Children of Non-American Ancestry in Hawaii." *Genetic Psychology Monographs* 21:119-284, May, 1939.
33. Stone, J. Joseph, "A Critique of Studies of Infant Isolation." *Child Development* 25:9-20, March, 1954.
34. Strang, Ruth, *An Introduction to Child Study.* (Rev. ed.) New York: The Macmillan Co., 1949.
35. Strickland, Ruth G., "Factors that Influence Language Growth: School Influences." *Elementary English* 29:474-81, December, 1952.
36. ——, *The Language of Elementary School Children: Its Relationship to the Language of Reading Textbooks and the*

Quality of Reading of Selected Children. Bloomington: Bulletin of the School of Education, Indiana University, July, 1962.

37. Templin, Mildred C., *Certain Language Skills in Children.* Minneapolis: The University of Minnesota Press, 1957.
38. Terman, Lewis M., et al., *Mental and Physical Traits of a Thousand Gifted Children.* (Genetic Studies of Genius, Vol. I.) Stanford, California: Stanford University Press, 1925.
39. Wann, Kenneth D.; Dorn, Miriam S.; and Liddle, Elizabeth Ann, *Fostering Intellectual Development in Young Children.* New York: Bureau of Publications, Teachers College, Columbia University, 1962.
40. Watts, A. F., *The Language and Mental Development of Children.* London: George G. Harrap and Co., Ltd., 1944. Boston: D. C. Heath and Co., 1947.
41. Wells, Charlotte, "Factors that Influence Language Growth: The Child's Equipment for Language Growth." *Elementary English* 29:348-55, October, 1952.
42. Witty, Paul, and Kinsella, Paul, "Televiewing: Some Observations from Studies, 1949-1962." *Elementary English* 39:772-79, December, 1962.
43. Wood, K. S., "Parental Maladjustments and Functional Articulatory Defects in Children." *Journal of Speech Disorders* 11:255-275, 1946.
44. Zachry, C. B., and Lighty, M., *Emotion and Conduct in Adolescence.* New York: Appleton-Century-Crofts, Inc., 1940.

LANGUAGE DEVELOPMENT IN THE PRESCHOOL YEARS

A great deal of new knowledge about what children do as they learn their language has been amassed in very recent years, in fact, more of it than in all the years preceding. General interest in language together with recently developed techniques for recording and processing it have produced a surge of interest in the language of children and valuable information concerning it. A number of studies were done in the 1930's but little was learned until fairly recently about the ways in which children's language develops and what they can do with it. Now, as a result of intensive study of the language learning of individual children and extensive recording of the language of groups of children, there is new evidence of what children do as they learn their language.

The new information is coming from a variety of sources. The methods and techniques of the descriptive linguist are being combined with those of the psychologist, giving the psychologist scientific methods for the study of language and the linguist insight into the psychology of learning. The work of the psycholinguists has been limited largely to the language of preschool children and how they acquire it. Researchers in English and education have studied the language of school children and provided information which can serve as a basis for curriculum and textbook production. Little by little, knowledge is accumulating about how a child progresses from his first word to the infinite sentences he can produce as an adult.

Actually, no one knows just *how* children learn their language but evidence of *what* they do as they learn it calls for some revision of popular notions about the early years. Much of the evidence can be verified by parents who have been interested in observing their child's language development but the significance of some of these observations is only now coming to light.

Parents watch with deep interest and some concern for evidence of the mental capacity of their child. Physical development which follows the normal pattern reassures them about his physical inheritance and the quality of care they are giving him. The language development of the child tends to afford them similar reassurance regarding his mental capacity. Perhaps that is the reason parents experience such pleasure in the first words a child speaks and what he does with language between this time and the time he enters school.

☐ A CHILD'S FIRST USE OF HIS VOCAL APPARATUS

Speech is a form of behavior which is very complex and lies within the power of man alone. Efforts have been made to teach anthropoid apes to talk, but though they do display an intellect somewhat like man's in certain respects and a language a little like man's in totally different respects, there is no close correspondence between the thought and speech that is characteristic of man and the achievement of any other creature (47, p. 41). No other form of behavior in which human beings engage requires such intricate patterns of muscular reactions, all of which must be perfectly and delicately coordinated if there is to be communication.

Three groups of muscles are involved in human speech: the muscles of respiration which produce the necessary air flow and pressure, the muscles which control the vocal cords to produce sound, and the muscles of the tongue, jaws, and lips which shape the sound. All of these must be coordinated and work in perfect harmony or speech will be defective.

The physical apparatus for the production of speech sounds is all present when the child is born. The first use comes at the moment of the intake of breath in what is called the "birth cry." Thereafter the baby's vocal expression is as diffuse for a time as his other muscular reactions, the waving of his tiny arms, kicking and squirming. The muscles of the face, the thorax, and other parts of the body are all involved when he cries violently. During the early weeks the baby attaches no meaning to his cries. They are not for the purpose of communication, but are associated with his bodily condition and are most likely to occur when he is hungry, or when he is wet or otherwise uncomfortable. The cries of very young babies differ, and the cries of the same baby vary from time to time in pitch, loudness, and quality of sound. Many mothers feel that they can distinguish easily the cries of hunger, pain, fright, and the cry which denotes loneliness and desire for attention, though some authorities question this.

Experimental study of infant crying carried on at St. Mary's Hospital, in Rochester, Minnesota, in connection with the Mayo Clinic, appears to indicate that even a tiny infant cries only when he has physical or emotional needs which call for attention.[1] Ignoring the notion current among many people that

[1] Katherine E. Roberts. "Babies Don't Cry for Fun." *Parents' Magazine* 21:22, 154-157, Nov., 1946.

much of a baby's crying is for exercise and that he should be left to cry if the mother or nurse feels that physical welfare does not call for attention, the attendants in the hospital nursery were instructed to give a baby comfort and reassurance the moment he cried through picking him up or meeting whatever need appeared most logical, so that crying was kept at the lowest possible minimum. Mothers were asked to continue this watchful care when the baby was taken home from the hospital and to record their best judgment as to the reason for the baby's cry, whenever it occurred, and the frequency of the cries. Crying was kept at a very low point through such care and there were noticeable results in even-tempered and smooth personality development. The vocalizations during the first days of life tend to be distress signals and call attention to the baby's complete helplessness. Though man in maturity goes beyond all other living beings in his ability to communicate, he is the most helpless of all infants.

Probably the most significant studies of infant speech are the studies of Irwin and his associates at the University of Iowa. They found four vowel sounds appearing with appreciable frequency in the vocalization of 40 newborn babies whom they studied during the first few days of life (19). In this study of infants' speech the researchists utilized the International Phonetic Alphabet to make their records and found high agreement between observers. In a study of the speech sounds used by 95 infants it was found that the average infant uses about seven different sounds in the first two months and that the total has reached approximately twenty-seven sounds by two and a half years of age (4). It appears that vowel sounds predominate in this early vocalization by a ratio of about two to one. This ratio is reversed by the end of the first year and by two and a half years there appear to be about one and one-half times as many consonant type sounds as vowel sounds uttered. By the age of two and a half the child uses practically all of the vowels needed for adult speech but only about two-thirds of the consonants. During the first two months of the infant's life vowel sounds were uttered about five times more frequently than consonant sounds but the two appear with about equal frequency by the age of two and a half years. During the first year there was no noticeable difference between the performances of boys and girls but after that girls appeared to utter a slightly larger number of types of sounds than did boys.

Another interesting point brought out by the studies deals

with the use made of the speech mechanism in producing these early sounds. The vowels uttered by newborns were made with the front part of the oral cavity more frequently than with the back part. In the course of vowel development during the first year there was increasing use of back vowels (20). Irwin found the trend in the use of consonants to be opposite to that of vowels (19). The aspirate sound *h* is used a great deal by six-months-old babies as well as other consonant sounds originating at the back of the oral cavity. The place of phonation for consonant sounds appears to be first back, then front, whereas the place of vowel sounds is front, then back. Lewis holds that sounds made with the back part of the oral cavity are those associated with states of comfort, such as feeding, while those made with the lips occur more often when the infant is in a state of discomfort. The hungry infant uses a variety of anticipatory mouthing movements (27). It is interesting to note that in many languages the baby's first word for mother combines a front consonant with a back vowel—*mama, mummy, mommie*, or something similar.

□ EARLY FORMS OF COMMUNICATION

The mother's earliest form of communication with the baby is probably through her hands. If the hands that pick him up are gentle, loving and comforting yet firm, solid, and dependable, they give him a sense of security, of being loved. Ability to trust begins at this point (45). Later he responds to his mother's smile with sparkling eyes and with a smile. He can laugh aloud by sixteen weeks. He recognizes adult attention; he coos, gurgles, kicks, and waves his arms in response to smiles and pleasant, familiar-sounding voices; but he grows tense and quiet and may break into tears if the voice is harsh, loud, angry, or scolding.

The child is responsive to inflections and intonations before he is aware of the exact sounds of vowels and consonants. When he has learned to wave in response to the sounds "bye-bye" he may wave also in response to other words of similar sound if they are spoken in the same tone of voice.

Gestures come into use as soon as the child has achieved control of the muscles of arm and upper trunk. He may grunt and reach for a toy that is just beyond his grasp, or he may vocally and forcibly reject an object he does not want, and reach for and accept with sounds of approval one he desires.

☐ THE BABBLING PERIOD

Discovering the possibilities of his own body is one of the infant's earliest forms of learning. A young infant will watch with great interest the movement of his hand without appearing to realize at first that he is causing the movement, that the hand is part of him. An infant plays with his vocal apparatus in much the same way. He blows bubbles, spits, gurgles, and sputters for the sensory pleasure it affords him. He appears to come to the realization that he is the producer of the sound he hears, that he can make it at will, and he repeats it over and over with evident enjoyment.

There is tremendous variety in the sounds uttered by the infant in the babbling period and many of the sounds defy spelling in our alphabet. Children who are hearing only English sounds in their enviroment appear to be making German umlaut sounds, French guttural r's and other sounds it would be impossible to describe (30). The babbling often consists of repetition of identical or similar syllables such as *mama, dada, bye-bye, choo-choo,* and the like. There may be more repetition than variety at this stage; an infant may have one or two combinations of this sort that he uses persistently for a time. Babbling which appears to be direct response to a person may begin between two and six months of age.

Singing tones are noted in the vocalization of some babies at an early age. Some hum or croon; other trill up and down the scale. There appears to be wide range in the age at which singing tones are first used.

Inflection and intonation similar to that found in adult speech have been noted at about nine months of age. Shouting to attract attention, calling in scolding or warning tones, squealing with delight, grunting, grumbling, and growling all appear before the first comprehensible word. It would be interesting to know whether the expressive tones the babies used were a normal outgrowth of development or whether they were acquired by imitation of the tones used by adults (35).

The speech of infants may begin to take on conversational form by ten or eleven months (35). Two dissimilar syllables may be combined and used in conversational tones. Later the infant may appear to jabber in sentences with inflections that are declarative, interrogative, or exclamatory. Such conversational jargon may be carried over and mixed with early comprehensible speech.

During the first six months of life the child is exercising his vocal apparatus and learning to form many of the sounds needed for articulate speech. In the course of the second six months he learns in his vocal play to utter at will the sounds that strike his fancy and he repeats them over and over again. He gives himself an amazing amount of practice without any loss of interest.

☐ ASSOCIATION, CONDITIONING, AND MOTIVATION

Jespersen has said that children would never learn to talk if they were surrounded exclusively by thinkers who used language as a means of communicating thought. Luckily for children, in their earliest years they hear mother, nurse, and other women (and children) talk endlessly, with everlasting repetitions about the things and events close at hand. "We must then never forget that the organs of speech besides serving for the conveyance of thought, and before they begin to be used for that purpose, are one of mankind's most treasured toys, and that not only children but also grown people, in civilized as well as in savage communities, find amusement in letting their vocal cords and tongue and lips play all sorts of games" (24, p. 8).

These endless repetitions of words in situations where meaning is evident condition the child's own vocal responses. Mother says, "Here is your bottle, your good bottle. Take your bottle," and the child learns to associate word with object. Or she says each evening, "Here comes Daddy. Here's your Daddy," and the child echoes "dada" or eventually *Daddy*. The adults in his environment respond with pleasure and more repetition of the word and the child repeats the pleasant response. Association, repetition, and the conditioning that results from satisfying reaction motivate attention to speech sounds and effort to reproduce them. Faith in himself and faith in his ability to make his body do what his mind wants it to do, begins to grow.

☐ THE FIRST WORDS

It is difficult to spot the first comprehensible word used by a baby because of the problem of distinguishing between the chance expression of a familiar sound and the real and meaningful use of a word. Words are usually understood before they are used and the time at which they are first used may depend upon the motivating situations in which the child finds himself. Authorities agree that the average age for the appearance of the first word is about eleven months. The first word is usually a monosyllable or a reduplicated monosyllable such as "mama" or "bye-bye." The single words are eked out with gestures and inflection that give them the force of whole sentences. These single words may be expressed with varying emotions.

Most researchers agree that the child does not learn to make new sounds by imitation. Adults call attention to the sounds in the child's own repertoire which are the closest approximation to real words and those are repeated most often (21). A child may learn new groupings of sounds through imitation but they are all sounds he already uses spontaneously. It is interesting to consider the imitative words the child uses at about this time. "Bow-wow," "meow," "tick-tock," and "choo-choo" may have been picked up from the parents or older children, not invented by the babies themselves. Some children apparently make little or no use of such words while others retain them for quite a long period.

Watts calls attention to the fact that many instances of duplicated sounds indicate that this is a natural impulse, not just something learned from adults. It is interesting to note the use of such symbol sounds the world over; for instance, children in Germany call a dog *wau-wau,* and the Russian term is the same; in France it is *oua-oua;* in Holland it is *waf-waf;* in Japan it is *wan-wan,* as compared with the English pet name *bow-wow* (44).

Little children use words less precisely than adults. "Daddy" may mean any man for a time and "bye-bye" may mean riding in a cart or putting on cap and coat. Stern tells of the misconception of one of his own children. They often said 'eins, zwei" (one, two) in time with their steps as they walked; this child later referred to a walk as an "einschei" (40). With many children, words appear for quite a time to indicate general association rather than specific meaning.

Babies begin to use jargon at about fifteen months and many use it predominantly until they are about two years or a little older. Their inflection and expression may be so like that of adult speech that it is difficult at times to realize that they are not saying understandable words. As vocabulary increases jargon diminishes quite naturally because language is becoming a useful tool. When the child discovers that words have power to bring results, he usually makes rapid progress in acquiring them. Increase in sheer quantity of talking comes with increase in vocabulary and language power.

■ *The monologues of two-year-olds* – By two and a half many children are carrying on long monologues. Daytime monologues tend to follow the sequence of the child's play. He appears to think aloud as he wraps up the doll for a ride in his little cart, piles blocks one on top of the other until they fall down, or scoops and pats the damp sand to make a cake. Speech is an accompaniment to action and is in itself satisfying to the child. He cannot yet carry on inner speech; overt speech and thought tend to be one and the same at this level.

Mothers have long known that some children talk to themselves before they fall asleep at nap time and especially at evening bedtime. A. A. Milne, who has shown particular sensitivity to children's ways of thinking and reacting, has portrayed this creatively in his poem "In the Dark" in *Now We Are Six*.

Ruth Weir, of Stanford University, made a scientific study and analysis of the pre-sleep monologues of her son Anthony between the ages of 28 and 30 months (45). She recorded his bedtime soliloquies on tape by remote control. Here is evidence of a child's play with language – play which is clearly practice of language forms he is mastering. Typical of the material of the soliloquies are transformations such as:

> Bobo go take off the hat
> Bobo took off the hat

and many instances of practice with ideas and words which interested him during the day –

> A phone call book
> Phone call book
> This is the
> Book
> Another phone call book
> This is light
> One light
> This is light on it

This egocentric speech may constitute, according to Vygotsky, an intermediate link between overt and inner speech. He hypothesizes that speech is internalized psychologically before it is internalized physically.

> Egocentric speech is inner speech in its functions; it is speech on its way inward, intimately tied up with the ordering of the child's behavior, already partly incomprehensible to others, yet still in overt form and showing no tendency to change into whispering or any other sort of half-soundless speech (47, p. 46).

The sequence Vygotsky sees is from overt speech through egocentric speech to inner speech.

As a result of his investigations of children's speech, Vygotsky concluded that mental operations generally develop in four stages. The first he calls the primitive or natural stage in which the child plays with sound in a primitive way. This stage of babbling and jargon is a stage of preintellectual speech and preverbal thought. Thought and speech are beginning to develop but separately and without clear relationship to each other. The second stage Vygotsky calls the stage of "naive psychology" in which the child's speech may run ahead of understanding. This stage is characterized by correct use of grammatical forms and structures before the child understands the logical operations for which they stand:

> He masters the syntax of speech before the syntax of thought.– (He) learns relatively late the mental operations corresponding to the verbal forms he has been using for a long time.
>
> With the gradual accumulation of naive psychological experience, the child enters a third stage, distinguished by external signs, external operations that are used as aids in the solution of internal problems. That is the stage when the child counts on his fingers, resorts to mnemonic aids, and so on. In speech development it is characterized by egocentric speech.
>
> The fourth stage we called the "ingrowth" stage. The external operation turns inward and undergoes a profound change in the process. The child begins to count in his head, to use "logical memory", that is, to operate with inherent relationships and inner signs. In speech development, this is the final stage of inner, soundless speech (47, p. 46, 47).

Vygotsky is convinced that with the young child thought is initially nonverbal, that much of what seems thought is perhaps conditioning, as when the child runs to get his cap and coat when he sees mother preparing for a trip in the car. Likewise, the beginnings of speech are nonintellectual, that they actually do not involve thought. Even adults may carry on speech without actual thought, as when one recites a poem or sings a song to himself with no thought of what he is saying or answers a routine question mechanically. After speech and thought converge they operate in conjunction at times, separately at times.

□ THE WONDER YEARS—AGE TWO TO FIVE

An enthusiastic student of the language development of young children, Kornei Chukovsky, a writer and student of children's language in the Soviet Union, calls the child from two to five a language learning genius and is greatly impressed by the zeal with which the child works on his learning of language and his orientation in the world of things and people. "In truth," he says, "the young child is the hardest mental toiler on our planet" (5, p. 10). Studies of what children do as they master their language are indeed impressive.

Between the time when the parents' eager expectation is rewarded by what they think they recognize as a real word and the age of eighteen months, the child makes do with single word utterances into which his listeners can read far more meaning than the words actually express. As the child accumulates words, names for things in his enviroment, a word may become for the child part of the structure of the object it names, on equal terms with its other parts. The child does not think of the word as a sign but as one of the properties of the object, and he may demand a name for each new object he encounters.

Then begins a period of expansion of utterances into what has come to be called "telegraphic speech." The child says, "Daddy come." "Sweater off!" "See truck, Mommy." He appears aware first of the key meaning-bearing words in adult sentences, words that are pitched a little higher and stressed a little more sharply than the structure words in the sentences. Efforts at this time to induce him to repeat a complete sentence such as, "It belongs in the cupboard" or "I will not do that again" probably result in the echo responses, "Belongs cupboard" and "Do again."

A study by Brown and Bellugi of the acquisition of syntax by two young children is particularly interesting (3). In imitating model sentences uttered by their mothers, two children who were called Adam and Eve in the report (Adam aged twenty seven months and Eve eighteen months) preserved in every instance the word order of the model though they often omitted some of the words in the model utterance. The model "Daddy's briefcase" became "Daddy briefcase"; "Fraser will be unhappy" became "Fraser unhappy"; and "No, you can't write on Mr. Cromer's shoe" was reproduced "Write Cromer shoe" in the child's imitation. The authors hold that the child may repeat the order of the original sentence because he wants to say what the order says but it is also possible that he does so because his brain works that way and without comprehension of the semantic elements involved. It is interesting also that, as the models increase in length, the child's imitation remains two to three words in length.

Typical of mothers is the tendency to expand a speech pattern uttered by a child. To the child's utterance, "Baby highchair" the mother responded "Baby is in the highchair" and to "Eve lunch" she added, "Eve is having lunch." She kept the order of words in the child's utterance but fitted in the words and inflections that made the sentence complete.

Within a few weeks these children were producing utterances that were their own, not copies of models. A child said, "No I see truck" and his mother expanded the utterance to, "No, you didn't see it." Such utterances as "Why it can't turn off?," "Put a gas in," and "Cowboy did fighting me" were considered to be the child's own construction, not based on a similar model. "Somehow, then," the authors conclude, "every child processes the speech to which he is exposed so as to induce from it a latent structure" (3, p. 144). In the final stage of the study the children were replacing noun phrases with pronouns, for example, "Fix a tricycle" with "Fix it" and were using pronouns and noun phrases in the same utterance, as in, "Mommy get it my ladder" and "I miss it cowboy boot." It seems clear that this last step, the induction of latent structure, is by far the most complex (3, p. 131).

Lenneberg, of Harvard University and Children's Medical Center, writes in a recent publication:

> The onset of speech is an extremely regular phenomenon, appearing at a certain time in the child's physical development and

> following a fixed sequence of events, as if all children followed the same general "strategy" from the time they begin to the period at which they have mastered the art of speaking. The first things that are learned are principles—not items: principles of categorization and pattern perception. The first words refer to classes, not unique objects or events. The sounds of language and the configuration of words are at once perceived and reproduced according to principles; they are patterns in time, and they never function as randomly strung up items. From the beginning, very general principles of semantics and syntax are manifest. Even if the maturation scale as a whole is distorted through retarding disease, the order of developmental milestones, including the onset of speech, remains invariable. Onset and accomplishment of language learning do not seem to be affected by cultural or linguistic variations. . . . The ability to learn language is so deeply rooted in man that children learn it even in the face of dramatic handicaps (26, pp. 66, 67).

The child's intuitive awareness of principles of phonology and syntax is manifest in a number of situations. He early learns that the plural form of a noun ends in an /-s/ or similar sound. He adds a /-z) sound in "boys," an /-s/ sound in "hats," and an /-iz/ sound in "wishes." To be sure, he over-applies his new found principle to produce such combinations as "feets," "sheeps," and "gooses." The same awareness of principle is evident as he forms the past tense of verbs. The verb "played" ends in a /-d/ sound, "walked" in a /-t/ sound, and "waited" in an /-id/ sound. The child appears to understand the difference between the classes of words. He does not add an /-ed/ morpheme to a noun nor an /-s/ morpheme to a verb. He follows his pattern exactly, even with words which are irregular. He says, "I breaked my whistle and Daddy buyed me another one." Even when he begins to sense irregularities, as in the verb "bring" or in forming comparatives and superlatives, he applies his own generalizations fairly consistently. He says, "Look what I brang you," following the pattern of "ring" and "sing" or "My book is more better than yours," applying both regular and irregular forms in the same sentence.

Interestingly enough, the child appears at this time to be doing just what the common folk of England did after the conquest by William of Normandy in 1066. That was a period when only those whom Hugh Sykes Davies of Cambridge calls "the little people" used English and in approximately three hundred years regularized and simplified it at many points (7). He holds that, given another hundred years in their exclusive care, English might now form all of its past tenses by adding /-ed) to the present and all of its comparatives and superlatives by adding /-er/ and /-est/. Children's efforts show the same tendencies.

Jean Berko Gleason tells of an experiment in which a child was shown pictures of one mouse and of two mice and told, "This is a mouse and here are two mice." The examiner then asked, "What is this? and this?" Many of the children tested answered, "A mouse and two mouses," or in other instances "two gooses" or the "bell ringed," having only a second before heard the correct form. It appears that children can imitate only what they are already able to produce—what has already become a part of their repertoire (13).

Wick Miller is convinced that each child appears to create anew the phonology and grammar of his language. He says,

> The evidence supports the notion that the child develops a set of rules, tests the rules with the sentences he hears, and changes, modifies, abandons, and elaborates his rules in the light of what he hears (31).

Chukovsky, speaking of children's grammatical skill, says,

> . . . A child having no notion of grammatical rules uses quite correctly all noun cases, verb tenses, and moods, even when he uses unfamiliar words. This perceptive use of words is a most amazing phenomenon of early childhood. . . . children's locutions are often more "correct" than grammar and "improve" upon it. . . . Not in vain did Leo Tolstoy, addressing himself to adults, write, ". . . [The child] realizes the laws of word formation better than you because no one so often thinks up new words as children" (5, pp. 6 and 8).

Mrs. Gleason furnishes two examples of this from the talk of her own children. A child of two and a half was feeling put upon when someone asked her, "Who loves you?" and she answered, "Nobody." Later, when she felt better about it she was asked again, "Who loves you?" and she answered, "Yesbody," a creation by analogy which was clearly all her own. Another child of three asked, "Mommy, what do giraffes eat?" Following her mother's answer, "Well, they eat leaves, mostly," the child thought a bit and asked, "And what do they eat lessly?" Parents and teachers can furnish other examples. Particularly apropos was the reply of the little girl criticized for not obeying directions: "I misunderheard you." When one is six years old, "misunderheard" makes better sense in that context than "misunderstood."

Children's language inventions make it very clear that their language learning is not all imitation. Imitation functions of necessity in the learning of vocabulary items but the child very early creates sentences of his own that are not copies of adult sentences. Whatever it is that the child does, it is extremely complex, a remarkable type of theory construction, and he does it in an astonishingly short time. In her studies of the language of young, preschool children from average or above socioeconomic level, Paula Menyuk discovered that almost all of the basic structures used by adults to generate their sentences can be found in the grammar of children as young as 2 years, 10 months to 3 years, 1 month (32). The evidence appears to indicate that what is achieved is somewhat independent of intelligence, yet it is accomplished in a comparable way by almost all children. This appears to be true no matter where a child lives on the surface of the earth or what his mother language may be. It becomes increasingly clear that no theory of learning has yet been proposed which can possibly account for language learning.

☐ THE VOCABULARY OF THE PRESCHOOL CHILD

A number of people have studied the growth of vocabulary in preschool children. Some have attempted to enumerate the total vocabulary of a child during these early years and their results indicate a wide range of individual differences. For older children, especially children who are beginning to have some experiences apart from their parents, a sampling method is necessary. The most widely quoted estimation of the probable vocabulary of preschool children at various ages is that of Madorah Smith, which was done in 1926 and was based on a study of 273 preschool children (38). This material is given in Table 1 (38, p. 54).

A later estimate of vocabulary, done by Mary Katherine Smith and Seashore and based upon a sampling of an unabridged dictionary, placed the vocabulary of an average child in the first grade at 23,700 words, while the range of words ran, for the first grade children tested, from 6,000 to 48,800 words at this

TABLE ONE

Increase in size of vocabulary in relation to age*
(from Madorah E. Smith, 1926)

Age Group		No. of Children	Average I.Q.	Vocabulary	
years	months			no. of words	gain
	8	13		0	
	10	17		1	1
1	0	52		3	2
1	3	19		19	16
1	6	14		22	3
1	9	14		118	96
2	0	25		272	154
2	6	14		446	174
3	0	20	109	896	450
3	6	26	106	1222	326
4	0	26	109	1540	318
4	6	32	109	1870	330
5	0	20	108	2072	202
5	6	27	110	2289	217
6	0	9	108	2562	273

*These were words that children actually used in their recorded talk.

age. This was a study of words children reacted to with evidence of understanding, not words they actually used. This, and other studies, will be discussed in detail in Chapter 9. There is considerable confusion at present in the literature on vocabulary, but it is probably safe to say that the average child on entrance to first grade has a vocabulary of several thousand words (28). Whether the difference between the two sets of figures for this age is due to difference in technique it is hard to say. One element which needs to be remembered is the broadened experience of children of today, all of whom view television, listen to the radio, attend the movies, and have many out-of-home contacts. All new experiences, such as a trip to a farm, to the zoo, or to the seashore result in great expansion of vocabulary if an adult talks over the child's experience with him.

Nouns predominate in the vocabulary of the beginner in speech. Observers have estimated the proportion of nouns in the child's vocabulary at two years of age to be between 50 and 60 per cent. Smith found that at two years, verbs, adverbs, and nouns were used more frequently than adjectives and connectives. Pronouns, prepositions, and connectives are added later.

Watts characterizes the child's second year as the year of "*the naming activity*" (44). At some time during that year the notion appears to enter the child's mind that things have names and he puts forth great effort to learn them. "Wha's 'at?" is an oft repeated question and may be also the first sentence the child uses. The predominance of nouns in the early vocabularies of children is doubtless due to this naming interest and the fact that adults and older children in the environment point out objects and call them by name. "There is a car. See the car!" are both sentences involving other parts of speech as well as the noun, but the noun is the key word and the one repeated for emphasis.

Pronouns appear in the speech of fairly advanced children late in the second year. The pronouns *I*, *me*, and *mine* are used most frequently, though *you* is used a great deal in contacts with other children. The child has a fairly clear awareness of self long before he begins to use words to designate self. Often a child will use his own name in designating himself, just as he hears other people use it in speaking or referring to him. The use of pronouns increases with language growth, though use of an unusually large number of pronouns after the age of three and a half years may be a sign of immaturity (15). Proper nouns and common nouns tend to be substituted for the word *it* as the child grows more specific in his speech.

As soon as the child begins to use full and complete sentences the proportion of the various parts of speech which he uses follows the conventional pattern of the language. The beginning of the use of modifiers and of prepositions and connectives is significant because it marks the beginning of the use of more elaborate sentences and more specific expression. Usually a child enjoys using longer and more involved sentences.

By the age of three or four, children have mastered the sound system of the language. An occasional child may make sound substitutions, e.g., "The wady had a wittow dway tat" for "The lady had a little gray cat." This does not indicate inability to say the correct sounds but failure to perceive the difference between the sounds he makes in those words and the sounds others make. Children of six know a great many words by ear, tongue, and mind. Most of them are ready to learn the symbol-sound correspondences that must be mastered in order to read.

☐ TALKATIVENESS AS AN INDEX OF GROWTH

The spontaneity of a child's use of language is an indication of his sense of security. If he uses speech spontaneously, fluently, and clearly for his age he is growing in a satisfactory manner. It is true that there are wide individual differences in the amount of talking children do in a given amount of time. Personality traits and responses to various types of situations all show in a child's speech responses. Everything a child expresses in a given situation shows his personality.

Young children who feel comfortable and secure in the situations in which they find themselves, give their growing powers of speech a tremendous amount of exercise. A child of three or four has been estimated to be linguistically inactive only nineteen minutes of his waking day, with four minutes his longest period of silence. He says approximately 7,600 words per day at three years and 10,500 at five (1, 28). A study of the total number of words uttered by children in a nursery school during approximately three hours of morning session averaged from 402 for twenty-four- to twenty-nine-months-old children, to 1,772 for children from forty-two to forty-seven months of age. Four-year-olds are at an exceedingly talkative age. A child's loquacity has been found to increase considerably more rapidly than his vocabulary (23).

☐ LENGTH AND STRUCTURE OF REMARKS AS A MEASURE OF GROWTH

McCarthy is convinced that the most objective and reliable measure of the language of a preschool child is the average length of the responses he uses. This measure has been used in a number of studies and it appears "a highly sensitive index that reveals developmental trends from infancy to maturity and also reflects sex, occupational, and intellectual-group differences with remarkable consistency" (28, p. 168). Studies indicate that a child of 18 months is in a one-word-sentence stage though he may occasionally combine two words. By three and a half years the average child uses functionally complete sentences (sometimes structurally complete, also) and his sentences are about four words in length, though he is capable of using longer sentences on occasion. A 1957 study by Templin (42) found the average number of words per remark used by six-year-olds to be from six to seven. A later study by Francis (12) set the figure at ten to eleven words per phonological unit, that is, between the beginning and the falling intonation which indicated the end of the remark.

It appears true that children from higher socioeconomic levels and children with a higher level of intelligence use more words per remark than less favored children. There are differences also when children are talking to other children as compared with talking to adults. Children tend to use more words in talking to an adult than in talking to each other in free play situations.

The structure of sentences and their complexity are fully as important an index to growth as is the length of sentences. Incomplete sentences abound in the speech of young children, but the proportion of structurally complete sentences is evidence of increase in language power. Fisher, in her study of the language patterns of a group of very superior preschool children, found that the proportionate increase of complete to incomplete sentences was approximately threefold between two and five years of age (11). Repetitions in response and the proportion of nonverbal responses decreased during this period. Boys were found to use more nonverbal responses such as shakes and nods and other gestures and more repetition in their responses than girls, and their proportion of incomplete sentences was higher.

All the sentences of children from eighteen to twenty-three months were found to be simple sentences, but by the time the children reached four and a half to five years of age the proportion of simple sentences had dropped to 85 per cent. About 13 per cent of the sentences used at this age were complex, and 3 per cent were compound. The children studied were superior children who represented the higher occupational levels and were using all types of sentences by the end of the fourth year. Throughout the study, girls showed clear superiority over boys in all items that portrayed developmental tendencies. Children from less favored backgrounds would develop in the same manner but their development would be slower.

□ EXPERIENCE AND LANGUAGE

Mental development and progress in language move along together and are thoroughly interwoven through the preschool life of the child. New experience or increased experience in areas the child has partially explored results in advanced understanding, vocabulary, and knowledge. This advance is accompanied by advance in the content and form of the language the child uses.

Just as the baby's realization that he can produce sounds at will motivates him to an amazing amount of play and practice with his vocal organs, so each new step of mental expansion tends to result in new steps in language learning. At some time during the baby's second year the realization appears to dawn that things have names and he demands names for everything. Then he learns that speech can serve his purpose and this realization results in further effort. "Mama" turns Mother's attention to him and "ba" said persistently enough results in someone's retrieving the ball that has rolled away, and returning it to him.

Comprehension precedes speech in most instances. The baby recognizes his name and knows when he is being spoken to or talked about long before he can say his name or can answer. He demonstrates his comprehension through eye, hand, and body behavior; looking at the speaker or the object being mentioned; reaching for, patting, or manipulating the object; or obeying the simple, familiar command. Some of the babies studied by Shirley showed recognition of their names at 15 to 20 weeks and by 36 weeks could "pat-a-cake," shake the head for "no, no," smack the lips when asked, "Are you hungry?" or turn to look at the canary in the cage in response to the question, "Where is the birdie?" A child of 18 months who spilled cream on the kitchen floor was found wiping it up with a cloth he had brought from the bathroom (35). There were many evidences of comprehension and thinking before the end of the second year.

As soon as a child can manage to move himself about, he demonstrates his desire for experience. Most young children show this eagerness for experience very clearly through the persistence with which they seek to explore their environment, their determination to get at everything in the house which catches their attention, and their insistent wandering off from the play yard unless they are carefully watched or securely confined. They often resent having their explorations curtailed and express that resentment vigorously.

Repetition of pleasant experiences is thoroughly enjoyed by

the young child. He learns the routines of his day and by the time he is two and a half he may insist that they be carried out with ritual exactness. If his mother tries to shorten the procedure or omit a portion of it, he may protest. Repetition of thoroughly known experiences gives him a sense of security and repetition of less familiar ones is a source of increased learning. The mother who talks about the experiences in brief sentences as she carries them through with the child will find that language develops rapidly.

Dramatic play in which the child reproduces his experiences and those of the adults around him becomes a source of great pleasure. A three-year-old boy served tea very solemnly and intently for a long period of time while callers were present on business. He went to the kitchen door, pushed it slightly, then returned carrying an imaginary cup of tea and serving each guest singly without losing track of his progress about the group. No one gave him any attention except to thank him or to indicate preference for cream or lemon when he had supplied everyone with tea and was passing these imaginary items. He went through the entire process of serving and collecting the cups, then went contentedly off to another room and played with his toys. He had watched the procedure for afternoon tea in his home and took care of the matter for the early evening callers with quiet, self-contained satisfaction. He demonstrated accuracy of observation and reproduction which included voice and manner, social courtesies, sequence of procedure, and numerical accounting.

Dramatic play is important as an adjunct to concrete experience or as a preparation for it. Mothers have found that the best way to prepare a child for a new experience which might be disturbing to him is to tell him just what the procedure will be and to dramatize it, if possible, so that the child finds few unanticipated elements in the real experience when he encounters it.

Trips out into the neighborhood to shop at the market, to have his hair cut, to call on friends, or for any other purpose serve to enlarge the child's horizon and to give him new words and new material for thinking. The mobility of our population uproots many young children from stable, settled home life

The spontaneity of a child's use of language is an indication of his sense of security.

and makes it necessary for them to move about and adjust to many types of conditions which undermine their security and render some of them less stable emotionally. It does, however, enlarge their experience beyond that of most children of preschool age. Whether the expansion of experience can compensate for the lack of secure and stable living, only time and good home and school guidance can indicate.

The child who is introduced to stories, poetry, and books during his preschool years has another rich resource for language development. Finger plays such as "Pat-a-Cake" and "This Little Pig Went to Market" introduce him to Mother Goose and other poetry for the little child. His mother's stories about himself may be his introduction to the content of stories. As a mother puts her active, wriggling two-year-old into socks and shoes she may tell him a story about himself. "Johnny woke up when the sun shone in at his window. He called Mommy. Mommy said, 'Good morning, Johnny,' and lifted him out of his little bed. Then she washed his face and his two hands. Then she said, 'Time to get dressed now, Johnny.' She took Johnny up on her lap. She pulled on one blue sock. Then she pulled on another blue sock. Then she put on one little brown shoe. In went Johnny's toes. Pull! On went the heel. Mother laced up the shoe and tied a nice bow. Then she picked up Johnny's other little brown shoe. Pull! On it went and Mother tied that shoe, too. Now Johnny had on two blue socks and two little brown shoes. When she had finished dressing him Mother said, 'Time for breakfast.'" A two-year-old will listen with rapt attention to such a story and help with it where there is repetition. It is his own story and he loves it.

Picture books which enable the child to see his own experiences on the pages fascinate him. He identifies himself with them quite completely as he looks and listens to his mother's running account of the content of the pictures and names the objects on the pages. The book is his book and the ball in the picture is his ball. He fingers and points and tries to enter into the story just as Dorothy Kunhardt has provided opportunity for him to do in her little "first book," *Pat the Bunny*.[2] He will go through an animal picture book again and again telling what each picture is, what the cow, pig, duck, and other animals say, and what each likes to eat. He loves simple picture storybooks

[2] Dorothy Kunhardt. *Pat the Bunny*. New York: Simon & Schuster, Inc., 1940.

which tell of experiences similar to his own. What the effect of television on a young child may be is not yet known. Certainly it appears true that the child who lives in a home where radio and television pour forth sound all day must of necessity learn to turn off the sound and give little or no reaction to it or he could develop no inner life of his own. No one has yet measured the vocabulary young children pick up from television but it appears to be considerable. Some of the words they acquire are certainly not found in children's books. How much some of them learn of spelling and reading and the extent to which it influences later school work would make an interesting study.

☐ SOCIAL DEVELOPMENT

The expanding social life of the preschool child enlarges his opportunity for language development and increases his motivation for learning.

The baby's social world includes at first mainly his mother, with some contact with brothers and sisters and with his father. His mother is the source of his security and the center of his interest and affection. He learns very gradually to be content in the care of someone else and to enjoy contact with others. The ability to trust himself to unfamiliar people develops slowly. Playing on the lawn in his playpen or riding in his carriage brings him broader experience and enlarges his physical horizon as well as his contacts with people.

The use of language for communication is a mark of social growth on the part of the child. Piaget, in studies of French-speaking children in Switzerland, found relatively little real conversation before the age of seven and a half years (33). Teachers of English children have found evidence of conversation between children a year or two earlier than this, and studies carried on in the United States indicate that American children also reach the age of real interaction earlier than seven years (44).

The talk which accompanies the parallel play of young children is itself parallel, or collective monologue. Piaget has called attention to the tendency of children at this stage to carry on a line of chatter without appearing to expect other children to answer or caring whether they listen or not.

By the age of four it is possible for an adult to talk to the child in a more mature and man-to-man fashion. While the four-year-old is often out of bounds verbally, he is gradually learning to use language thoughtfully. By his fifth year, he is taking an interest in words and word meanings and his questions tend to be information-seeking ones. He likes to figure things out for himself and may attempt to answer his own questions through generalizations which are based on little experience.

Social contacts and experience are essential to language growth. The child with a rich experience background is using language confidently and effectively by age six. The child who lacks such a background of growth and experience enters the primary school with a distinct handicap. This handicap must be removed if he is to succeed in living up to his potentialities in the school program, since language is one of the major avenues of school learning.

Chukovsky, in the delightful book translated from the Russian by Miriam Morton, presents illuminating vignettes of the thought and fantasy of young children. He is a poet, a scholar, and writer of adult literature, and a member of "that small commonwealth of those who, having an intuitive kinship with children, fortify and extend it by observation, by scientific and psychological studies, and so increase our sense of wonder and delight in children and cast across the divergent theories of education a long shadow of universal wisdom" (5, p. VII). He says of the first years of childhood,

> That the thought processes of children do not change, only the symbols of their interpretation are adapted to the social structures of their day.
>
> That the child is "armored against thoughts and information that he does not yet need and that are prematurely offered to him by too-hasty adults."
>
> That the young child uses fantasy as a means of learning, and adjusts it to reality in the exact amounts his need demands.
>
> That poetry is the natural language of little children, and nonsense serves as a handle to the proportion of logic in an illogical world.
>
> That the fetish of practicality is a blight upon the literature of childhood. Chukovsky inveighs against those who "look upon every children's book as something that must immediately pro-

The thought processes of children do not change, only the symbols of their interpretation are adapted to the social structures of their day.

Cookie Jar

duce some visible, touchable, beneficial effect, as if a book were a nail or a yoke."

That "the present belongs to the sober, the cautious, the routine-prone, but the future belongs to those who do not rein in their imaginations."

Many parents can verify Chukovsky's evidence that children take only so much of adult wisdom as they can use at the time and that they employ it according to their own fancy. Instead of adapting themselves to the truth they frequently adapt the truth to themselves for the sake of an imaginary play situation (5, p. 27). The child who talks of animals as though he could converse with them and who personifies cars and other inanimate things is doing this. He knows that dogs do not talk and that cars and trains are not alive, but it suits his immediate needs to imagine that they are.

☐ HANDICAPS TO NORMAL SPEECH DEVELOPMENT

Children appear to differ in linguistic aptitude as well as in other aspects of development. Intelligence determines in large measure the quality of growth a child achieves and his rate of progress, but environmental factors enter in also. The child who is given intelligent and adequate adult attention and opportunity to learn to play with children has wholesome social motivation for speech development. The provision of childlike experiences which enlarge horizons and introduce new vocabulary serves to stimulate and feed intellectual curiosity and make the child an eager seeker after knowledge, and his language develops proportionately.

Lower levels of intelligence will result in slower than normal language growth. Each child will learn at his own rate regardless of the amount of deliberate stimulation he may receive. Native capacity cannot be changed, but environmental factors can be made as favorable as possible. Certainly the slow learning child needs the security of parental affection and approval of his efforts and his progress. Parental disappointment, overanxiety, and efforts to force growth only undermine the child's security and sense of adequacy and make learning even more difficult for him. Pressure results in emotional maladjustment which forms a serious stumbling block to learning.

Various types of physical handicaps can impede progress in

language development. Poor health requires physical care and protection which may cut the child off from social and intellectual stimulation. Impaired vision may restrict the child's experience both through the added physical protection he requires and because a major avenue of learning is cut off. The problem is even more serious for the child with a hearing handicap because hearing is essential to learning the sound patterns of language.

Defective speech mechanism may stand in the way of speech development. Cleft palate, harelip, or other malformation of the speech mechanism may prevent the development of adequate speech unless it is corrected and even then may require special techniques and training to compensate in a measure for the structural defect.

Parents often need help to distinguish between problems that are temporary and will be outgrown with intelligent care and guidance, and problems which require highly specialized treatment and extended therapy. Many three-and-a-half- and four-year-old children do some stuttering for a time. This appears to be due to the fact that ideas and eagerness to express them are running ahead of facility in expression. As the child has more language experience and gains in dexterity and confidence the stuttering tends to disappear. Stuttering which is the outgrowth of serious emotional tensions and other personal, developmental problems may require expert diagnosis and treatment over a long period of time.

☐ SPEECH AND PERSONALITY DEVELOPMENT

Speech development has clear and far-reaching influence on personality development. The child who acquires speech easily tends to make social contacts easily, to learn readily, and to become a secure, confident, and outgoing person. The child who has difficulty with speech finds social contacts difficult. He becomes self-conscious, tends to lack confidence in his own ability and worth, and may eventually shrink from social contact or become overaggressive to compensate for lack of ease in communication. In any case, his personality tends to become modified and often warped by his inadequacy in speech. Such a child needs protection from pressures, from undue attention to his problem, and certainly from criticism and ridicule. He needs affection and guidance which will give him a sense of security and help him to develop confidence in his ability to learn to hold his own in social situations.

The preschool years are years of great significance in the life of a child for a great many reasons. No aspect of development during these years is more important for his future life than his language development. It colors the attitudes, the potentialities for learning, and the acquisition of foundational equipment not only for these years but in a measure for the rest of the individual's life.

☐ SELECTED REFERENCES ☐

1. Brandenburg, George C., "The Language of a Three-Year-Old Child." *Pedagogical Seminary* 22:89-120, March, 1915.
2. Brodbeck, A. J., and Irwin, O. C., "The Speech Behavior of Infants without Families." *Child Development* 17:145-156, September, 1946.
3. Brown, Roger, and Bellugi, Ursula, "Three Processes in the Child's Acquisition of Syntax." *Harvard Educational Review* 34:133-151, Spring 1964.
4. Chen, H. P., and Irwin, O. C., "Infant Speech Vowel and Consonant Types." *Journal of Speech Disorders* 11:27-29, March, 1946.
5. Chukovsky, Kornei, *From Two to Five.* Berkeley: University of California Press, 1963.
6. Church, Joseph, *Language and the Discovery of Reality.* New York: Random House, 1961.
7. Davies, Hugh Sykes, *Grammar Without Tears.* New York: The John Day Company, 1953.
8. Durkin, Dolores, *Children Who Read Early.* New York: Teachers College Press, Columbia University, 1966.
9. Erikson, Erik A., *Childhood and Society.* New York: W. W. Norton and Co., Inc., 1950.
10. Ervin, Susan M., and Miller, Wick R., "Language Development" in *Child Psychology.* Yearbook 62, Part I, National Society for the Study of Education. Chicago: The University of Chicago Press, 1963.
11. Fisher, Mary S., *Language Patterns of Preschool Children.* Child Development Monographs, No. 15. New York: Bureau of Publications, Teachers College, Columbia University, 1934.
12. Francis, Sarah Evelyn, *An Investigation of the Oral Language of First Grade Children.* Doctoral Dissertation. Bloomington: Indiana University, 1962.

13. Gleason, Jean Berko, "Language Development in Early Childhood." Paper prepared for National Council of Teachers of English.
14. Gesell, Arnold, and Ilg, Frances L., *Infant and Child in the Culture of Today*. New York: Harper and Brothers, 1943.
15. Goodenough, Florence L., "The Use of Pronouns by Young Children: A Note on the Development of Self-Awareness." *Journal of Genetic Psychology* 52:333-346, June, 1938.
16. Havighurst, Robert J., *Human Development and Education*. New York: Longmans, Green and Co., 1953.
17. Hopkins, L. Thomas, *The Emerging Self in Home and School*. New York: Harper and Brothers, 1954.
18. Hughes, Marie M., and Sanchez, George L., *Learning a New Language*. Bulletin 101. Washington, D. C.: Association for Childhood Education International, 1958.
19. Irwin, O. C., "The Profile as a Visual Device for Indicating Central Tendencies in Speech Data." *Child Development* 12:111-120, June, 1941.
20. Irwin, O. C., and Curry, T., "Vowel Elements in the Crying Vocalization of Infants under Ten Days of Age." *Child Development* 12:99-109, June, 1941.
21. Jersild, Arthur T., *Child Psychology*. (Rev. & Enl.) Englewood Cliffs, N. J.: Prentice-Hall, Inc., 1961.
22. ———, *In Search of Self*. New York: Columbia University, Teachers College, Bureau of Publications, 1952.
23. Jersild, Arthur T., and Ritzman, Ruth, "Aspects of Language Development: The Growth of Loquacity and Vocabulary." *Child Development* 9:243-259, September, 1938.
24. Jespersen, Otto, *Mankind, Nation and Individual from a Linguistic Point of View*. London: Allen & Unwin, Ltd., 1946.
25. Judd, Charles H., *Educational Psychology*. Boston: Houghton Mifflin Co., 1939.
26. Lenneberg, Eric H., "A Biological Perspective of Language." *New Directions in Language*. Edited by Lenneberg. Cambridge: The MIT Press, 1966.
27. Lewis, Morris M., *Infant Speech: A Study of the Beginnings of Language*. New York: Harcourt, Brace and Co., 1936.
28. McCarthy, Dorothea A., "Child Development: Language." *Encyclopedia of Educational Research*. (Ed. Walter S. Monroe.) New York: The Macmillan Co., 1950 (Rev.) pp. 165-172.
29. ———, "Language Development in Children." *Manual of Child Psychology*. (Rev., Leonard Carmichael, Ed.). New York: John Wiley and Sons, Inc., 1954, pp. 492-630.
30. ———, *The Language Development of the Preschool Child*.

Institute of Child Welfare Monograph Series, No. 4. Minneapolis: University of Minnesota Press, 1930.

31. Miller, Wick, "Language Acquisition and Reading." Paper prepared for National Council of Teachers of English.
32. Menyuk, Paula, "Syntactic Rules Used by Children from Preschool through First Grade." *Child Development* 35:533-546, 1964.
33. National Conference on Research in English, *Factors that Influence Language Growth.* Edited by Dorothea McCarthy. Chicago: National Council of Teachers of English, 1952 and 1953.
34. Piaget, Jean, *The Language and Thought of the Child.* (Tr. Marjorie Warden.) New York: Harcourt, Brace and Co., 1926.
35. Shirley, Mary M., "Common Content in the Speech of Preschool Children." *Child Development* 9:333-346, Dec., 1938.
36. ———, *The First Two Years: A Study of Twenty-five Babies.* (Intellectual Development, Vol. 2.) Minneapolis: University of Minnesota Press, 1933.
37. Smith, Dora V., "Growth in Language Power as Related to Child Development." *Teaching Language in the Elementary School.* The Forty-third Yearbook, Part II, of the National Society for the Study of Education. Chicago: University of Chicago Press, 1944, Chap. IV, pp. 52-97.
38. Smith, Madorah E., *An Investigation of the Development of the Sentence and the Extent of Vocabulary in Young Children.* (Studies in Child Welfare, Vol. 3, No. 5) Iowa City: State University of Iowa, 1926.
39. Smith, Mary Katherine, "Measurement of the Size of General English Vocabulary through the Elementary Grades and High School." *Genetic Psychology Monographs* 24:311-345, Nov., 1941.
40. Stern, William, *The Psychology of Early Childhood.* New York: Henry Holt and Co., Inc., 1924.
41. Strickland, Ruth G., *The Language and Mental Development of Children.* Bulletin XXIII, No. 2. Bloomington: Division of Research and Field Services, Indiana University, 1947.
42. Templin, Mildred C., *Certain Language Skills in Children.* Minneapolis: University of Minnesota Press, 1957.
43. Wann, Kenneth D.; Dorn, Miriam S.; and Liddle, Elizabeth Ann, *Fostering Intellectual Development in Children.* New York: Bureau of Publications, Teachers College, Columbia University, 1962.
44. Watts, A. F., *The Language and Mental Development of Children.* London: George G. Harrap and Co., Ltd., 1944. Boston: D. C. Heath and Co., 1947.

45. Weir, Ruth, *Language in the Crib.* The Hague: Mouton & Co., 1962.
46. Witmer, Helen Leland, and Kotinsky, Ruth, *Personality in the Making: The Fact-finding Report of the Mid-century White House Conference on Children and Youth.* New York: Harper and Brothers, 1952.
47. Vygotsky, Lev, *Thought and Language.* Cambridge, Mass.: The M.I.T. Press, 1962.

language development in the nursery school and kindergarten

The interest that the American public and the government are taking in the educational possibilities of the preschool years is one of the most heartwarming developments of this era. Only a portion of the states have made kindergartens available for young children as a part of the public school system and until very recently nursery schools were practically all outside the educational system. Where they existed, they tended to be under philanthropic agencies, attached to education departments of colleges, or privately managed by cooperating parent groups or private tuition schools.

Experience in nursery school and kindergarten furnishes the young child with opportunity for language development which can scarcely be equaled in even the most favorable home. Sympathetic adults who are trained to understand the child's developmental needs provide him with the stimulation and guidance which enable him to make rapid strides. The learning environment is carefully tailored to fit his stature and capacities. Interaction with other children takes place in play situations which are adjusted to his social and intellectual level and is highly conducive to language growth. The program of simple experiences provides motivation for growth in vocabulary and in accuracy and maturity of speech. Improvement in speech and language is one of the clearest evidences of growth during these years.

Even before the present burst of interest conscientious parents were enrolling their children in nursery schools for a number of reasons. The one-child home finds it impossible to provide the child with the contact with other children which he needs. Crowded and unfavorable housing is causing parents to turn to the nursery school to give their child adequate freedom and materials for wholesome play experience. Young, untrained, and inexperienced mothers are feeling the need for help and guidance to do for the child the things they recognize that he needs but feel inadequate to provide. Mothers in some homes must be wage earners and are convinced that the child is best cared for by trained teachers in an environment carefully planned and arranged for children. The proportion of preschool-age children attending nursery school is growing very rapidly.

Two, three, and four are the usual ages for nursery school,

and five for kindergarten. Tremendous growth in language and other aspects of mental and social development takes place during these nursery school years. The two-year-old who enters nursery school may be just passing from the stage of jargon into that of intelligible speech. By the age of five, three years later, he is an inveterate talker and is employing all the language patterns used by adults in ordinary conversation. His fund of knowledge has increased vastly and his range of interests is as wide as his experiences have permitted. He has grown from the stage of individual and solitary play to interest in many types of group play, and from monologue as a running accompaniment to his individual play to ability to carry on conversations and real social interaction. These early school years bring great growth in articulation of sounds, pronunciation of words, sentence structure, and ability to communicate through meaningful use of words. The voice comes under better control and is made to fit the accepted pattern of the culture.

☐ GUIDANCE THROUGH LANGUAGE

The behavior of the very young child is guided largely through physical handling. The mother places the baby where she wants him, puts before him the play materials he is to use and takes from him the things he is not to handle. By nursery school age, guidance becomes increasingly verbal rather than physical. "Time for juice," "We wash hands now," "It belongs here," "John needs it when you have finished," "You can play with it again after nap," are typical guidance statements for the two-year-old child.

A three-year-old responds favorably to verbal guidance. The suggestion, "You could help Bill put away his blocks because he has so many," brings ready co-operation. "You might get another book," or "What can Mary have if you have this?" may solve the problem of two children whose desires conflict. The question, "What are the blocks for?" may bring more satisfactory use of equipment. "That is a secret," may curtail over-insistent curiosity.

By the time a child has reached the age of four there is less need for guidance through the use of key words such as "it's time to," "when you have finished," "might," and "could help." He can talk with the adult now in more nearly the fashion of intellectual equals. He listens when reasoned with and tries to follow through on adult suggestions. This may include learning to guide others through verbal means. A four-year-old boy who was carrying on a solitary building project with blocks was annoyed by the depredations of a two-year-old who continually took his blocks, and he complained to the teacher about it. He was given the suggestion, "You might tell Tommy that these are your blocks. Show him where he can get some of his own." The child tried the suggestion but came back with further complaint. "Suppose you tell him, 'No, no! You can't have these blocks. You play with *your* blocks,'" brought no better results. "Could you get him some more blocks, yourself, and tell him they are for him? Then send him away if he comes for more of yours," apparently solved the problem because there were no further appeals for help.

Five-year-olds are interested in verbal guidance and ask, "Is this the way to do it?" or say, "Tell me what I'm s'posed to do," or remind other children, "It's time to clean up now. Miss Brown said so. I'll sweep up the sawdust if you'll put these away."

☐ STIMULATION OF LANGUAGE GROWTH

Most young children develop speech at a normal rate and use it freely for their age and maturity level, but there are always some who lag behind the rest. This may be due to mental retardation, to poor hearing, or to some defect in the speech mechanism, but more often it is due to environmental conditions of one sort or another.

Some children are slow to talk because they have no need for talking. Their wishes and needs are anticipated and met without any effort on their part. A child who has learned to get what he wants through pointing, whining, and "baby talk" may feel little need for working on speech. The nursery school teacher who consistently fails to understand his methods of communication and waits for an effort at speech before satisfying his wants will soon have him talking. If talking brings the satisfaction of those wants promptly, together with praise and encouragement for his achievement, he will soon go beyond the compulsion of the teacher's method to other talking.

Occasionally one finds a child who uses speech only when it is necessary to use it, because the home standards set for him have been too high. The child's silence has become his protection from correction and criticism. In school his speech is accepted as it is and he is drawn into activities which encourage him to talk. The teacher may join in his activities or encourage him to participate in hers so that there is opportunity for her to chat with him over things that really interest him. His response may be a single word at first, but the responses lengthen as the child grows in confidence in his ability to talk.

Both of these types of children respond to play materials and activities that encourage talking. Dramatic play with toy trains, boats, and people leads to some verbal exchange and sometimes to conversation. A toy telephone interests almost any child in talking. Sitting with a group of children to play with clay usually results in interchange of remarks, but drawing with crayons, painting, or constructing things of wood—anything which requires the child's close attention—is apt to be carried on in silence (8). Playground apparatus such as climbing structures, slides, and sand boxes stimulates social reactions, while wheel toys may be used by the child for solitary play. Rhythmic activity and sitting in a small group at lunch time tend to stimulate talk.

□ LEARNING FROM THE TEACHER'S EXAMPLE

A requirement for certification of teachers in all states is that the teacher have sufficient background of schooling to speak standard English. To children who come from areas in which the neighborhood dialect is less than standard, the teacher's English may seem almost a foreign language. It takes a long time for a child to acquire standard English (the English of educated people in his geographic area) if home and community language differs greatly from this. The sooner the child can be exposed to the language he needs to acquire, the better is the prospect that he can master the English he needs to rise above the level of his environment. Much of the child's way of using language is learned through imitation, so the example set for him by the teacher is of the utmost importance. The teacher's voice should be quiet and low pitched; her enunciation should be clear; the articulation of sounds accurate; the pronunciation of words and the grammatical structure of sentences always correct.

The quality and pitch of the teacher's voice are important not only because they are unconsciously imitated by the children but because they set the emotional tone for the room. A high-pitched or loud voice causes children to be noisy, irritable, and difficult to guide. A quiet, low-pitched voice helps to keep children relaxed, poised, and on an even keel. Every teacher has had the experience of an occasional bad day caused by fatigue, emotional strain, or physical ill-health when her own voice and manner were less controlled than usual and has found the children particularly noisy, quarrelsome, and lacking in control. Children sense the emotional climate which the teacher provides and respond accordingly.

The use the teacher makes of language is a part of the child's learning experience. Jean had fallen on the gravel and bumped her knee and was lying there crying. The teacher said quietly, "Let's brush off your knee. Then you will feel better." Later another child fell in playing and Jean helped her up, brushed her off, and turned away saying, "Now you feel better, don't you?"

Forms of courtesy and other suitable methods of expression are learned through example. The teacher's casual and friendly attitude toward each child is carried over by the children into their contacts with each other. The courtesy of her responses to them causes them to respond to each other in similar spirit and at times to use the forms of expression which the teacher has used. True courtesy is a matter of consideration and feeling for others even more than of words. It will take the child years of experience to achieve it, but falling into the pattern of the teacher's response forms a good beginning.

The child's first awareness of the functions of written language may come through the teacher's use of it. A note to the child's mother telling of an early dismissal for a teachers' meeting, a memorandum about the mat he needs to sit on at school, or a note to a child who is sick introduces the nursery school child to the uses and values of written language.

☐ THE TWO-YEAR-OLD IN NURSERY SCHOOL

The average two-year-old in nursery school understands what is said to him and can answer simple questions. He is using less and less of jargon, and is beginning to employ three and four word sentences such as "Tommy do it" and "Mama come home now." Some studies have set the vocabulary of this age level at about 270 words, though Gesell indicates a possible range from

12 to 1,000 words (9). The child of two uses a large proportion of nouns, few pronouns other than those which refer to himself, and very few prepositions and conjunctions. He has difficulty with the sounds of some letters, particulary *f*, *v*, *s*, *b*, and *r*, and more trouble with the final sounds of words than with the beginning or middle (8). The two-year-old carries on a running monologue which accompanies his activities, but he rarely talks to people except to ask, "What's that?", to respond to questions, or to approve or protest what is being done.

Both at home and at school, the two-year-old is learning ways to get what he wants and to do what he wishes to do. Sometimes he shows an amazing ability to detect techniques that work and he uses them persistently. Because he is actively exploring his environment he encounters frequently the "No, no" of adult prohibition, and he protests the frustration of his wishes both vocally and physically. His aggressive actions usually do not last long, but he shows great persistence at points where his interest is strong.

The two-year-old is beginning to be interested in pictures, rhymes, and stories. He likes to have a story repeated over and over and he tolerates no variation in the telling. Stories deal with his own experience and things in his own environment which he can understand. He enjoys repeating words and sounds regardless of meaning. Finger plays and simple nursery rhymes intrigue him.

Some two-year-olds use jargon and gestures to take the place of words. The teacher studies such children to determine whether the retardation is due to malformation of the vocal apparatus, mental retardation, or defective hearing. If none of these appears to be the cause, it is probable that natural incentives to talk and prompt satisfaction of the child's desires when he makes an effort to talk will improve his speech very rapidly. Placing him with other children who are talking usually causes him to talk in order to participate.

□ THE THREE-YEAR-OLD

The child of three has advanced considerably beyond the two-year-old level. His articulation is fairly clear, his vocabulary has reached 900 or more words, and his sentences are longer and more complex. He is using more pronouns and prepositions, and his sentences are more mature. His fund of information is growing rapidly and his perception of size, number, and spatial relationship is growing (9).

The three-year-old plays with older children fairly frequently, but he still enjoys going about his own individual activities in the presence of a group. Groups change constantly and the span of attention for any single activity is usually short. There is some social interaction and real communication. There are occasional brief conversations when interests coincide momentarily, and there are also quarrels when interests overlap. These quarrels are quickly forgotten.

Dramatic play becomes of interest to children of this age and they play house, store, or doctor in their own way, often with little regard for accuracy of timing or details.

The three-year-old likes stories that are more advanced than the simple stories of the two-year-old, but here-and-now stories are still enjoyed if they involve a slight plot or pattern of action.

□ THE FOUR-YEAR-OLD IN SCHOOL

The four-year-old child is ready for many types of activities. His vocabulary is now expanded to about 1,500 words and is increasing rapidly. His loquacity is increasing even more rapidly. He talks a great deal, exaggerates, boasts, tells highly fanciful tales, and is often verbally out of bounds (10). He likes new and different words, silly language, and rhyming.

The sentences of a four-year-old have grown in length and complexity. He can use the language patterns of ordinary adult conversation but he misuses words and sometimes invents words to meet his needs.

The span of attention of a child of four is increasing rapidly and he finds satisfaction in thinking some things through for himself. His reasoning may lack adult logic and he may arrive at generalizations from very little knowledge or experience, but he is satisfied with his conclusions.

Social development is evident in the increase in the amount of group play in which the child participates and the increased size of the group with which he can interact and cooperate. Solitary play is seen less frequently though there is a good deal of independent activity, often paralleling the activity of other children and accompanied by a flow of remarks if not actual conversation.

The interest in stories and poems is now very keen and the

child of this age likes to be a member of a group of listeners. *Peter Rabbit, Little Black Sambo,* and many of the old folk tales – "The Three Bears," "The Billy Goats Gruff" and others of their kind are always favorites. Marjorie Flack's *Ask Mr. Bear* and *The New Pet*, Helen Puner's *Daddies and What They Do All Day,* and Lois Lenski's books about the Small Family are satisfying extensions of children's own thinking and experience. The child enjoys looking at picture books and will often pore over a book for several minutes at a time. Picture books of animals, farm life, trains, ships, and airplanes always fascinate. Such books as Ethel Berkley's *The Size of It* – a giraffe is tall and so is a building – and *Up and Down* help children to think in terms of comparison.

Some four-year-olds enjoy having an adult print the child's name on his products. He may recognize the first letter of his name and those of others in the family. An occasional child of this age will try to print his own name, probably using many separate strokes for each letter.

□ THE FIVE-YEAR-OLD IN KINDERGARTEN

The five-year-old uses speech almost constantly. He talks to everyone. He is interested in words and meanings. Most of his questions are information-seeking ones. He has learned as much as he could from his home and neighborhood environment, from stories, and from the movies and television if they are available to him, but his information is spotty and limited at many points (8). He finds it difficult to distinguish fact from fantasy. Figuring things out for himself gives him great satisfaction. He generalizes very readily on even a single occurrence. Some kindergarten children were discussing whether babies had teeth. Another child responded that babies did have teeth because his baby sister had some. "Girl babies have teeth and boy babies don't" was a conclusion satisfactory to the group.

The child of five years is speaking about as well as the adults in his environment. His patterns of grammatical usage conform to theirs for the most part and he is aware of and criticizes speech which deviates. He is beginning to use language thoughtfully. He may evaluate tasks, saying that this one is easy and that one hard. He can define familiar words in terms of use: "An orange is to eat"; "A doll is to play with."

Many children of five years are interested in books and turn to them frequently both for pleasure in the pictures and to rethink a story that has been read to them. Some children of this age will watch pages closely when an adult is reading to them, noting words that are repeated, or the name of a character, and following the print as well as the pictures. Some can tell the story from a simple book, turning the pages at the correct points in the story. Wanda Gag's *Millions of Cats* and *Gone is Gone,* Marjorie Flack's *Angus and the Ducks,* Inez Hogan's *The Bear Twins,* Mariana's Flora McFlimsey stories and the like are all enjoyed over and over. Carl Memling's *What's in the Dark?* Virginia Burton's *The Little House,* Robert McCloskey's *Make Way for Ducklings,* and such picture books as Illa Podendorf's *Animal Babies* expand children's experience and give them material to think with.

Five-year-olds who have listened to the reading of ABC books or played with alphabet blocks may ask the spelling of simple words from time to time. They may know the words *hot* and *cold* on the faucets or *stop* and *go* on the signs and may recognize their own names in print. Some of them like to learn to print their names or to dictate material for an adult to write, as in a letter to Daddy or a note to a child who is ill. An occasional five-year-old may become keenly interested in writing and through it begin to take an interest in learning to read.

Children of this age like to link their home and school experiences through bringing a favorite toy to school or bringing things of special interest to show to the other children. They also like to take home the pictures they have drawn and the things they have made. They adjust well to school and appear to enjoy both the routine and the activities. Transitions from one activity to another are made with relative ease. These children can participate in a group activity for about twenty minutes, but their activities tend not to be highly social. There are bursts of energy in carrying out projects, and the child likes to complete a task (10).

☐ LEARNING THROUGH EXPERIENCE WITH THINGS

A child of two is learning a great deal through sensory contact. He likes to play with objects of different shapes and sizes. He fingers them, sensing their texture and other properties, perhaps shaking or pounding them or testing them with his tongue.

Learning the properties of common objects requires many contacts and experiences. Adults speak of this doll as *big,* that one as *little;* this block as *heavy,* that one as *light;* this toy as *hard,* that one as *soft.* Mental growth comes through many types of sensory experience.

A large portion of the nursery school day is spent in playing and working with materials. The two-year-old likes to drop objects of different sizes and shapes through similarly shaped holes in the top of a box or can, and having done so dumps them all out and starts again. He loads his tiny cart with blocks and toys of all sorts and pushes or pulls it about the room. He misjudges distances and spaces at times and finds it impossible to proceed until he has become disentangled or has adjusted his efforts and equipment to the space. He splashes color on a big sheet of newsprint paper or paints the playground sidewalk with a broad brush and a bucket of water, watches it dry, then paints it again. He molds, pats, and tunnels the moist sand, packs it into a bucket or sifts it in an old sifter. This is not a "No, no! Mustn't touch!" sort of world but one filled with opportunities to learn what is meant by words denoting size, weight, texture, and other properties. Gradually, through playing side by side with other children he learns *mine* and *yours* and simple quantitative concepts, and he discovers the relative meanings expressed by words: a *little chair* for him to sit on and a little chair for the *doll* are quite different. He learns to put *on* his cap or to hang it *in* his locker cupboard. He finds that to get things out is followed later by helping to put things back where each belongs. It takes many experiences to make words other than nouns take on meaning and fit into the child's speech. Here is a world his size with things in it that are designed for just such exploration as he delights in and needs.

The nature of the child's exploration changes with the years. A three-year-old is less apt to be dropping objects through matching holes but he likes to pound nails in a soft wood block or fit peg toys in a peg board or string large wooden beads on a string. He smears finger paint, reveling in its texture and the variations in pattern that his hands can trace. He pounds, pokes, shapes, and reshapes clay, not so much for the purpose of producing something with it as for the joy of the doing. He may put together simple wooden puzzles of five or six pieces. His block towers are higher and more steady, and his play with toys may take on a dramatic quality as he plays house or train.

The four-year-old is still a busy explorer, learning the properties of things, their uses, how to make them work, and what makes them go. His manipulation of objects is on a higher level; he experiments with them and uses them in a variety of ways. Small kegs, boards, and a sawhorse or two can be set up as a runway for balancing and jumping at one moment, and become a complicated railway system the next moment by the addition of a toy engine or train, though a box or block with appropriate sound effects produced by the engineer will serve almost as well.

The five-year-old wants to find out about things. He investigates, examines, and questions. He wants to know how things work, where they come from, what they are made of, and is curious as to the weight, strength, taste, and smell of all sorts of materials. Crayons, paints, scissors, woodworking tools, and gymnasium apparatus all challenge him. He experiments with all of them and tests his abilities in utilizing them. He is fond of books and knows that books are sources of information and can be used to prove a point (8).

Block play is of special interest to boys at this age. It is usually group play that is highly co-operative and frequently holds attention over a period of several days. Elaborate structures are made: two-story houses, fire stations, stores, airports, ships, trains, almost anything that can be used for dramatic play. Building energy is then turned into play in which the children's concepts of adult life are portrayed through dramatic action. Though girls do less of the building they are frequently drawn into the dramatic play. Dramatic play of all types interests both boys and girls at this age.

Putting together puzzles, constructing in wood, working with clay, paint, and other materials develop knowledge of the properties and uses of materials and the ends they can be made to serve.

☐ LEARNING THROUGH EXPERIENCE WITH CHILDREN

The two-year-old has been busy for some time learning how to respond to adults and how to get his own way with them. In many instances, he has developed surprisingly useful techniques. When he comes to nursery school he likes to be near other children but he treats them as though they were inani-

mate objects, not people. He may hug another child, snatch something from him, or push him out of the way without any interest in what the other child does and says unless the victim protests loudly and vigorously, in which case the child may watch him with curious interest. He is gregarious but carries on little or no social contact with children who are playing near him, each intent on his own play interest.

By the time children are three years old they play together fairly frequently but each still enjoys going about his own individual activity in the presence of a companion or a group. Groups change constantly and the span of attention for any single activity is usually short. There are occasional brief conversations when interests coincide and there are also quarrels when interests overlap.

Social development at four years of age is evident in the increase in the amount of group play in which the child participates and the increased size of the group with which he can interact and co-operate. Solitary play is seen less frequently, though there is a good deal of independent activity accompanied by a flow of remarks if not actual conversation.

Four-year-olds are learning how to deal with people. Jan was carrying on a highly satisfying housekeeping play in the doll corner when a very active and boisterous little girl rode up on a tricycle asking to play, too. Jan's instant response was, "All right, you be the father." No sooner had Sally dismounted from the tricycle and parked it than Jan met her at the door with, "We've just had breakfast so now you go to work. You have to go to work all day. I'll see you tonight," and she waved her off. The strategy brought the opportunity Jan wanted to continue her play. Foster and Headley tell of the skill in leadership of Lawrence, a four-year-old boy, who turned aside a destructive child who wanted to play in the block house a group had just completed by saying, "Would you like to be our dog?" Then he added, "We don't let the dog in the house, but all this end of the room is the yard and you can run around it and bark real loud!" (8, p. 12)

Five-year-old children do relatively little solitary play but there is often parallel play carried on by two children or a larger group. While groups of two predominate, there is an increasing

Block play provides an opportunity to find out how things fit together and how much they weigh, and forms a basis for dramatic play.

amount of play in larger groups. Often the play appears more highly co-operative than it is in reality. Each child goes his way with little concern for the group, though the pattern of the play may fit together. Both large and small groups shift continuously. There is a great deal of imaginative dramatic play in which both boys and girls ignore sex in order to play the parts they want to play. Much of the play centers around the house. They can turn almost any set-up into a house where they imitate adult activities. Dolls are no longer lugged about by an arm or leg, clothed or unclothed, as they were earlier, but are cared for like real babies.

Children of this age are expanding their interests in many directions. Not only are they interested in all that people are doing in the neighborhood but they are interested also in the storybook characters of folk tales, poetry, and realistic stories, and they call for their favorites over and over again. Some of the children are interested in certain television and moving picture characters which are aimed at their level.

Kindergarten teachers often teach children to use people as resources for learning. They suggest that the children ask mother, daddy, the groceryman, or the postman for information that is needed. Two children in a summer kindergarten were carrying on the typical five-year-old "'tis not," "'tis so" sort of dispute about the lawfulness of the use of firecrackers in the town. The teacher called their attention to the need for real information. At the end of the session, the group took their question to the traffic policeman on the school corner for authoritative information. They were shown not only the need for information to back up their assertions but also that information can be had from people who are authorities in the area. Learning to deal with both adults and children is an important part of preschool education.

☐ LANGUAGE OPPORTUNITIES IN THE NURSERY SCHOOL

A satisfactory nursery school program provides large blocks of uninterrupted time for individual activities of the child's own choosing. Often the first part of the day is devoted to outdoor play with a variety of simple play materials and apparatus and plenty of space for individual activities as well as opportunity for group play. Children have unlimited opportunity to learn through the manipulation of material and through contacts with other children. Adults provide only as much guidance as is needed for the welfare of each individual child. Indoor play is again self-chosen, with freedom to explore the possibilities of materials and play with them as the child wishes. Language functions here and there in interaction between child and child and between child and teacher. Children learning through first-hand experience in such an atmosphere require relatively little verbal guidance.

Transitions from one activity to another are not mass movements but take place gradually. Children are guided one at a time or in small groups to put away their toys, take care of toileting, wash their hands, drink their midmorning fruit juice, or get ready for rest or lunch. At any one time, children about the room may be at various stages in the morning's routine. Groups at the lunch table are small, and guidance can be given very simply and quietly.

Opportunities for music, rhythms, stories, and conversation are offered to small groups of children, especially at the ages of two and three. The teacher may sit down at the piano and let those children who wish gather about her for songs or rhythms. Other children may go about their individual activities, listening or not, as they wish. An offer of a story may draw a few children or a larger number. Some may come and go without disturbing the group as the story progresses. Four-year-olds are often ready for more group listening and participation. They may be interested in opportunities to share home and school interests and to tell stories of their own creation.

☐ LANGUAGE IN THE KINDERGARTEN

Language functions almost constantly throughout a kindergarten day; in fact, rest periods are probably the only time in which it is omitted. Conversation begins as the children enter the room and forms an accompaniment to the removing of wraps, selecting materials for work and play, and much of the activity of all work and play time. Children of five are increasingly able to listen to each other and to react to the thinking of others. The kindergarten day includes periods set aside for talking and planning together, sharing interests brought in from home and community, and discussing the work that is being done by groups and individuals.

The midmorning "snack" period for milk or fruit juice or the noon lunch period, if the kindergarten has a full-day program, offers a special opportunity for pleasant visiting together about many subjects. Often the subject matter for conversation comes from the children, but if they offer none or talk degenerates into idle or silly chatter, the teacher is ready to introduce new material. Conversation material ranges from pets, weather phenomena, excursions, holidays, seasons, and birthdays, to means of travel, television programs, and movies. Children draw on their past experience for the material for their conversation, just as adults do (1, 8).

A period for stories and poetry is a part of the daily program, and children are encouraged to select material from the library table for the teacher to read and to express their preferences and their reactions. Dramatization of folk stories or stories of real experience interests many children and is carried through with evidence of clear imaginative thinking and little need for properties.

Making up original stories is a consuming interest of some groups and of some children in all groups. If the teacher tells stories well the children will put into their stories the action and dramatic interest they enjoy in the stories told to them. One kindergarten teacher has a large scrapbook for each new group of children. She puts a camera snapshot of each child on a page that is to be all his own for the stories he tells. Children are encouraged to dictate stories when they wish to do so, and the stories are copied onto the child's page in the book. New looseleaf pages are added as they are needed. The time comes when the children say, "Read our book today. Read John's story about the baby bear up in the tree."

The contribution of the kindergarten to the growth and development of children is still not understood by all parents or even by all teachers and administrators in elementary schools. Evidence of this is the number of kindergartens one finds about the country in which reading is being taught to five-year-olds whose language development is far below the reading stage. Reading is not just word recognition. It is a matter of associating meaning which exists in the reader's mind with word symbols on a page. Many five-year-old children have not had enough experience to build the necessary background for such association. A kindergarten year filled with rich opportunities for language development and a wide variety of experiences is far better preparation for success in reading than any amount of premature exposure to the reading process itself.

A small proportion of children have made a start on learning to read before they come to kindergarten or first grade. Durkin (7) has studied some of these children to ascertain the source of stimulation for their interest and who in the child's home environment helps him with it. This small number of children can be given opportunity to continue their interest in kindergarten through the availability of picture and story books to examine or to read, the making of signs or labels for occasional classroom activities, and the dictation of original stories. Daily experience in listening to stories and poems told and read and opportunities for dramatic play further their interest in reading. They are given help with any self-initiated reading activities as they ask for it, but reading is not formally taught to them in the kindergarten.

All kindergarten teachers give thought to the development of readiness for reading through the building of interest in stories and books, ability to pay attention and the development of vocabulary and power in the use of oral language. Many kindergarten activities help to develop the visual and auditory discrimination and correct articulation each child needs in order to master the symbol-sound correspondences of reading. More attention is given to this in Chapter 13 which deals with reading.

Experience and knowledge which fall into the social studies and science realms abound in the kindergarten. The children are keenly interested in everything in their environment. They bring in quantities of nature material, from leaves and acorns in the fall to the first dandelion, cocoons, caterpillars, earthworms, toads, and discarded birds' nests. Even a walk around the block is invariably productive of some sort of nature interest. Their questions cover all aspects of nature, from "What makes the water in the fountain blue?" to "Where does the sun go at night?" Stories and picture books help to sharpen curiosity about natural phenomena as well as to answer questions.

There are excursions out into the environment for many purposes. The children watch the building of a house in the neighborhood from excavation to the day of moving in. A trip to a farm provides material to talk about for many days. A ride on a local train from the home station to the nearest stop and back on the bus or in their mothers' cars gives them opportunity to ask and answer innumerable questions. Just a trip across the street to the nearest grocery store for the Halloween pumpkin enlarges experience with buying and selling and the courtesies necessary for purchaser and salesman. It offers, in addition, opportunity to discuss safety in crossing streets, seasonal products in the store, and the fact that one buys some things by the pound and others by the dozen, quart, or in various packaged forms. Innumerable planned and incidental experiences afford new vocabulary, new concepts, and new material to think and talk about.

A year in kindergarten adds immeasurably to the child's stock of experiences, meanings, and words. Freedom to talk and experience increase the fluency and ease with which a child talks and the maturity of his use of language. The language gains are clearly evident to parents and help to prepare the child for the work of the primary school. A discerning young father remarked that his kindergarten-age daughter had "blossomed in language," and that it was "beautiful to watch."

The kindergarten introduces the child to many forms of language experience which will be carried forward to higher levels of independence in the elementary school. He learns to speak freely and to listen when others speak. He learns to contribute clear ideas, clearly expressed. His interest in books and stories is fed and extended in preparation for learning to read for himself at a later time. He learns to dictate stories, poems, songs, records, notes, and letters for someone else to write down and, in so doing, forms some fundamental concepts and attitudes regarding the use of written language. He learns to seek information through questions, observation, experimentation, and other means in order to satisfy his desire for knowledge. And he learns to use language with people.

☐ CARING FOR INDIVIDUAL DIFFERENCES

Not all children develop at the same rate or in the same way. The teacher of young children studies each one and plans the guidance of each in relation to his needs. The inarticulate child is helped in many ways to gain confidence and satisfaction in the use of language. The aggressive child is taught to give attention to the needs and interests of others. The child with a

Nursery school and kindergarten add greatly to the child's stock of meaningful words. Freedom to talk and experience increase the maturity of his use of language.

serious defect is referred to specialists for diagnosis and treatment. Guidance is provided through the use of materials, through grouping according to need, through firsthand experiences, and through the use of language. The language program of the nursery school and kindergarten is designed throughout to develop language power and the solid background of experience with things, people, information, and ideas which are necessary in order to use language in wholesome living.

□ HEAD START PROGRAMS

A major value of Head Start programs is the opportunity they afford children for language development. Many children from culturally disadvantaged homes have had relatively little stimulus to develop language—in fact some have found silence safer and more comfortable. It appears characteristic of these homes that there is very little talk and practically none addressed to the child except orders and discipline. Whereas, in the example of Adam and Eve cited in Chapter IV, the mothers gave children models of sentences built about the child's own utterances, there are few models of any kind in the homes of these children. They have had little experience in being guided by language and practically none to help them think with language.

In a middle class home, if a mother wishes the children to be quiet so that Daddy will not be disturbed, she is apt to explain to the children, more than once if necessary, "Daddy is tired and wants to rest and read his newspaper. You have had all day to play noisy games. Now let's look at picture books or get out the crayons so you can be quiet until bedtime." The mother in the less advantaged home is more likely to shout, "Shut up!" or "Get out!" than she is to explain the need for consideration and help the children practice it. Because the nursery school teacher does try to help the children learn to think, she may seem to them very "talky" and they may find it difficult at first to listen to so much talk. The teacher's questions will tend to be questions that stimulate thinking, that call attention to cause and effect, and that encourage the child to develop his imagination and to go beyond visible facts to further possibilities.

Each child will bring to the Head Start program the language he has been able to acquire in his environment. It will tell the teacher three things: the quality of his usage will tell her the kind of language used in his home; his vocabulary will tell her the extent of his experience; his nouns will tell what things he has encountered and can name, and his verbs will help her understand the experiences he has had. The way he uses language will tell the teacher something about his self-concept. If he speaks freely and confidently, he has a wholesome concept of himself; if he hangs his head and is silent or answers in monosyllables, he will need a great deal of support and guidance to rebuild his attitude toward himself. The child's language cannot tell the teacher how bright he is.

Many of these children bring to school language that is not only meager but also substandard according to the school's value system. The first and most important attitude for the teacher to assume is one of complete and sincere acceptance of the child's dialect, whatever it may be, but her own response must be in her own dialect, the English the child must later add to his repertoire. If he enters school with little language and becomes comfortable and happy there he will soon be accepting the teacher's speech as his model. She will have innumerable opportunities to help him. If he says, "He go he house," the teacher will probably answer, "Yes, he is going home, isn't he." or if a child says, "She bes my friend." the teacher will answer, "I'm glad she is your friend. It is good to have a friend."

Enriching the children's experience is a major goal of the Head Start program, which offers valuable opportunity for language. Language and experience must operate together if the child is to gain the values that are there. A child might be given the most interesting kind of experience and yet come back with no new words and no new ways of expressing what he saw unless the seeing was accompanied by talk. If the visit is to a farm, there will be talk which includes such words as "pasture," "fence," "silo," "tractor," "milking machine"; if to a market there will be talk of "shelves," "packages," "vegetables," "fruits," "scales," "cash register," and the like. Children's eagerness for experience includes concern for ways of thinking and talking about it, if the school gives attention to lighting the spark.

Of all the values Head Start can offer, none exceeds the possibilities for language development. Through language and warm, comfortable human interaction children absorb both ideas and values.

☐ SELECTED REFERENCES ☐

1. Association for Childhood Education International, *Basic Human Values*. Washington, D. C.: Association for Childhood Education International, 1962.
2. ———, *Knowing When Children Are Ready to Learn*. Washington, D. C.: Association for Childhood Education International, 1947.
3. ———, *Reading in the Kindergarten*. Washington, D. C.: Association for Childhood Education International, 1962.
4. Brown, Roger, and Bellugi, Ursula, "Three Processes in the Child's Acquisition of Syntax." *Harvard Educational Review* 34:133-151, Spring, 1964.
5. Chukovsky, Kornei, *From Two to Five*. Berkeley: University of California Press, 1963.
6. Church, Joseph, *Language and the Discovery of Reality*. New York: Random House, 1961.
7. Durkin, Dolores, "Children Who Read Before First Grade." *Teaching Young Children to Read*. Bulletin No. 19, U. S. Office of Education. Washington, D. C.: Superintendent of Documents, 1964.
8. Foster, Josephine C., and Headley, Neith E., *Education in the Kindergarten* (3rd Ed.). New York: American Book Co., 1959.
9. Gesell, Arnold, and Ilg, Frances L., *Infant and Child in the Culture of Today*. New York: Harper and Brothers, 1943.
10. Gesell, Arnold, and Ilg, Frances L., *The Child from Five to Ten*. New York: Harper and Brothers, 1946.
11. Hammond, Sarah Lou, *Good Schools for Young Children*. New York: The Macmillan Co., 1963.
12. Heffernan, Helen, and Todd, Vivian E., *The Kindergarten Teacher*. Boston: D. C. Heath and Company, 1960.
13. Hughes, Marie M., and Sanchez, George I., *Learning a New Language*. Washington, D. C.: Association for Childhood Education International, 1958.
14. Hymes, James, *Before the Child Reads*. Evanston: Row, Peterson and Co., 1958.
15. Lambert, Hazel M., *Early Childhood Education*. Boston: Allyn and Bacon, Inc., 1960.
16. Loban, Walter D., *The Language of Elementary School Children*. Research Report No. 1, Champaign, Illinois: National Council of Teachers of English, 1963.
17. Mackintosh, Helen K., Chairman, *Children and Oral Language*. Washington, D. C.: Association for Childhood Education International, et al, 1964.
18. McCarthy, Dorothea A., "Language Development in Children." *Manual of Child Psychology*. Leonard Carmichael (Ed.). New

York: John Wiley and Sons, Inc., 1946, Chap. X, pp. 476-581.

19. Munkres, Alberta, *Helping Children in Oral Communication.* New York: Bureau of Publications, Teachers College, Columbia University, 1959.

20. Olson, Willard C., *Child Development.* Boston: D. C. Heath and Co., Second Edition, 1959.

21. Piaget, Jean, *The Child's Conception of the World.* New York: Harcourt, Brace and Co., 1929.

22. Read, Katherine H., *The Nursery School.* Philadelphia: W. B. Saunders Co., 1960.

23. Rosenthal, F., "Some Relationships Between Sociometric Position and Language Structure of Young Children." *Journal of Educational Psychology* 48:483-497, December, 1959.

24. Rudolph, Marguerita, and Cohen, Dorothy H., *Kindergarten – a Year of Learning.* New York: Appleton-Century-Crofts, 1964.

25. Sheehy, Emma Dickson, *The Fives and Sixes Go to School.* New York: Henry Holt and Co., 1954.

26. Smith, Henry Lee, Jr., *Linguistic Science and the Teaching of English.* Inglis Lecture. Cambridge, Massachusetts: Harvard University Press, 1958.

27. Templin, Mildred C., *Certain Language Skills in Children.* Minneapolis: The University of Minnesota Press, 1957.

28. Wann, Kenneth D.; Dorn, Miriam Selchen; and Liddle, Elizabeth Ann, *Fostering Intellectual Development in Young Children.* New York: Bureau of Publications, Teachers College, Columbia University, 1962.

listen learning
to listen

The gist of a little booklet on listening distributed to the foremen and managers of one of the Gary, Indiana, steel mills is summarized with a series of exhortations, as shown on the next page. Business executives and leaders in many realms have become aware of the economic and social values of good listening and are urging their workers to cultivate good listening habits. The schools have been slow to recognize the need for teaching listening as one of the basic language skills.

The four ways in which language functions in school and in life are in listening, speaking, reading, and writing. Listening is the first to operate in the life of a normal individual and the one he uses more than any other. Yet emphasis on helping children learn to listen is a comparatively recent emphasis. It stems from two facts—neither of them new. One is the realization that hearing and listening are not the same thing and that listening must be learned, and the other is the fact that interest in television, talking pictures, and radio is causing children to spend more time in listening than ever before.

Until very recently, there were few studies of listening as compared with other areas of the language arts. Since 1949 when Wilt called attention to the classroom time children spend in listening, a number of researchers have worked on the problem and their studies have been reviewed in educational journals (14). For the most part, these studies have been concerned with listening experiences in school, how to measure listening ability, ways of improving listening, and the relationship of skill in listening to achievement in other school work.

Perhaps the earliest study of listening was that of Rankin, who found in 1928 that of all the time people spent daily in communication, approximately 42 per cent was spent in listening, 32 per cent in speaking, and the remaining 25 per cent in reading and writing combined (9). The proportion of listening has probably increased in the intervening years. Wilt's study of teachers' estimates of the amount of time children spend in listening and the actual time clocked through classroom observation, brought forth some interesting data (14). She found that children spend an average of more than two and a half hours in listening during a five-hour school day. This was more than twice the amount of time teachers had estimated and bore out the fact that Corey had found earlier, that teachers outtalk the pupils by a considerable margin (2).

HERE IT IS IN A NUTSHELL*

TO LISTEN BETTER . . .

Avoid These	*Do These*
Preoccupation Daydreaming Prejudices	Recognize the importance of listening well Make listening an active process Use the full time for listening Open your mind to new ideas
Wrong attitude Self-centeredness Closed-mindedness Argumentativeness	Straighten up and lean forward Look at the speaker Be alert all over Show interest in your face Take brief notes Ask questions
Busy-ness Jumping to conclusions Stereotyped thinking Passive listening	Look for the speaker's purpose Look for main ideas Distinguish facts from opinions Analyse the speaker's reasoning Apply what is said to your own interests

If you forget some of these, use the Golden Rule of Listening:

LISTEN TO OTHERS AS YOU WOULD HAVE THEM LISTEN TO YOU

Parents and teachers have always exhorted children to "listen" and to "pay attention" to what is said to them but rarely have they given children any real help in doing so. The curriculum guide of a large city school system recommended these rules for good listening in the primary grades: "Sit up straight. Keep your hands still. Keep your feet still. Look at the speaker." It is conceivable that all of these injunctions might be followed

*A Help-Your-Self Booklet, No. 5901. Copyright 1958. New York, New York.

to the letter with no listening at all. Sometimes adults are content with children's response but frequently they are dissatisfied with it. Only fairly recently has there been any systematic effort to study listening to discover how children learn to listen and what help they need in order to make their listening skills effective.

Children need to be taught that listening is a complex mental process that requires effort and thoughtful attention. As one listens he does four things simultaneously. First, he recognizes the sound patterns that he hears. If the patterns were in an unfamiliar language, he might hear them equally clearly but be unable to recognize them. Second, as he recognizes the sound patterns he puts meaning into them. The fact that he can attach no meaning to sounds in a foreign language proves that the meaning is not in the sounds but in the mind of the listener who recognizes the sounds. Third, he reacts to the sounds with his own background of experience. If the sounds deal with things or ideas that are outside his experience, he may be unable to react to them or he may attach to them meaning quite different from what the speaker intended. Fourth, he puts the material into perspective. A speaker who speaks English helps the listener with this process because in English one uses pitch, stress, and pauses to accent peaks of meaning. A teacher may say to her class, "If you put your work away quickly and quietly, we may have time to play a game." In so doing, she probably gives some emphasis to "if," "work," "away," "may," and "play" and special emphasis to "quickly," "quietly," "time," and "game." These are the meaning-bearing words which set the condition and propose the reward. The pause after "quietly" makes the reward stand out clearly. The other words which make the English sentence complete are fillers which carry less of critical meaning; the children might, in fact, catch the meaning without them.

In his experience with listening, the listener frequently does a fifth thing: he incorporates all or a portion of what he hears into himself. In other words, he remembers whatever parts of it mean enough to him to be remembered.

Listening corresponds to reading in what it demands of an individual, though it utilizes oral symbols and sounds, while reading utilizes marks on a surface. Listening and reading are both mental processes calling for thought and reaction. They differ in some important respects. As one listens to a person who is speaking, the reaction and interpretation he gives to words are colored by the attitude, the facial expression, voice, and bodily gestures of the speaker. Written words tend to be more impersonal unless one knows the writer well enough to read his attitude into his written words. When the words are impersonal, the reader builds his reaction almost entirely from the words themselves. If one's attention wanders in reading, he can go back and pick up the dropped threads. In listening, a portion of what was presented is lost. In reading, one can stop to ponder on points suggested. In listening, one must stay with the task and absorb the sound meaning at the rate at which it comes. One has no control over it.

Listening to words and sounds through radio requires the listener to put meaning into sound without any sensory impression other than hearing. Interest in radio, consequently, comes later than interest in television where the child has visual help in putting meaning into sounds and interpreting them. A child growing up in a home in which the television or radio pours forth sound all day, must first of all learn to cut the sound out of his consciousness or he could develop no inner life of his own. Later, the school calls upon him, on occasion, to listen to and learn from such disembodied sound. On the same point Bell says of English children:

> The child begins to listen with a *desire* to understand what is being said. Every teacher has experienced that strange blank impenetrable cloud of unawareness which veils the minds of very young children. From time to time they will emerge and make direct contact with our minds. But, except during those rare moments, it seems often useless for us to speak, for having ears they hear not. I am not sure but that this is more noticeably the case now than it was twenty years ago. And I am tempted to attribute this voluntary deafness to the fact that almost from birth, many children now have lived all their waking hours against a background of noises from the wireless set (1, p. 66).

Television has caught the interest of even young children as radio never could, because the pictures and action help to invest the sound with meaning and furnish the child with material for the building of his own mental pictures.

☐ KINDS AND STAGES OF LISTENING

Listening and speaking go hand in hand; it is almost impossible to deal with one without the other. Listening is intake which is concerned with expansion of the self, while speaking is the outgoing, expression aspect.

Children come to school varying greatly in their ability to listen. The skill they have attained is the product of their environment and their experience, influenced, of course, by auditory acuity and mental capacity. Interest plays a large and significant part in learning and in achievement. If a child's environment has awakened interests and his curiosity has been fed, he can enter into new interests and expand old ones with zest and energy. If he has had opportunity to develop few interests or has found little help in satisfying his curiosities, his mind may not reach out for new listening and learning experiences. The maturity of a child's listening is dependent in part on the way he has been listened to. Milner's study showed higher language attainment in school on the part of children who had experienced give and take in home conversation (6). If they had had opportunity to talk and had been listened to, their achievement was at a higher level than that of children who had had little or no opportunity to talk and be listened to by significant adults in their environment.

One finds in children's responses a number of kinds, levels, or types of listening. The list progresses from less mature to more mature levels and includes:

> Little conscious listening and then only when interest is closely related to the self: easily distracted by people and things in the environment.
> Half listening: holding fast to own ideas and waiting to insert them at the first opportunity.
> Listening passively: apparent absorption but little or no reaction.
> Off again—on again listening: mentally entering into what is said if and when it is closely related to own interests.
> Listening: responding with items from own experience as result of associations brought to mind.
> Listening: some reactions through questions or comments.
> Listening: some genuine emotional and mental participation.
> Listening: a meeting of minds (12, pp. 42, 43).

All of these types of listening are found among adults as well as among children. Probably every individual responds at times in each of these ways, depending on his interest, his knowledge of the subject, his attitude toward the topic or the person speaking, and his physical and emotional condition at the moment. Really entering into the thought of others with self-forgetfulness is a mature response. Few young children are capable of it and then only for brief periods when the material being dealt with touches their own lives intimately. An experienced teacher can tell by watching children's faces how deep their listening is going and when and where they get off the track. At the beginning of the year many six-year-olds only half listen to the contributions of others. They can bring to the listening little from their own experience; they are distracted by the unfamiliar elements in the situation; or they are in the habit of saying what they wish to say whenever they wish to say it and are struggling to hold on to the ideas they wish to express until they find an opportunity to pour them forth. Often one can tell by watching their eyes and faces what kind and quality of listening is taking place. With understanding guidance, most children expand their listening powers as the year wears on. They take pride in their growing power to discipline their listening and talking to bring about a meeting of minds in group planning, discussion, and other situations which call for group interaction.

Listening has been classified also as passive or marginal, appreciative, attentive, and analytical listening (7, p. 81). *Marginal* listening is the kind a housewife does as she makes the beds or sets the table with the sound of the radio in the background of her consciousness. Many of today's high school and college students insist that they can study as well or better with the radio on. They appear to have it "turned low" as far as consciousness is concerned, yet to be sufficiently aware of it to stop to listen attentively when something of special interest is said. Children learn very early to tune out what they do not care to listen to, yet are quickly aware of a voice calling them back to attention. Listening to a concert, a play, or a story may be *appreciative* listening—often with an element of the creative in it as the mind builds its own mental pictures and moods. Teachers and parents strive for *attentive* listening when they are giving directions and instructions to children. Attentive listening is also called for in making plans, in discussing problems, and in evaluating in all of its forms. *Analytical* listening is the kind one hopes may operate in listening to political campaign speeches or any others designed to sway the opinions and influence the behavior of the listeners. Recognition and analysis of propaganda calls for this kind of listening.

All of these forms of listening are found in any classroom. Marginal listening undoubtedly takes place when children are asked to work independently while the teacher works with a small group. Yet they must be alert to the time when the teacher again turns her attention back to the whole class or shifts her attention to other individuals or groups. Appreciative listening is the purpose for which the teacher reads or tells stories or poetry to the class or plays recordings of music or literature. Attentive listening is called for at many points throughout every school day. Analytical listening may function less frequently in the elementary school, though it is evident in all problem-solving situations.

□ "LISTENABILITY"

A good deal of study has gone into the matter of what makes printed material easily readable. Clear print, good space or leading between lines, good margins, sentences and paragraphs not too densely packed with concepts, and the like, are all aids to readability. There are parallel points which are important to listening. Speech sounds uttered in a pleasant voice, loud enough to be easily heard, flowing rhythmically and not too rapidly, can be listened to without strain. The pronunciations and the pattern of the sentences must be familiar and conventional enough to require no extra effort to understand them. As in material for reading, material for children's listening cannot be too closely packed with concepts. Ideas need to be spread out and spaced, not compressed, so that children have time to catch and absorb each one. Unfamiliar words must be woven into context which gives clues to their meaning.

Readiness for listening is fully as important as readiness for reading. At all age levels, physical conditions conducive to good listening need to be provided. A relaxed, quiet atmosphere, a comfortable physical setting, and a minimum of distractions, are all aids to listening. Preparation for listening—an introduction which catches children's interest or provides them with a purpose for listening—paves the way for thoughtful, concentrated listening. Teachers find such preparation particularly important before the presentation of a film or a lesson on television. There must be opportunity, too, for reaction and at times for doing something about or with the material acquired through listening. Children are not empty cups to be filled. What a child gains through listening, as Bell has indicated, is gained because there is within the child *desire* for understanding of what is said (1). He must mentally reach out for it and garner it himself if it is to become a part of him.

☐ PRESCHOOL EXPERIENCES IN LISTENING

Preschool listening experiences of young children differ greatly in detail but have much in common no matter what the type of home from which the child comes. Every child has learned his language through listening. If he lacks ability to distinguish sounds clearly there may be defects in articulation but for the most part his speech mirrors that of his environment.

As a young child, he has grown quite easily into the habit of listening when speech is addressed to him directly. He has listened, also, to interchange of talk in the family group. To this he has probably given attention if it seemed to concern him and was within his understanding, otherwise he has let it pass him by. Unless he has gone to nursery school or Sunday School he has had little or no experience with listening as part of a larger group. What experience he has had with listening to stories told or read usually has been in situations in which the stories were addressed to him.

The preschool child has learned to respond to his mother's verbal guidance. He knows what is expected of him. He has probably learned to distinguish between suggestions which he is free to utilize or not, as he chooses, and commands or directions which call for obedience. He has learned under what circumstances he can safely turn a deaf ear to what is said to him and what are the danger signals in tone of voice, words, and attitude which call for attention and conformity to adult wishes.

The young child's talk with his playmates is often not of the level he uses in talk with adults. Words combined with action and fragments of sentences have often sufficed to carry his meaning to his contemporaries. Action on the part of the other child has frequently been satisfactory without verbal response.

The child before school age has formed many sound associations—the kitten scratching at the door, the dog barking, his father's car coming into the driveway, the buzzing of flies, the sound of the wind–these and many other sounds have taken on meaning. Children bring to school varied backgrounds of listening experience but all who can hear have well-established listening habits of one sort or another.

□ LISTENING PROBLEMS OF THE PRIMARY SCHOOL CHILD

Some beginners find it very difficult to acquire the listening habits needed in first grade. Here are many children, and much of what the teacher says is directed to a large audience, not to the child as an individual. The teacher's methods of guiding through words may differ greatly from his mother's methods. Often there are detailed instructions for doing certain things. There is a great deal that is new to take in, react to, and remember. First grade teachers, especially, need to be infinitely patient in helping children adjust to the group methods and the more impersonal contacts and guidance of the primary school years.

One of the difficult tasks for some children in the primary grades is to learn when to give full attention and when to give only marginal or no attention to what the teacher is saying. When she is speaking to the entire class or to a group of which the child is a member, he must give full attention. When she is working with a group which does not include him, he must learn to cut out what she is saying or give only marginal attention to it so that he can concentrate on what he is doing. It takes time for young children to learn what is called for in each situation and also to learn to make the transitions from one kind of listening to another.

The period during which a young child can listen attentively is short at first but gradually lengthens as he gains experience and becomes secure in the classroom. It is better for the teacher to study the children's listening span and accept it as it is than to struggle to hold them to a longer period of listening than they are ready for. Listening can scarcely be forced. If the teacher is unduly persistent and strenuous in her determination to hold children to attentive listening beyond what they can give comfortably, the tension created may, in itself, stand in the way of good listening.

The length of time a young child can listen depends more than anything else on his interest in the subject of the moment. The length of time he can give attention to planning a party for his mother or a trip to a point of interest is probably longer then he can devote to planning for a reading lesson. The attentive listening he can bring to a story that catches his interest differs from the listening he can do to directions for filling blanks in his workbook, if that is the task in hand. He may be able to listen for a longer period to what the teacher is saying than to another child, though the opposite may be true if the other child is relating an experience which touches intimately the child's own experience.

Primary grade children profit from an occasional discussion of listening and the setting of definite purposes for listening. This is especially true of sharing, planning, and discussion situations. The importance of listening in order to fit one's own contribution into the total, or in order to weigh alternatives and arrive at a decision, can be increasingly understood and acted upon by younger children.

Children need help to understand what other children will listen to. The boy who said, in answer to his mother's suggestions regarding the sharing of his travel experiences with his class, "Oh, that's the kind of stuff grownups always want kids to tell but kids aren't interested in it," was aware of what would be listened to with interest and what would not.

☐ HELPING CHILDREN GROW IN ABILITY TO LISTEN

Conversation is a two-way process which calls for as much listening as talking. Opportunities for free conversation before school in the morning, during the lunch period, or at times during the course of certain kinds of work accustom children to the give and take of real conversation. They can learn very quickly that only one person can talk at a time if others are to listen, that the speaker must have something relevant to say, that he must say it clearly, and that no one speaker can monopolize the talking time if real conversation is to take place.

Periods for sharing are especially important to primary grade children. Beginners are still learning to adjust to school living; bringing things from home to show and telling about home and family experiences helps to pull together the two major segments of their world. A child's own contribution is frequently of far greater importance to him than anyone else's contribution. He enjoys having others listen to him with interest and attention but is often far less interested in listening to the contributions of others. Sometimes he can listen attentively for a time. Then a remark by someone else gears in with experiences of his own and he relives his experience, rather than that of the other child. Waiting for a turn to talk is not always easy. Talking himself, for only a brief minute, then listening to others talk for a much longer period, collectively, is also difficult. Patience and understanding are needed to help him make the necessary adjustments.

Even third grade children sometimes need help at some of the same points. Contributions tend to be longer now, and the child's own turn may come less frequently. Also, more of the contributions may be further from the child's own immediate experience because horizons widen considerably by the age of eight.

Periods in which children share the books they have read or report on their findings in social studies and science may call for more real effort to listen because the material is third-hand now, and even farther removed from the listener than someone else's first-hand experience. Also, listening in these areas sometimes calls for critical analysis and this presents new listening problems for most children. They need a great deal of help to learn how to evaluate and also how to express their evaluations courteously and sympathetically. They are confronted at times with evidence which they react to negatively and must learn to give it a hearing and weigh it fairly, presenting reasons for their unfavorable reactions.

In the primary grades, definite time is set aside almost daily for appreciative listening. Story period is looked forward to by most children. They can listen attentively and appreciatively for several minutes if the teacher reads well and if the stories and poetry she reads are well selected. Ability is growing to listen to music and to appreciate it if the selections are not too long and if they have rhythmic and tonal patterns that are simple enough for them to enjoy.

The school's use of audio-visual materials affords children guided experience with some of the kinds of listening they do at home. In listening to radio or viewing television, children take the programs as they come. Rarely is there any preparation for the material of the program. Teachers have found, however, that children gain a great deal more from their listening and viewing if the teacher has previewed the material and can introduce them to the ideas that are coming and help them to know what to listen or watch for. A mind set toward the material that is coming and some goals to strive for make the experience far more valuable than just going into it "cold." Also, in the use of audio-visual materials at school, it is possible to repeat the experience after it has been discussed, to clarify points that are hazy, to catch elements that have been missed, and to sharpen and deepen impressions. Such experience and guidance may add value to home listening and viewing through helping children to make them a thinking process.

☐ IMPROVING LISTENING AT THE INTERMEDIATE GRADE LEVEL

All of the kinds of listening that have been discussed appear also at the intermediate level. Some children have developed fairly mature listening habits which they use most of the time though they regress to less mature levels on occasion. Other children are little more advanced in their listening habits than they were in the early grades. Intermediate grade children are better able to analyze their own listening habits, to set definite goals for self-improvement, and to work toward them than are younger children. At this level, children profit by the experiences of analyzing listening as discussed on page 129.

The work of the intermediate grades calls for more of analytical listening than does the work of the earlier grades. Children can begin to compare sources and to check what they hear for reliability. With guidance, they can look into the qualifications of speakers, become aware of biases, and learn to look at all sides of controversial issues which are within their understanding. They can learn to withhold judgment until the facts are in and learn to let reason and knowledge guide their judgment rather than emotion or personal interest. All of this development will take place slowly. Children will do well at some points and be proud of their gains but slip back to less mature levels at other times. Interest in improving their listening habits and their attitudes toward what they hear is highly important. The more practice they have under guidance the more surely will good habits take root.

☐ EVALUATING CHILDREN'S LISTENING

Analyzing with children what one does in his mind as he listens, helps them to understand the process of listening, recognize its complex demands, and appreciate the need for giving mental effort to it. Such analysis could be carried on as early as third grade and should be repeated more than once at each grade level.

There are times when the teacher should interrupt a sharing, planning, reporting, or discussion period to evaluate with the children the listening they are doing. If poor listening is creating a problem in carrying on their work, calling attention to the problem and setting up objectives of good listening may put a situation that is deteriorating back into working order. Or, if the period has gone well, the teacher may wisely call attention to the elements of good listening that made the successful experience possible. Children can set up their own standards for listening and check themselves against their standards both individually and as a group.

☐ TELEVISION AND CHILDREN

Television is so much a part of the lives of vast numbers of children that it must enter into any discussion of the language arts. Perhaps it fits into the area of listening as well as into any other part of the total discussion.

> In the decade of the 1950's, television came to dominate the nonsleep, nonschool time of the North American child. One-sixth of all the child's waking hours, from the age of three on, is now typically given over to the magic picture tube. During the first sixteen years of life, the typical child now spends, in total, at least as much time with television as in school. Television is probably the greatest source of common experience in the lives of children, and, along with the home and the school, it has come to play a major part in socializing the child. (10, p. 12)

The most extensive study to date of the time children spend in viewing television is one reported by Schramm and others in 1961. They found children in the San Francisco area spending 14 hours per week at Grade I and approximately 18 hours per week at Grade VI. Sixth grade children in relatively isolated towns averaged nearer 23 hours per week watching television. The conclusion of this study of nearly 3000 children and the parents of some of them in towns and cities of western United States and Canada was that viewing seemed to benefit the dull child and some bright ones (who choose more intellectually stimulating programs) more than the average child. The evidence did "nothing to controvert the conclusion that (after the early years, at least) television does not markedly broaden a child's horizon or stimulate him intellectually or culturally. This is not to say that television does *not* stimulate or broaden a child;—it probably does not do those things to a greater degree than would be done without television" (4, p. 97). A report by Himmelweit and others of research done in England in 1955 and 1956 arrived at the same conclusions.

Ten years of study of the television viewing by children in the north area near Chicago have been reported by Witty. Elementary school children averaged a little more than 21 hours a week of televiewing and high school students more nearly 14 hours. Children scoring well on achievement tests spent fewer hours viewing television than those whose scores were low (14).

All of this means that teachers could well follow on television some of the better programs that are suitable for children, discuss the programs with them, and find ways to encourage children to turn on the better programs at home and use or recognize the results of their viewing at school. Several years ago a teacher in St. Paul reported preparatory work on the part of her sixth grade for each week's program of *You Were There*. The children took note each week of the topic announced for the next week's program. They read and discussed background material at school, then viewed the program at home. They came to school the next day discussing how reliably the program had presented the historical facts as they had read them, where liberties were taken for dramatic effects, what elements were clear and trustworthy and where misinterpretation might result. Surely such experience would make children more discriminating listeners and viewers of other programs as well.

More and more of leisure time is being spent, by children and adults alike, in recreation that is comparatively effortless absorption. For wholesome development, children need to be helped to set standards for their recreational experience and to learn to interpret and to evaluate what they hear and see.

□ SELECTED REFERENCES □

1. Bell, Vicars, *On Learning the English Tongue*. London: Faber and Faber, 1953.

2. Corey, Stephen M., "The Teachers Outtalk the Pupils," *School Review* 48:745-52, December, 1940.
3. Duker, Sam, "Listening." *Review of Educational Research* 31:145-51, April, 1961.
4. Himmelweit, Hilde; Oppenheim, A. N.; and Vince, Pamela, *Television and the Child.* Published for the Nuffield Foundation. London: Oxford University Press, 1958.
5. Lewis, T. R., "Listening." *Review of Educational Research* 28:89-95, April, 1958.
6. Milner, Esther, "A Study of the Relationships between Reading Readiness in Grade One School Children and Patterns of Parent-Child Interaction." *Child Development* 22:95-112, June, 1951.
7. National Council of Teachers of English, Commission on the English Curriculum, *Language Arts for Today's Children.* N.C.T.E. Curriculum Series, Vol. II. New York: Appleton-Century-Crofts, Inc., 1952, pp. 71-105.
8. Postman, Neil, and associates, *Television and the Teaching of English.* New York: Appleton-Century-Crofts, Inc., 1961.
9. Rankin, Paul T., "The Importance of Listening Ability." *English Journal* 17:623-30, October, 1928.
10. Schramm, Wilbur; Lyle, Jack; and Parker, Edwin B., *Television in the Lives of Our Children.* Stanford: Stanford University Press, 1961.
11. Shane, Harold G., and Mulry, June G., *Improving Language Arts Instruction through Research.* Washington, D.C.: Association for Supervision and Curriculum Development, 1963.
12. Wilt, Miriam E., "Children's Experiences in Listening." *Children and the Language Arts.* (Herrick, Virgil E., and Jacobs, Leland B., compilers.) Englewood Cliffs: Prentice-Hall, Inc., 1955.
13. ———, "A Study of Teacher Awareness of Listening as a Factor in Elementary Education." *Journal of Educational Research* 43:626-36, April, 1950.
14. Witty, Paul, and Kinsella, Paul, "Televiewing: Some Observations from Studies, 1949-1962." *Elementary English* 39:772-79, December, 1962.

SPEAKING AND LISTENING IN THE PRIMARY SCHOOL

Because ours is a highly mobile population and families are free to move to any part of the United States as they like or as circumstances require, the children in any primary school classroom may speak a variety of dialects of American English. Schools in California contain many Negro children from the deep south, Spanish-American children, and children from Asia and the Pacific Islands, as well as other migrants speaking the dialect characteristic of the northeastern and central states. Cities like New York, Chicago, Gary, and Wilmington, any industrial city, may present many differences in home dialect. If, however, the community is a settled one, a single dialect may prevail. And if, as is sometimes true, the children in a first grade class have had kindergarten or other organized preschool experience, their months under the guidance of a teacher may have given them a fund of common experiences and the common language built about those experiences. In any case, each child brings to the primary classroom the language of his own previous experience – the language acquired through his home, neighborhood, and preschool living.

One of the avowed purposes of the primary school is to improve the language skills and usage of children. The primary school has always accepted this responsibility though the methods applied to attain its ends have changed greatly with the years.

During one period of school history teachers considered their first task in the primary school to be that of subduing and silencing little children. They fastened them, almost literally, into seats screwed to the floor in formal rows and taught them to listen while the teacher talked. Children who had been unceasingly active in their preschool living were now taught to be inactive little puppets, moving only when activated by the teacher's commands. Children who had learned all that they knew through talking, asking questions, and firsthand experiences were required to lay aside these well-developed learning techniques and learn almost solely through obedience to commands. They were given "language lessons" instead of language experience and taught the mechanics of reading by teachers who in many instances knew nothing of the level of language power each child had attained and the background he brought to the black symbols on the page.

The first goal in language development in the modern school

is to free the child so that he talks easily and confidently. Until a child will talk freely the teacher has little opportunity to learn the level of language development he has attained and what help he needs. It is impossible to improve the language of a child until there is some language to improve.

□ FREEING THE CHILD TO TALK

The first efforts of the teacher in the primary school are planned to help each child feel comfortable, relaxed, and at home in his new school environment. Anxiety and insecurity are not conducive to good adjustment or good learning. In order to give them a comfortable sense of at-homeness, the teacher helps the children explore their school environment to see how it operates and to meet the people with whom they will be associated. Even children who have attended kindergarten profit by such orientation. In the classroom, the children share freely their own home and neighborhood experiences. They bring toys and other treasures from home to show and talk about. They work and play with many types of materials and express their ideas freely through the use of crayons, paints, clay, construction materials, and toys. They sing, talk, dramatize, play games, and listen to stories.

During this period of orientation and adjustment the teacher differentiates her guidance to fit the needs of each child. The confident, aggressive child is helped to see his need for taking turns in talking and for listening and reacting constructively to what other children are saying. The timid, insecure child is drawn into interests in which he can lose himself and is guided into informal work and play situations with other children.

An informal room arrangement and movable furniture are assets to a good language program. Furniture can be pushed into cluster groupings for various purposes so that those children who wish to carry on similar activities can be placed together. A group can work with clay in one section of the room while other groups look at picture books, play in the playhouse, build a hutch for the pet rabbit, arrange nature materials they have brought in, put together picture puzzles, or carry on individual activities as they wish. Many children will talk freely with a small group before they are ready to face the entire class and make a contribution.

It would be impossible to overemphasize the value of informal room arrangement and organization to a good program of language growth, especially in the primary school. Children, as well as most adults, talk better in informal, face-to-face contacts than they do in highly formalized, impersonal situations. There is nothing inspirational about talking to the backs of heads and nothing more terrifying to many children than to be required to stand before an impersonal mass of faces, dotted at even intervals throughout the length and breadth of a large room. Even children who speak freely and well in out-of-school situations find adjustment difficult in the formalized atmosphere of some classrooms. A modern schoolroom with carpeted floors or at least a rug that can be unrolled for the children to sit on makes good face-to-face interaction in large or small groups easy to attain.

It takes a great deal of experience with language to develop it to the point where it is a ready and effective tool for all kinds of use. Schools no longer strive to keep children silent for the major part of the day and then work intensively on language improvement during a single "language period." Language is both an end and a means to an end in almost all of the work of the day. The teacher works with language from the time the first child comes to school in the morning until the last one goes home at the end of the day. The entire curriculum is a language curriculum. Language is thought of as a means of operation, as an avenue of enrichment and learning, and as a means of expression. It is an essential part of individual and group living.

☐ FOLLOWING UP THE HEAD START PROGRAM

Studies have demonstrated that a good Head Start program may raise a child's intelligence quotient several points through even a few month's experience. It is particularly distressing to learn that the Head Start gains are almost entirely lost in a very short period in some first grades. The child has made his gains in the Head Start program through a rich program of guided experience and constant encouragement to add to and improve his language through free use of it. The kind of first grade experience which puts a premium on silence and obedience, the filling in of workbooks, and drill on reading skills makes little or no use of the child's gains, and because they are so new to him and he has had at best only a few months to practice them, they soon disappear—a tragedy for the child and a sad waste of potential for society.

Children from culturally disadvantaged homes need a great deal of time and opportunity to use and continue to improve their oral language. Oracy, the ability to communicate in their dialect, is for them a first need, though work toward literacy can be carried on very profitably if it is built on the language-experience approach to reading, which appears to bring good results in the schools utilizing it. This approach is presented in Chapter 11.

☐ LISTENING, SPEAKING, READING, AND WRITING

There are four aspects of language with which the school is concerned: listening and speaking, reading and writing. Listening and reading are the intake aspects of language, the means by which one enriches himself and adds to his stock of interests and knowledge. Speaking and writing are the outgoing aspects, the means through which one expresses himself and communicates his thinking to others.

Listening and speaking are of first importance in the primary school; they are the aspects of language the child needs first. The written symbol form of language is learned after the child has gained proficiency in the use of the oral form. This was true of the development of the race and it is true also of the child. The school does not wait to perfect a child's language before teaching him to read and write but it does seek to build facility in the use of oral language to the point where it forms a working foundation for the learning of written symbols.

Teaching a child to observe accurately is important also. Children as well as adults look without seeing and see without comprehending until they develop the background of knowledge and experience which is essential to accurate observation and true comprehension of what is seen. This precedes and accompanies the development of both oral and written language.

☐ THE GOAL OF EASY USE OF LANGUAGE

The first requisite to easy, useful language is *an atmosphere in which language can flourish.* Talking must be legalized—

the atmosphere must be one which not only permits talking but actively stimulates and encourages it.

The second requisite for easy use of language is *a happy, wholesome relationship between the teacher and children and among the children themselves*. Wholesome human relationships result in communication which is wholesome and stimulating. Whether the wholesome flow of communication brings about good relationships or whether the high quality of human relationship brings about good communication does not matter. The important point is that one is essential to the other. The emphasis on sociometric studies has called attention to the presence and the problems of the isolates and misfits in school groups—those who are ignored or excluded from participation in the give and take of classroom living. Many times the evidence points to the fact that the isolate has become lost because of his inability to communicate with other children because he has a speech defect, comes from a foreign background, or uses speech in a manner different from that of other children. A child may be excluded by the children because he is "bossy" and overaggressive in his use of language, because he is inept in making contacts with people, or because he cannot fit into a group as a co-operative, participating member. Improving the relationships within a group improves interaction and communication.

Helping a rejected child to make himself acceptable to the group and helping the group to take him in is definitely a language problem. James had come to the first grade in November as a transfer from another school. He was quiet and unobtrusive for a time, then began to be complained of by the children because he damaged their clay work, tore their drawings, and took the ball on the playground and ran off with it. The underlying problem was revealed when the parents were called in for consultation. The father's occupation had caused the family to move many times and James had attended two kindergartens and started first grade in another school. The children of the present first grade had attended school together for more than a year and formed a well-knit cohesive group which did not open up and take in the newcomer. James had reached the point of concluding that even unfavorable attention for his behavior was better than no attention at all. The father and mother had transferred their church membership, joined some local clubs, and were finding a place in the social life of the new community. Six-year-old James had no techniques for similar accomplishment in his school group. When his mother invited children to come home after school to play with James and the teacher helped him to find a place in the activities of his group, the behavior problems disappeared and James became a happy, contributing member of the class.

The third requisite for easy use of language is the presence of *many dynamic ongoing interests.* These interests will be of assorted types. Some will be interests in which the entire class participates, others will be interests carried on by small groups, and there will be many individual interests.

Language development comes through the use of language. The child has spent five or more preschool years in building a language background of words and meanings before he is ready to learn to recognize those words and meanings when they appear in the form of little black symbols on a printed page. Linguists and teachers of foreign languages maintain that, to learn a language, attention should be given first to the oral language. Work with the written form of the language should wait until some mastery of the spoken language has been achieved. In dealing with the native language, efforts to teach a child to read before he has command of the oral language may be harmful to future attitudes and achievement. It is the task of the primary school to keep the vocabulary of words and meanings pushing on ahead of the reading vocabulary throughout the primary years in order to give the child an increasingly broad working vocabulary to utilize during the years which follow in the intermediate school. Traditional schools have often put the child on a language learning plateau in the primary grades and cut him off from all opportunities to build vocabulary and language power. They have centered his entire attention upon learning to recognize the printed symbol form of *known* words, but have given him little or no opportunity to engage in experiences which would expand his vocabulary of words and meanings in preparation for the advanced work of the later grades. They have turned off the fountain at its source. A rich program of work with literature, social studies and science is necessary to expand the child's experience with language and lay the foundation for later work.

Language must be used if it is to expand and grow in power. Many opportunities for growth in language power can be made available in any classroom.

☐ LANGUAGE AT WORK IN FREE AND DISCIPLINED SITUATIONS

Oral language serves many purposes in the daily life of a group of children in the primary school. They use language in at least the following ways and probably others as well:

Talking	Reporting
Conversing	Explaining
Sharing	Evaluating
Planning	Solving problems
Discussing	Expressing creative thinking

■ *Talking* takes place as the children come into the room in the morning, as they work about the room getting ready for the day, and as they carry on their individual and group interests. It may be a matter of occasional remarks or assertions about what is being done, or suggestions, reminders, comments, or criticisms of what the individual or others about him are doing. It is spontaneous, unorganized, and completely random. It helps the teacher understand children's interests and needs.

■ *Conversing* may take the place as children carry on activities around a worktable or drink their fruit juice or milk at mid-morning lunch. It may deal with the activity at hand or with some other topic of mutual interest. It involves contributing and listening to the contributions of others and reacting to them. It differs from just random talking in that it involves a meeting of minds, a thinking and talking together on a subject that is, at least for the moment, of mutual interest. Conversation is more apt to occur between two children or in a small group than in a large group. It involves real interaction, a tossing of the talk back and forth, and contributions from the thinking of the participants.

■ *The sharing period* is looked upon with happy anticipation in the primary grades. Young children enjoy bringing things from home—treasures that interest them especially, or tales of their out-of-school experience to share with the group. Mere showing of what he has brought may be all that a timid child can manage at first. Later he will respond to the teacher's questions with monosyllables or phrases. Still later, he will tell the teacher about it, then repeat what he has said to the group if he is asked to do so. Finally the time will come when he can face the group and make his contribution without help. Sharing items of home experience with the school group helps to bridge the gap between home and school as well as add to the richness of school experience.

■ *Planning* takes place almost daily in the life of the classroom. There is often a planning period for the entire class as soon as the children have gathered in the morning. Planning requires that all participants discipline their thinking, listening, and speaking. There is a task to be accomplished and all must keep their minds centered on the goal. Talking about unrelated matters must be guarded against because it interferes with the work of the group. Each child must listen thoughtfully and weigh the contribution of each speaker to determine its value and its suitability to the solution of the problem under consideration. Each participant must try to make his contribution serve the purpose of the group. Children can learn, through experience, the way in which language must be utilized to meet a classroom need. The teacher tends to be the leader and the children work through with her any plans that are needed for the work of the day or for any part of the day that differs from their usual plan of operation. Points may be formulated and recorded on the chalk board for later reference. All children are encouraged to participate and to feel a sense of responsibility for the ongoing activity of the group.

Planning may occur at various points during the day. It may involve two children, a small group, or the entire class, depending on the situation. Planning calls upon children to keep their attention centered on the problem under discussion, to approach it in a practical and realistic manner, to evaluate the suggestions that are made, and to select the one or ones most suitable for the purpose. It calls for disciplining their listening and talking to serve a social end. Learning to plan and to follow through with plans is an important part of the child's education.

■ *Discussing* may enter in at a number of points. Several plans may be presented for the carrying out of an interest and the children discuss the merits and problems of each in their effort to select the most feasible and valuable plan. Perhaps the children have listened to or read a story; they discuss what occurred in it and their reactions to it, and deepen, through discussion, their understanding of what the writer sought to convey. Or they have taken a trip to visit the fire station, the post office, or a farm and they discuss the points they found most interesting, the information they have gathered, or the possible ways of following up and utilizing what they have learned in carrying on projects they have planned for the classroom.

■ *Reporting* is called for in the working out of all types of projects. Reports of plans may be the first step and progress reports will follow any work period. Children may find information to answer questions and report their findings to the group. News reports are of interest whether the news is drawn from the television, radio, printed material, or firsthand experience. Stories and books may afford material for simple reports from time to time. Children who are beginning to read independently often find great pleasure in advertising a book through a brief report so that the interest of other children is stimulated and they are led to read the book. Reporting achievement to parents is always of interest and children enjoy preparing a summary report of the work they have completed to present in oral or dramatic form for another grade. In every case, determining what they will talk about, thinking through relevant material, deciding what to say first and next, and the final oral presentation (or possibly the writing of it), all call for disciplined thinking and use of language power.

■ *Explaining* a project and the method by which it was achieved becomes necessary from time to time. Explaining a process or giving directions for the playing of a game calls for sequential thinking and attention to audience reaction. It requires clear thinking, careful attention to detail, and well-ordered presentation to make an explanation meaningful to the listener. Children like to explain the pictures they have crayoned or painted as they show them to the group. The explanations of young children are apt to be mere enumerations of points. Older children will bring out cause and effect relationships which explain the reasons behind the facts. The explanations of young children, like their definitions, tend to be stated in terms of function: "The ladder has rungs like this so you can climb it." Later, they will generalize and fit phenomena into their respective categories.

■ *The solving of problems* is done democratically in a modern classroom if the problems are within the children's ability.

"Is it wise to run about in the classroom when there are so many sharp corners on furniture?" "John's costume does not fit and the material has all been used. What can we do about it?" "State and town policemen wear different uniforms and seem to do different things. How can we find the differences in the work of the two?" These are all problems which might arise in any primary school classroom. Solving them calls for clear recognition of the problem, thinking of and searching for solutions, working through the methods agreed upon, and evaluating the end result. All of this involves language and language used with a purpose. Children grow rapidly in ability to recognize a problem, define it, and work out a solution for it when they have repeated experiences in solving real problems.

■ *Evaluating* is not the final step of a process but a part of the process from beginning to end. Children as well as adults need to stop now and then to ask, "Where are we now? How much have we accomplished? Are we satisfied with it? What do we need to do next?" Through guidance in evaluation children learn to take note of strengths as well as weaknesses and to commend the good points of a piece of work before commenting upon or criticizing the unfavorable points. They learn that the giving of unfavorable criticism obligates the critic to make constructive suggestions for improvement. They learn also that criticism expressed in a sympathetic and kindly manner is easier to take and results in more favorable response than sharp, unsympathetic, and destructive criticism. Through guidance in evaluating they can begin to sense the effect of words upon human emotions and the effect of emotional reactions upon human relations.

■ *Expressing their own creative thinking* gives satisfaction to people of all ages. Children of primary school age enjoy telling stories of their own creation and composing material for the teacher to write. This is an important aspect of language development which will be dealt with more fully in Chapters 11 and 13. It fits into the reading and writing program as well as into the program of oral language.

Ease in the use of language is the product of a great deal of language experience under many types of circumstances and in many situations. Ease comes only with confidence and a deep sense of adequacy, with the inner conviction that one can depend on his use of language to make his meaning clear and intelligible to others. Poor speech, inadequate vocabulary, or noticeable departures from commonly accepted usage make any individual, young or old, feel uncertain of the response his efforts will bring forth and consequently make him hesitant and in every way insecure. Easy command of language is a goal to be sought for each child.

☐ THE GOAL OF CLEAR, INTELLIGIBLE LANGUAGE

Jespersen, the noted Danish philologist, lists three stages or levels of language: intelligible language is the minimum level; correct language is the next and more exacting level; and finally, good language which may, at the top of the scale, be both clear and beautiful (14). Intelligible language is the first need in the primary school so that the child can express himself with ease and with confidence that he will be understood. An old Japanese primer begins with the statement, "Dear little children, good little children must learn to use elegant language." The polishing and refining of language is not considered the task of the primary school; that comes later. In the primary school intelligible, useful language is the first requirement.

Clarity of speech and language has a number of aspects. It involves accurate articulation of sounds, clear enunciation, pronunciation which can be understood, usage which fits commonly accepted standards, and choice of words which carry the meaning that is intended.

■ *Articulation* of the sounds of the language still presents a problem for some children on entrance into the primary school. The majority of children are forming most sounds correctly, but there are a few in almost any group who substitute sounds or manipulate their lips and tongue in such manner that the sound produced for a letter differs from the accepted sound for that letter. Again, teachers must consider regional dialects in determining what to correct.

A 1957 study by Templin (29) appears to be the most recent and reliable study of children's articulation of sounds. She found children articulating correctly at three years of age practically all of the vowel sounds of English. Unless they are experiencing special difficulty, children appear able to articulate the consonant sounds at the following ages (the letters represent speech sounds, not letter names as used in spelling):

3 years:	m, n, ng, p, f, h, w,
3.5 years:	y
4 years:	k, b, d, g, r
4.5 years:	s, sh, ch
6 years:	t, th, v, l
7 years:	th (voiced) zh, j

The only sound Templin tested that was not produced correctly by 75 per cent of the children tested at the oldest age, 8 years, was the *hw* sound. Linguists have found that, in some regions of the United States, no distinction is made by speakers of any age or socio-economic level between *w* as in "wish" and *wh* as in "what."

Many children are able to form these sounds much earlier than the ages indicated, but these are the latest ages that can be considered usual for the development of facility in the use of the sounds. In the sounds of *s* and *z* distortions occur when children lose their deciduous teeth in front, and a few children require help to correct the pattern when they have their permanent teeth. The development of skill in articulation lags behind with some children, but if they are progressing fairly steadily along this path they should not be considered defective.

Deficiencies or inaccuracies in hearing are responsible for substitutions and poor articulation in some children. If a child learning to talk does not perceive correctly the sounds made by adults, he forms the sounds as he hears them. Unless he is given help, he continues to practice the sounds as he first learned them until, by the time he enters school, he finds it difficult to make corrections in the articulation of them.

Local pronounciation of vowel sounds constitutes a spelling problem in some areas of the country and with some children. Children in southern Indiana who say *min* for men and *far* for fire have great difficulty in spelling vowel sounds correctly even in the commonest words. Such dialectic problems must be taken into account in various regions in teaching spelling.

A child who is progressing in articulation of sounds even though he is behind schedule probably needs no remedial help. A child who has "ironed in" certain incorrect forms and does not perceive any difference between what he says and the sounds used by others, will need help to understand his problem and correct it. More definite help with improving articulation will be found in Chapters 9 and 17.

■ *Enunciation* is a matter of clear-cut handling of beginnings and endings and of giving each syllable its full value. Many amusing stories are told of children's confusions which grow out of the poor enunciation of adults. An English professor once remarked that he was a good-sized boy before he knew that "neck 'n' ears" was not all one word. Children often ask for help with spelling "how'z it," "gon-to," and the designation of division in arithmetic as "gozinta" is a classic.

The teacher's own example of clearly enunciated speech is perhaps the most potent force for improvement. Children can be encouraged to carry on many types of activity that demand clear enunciation. The dramatization of a story falls flat if the audience cannot understand what the characters are saying. Making reports to an audience encourages children to put forth effort to be understood. The sharing period, too, demands speech that can be understood with ease or the children listening lose interest. Dramatization of radio broadcasts (or real ones) motivates effort to enunciate clearly, and choral reading can also be used for motivation.

Enunciation is important in learning to spell. People who make many and persistent errors in spelling are often found to be spelling exactly what they are saying. It is difficult for most children to remember the spelling of a word by rote memory alone. Even though the word is partially irregular it gives the child some association to tie to if he is taught to enunciate the word very clearly as he learns to spell it.

■ *Pronunciation* tends to be learned from the family at home and from other people with whom the child associates. The mispronunciations of young children may be due to lack of careful attention to a word, to difficult sounds in the word, or to attempts to make it match other similar words, as when the child uses *brang* as the past of *bring* to match *rang–ring* or *sang–sing*. Often it is learned from the mispronunciation of others.

Again, the teacher's own example is especially important in helping children to give attention to pronunciation and to feel a sense of obligation to use the approved form, the form used by educated speakers in his area. Developing such a sense of obligation is difficult to do if the form the child uses is the accustomed form in his environment. If this is the case, he may absorb or copy the correct form if it is used often enough in schoolroom activities to help him register a clear sound image of it. The factor of unconscious imitation is a potent one. If, however, the word is pronounced differently in his environment, he tends to change his pronunciation only if motivation is sufficiently strong to make him want to substitute the form he hears at school for that which he hears away from school.

■ *Grammatical usage* problems have to be considered in the language program of most communities. The primary school child mirrors the language usage of his home and community. This usage is acceptable to him because the people who use it are acceptable to him. He has no standards other than those of the culture in which he lives. Usage which deviates from that of his culture milieu may sound strange and different to him if he has a keen ear for language, but it does not sound better or correct; he may even think it queer or amusing.

The best antidote to hearing poor language in the home is hearing quantities of good language at school (26). Many adults, as well as children, tend to copy the speech that is used in talking to them. It is difficult not to be influenced by the speech of a stutterer or a person with a foreign accent. It is almost impossible for an individual to keep his Southern accent unmodified if he lives for a period of time in Minnesota, or to avoid acquiring a Southern accent if he lives for a time in Georgia or Texas. A very real asset to the language program is the fondness the child feels for his primary school teacher, if she is the type of person who should teach younger children. Parents can vouch for the fact that the child can imitate his teacher's voice, speech, mannerisms, and attitudes. This tendency to emulation places heavy responsibility upon the teacher for consistency and quality of personal behavior.

The child's ability to imitate and absorb the sound patterns he hears about him is both asset and liability in a language improvement program. The number of hours a child spends apart from the influence of the school is much larger than the number of hours he spends under the guidance of the school. His ears are assailed by the home and community pattern of language far more of the time and this sheer overbalance of the time element presents serious problems. As a consequence, motivation is of the utmost importance. If the child sees value in learning new patterns and wants to learn them, he will succeed, but if he does not care about them they will remain unlearned. Stimulation and motivation which results in an inner desire and drive to improve is the most important element in language improvement. More detailed suggestions for improvement will be found in Chapter 15.

■ *Choice of words or diction* is an important element in clarity of language expression. The words one chooses determine the mental pictures that are built up in the mind of the listener, the train of thoughts that is set in motion, and the emotional reaction that is engendered. Many situations arise in classroom living which enable children to see that unfortunate choices of words result in confusions, misunderstandings, and at times even hurt feelings, resentment, and anger. There are many opportunities to weigh words and evaluate their service to a recognized purpose. Perhaps the children are dictating a note to the principal asking his help in planning a trip and they decide to change the sentence "We want you to help us" to read "We would be glad if you could find time to help us" because the first sentence sounds too demanding. Or the group is writing a composite story and the sentence "The boy went down the street" fails to paint a clear mental picture of the boy, his action, and the setting so they try many words, as "The boy hurried eagerly on his way down the street" or "The boy loitered along the street looking lazily into the windows" until they have sharpened the outlines of the picture they want to paint.

The goal of clear, intelligible speech and language cannot be achieved in the primary school—it can only be set in motion there; all successive levels of education must carry it on through the intermediate grades, the junior and senior high schools, college, the graduate school, and life itself through the years that follow formal education. If individuals are motivated to want such a tool and to see real value in it, they will develop it through self-discipline and individual effort.

■ *Intonation* is another element to be considered in developing clarity of speech. In speaking English, pitch, stress, and pauses help to carry meaning. Children will enjoy playing with an occasional sentence that is used by a child to note what changes of meaning can take place through changing pitch and stress. The question, "Where are you going?" can carry a number of shades of meaning, depending upon the words that are emphasized. Children can begin to recognize that some words are clotted together in speech and others held apart by pauses, as in the sentence, "My Uncle John, who just came to visit us, brought me a present." This recognition begins to pave the way for punctuation in their own writing later on.

☐ THE GOAL OF LANGUAGE THAT SUITS OCCASION AND NEED

Different cultures develop different forms of language response which they consider suitable. The language training of Japanese children includes careful training in forms of courtesy to be addressed to father, mother, teachers, and others to whom the child is taught to show special respect. Just as a bow of greeting to a workman may be of one sort and the bow with which one greets an honored guest who comes to one's home of another sort, so must the language used fit different occasions and needs. A democratic society does not have special forms of courteous language to be addressed to people in high places and other forms for informal, daily use but it does have conventional forms of language behavior which children need to learn in order to operate satisfactorily in that society.

The use of certain accepted forms of courtesy helps to keep the machinery of human relationships oiled and running smoothly. The child of primary school age learns those forms chiefly through imitation in situations in which the forms are used consistently by the teacher and in which he is able to sense the contribution they make to attitude and relationships. If the teacher invariably uses the accepted words of courtesy in asking or accepting service from the child and does so in a spirit of consideration and kindliness, the child will pick up the forms or can be guided into doing so very easily. A suggestion when he forgets, and a smile or word of commendation when he remembers, are all the motivation a child needs if they are applied consistently and in a constructive, helpful spirit.

Learning to greet people who come to visit, to give and receive introductions, to thank the hosts or entertainers when one leaves after enjoying hospitality or entertainment is a matter of opportunity and practice. As new children come to the school or parents and visitors come in, children can be introduced to them and taught how to acknowledge introductions. They learn to be guests and hosts through being invited into other classrooms and through inviting other classes or parents or friends into their own classroom for a Halloween party or to sing Christmas carols, see a dramatization, hear about a trip, see some work which has been done, or share in games and rhythmic play. As they practice being guests and hosts they grow in the poise, ease, and thoughtful control with which they conduct themselves and meet their obligations. It is not a matter of formal teaching but rather one of concrete application. Children learn by doing in this as in everything else. Informality and genuine thoughtfulness for the comfort and happiness of others are more important than the words that are uttered. The words merely indicate the underlying feeling of friendliness and consideration which, after all, is the true courtesy.

Present-day courses of study call attention to the need for teaching children courtesies connected with the use of the telephone. There are opportunities to do this as plans are made for excursions of various sorts, or as use is made of persons in the community whose experience could be drawn upon to answer the children's questions and add to their knowledge of interests being studied.

There are occasional opportunities to make announcements and learn the need for careful planning to make sure that all necessary facts are presented as clearly and concisely as possible. Announcing a play to an audience, announcing special activities to other grade groups, announcing services the group is offering or appeals for help with various causes such as Junior Red Cross, a newspaper collection, or a Thanksgiving collection for charity gives children concrete experience.

Even though children may not have acquired enough skill and co-ordination to write notes and invitations, they can learn a great deal about suitable forms. As they formulate and dictate a note of invitation they notice the way in which it is being worded and the form in which it is written. Primary school children learn why and for what purposes one writes notes as well as how notes are written. If a child is ill they are encouraged to dictate a note expressing sympathy; a note is prepared to congratulate a group that has put on a fine assembly program; notes of request and of thanks and appreciation are called for at many points. It is fully as important for children to learn suitable occasions for such expression as to learn how to put it on paper in correct form.

These are matters of suitability of expression in the give and

take of classroom living. What is suitable to say to another child may not be suitable to say to an adult. Americans tend to demand very little respect for age in the training of children but there is a place for some of it, perhaps more than has become our custom.

☐ THE GOAL OF ORIGINALITY IN THE USE OF LANGUAGE

A language is a system of sounds and meanings held in common by many people, while speech is an individual's use of language; it is his own expression and he is the producer of it. A language is, of necessity, an accumulation of accepted custom in the form of sounds, inflections, meanings, and patterns of expression. It is this, or a portion of it, that the child is expected to learn but his use of it remains his own. Children use language in interesting and colorful forms. They express their own individuality through the use of it.

It would be as unfortunate for the language of all children to be poured into the same mold as for all potential researchers and inventors to be required to operate entirely within the realm of known facts. In order to preserve the imagination, uniqueness, and originality of children there must be opportunity for them to be themselves and to express themselves creatively in their own way. There must be opportunity to enjoy fanciful material as well as factual and realistic material and opportunity to make up stories, original dramatic play, games, and art creations. Expression is essential to mental health and wholesome intellectual development.

Oral expression can take many forms. It may be sentences for the teacher to put into a chart story as a first step in reading. It may be thoughts for a letter, or facts for a record which the group is composing. Often it is storytelling just for its own sake.

Some of the stories a child tells may be true or almost true stories about himself and his experiences and some will be vivid, fanciful tales in which he displays his power of imagination and creative invention to the full. Usually he tells the stories for the pleasure of the telling and for the audience reaction he receives. As he grows in ability to tell a series of incidents or a somewhat coherent story, he enjoys having it

The first goal in language development . . . is to free the child so that he talks easily and confidently. An informal room arrangement will allow the children to create small groups they can talk to comfortably before they are ready to face the entire class.

written down for him. It gives him a sense of power and achievement to have the tale he is telling put down in black marks on a sheet of paper even though he cannot yet read them. As soon as he reaches the point where he can make his hand do what his mind wants it to do he will find satisfaction in writing his stories himself.

Teachers in England as well as in the United States are putting greater and greater emphasis on the importance of developing the young child's skill in spoken English. Attaining natural ease and fluency is far more important at this stage than correctness. In nurturing spoken language, we should be careful to do nothing that will produce tension or lack of courage. Bell, of England, is convinced that the basis on which good standards of English must be built is "the gift of free and natural speech" (3, p. 33). The goals he lists for the teaching of English are three: (1) Honesty and individuality of thought. (2) Freedom clearly to express that thought to others. (3) A capacity and desire to share life with the great writers (3, p. 12). The English have, in fact, created a new term to parallel the term "literacy." They call work with oral language the development of "oracy" and consider it an important part of the school's responsibility.[1]

A child will not write better than he talks. Writing is an extension of talk. If the child is allowed to grow into writing with ample help in putting his ideas on paper, the content of writing will become, during the elementary school years, as good as the child's talk. If he is not given adequate encouragement and help, his writing may be far less good than his talk. But it will never be better. It is on oral work, and on that alone, says Cutforth, another English writer, that skill in written work eventually depends (4).

It is likewise true that a child who lacks ease and fluency in speech will find reading difficult. He will not be able to make sense in his reading of sentences that differ greatly from those he says. The inarticulate child, the child hemmed in by fears, inhibitions, and insecurities so that he talks in fragments and then only when he is called on, will have great difficulty in putting meaning into complex sentences such as he never speaks. He will be completely unable to read them aloud with fluency and clear interpretation.

[1]"Some Aspects of Oracy." National Association for the Teaching of English. *Bulletin,* Volume II, Number 2, Summer 1965, University of Nottingham.

Growth in oral language is one of the most important elements in the entire program of the primary school. It is not a matter of course of study and lessons but of rich and varied experience and constant practice in the use of language. The child who comes through these years with confident and easy use of language in all its forms has a good start not only toward the education furnished by the school but toward self-education and toward a successful and happy life.

☐ SELECTED REFERENCES ☐

1. Almy, Millie Corinne, *Children's Experiences Prior to First Grade and Success in Beginning Reading.* Teachers College Contributions to Education, No. 954. New York: Bureau of Publications, Teachers College, Columbia University, 1949.
2. Association for Childhood Education, *Portfolio for Primary Teachers.* Washington, D. C.: Association for Childhood Education, 1945.
3. Bell, Vicars, *On Learning the English Tongue.* London: Faber and Faber, 1953.
4. Cutforth, John A., *English in the Primary School.* Oxford: Basil Blackwell, 1954.
5. Dawson, Mildred A., *Language Teaching in Grades 1 and 2.* (Rev. Ed.) Yonkers-on-Hudson, N.Y.: World Book Co., 1957.
6. Francis, Sarah Evelyn, *An Investigation of the Oral Language of First Grade Children.* Unpublished dissertation. Bloomington: Indiana University, 1962.
7. Gans, Roma; Stendler, Celia Burns; and Almy, Millie, *Teaching Young Children in Nursery Schools, Kindergarten, and the Primary Grades.* Yonkers: World Book Co., 1952.
8. Gesell, Arnold, and Ilg, Frances L., *The Child from Five to Ten.* New York: Harper and Brothers, 1948.
9. Hatfield, W. Wilbur, (Ed.), *An Experience Curriculum in English.* National Council of Teachers of English. English Monograph No. 4. New York: D. Appleton-Century Co., Inc., 1935.
10. Heffernan, Helen, *Guiding the Young Child.* (Rev. Ed.) Boston: D. C. Heath and Co., 1959.
11. Herrick, Virgil E., and Jacobs, Leland B., (Ed.), *Children and the Language Arts.* Englewood Cliffs: Prentice-Hall, Inc., 1955.
12. Hildreth, Gertrude, *Readiness for School Beginners.* Yonkers: World Book Co., 1950.
13. Hughes, Marie M., and Sanchez, George I., *Learning a New Language.* Washington, D.C.: Association for Childhood Education International, 1958.

14. Jesperson, Otto, *Mankind, Nation, and Individual from a Linguistic Point of View.* London: Allen and Unwin, Ltd., 1946.
15. Lee, Dorris M., and Allen, R.V., *Learning to Read Through Experience.* New York: Appleton-Century-Crofts, 1963.
16. Loban, Walter D., *The Language of Elementary School Children.* Research Report No. 1, Champaign, Ill.: National Council of Teachers of English, 1963.
17. Mackintosh, Helen K., (Ed.), *Children and Oral Language.* Washington, D.C.: Association for Childhood Education International, 1964.
18. Martin, Clyde, "Developmental Interrelationships Among Language Variables in Children of First Grade." *Elementary English* 32:167-71, March, 1955.
19. Monroe, Marion, *Growing into Reading.* Chicago: Scott, Foresman and Co., 1951.
20. Munkres, Alberta, *Helping Children in Oral Communication.* Practical Suggestions for Teaching, No. 19. New York: Bureau of Publications, Teachers College, Columbia University, 1959.
21. National Council of Teachers of English, Commission on the English Curriculum, *Language Arts for Today's Children.* N.C.T.E. Curriculum Series, Vol. II. New York: Appleton-Century-Crofts, Inc., 1954.
22. Olson, Willard C., *Child Development.* (2nd Ed.) Boston: D. C. Heath and Co., 1959.
23. Russell, David H., *Children's Thinking.* Boston: Ginn & Company, 1956.
24. Shane, Harold G.; Mulry, June Grant; Reddin, Mary E.; and Gillespie, Margaret C., *Improving Language Arts Instruction in the Elementary School.* Columbus, Ohio: Charles E. Merrill Books, Inc., 1962.
25. Shibles, Burleigh H., "How Many Words Does a First Grade Child Know?" *Elementary English* 41:42-47, January, 1959.
26. Smith, Dora V., "Growth in Language Power as Related to Child Development." *Teaching Language in the Elementary School.* The Forty-Third Yearbook, Part II, of the National Society for the Study of Education. Chicago: University of Chicago Press, 1944, Chap. IV, pp. 52-97.
27. Strickland, Ruth G., *Guide for Teaching Language in Grades 1 and 2.* Boston: D. C. Heath and Co., 1962.
28. Strickland, Ruth G., *The Language of Elementary School Children: Its Relationship to the Language of Reading Textbooks and the Quality of Reading of Selected Children.* Bulletin of the School of Education, Vol. 38, No. 4. Bloomington: Indiana University, July, 1962.

29. Templin, Mildred C., *Certain Language Skills in Children.* Minneapolis: The University of Minnesota Press, 1957.

30. Winter, Clotilda, "Interrelationships Among Language Variables in Children of First and Second Grades." *Elementary English* 34:108-13, February, 1957.

SPOKEN LANGUAGE IN THE INTERMEDIATE SCHOOL

Children have only to read the newspapers and listen to newscasts on television to understand the importance of oral language in the world today. A few days of attention to the mass media would make them aware of the amazing proportion of the important work of the world that is being done through talking and listening. The newspapers and television feature almost daily the visits of foreign leaders and dignitaries to the United States and the visits of our leaders to other countries for face-to-face discussion of significant and far-reaching problems and policies. Representatives of many countries meet at stated times and places to share their thinking and strive for consensus on basic issues of importance to the entire world. National and state problems are solved through oral interaction by the Congress and the state legislatures. Local news in any community is filled with evidence of the place of oral language in the activities of clubs, labor unions, churches, and social and professional groups of all sorts. All such work in the United States is carried on in English and so is much that is done on the international level. The development of speech instruments—the telephone, record player, radio, talking pictures, and television—makes this the era of the spoken word. The power of speech has become virtually unlimited. International radio spreads the influence of a single voice throughout the world. The significance of this fact is so great that the Congress of the United States appropriates funds for a Voice of America to carry American thought, as a part of national policy, even to areas of the world where it is officially unwelcome. This is not always in English, though it often is. Studying English has become a requirement in secondary education in many foreign countries, and study of it begins at the elementary level in some foreign schools.

English is our language, yet boys and girls graduate from our secondary schools speaking and reading it poorly. The materials available for teaching—textbooks, reference materials, literature, and other library resources, films and recordings—are plentiful and some of them are the finest that have ever been produced. The attitude of schools toward the teaching of English and the methods they employ appear to be the problem.

It is one of the curious and unfortunate facts regarding education in the United States that the teaching of language becomes highly formalized and divorced from actual use in many elementary schools at just the period when children have achieved sufficient power in the use of language so that they can begin to refine the quality of their personal language and extend its usefulness into new forms and fields. Even schools which carry on good programs of language development in the primary grades may, beginning at the fourth grade level, reduce the quality and quantity of the children's experience in the language arts to a program centered almost entirely on a textbook. The development of skills becomes important as children reach more advanced levels, and no one could wisely underestimate that need. The problem is one of how to achieve the skills and what is the role of each of the available forms of material and experience in achieving them.

The language skills are not subjects and cannot be, though there are some understandings to be developed and some knowledge of operating procedures to be learned in connection with each of them. One cannot read *reading* and write *writing;* when one talks, reads, or writes he must talk, read, or write about *something.* There must be some content, whether it be trivial or profound; whether it deals with language itself or with social studies, literature, arithmetic, art, music, or items of personal or community interest. It is a major challenge to teachers and curriculum makers to find ways to make the experience of children vital, practical, and meaningful. They need to emphasize the kinds of experience which build the language skills that are needed and build them in such manner that they are not surface veneer but a part of good living.

Taking time with an intermediate grade class to analyze the way in which language functions in the adult world could provide excellent motivation for intensive work with language in the classroom. Children need to understand the reasons for the work they are asked to do and to be clear about its values in life outside the classroom. Boys and girls of this age are keenly interested in language and can develop pride in their growing understanding of it and their power to use it well in all types of real-life situations.

☐ THE NEED FOR ORAL LANGUAGE IN THE INTERMEDIATE GRADES

Experience in the use of oral language is fully as important in the intermediate grades as in the primary school. All of the uses and values which operated at the earlier level are needed here, as well as others connected with the advanced materials, concepts, and processes which are included in the curriculum for older children. New subject matter is called for and more advanced textbooks bring new demands.

Whereas the textbooks of the primary grades utilized, almost exclusively, vocabulary which the children understood and used, the textbooks of the intermediate grades include vocabulary which is foreign to the children's experience and which is not a part of their working stock of meanings. Not only do intermediate grade textbooks in the content areas employ words which are unfamiliar to many children but the density of the content itself has increased. Each sentence is weighted with meaning and each paragraph closely packed. Someone has referred to American textbooks as masterpieces of compression, an apt description of many of them. Also, the books introduce abstract concepts with which children need a great deal of help. Abstract concepts develop slowly through the expansion of experience, through discussion, and through application in many situations.

As children advance through the grades, they need to be made increasingly aware of the fact that written language differs from oral language. Middle grade children have for years employed in their speech all of the kinds of sentences that adults employ. The children's sentences tend to be structured more loosely and they use more run-on sentences composed of coordinate parts than educated adults use even in informal talk. But written language is more formalized and compact in its portrayal of ideas than is oral language.

Watts, the English researchist, has said that, "Where textbooks, the natural habitat of the abstract term, abound most, ignorance finds it easiest to disguise herself" (36, p. 28). He calls attention to the need for having children discuss freely the material they are reading and studying because all too often the meanings are hazy and reside "in the twilight between clear knowledge and blank ignorance" (36, p. 21). They need to be drawn out into broad daylight, applied to personal experience, and thoroughly linked with as many types of association as possible and then used in some form before they fit securely and comfortably into the child's own accumulation of knowledge.

☐ COMMUNICATION THROUGH SPOKEN LANGUAGE

The basic and fundamental use of spoken language is in communication. By the time young people leave the secondary school some of them are keenly interested in speech as an interpretative art for the interpretation of drama, verse, and prose. The theater, radio, motion pictures, and television appeal to a number of them as vocations, and interpretative skill and artistry are essential in many branches of such work. The school should keep in mind this aspect of language need and develop it both from the point of view of the consumer, for every individual is a consumer, and from the point of view of preparing interested individuals to become producers. But the main concern of the school is the use of speech and language as means of communication. This is the foundation for everything else in education.

Speech as a means of communication has two main functions. We use it as a means of causing others to act: we instruct, persuade, command. Or we use it as a means of causing others to think or feel, often with no intention of causing them to act. Speech is used in an endless variety of ways for the purpose of causing others to act. They range from casually motivating comment such as, "The thermometer reading is thirty degrees this morning. This is a day for warm coats," to the vigorous, purposeful persuasiveness of the loud-speaker directing traffic at a busy street corner or the insistent urging of radio commercials. One uses speech to cause others to think or feel when he creates contacts and pleasant recognition through greetings such as "How do you do?" or "A lovely day, isn't it?" He uses it for its thinking and feeling value when he uses it creatively in writing poetry or prose for others to share. Speech combines both the motivation to act and the motivation to think and feel when one tries to put his listeners into the right frame of mind in order to influence behavior and attitudes.

The responsibility of school is to so develop children that they can speak clearly, expressively, and effectively in all situations in which speech is required, from informal everyday conversation to the giving of a formal report or address. The community as well as the world needs informed and responsible citizens who are also articulate.

No matter what his occupation, every individual in the role of citizen must be able to explain his ideas and when necessary to persuade and convince others of their worth. As a worker, he may need to analyze, organize, and effectively present his demands for conditions which he needs for productive work. If he is called upon to serve as a manager or leader, he will need skill in giving directions, explaining processes, inspiring cooperation, and maintaining the level of human relations necessary to maximum effectiveness in the production of whatever sort. Children can begin to analyze the language requirements of workers in selected vocations and civic enterprises to learn the quality of language it takes to succeed in various aspects of adult life. This is particularly important for children who speak a nonstandard dialect. They must be made aware of the value of adding the prestige dialect which will be an asset in any social or vocational area they may later wish to enter.

☐ LISTENING IS IMPORTANT

Continuous development of the art of listening unquestionably goes hand in hand with progress in speaking. Good conversation is impossible without good listening because it calls for real interaction. To understand instructions requires a high quality of listening, and there is great need for critical listening. The complex forces pressing in on every individual in these days call for ability to listen with discrimination as well as with sympathy and understanding because of the constant barrage of all kinds of material which bombards the ears from radio, television, motion pictures, and other sources.

Opportunities for learning to listen occur in all situations in which the spoken word is used. The listening opportunities in some classrooms are confined almost entirely to listening to directions, and the responsiveness of the pupil is confined to accurate following of the directions. His purposefulness is therefore limited to purposing to conform to what is expected of him in order to stay out of trouble. Some of that kind of listening is essential in life outside the classroom in such experiences as learning to drive a car or learning to light the gas in the kitchen oven for baking. There are many situations arising constantly in the life of every individual which call for critical and discriminating listening and for the mental responsiveness that is real thinking. Listening and speaking operate together and complement each other in the sketch of activities which appears later in this chapter. Children grow in one aspect of oracy (see p. 162) as they grow in the other and gradually attain proficiency in both.

☐ KEEN INTEREST IN COMMUNICATION

Children of nine years of age and on through adolescence are deeply interested in all aspects of communication. They are drawing away from the close home ties that have held them, and they want, more than anything else, to be persons in their own right. If their natural zest for learning has not been destroyed by a barren skill-drill type of program in the primary grades, they are hungry for experience and knowledge. They are equally eager for new skills. Anyone who doubts that point needs only to watch a boy practicing to pitch for his baseball team or a girl working on a scouting project to be convinced.

Children of eight to twelve years of age find word meanings fascinating and will make a game of the quest for new words if they are stimulated to do so. They enjoy playing anagrams and a variety of spelling and word games. Learning to use the dictionary independently can be an adventure.

Boys and girls during these years are keenly interested in language itself. The eagerness with which they lay hold on each new bit of slang that comes their way is proof of that fact. Any colorful or tangy expression is put to use as quickly as possible. Both boys and girls like easy, catchy phrases and new words to substitute for worn and commonplace ones. This is the period in which gangs and clubs predominate, each with its secrets of password and slogan. Secret languages are created or learned from more accomplished older children. Pig Latin or its equivalent may be used exclusively in communication between pals and members of a club or gang. There are codes and records which are guarded with great care.

☐ SLANG AND OTHER UNAUTHORIZED LANGUAGE

Slang is unauthorized language, most of which remains forever outside of dictionaries and the circle of accepted usage. But occasionally an expression which is originally slang appears to fill a need, becomes accepted, and finds its way into authorized usage. New patterns in speech, if used widely enough, are accepted into the language family in the course of time. Such expressions as "blah," "rubberneck," "stunt," "debunk," "phony," and "highbrow" may never be lifted out of the slang classification but they are here to stay and are widely accepted.

Slang is inadmissible but usually inoffensive language. Some of it may seem silly and unwarranted to an adult but often it appears to meet a need during the years when vocabulary is still limited. At least it provides a type of satisfaction; it gives a child an opportunity to show off, to feel himself a "good sport." There is an element of "smartness" in it for him. He enjoys the reaction of adults, the sense of mildly shocking or displeasing them. It is all a part of the process of weaning himself away from adult domination and becoming a real person.

Swearing is also unauthorized speech but of the offensive sort. Just what words an adult finds offensive depends upon his background. For example, the word "lousy," used rather commonly by some people, is highly offensive to others. A child may use an unauthorized word at first quite innocently, without awareness of its meaning. Often, if the word receives no recognition he drops it and returns to accepted forms. If, however, it does create a sensation in the home or school group, he may use it freely for its shock value and the satisfaction it affords him.

Hurlock tells the story of a mother who handled successfully the problem of desire for colorful and catchy language on the part of her sons. When they acquired the expression "O Lordy," she called their attention to the fact that it was commonplace and suggested that they try "Horrors!" with proper inflection, instead. When they started to say "O. K." or "Okey-doke," she introduced them to the English expression "Righto!" The substitute words were copied by neighborhood boys, who appealed to her frequently to "think up" some more words for them (19).

Disappointed or distraught parents complain to intermediate grade teachers from time to time that the son whose language was of high quality in his early childhood now talks like a street urchin and they are at a loss to know how to correct him. It is some comfort for the teacher to be able to tell them that a boy of this age feels a strong need to be like his school companions in every way, speech as well as cut of hair and style of clothes. As he grows older and reaches the age when he wishes to impress the girl of his choice or desires to be sophisticated, the early family training and example will stand him in good stead.

A characteristic, even of adolescence, in these days is fondness for the specialized language of the gang. "Penny," in the comic strip, is the prototype of many girls of her age. The story of the mother who went to an adult education center asking for an evening course in modern language so that she might understand her teen-age daughter, is not difficult to believe.

Interest in language is present in all normally developing children of the middle and upper school years. It presents a challenge to teachers to catch and use that interest in developing easy, clear, and effective use of commonly accepted and standard English forms for both oral and written expression.

☐ CHARACTERISTIC LANGUAGE ABILITIES AND INTERESTS

Children of nine to twelve years of age have the widest range of interests of any age group and, if they are physically well and well cared for, lead active, strenuous lives. They are alert to everything going on about them and their intellectual curiosity is unbounded. There are sex differences in behavior and interests but both boys and girls are avidly interested in all types of real-life activities. They show independence and initiative, interest in fair play, and a fairly well-developed sense of humor with ability to enter into humor directed toward themselves as well as others.

These children talk freely in their own age groups and can converse with adults and enter into family and class discussions with ease and confidence. They have sufficient control of small muscles and eye-hand co-ordination so that they can express their ideas in writing without undue strain or effort. They are reading widely in magazines as well as books (unless their school experience in learning to read has left them with little interest in reading), and vocabulary is growing rapidly. They vary widely in skill in reading but all recognize reading as a means of extending experience and learning about other times, places, and people. Most of them can read for pleasure and to follow individual interests.

Interest in story content varies but the earlier interest in imaginative material has been largely displaced by interest in fact and realism, though some still like fairy stories and many show an almost insatiable appetite for comics and adventure tales. Children of this age range are becoming interested in reading material dealing with travel, true adventure, biography, nature, and science. Boy and girl interests separate at some points, but even at twelve years of age girls read almost all of the books that boys like, and there are many that are equally popular with both sexes. Boys are less interested in books of home and school life and certain types of stories of sentimental nature, but reading tastes and interests are somewhat similar.

Parallel with this interest in personal expansion through reading and firsthand experience is interest in many types of expression. Children of middle and upper grade age enjoy telling and writing stories and planning, writing, and producing plays and other types of programs. They enjoy giving reports and reviews of books, movies, and television programs.

Club interests are important during these years and provide opportunities for a variety of types of expression as well as some rudimentary knowledge of parliamentary procedure and opportunity to practice social courtesies. Children of this maturity level can plan a course of action and follow it through to a satisfactory outcome without a great deal of assistance. They like to work out their own rituals and to have secret codes and means of communication. They are collectors, both as individuals and as groups, and enjoy owning, using, and sharing their materials. Collecting is of vast importance to this level.

Their developing interest in science and in national and world affairs affords the children opportunities to learn to do scientific thinking, to weigh evidence, and to draw conclusions based on information secured from several sources. They learn to use source materials, to do critical and analytical thinking, and to evaluate both their materials and their methods. They are capable of carrying problem solving through all of the necessary stages to a final solution and a thorough and careful evaluation.

Children of all ages respond to the media of communication. Studies show that they view television an average of more than three hours a day and many of them attend the movies one or more times per week (37). Radio is still liked but television is a consuming passion of most middle grade boys and girls.

Before they are twelve years of age, most boys and girls are interested in human behavior, in social problems, and in problems of right and wrong. They have been accepting the ethical standards of their parents and the community without very much thinking or very keen awareness of the principles which were operating. Now they are becoming increasingly aware of the inconsistencies in human behavior and are questioning or at least analyzing the standards which they find operating.

The preadolescent as well as the adolescent needs help to understand himself and why he thinks, feels, and acts as he does. He needs to learn ways to satisfy his basic needs for love, success, belonging, and approval, and to recognize the needs of others and their efforts to gain satisfaction. He can begin to understand what causes others to behave as they do and to put himself in another's place. He needs to learn that all people experience disturbing emotions such as anger, fear, and jealousy, and to grow in ability to face them and work toward happier feelings. Literature can be of special value in helping him understand people: their motivations, why they behave as they do, how experiences change them, and how they interact in groups under varying circumstances. All of this helps him understand himself as well. He can learn to find sensible ways to "let off steam," and through appreciating and building upon his strong qualities learn to improve or compensate for his weak ones. He needs to develop an awareness that there is distinct harm in keeping feelings "bottled up" and to recognize how such feelings may come out in teasing, bullying, headaches, or other forms which are equally unsatisfactory. He is mature enough at this age to learn the value of turning to writing about the feelings, drawing, dramatization, music, some consuming hobby, or even a punching bag to relieve unhappy feelings in wholesome and legitimate ways. Bibliotherapy, the right book at the right time, may help him solve his problems through seeing how others solve theirs and how they gain strength and growth through their solutions.

Boys and girls of the preadolescent and early adolescent years can begin to understand the value of learning techniques for making and keeping friends and for working with people. They are interested in learning how to disagree with others without quarreling, how to work co-operatively with others, and how to enter into social situations as host and guest. They enjoy planning and producing programs of sharing and entertainment and learning various ways to make social contributions. They are not all equally ready for these experiences and sometimes girls, because of their greater maturity, appear ready before boys do, but all see value in learning to understand their own needs and those of others and developing techniques for meeting them.

☐ A SUITABLE ENVIRONMENT FOR LANGUAGE GROWTH

Language abilities thrive and grow in a climate and under environmental conditions that are suitable and stimulating, and actually suffer a setback in situations that dam up their potentialities and channel practice into lifeless and artificial learning situations. It is as true in the intermediate grades as in the primary that immovable furniture and rigid classroom organization and time schedules are highly detrimental to good language development. Children of all ages (as well as adults) use language best in situations where it really functions and in face-to-face relationships.

Flexibility in arrangement and movable furniture found its way into primary classrooms more rapidly than into intermediate grade rooms, but it is an asset of great importance in work with older boys and girls. Nine- to twelve-year-olds can work successfully in committees and interest groups and through group activities can meet individual needs and carry on a varied and intensive learning program. The range of ability found within a group of children in any area of work during these middle years is at least a five grade range, so that exclusive emphasis on mass work could not possibly meet the needs of all. Also, children during these years have an amazing number of interests and show a great deal of initiative and energy in carrying through many types of work which are related to their interests. A formal program centered largely on skills is highly wasteful of time and energy and distinctly boring to children—a condition not at all conducive to learning. Movable furniture is now found in nearly all of the intermediate grade classrooms of the country, though not all intermediate grade teachers utilize its possibilities for the growth of the children in the room. A challenging working environment is possible in any classroom in which teacher and children work together cooperatively to achieve that end.

The materials and equipment necessary to the setting up of a challenging classroom environment are known to every teacher. Bulletin boards which children help to arrange provide stimulation for thinking and constructive work in all the content areas of social studies, science, and literature. They can be used also to sharpen the children's interest in current happenings and to open up new areas of interest. Book collections are indispensable and should contain material on a variety

of subjects and covering a range of levels of reading difficulty. There are a number of good magazines for children which stimulate interests and suggest activities. Working tools, such as encyclopedias, dictionaries, maps, globes, and visual aids need to be arranged for free and easy use. Materials for expression—paint, clay, and raw materials of a number of kinds appropriate to the current group interests—are needed for individual expression. A good learning program gives as much thought to expression as to impression. Tables, shelves, cases, or even window ledges for hobby displays and collections stimulate individual initiative and provide material for spoken and written language. Children are highly resourceful and bursting with ideas for improving and enriching the working environment if they are encouraged to give thought to the problem.

Language development takes place best in an atmosphere of stimulation and challenge or at least a permissive atmosphere. Expression needs to be made legal so that children do not feel that they need to cover up and hide their individual interests and concerns when they come to school, but can express them and build upon them whenever they can be used in the ongoing program of experience. The relaxed, natural atmosphere which is characteristic of a stimulating, wholesome classroom is the best situation in which to help individuals develop language power. It provides incentives for the use and improvement of language. It gives children the nice balance between freedom to be themselves and guidance in self-improvement which carries them along to ever higher levels of attainment. A teacher who has faith in herself and faith in the children can create such an atmosphere in any type of school. Middle grade children need the challenge and support which come from friendships and from happy working relationships with their classmates within the school organization.

□ LANGUAGE IN THE PERIOD BEFORE SCHOOL BEGINS

Except during the early days of good weather or the baseball season, boys and girls come into the room singly or a few at a time, visit with the teacher or with their friends, and then

Children of all ages . . . use language best in situations where it really functions and in face-to-face relationships.

set about the doing of classroom chores or work of their own choosing. This gives the teacher opportunity to become thoroughly acquainted with each individual, to enter into his interests, and to guide him into new or more profitable ones, if need be. It gives her opportunity to locate the children who stand out alone, lacking the personality, the techniques, or the social acceptability to become a part of the group activity. The sense of freedom and comradeship leads to spontaneous expression, which is a starting point for good human relationships as well as good learning.

This is a time for work with special individual projects such as science experiments, map making, keeping a personal or classroom diary, recreational reading, or individual work for the improvement of skills. Children may use the time for gathering material from the school library, planning or practicing a play, arranging a bulletin board or exhibit shelf, interviewing people whose help is needed for a project, or doing individual imaginative writing. There are limitless potentialities in this time, all of which are valuable for language development.

☐ INTERRELATED WORK IN SOCIAL STUDIES AND LANGUAGE

Good work in the social studies is also good work with the language arts. Boys and girls in the intermediate grades are pushing back horizons and operating in a larger world of interests, knowledge, and vicarious experiences. Too often in the past this has been largely textbook work: studying, answering questions, and giving back what has been read from the books. It is in textbook work like this that Watts finds ignorance can go undetected and unchallenged. Many children can give back what they have read without any understanding.

The best teaching is probably the kind that stimulates children to set up problems and formulate questions and then search for answers. The textbook may be a first source to turn to in finding answers or it may be used later to pull together, organize, and summarize the findings. In any case, it is only one source of learning material and one which must be used with insight into the values and the problems it presents.

The social studies interests of the middle grades take children away from the things they know through firsthand experience and expose them to ideas and factual content that are remote in geographic space and often also in time. When children first work in a new area their thinking is vague unless they have had enough similar experience to find the ideas dealt with in this new area familiar and easily understood. As they gather material and express their newly developing concepts, they form new associations and make comparisons with old knowledge until what has been imperfectly understood becomes clearer.

☐ UTILIZING OPPORTUNITIES TO TEACH ABOUT LANGUAGE

Every opportunity should be utilized in all subjects to teach children about language. They should learn that all peoples in all times and places have had languages which adequately met their needs. There is no such thing as a primitive language though there are still oral languages in remote parts of the world which have no form of writing. Children can become aware of the way languages influence one another through the borrowing of words. English has borrowed mainly, of course, from French, Spanish, and American Indian languages as well as from Latin and Greek. Some languages have borrowed a script, as Japanese has borrowed the written characters of Chinese and Persian has borrowed the Arabic script. Many of the languages of Europe including English use the same alphabet derived from the Phoenician.

Any study involving the historical development of a people provides opportunity to call attention to the growth and development of their language. The proportion of literate and educated people in a country is closely related to the form of government of the country. The history of the movement of people from place to place on the earth's surface explains the geographic distribution and spread of languages. English was taken to South Africa, Australia, and New Zealand and Spanish to most of Central and South America, supplanting the languages of the indigenous natives. Bismarck once said that the most significant political fact of the 18th century was the establishing of English as the language of North America.

Science is helping to draw together the languages of the world. When a scientist in one country develops a new process or product or isolates and verifies a scientific phenomenon, he selects or coins words to name or describe his work. Those same words are taken, almost without change, into the languages of other scientists, in other countries, working in similar realms. Eventually, these borrowed words may become a part of popular language, not just the exclusive property of scientists.

The mass media and the present intermingling of people from all parts of the world will almost certainly influence language. Students, farmers, industrialists, and professional people of all sorts are traveling, working, and studying in many parts of the world. Attention to language and its place in the on-going development of the people of the world is important in many areas of study.

So much has been said and written in the past about the verbalism found in the schools that some teachers are in danger of falling into a very natural error. Cutting down on the amount of discussion is not the need, but rather more of concrete experience, wider reading, especially in books other than textbooks, wise use of carefully chosen audio-visual aids, and more opportunity for children to talk their way through to clarity. Unless children are encouraged to talk freely about their work and play and especially about the material they are studying, how can the teacher discover what words or concepts they lack and what, if anything, they think (36)?

Many textbooks present factual material in fairly condensed form and with relatively little space given to illustrations, both verbal and pictorial, which expand and explain the content. For the brighter and more mature children in a group this may be sufficient to enable them to form clear mental pictures and to develop the necessary concepts. Other children, and probably the most capable ones also, need opportunity to expand the material and to weave it into a clearly designed mental fabric. Many books are being made available to serve this purpose. The child who has read Laura Ingalls Wilder's book *Little House in the Big Woods*, and has followed this family as it moves through the Midwest in succeeding books has a clear and intimate picture of the hardships and satisfactions of pioneer life. *Henner's Lydia; Thee, Hannah!; Skippack School,* and the other books by Marguerite de Angeli give children a picture of the Amish, the Quakers, the Pennsylvania Dutch, and others who settled Pennsylvania as no textbook can paint the picture. Such books fill in the outlines sketched or suggested by textbooks and make a period of time and a distant place come to life for the children. They make people of different background real people whom children enjoy regardless of nationality, race, or socioeconomic level.

In a sense, this bears out a point repeated more than once by Watts. He is convinced that children of intermediate grade age are unready for the study of history except as it deals with the lives of individuals in the form of simple biographies (36). Gesell, on the other hand, found nine-year-olds expressing marked interest in history as well as in biography (15).

The value of any social studies program to children from nine to twelve years of age depends in large measure upon the way in which they are made ready for attack upon the program. If the study grows out of the current interests of the group and is closely related to their own experience, it proves no problem. If, on the other hand, the study to be undertaken as a part of required curriculum experience is more remote, the matter of readiness needs to be taken into account. A sixth grade teacher, realizing that a study of the Middle Ages would be a difficult requirement to meet with her group of children, read with the group and carried on a variety of exploratory experiences to introduce children to some of the vocabulary of the period and to give them a little of its romantic flavor. When they had reached the point at which such words as *squire, page, knight, castle, turret, drawbridge, monk,* and *monastery* held some meaning, she encouraged the children to read of Robin Hood, King Arthur, *Gabriel and the Hour Book, Adam of the Road,* and other stories of the period. Reading around a center of interest provides excellent material for language growth if care is taken to insure genuine understanding. Genuine understanding is further developed by dramatization.

☐ SOCIAL STUDIES AND LANGUAGE SKILLS

It requires great effort to prevent modern boys and girls who are fed snatches of material of many sorts by television and movies from being satisfied with surface knowledge and fragmentary pictures. It is far too easy for them to flit from one interest to another without ever digging deep beneath the surface and really working to develop clear thinking and concepts that are sufficiently substantial to serve as foundation for further study. Such thinking cannot be developed through the pressure and forcing tactics of required assignments and rigid checking, but it grows admirably in situations in which real interest is the motivating influence.

Work in the social studies is especially fruitful in language growth because it not only utilizes the content being studied to develop clearer thinking, better speech, and more effective writing, but children learn social techniques as well. Many classes begin their study with discussion of what the children know about the subject to be considered and the formulating and listing of questions for later work. Group planning follows and there are progress reports from time to time as the work is carried on and also periods devoted to evaluation of both the findings and the methods of work being employed. There are many opportunities for sharing the material the children are reading and gathering from various sources. This is accomplished through conversation and discussion as well as through oral and written reports. Learning to ask and answer questions clearly and concisely is in itself an important achievement which requires study and practice. Learning to take reading notes and to organize them for presentation also requires skill and practice.

Written language is called for at a great many points, from personal note-taking to correspondence and writing for the school newspaper. Writing to ask for material and gaining the necessary permissions for trips will call for business letters. Personal letters may be written to ask questions, to plan conferences and interviews, and to express appreciation for cooperation. Creative writing may be stimulated at many points.

The social studies provide many controversial questions which need to be discussed. Children should be taught to read all factual material critically and analytically. Through the discussion of controversial questions they learn the specialized skills that are needed by both speaker and listener: how to catch the main points, weigh and evaluate them; how to disagree courteously; how to present a point and back it up with evidence; and how to follow through and gain recognition of the point one is making. All children need to learn the art of persuasion as well as the art of critical listening. Children of elementary school age are not ready for the more formal techniques of debate, but they will find many occasions for the discussion of controversial issues. They can learn to word the question clearly and to identify the issues on both sides. They can learn also how futile it is to argue without information, and can be taught to assemble evidence and organize it in forceful and persuasive manner.

Social studies interests may culminate in written reports or graphic portrayal of significant points through the use of crayons, paints, clay, or construction materials. The writing and production of a play or a radio broadcast often serve as a satisfactory final summary of what has been learned.

Evaluation is not only a part of the study all along the way, but it is also an important final step. A sixth grade group which had spent a semester studying the British Commonwealth of Nations planned and carried through a valuable program of evaluation. So much material had been gathered that the question was asked as to what facts or knowledge the group needed to master to possess some pegs on which to hang later reading and thinking. They divided into six working groups and each group prepared a list of ten important points for a final test. During the course of this preparation each group reviewed the significant points of the study with great thoroughness, comparing and evaluating the points with care. Chairmen of the various groups then worked with the teacher to compile a composite list and to record the frequency of occurrence of the various questions submitted by the groups. From this list the teacher composed a test which the children wrote. As a final step, their answers were evaluated through class discussion. The entire evaluation project provided practice in clear thinking which called for precise expression, as well as excellent experience in summarizing a quantity of material and pulling out and weighing the points of greatest significance. The evaluation was, in itself, a learning experience of great value.

Combining and interrelating work in social studies and English is both logical and fruitful in so many ways that a number of junior high schools are experimenting with programs which combine these subjects under a single teacher and take them out of the departmentalized organization. The study of a geographic area, a period in history, or a movement is incomplete without study of the art, music, literature, and other cultural interests and expressions which accompanied it. Children need to study them together in order to understand the strands of interrelated influences which shape the lives of men. Language is a tool which man has used for countless ages. He has developed new uses and new forms of expression as well as new words as he has had need for them. No study of the social development of man could be complete without attention to man's uses of language for expression as well as for the everyday business of living. Children's respect for language grows as they use it as a tool in carrying on various types of enterprises and as they study its place in the whole ongoing movement of civilization.

☐ LANGUAGE VALUES IN THE SCIENCE PROGRAM

The scientific method which is basic to all modern progress is a method of thinking and reacting which is related to language at all points. Science is an active, dynamic field, constantly demanding willingness to make new observations, to repeat experiments, to consider new facts, and to challenge earlier conclusions. All science work for children should have as its most important objective the development of a method of thinking and learning which is applicable to any subject and any situation. Craig calls attention to the need for developing open-mindedness. He reminds us that, while childhood is a period of eager learning, it is also a period in which children can acquire dogmatic traits and learn to accept and vigorously adhere to the prejudices, superstitions, and unreasoned attitudes of the adults with whom they have contact. Open-mindedness calls for willingness to consider new information, to distinguish between fact and fiction, to challenge old beliefs and subject them to scrutiny in the light of authoritative information. The critical-mindedness which is forever seeking better explanations, experimenting to learn and to check facts – this is needed in all aspects of complex modern living. Children can learn through their work in science how to do intelligent planning so that they are not dependent upon guessing, haphazard thinking, or biased or unreliable information. They can learn to bring to bear upon the solution of problems the best thought, techniques, and information that can be made available to them.

Dora V. Smith calls attention to the need of children for "direct, positive instruction in how to attack their problems by means of the logical procedure of (1) defining a problem, (2) collecting and evaluating material related to the problem, (3) organizing it so that its relationship to the main topic and to other ideas bearing upon the topic is clear to the reader or listener, and (4) presenting it effectively for others" (34, p. 64).

She calls attention to the fact that such procedure should be applied to any and every activity of the school day. All work in science must of necessity follow such a plan and result in increasing ability to carry on scientific thinking as children grow from year to year. The problems in the kindergarten or primary school may deal with such matters as how to feed the pet rabbit and what kind of pen it needs; what happens to the water in the bowl on the radiator; why the leaf floats on the water while the stone sinks; or what the plants need in order to grow. Older children will be interested in everything: earth science, astronomy, atomic energy, or any other matter that comes to their attention. Space exploration is of tremendous interest to all of them.

Through their work in science, children can learn to present their thoughts accurately and precisely in carefully chosen words and in sentences which are clear and pointed. They can learn to distinguish clearly between the place and functions of imaginative and intuitive thinking and scientific thinking. Basically, all work in science is also work in language and helps to develop language power.

□ MATHEMATICAL THINKING

Specialists in arithmetic are facing the fact that many children develop a distaste for mathematics and actual fear of it because of the teaching methods that are used. Year after year, college students preparing to be teachers express fear and dread as they enroll in courses in general mathematics which are a part of the teacher education program. Many of them beg to be permitted to postpone them as long as possible. No other course requirement produces that reaction. When they are encouraged to discuss their attitude and try to analyze it, their thinking turns to unhappy experiences with arithmetic in the elementary school. All of these students learned to manipulate symbols and processes well enough to meet the basic requirement of the elementary school. But they were so lacking in understanding of what they were doing that they are afraid to approach mathematics on a higher level.

Dull children are by no means the only ones to have difficulty with mathematics. Several intellectual leaders have recorded the fact that school mathematics was a painful experience and one from which they profited little. Many adults dread the preparation of income tax returns not so much because of the money outlay required as because of the arithmetic that is called for and the need for accuracy. A great many people would rather accept a bill and write a check for the total indicated than keep records and carry on their own computation in order to check it for accuracy.

Developing number sense is developing vocabulary and meanings. A large number of quantitative and relational words must be learned as well as the number words. In fact, approximately twenty-five percent of all common words in daily use are quantitative in nature. Words for processes and the meaning and significance of processes come later. Verbal problems in arithmetic seldom call for only symbol manipulation and number knowledge. The development of concepts in mathematics begins with concrete experience and moves to the symbolic and abstract. Solving a verbal problem when the only stimulation comes from the printed words describing a situation, or from the sound of the teacher's voice, is very much more difficult for children than working out the problem through manipulating actual materials.

The new mathematics being taught in the schools gives careful attention to mathematics as a language. Each concept is carefully developed and forms the basis for the next concept. It is assumed that the basic concepts of mathematics can be so taught that they are intelligible to children at all levels of the educational ladder.

☐ LANGUAGE AN ALL-DAY PROGRAM

There is no phase of the work of the intermediate grades that does not lend itself to the development of language power. The wide range of interests of the nine- to twelve-year-olds and their increased attention span make it possible to carry on many types of classroom interests. There will be interests which are common to the entire class, those shared by only a group, and individual interests and hobbies as well. Some interests will be carried through intensively over an extended period of time as major units of interest. Others will be dealt with intensively for a brief period and added to intermittently as new material comes to light or a child wishes to return to or add something to the study. Other interests will be picked up and dropped as the children may desire at any time during the year. Perhaps a fourth grade group makes a study of regional history and current affairs in the community and surrounding area a matter of intensive study for a semester or longer. They may become interested in the reasons why a community was established at that spot and give concentrated attention for a time to the topography of the land and its resources. They will come back to this from time to time as they find related material or wish to make new applications. In the meantime they may carry on an extended study of weather, giving attention to it periodically so that they come to understand that climate is a composite of all the types of weather conditions found at all consistently in the area. They may also be giving attention to apparently unrelated matters such as the new uses of atomic energy, space flights, good books to read, American folk music and dances—any interest that is strong enough to call for attention.

Oral language, written language, and reading all develop together. The children as well as the teacher need to have some goals in mind so that they are always consciously moving forward toward them. Various aspects will be emphasized as there is need for them. Occasionally, a problem will be selected, discussed, and worked upon, and some standards set toward which the group will work. Group and individual evaluation will take place as it is needed, through discussion or individual conference. Children can give concentrated attention to a personal need only when they see it clearly and know what they can do to remedy it. They need to see evidence of growth as they go along in order to maintain their interest and efforts to improve.

□ ESSENTIAL SKILLS FOR SPEAKING AND LISTENING

Certain language skills are necessary for personal, civic, and occupational competence. Each type of skill is introduced wherever the need for it appears first, and it is given a forward push by each succeeding experience in which it is used if both teacher and children are gradually evolving standards for its improvement. Children have occasion to carry on informal conversations and more purposeful discussions, to ask and answer questions, to give and follow directions, to make plans, to give reports, and to criticize and evaluate. They need to learn simple parliamentary procedures for making decisions and carrying on democratic action. They have occasion to listen to television and radio and perhaps to participate in broadcasting. They also participate in dramatization both as players and as audience. They need to learn certain social procedures such as methods of introducing people and the responsibilities of hosts and guests for making social situations pleasant.

Developing skills in speaking and listening is a continuous program. No element can be assigned to the course of study for a given grade level to be attacked, practiced, and mastered at that grade level. Each of the needed elements of skill must be introduced whenever children have need for it and are intellectually and emotionally ready to work on it. Work must be continued from level to level, in life situations where it really functions, until children have reached the point of confident and effective use of the skill in all situations in which it is needed. At times it is profitable to examine a skill, discuss it, work on it through direct attack and practice, then fit it back into the total program of use. The method of direct attack is used infrequently in the primary grades, perhaps not at all until Grade Three. Even in the intermediate grades it is valuable only if the use of the skill is essential to experiences the children are having and they recognize its value and their need to improve their own level of skill. Practice without genuine motivation has little carry-over value.

■ *Sharing experiences through informal conversation*— Many of the conversations children carry on are informal interchanges of comments and thinking with no problem to be solved or decision to be made. A small group may assemble around a center of interest such as a display table, a bulletin board, or a work project. This informal sharing of reactions in a small group makes it possible for children to respond freely in their own way and may draw even a timid child into the circle of participants.

Standards for growth in power to carry on conversation are expanded as the children are ready for new points of emphasis and higher goals. Primary grade children need to be encouraged to participate, to take turns, to listen courteously, and to say something which will interest the group. They can learn gradually to stick to the subject they have chosen and to suit voice and speech to the needs of the situation. Intermediate grade children are still working on these points but are ready to add others which are probably not new to the group but have received less direct attention (34). Appropriate objectives call for knowledge of and practice in these matters:

When and how to get interesting material for conversation
What topics are appropriate for different types of occasions
When and where it is appropriate to talk
How to change a topic tactfully if it becomes unpleasant for participants
How to interrupt and when to do so
How to express feelings, likes, and dislikes without undue emphasis
How to differ with another's view and do it tactfully and courteously
How to avoid embarrassing others through attitude or speech
How to draw others out and encourage them to participate through showing sympathetic interest in what is said and asking pertinent questions
How to use a pleasant, conversational voice and manner
Acceptance of responsibility for saying only what is true and reasonable

The standards which evolve from experience and advance progressively from level to level follow this general sequence:

1. Emphasis on freeing the individual and encouraging him to participate
2. Emphasis on increasing recognition of responsibility to others and the development of group consciousness
3. Emphasis on interplay of ideas and meeting of minds
4. Emphasis on responsibility for the value and the accuracy of one's remarks
5. Emphasis on the improvement of personal techniques such as voice and mannerisms
6. Emphasis on training for leadership in the carrying on of group processes

Since standards cannot be assigned to any grade level, the teacher needs to be aware of the progress individuals are making and sensitive to their needs. Then she can feed in new ideas as the children are ready for them and guide both group and individuals in pushing the standards on ahead and climbing toward them. Standards that are too low retard growth; standards that are set too high discourage it. If children are guided into recognition of next steps in the refinement and improvement of conversation as these are called for by experience, the growth will be continuous and consistent with the needs of each individual.

There will be face-to-face conversations at school but children may carry on similar conversations by telephone. They learn from experience the need for clear expression where the voice must carry the full meaning without reliance upon facial expression or gesture. They learn also to listen carefully and to attend to any directions or plans. Through school discussion, dramatization, and experience, they can be guided into an appreciation of effective and considerate telephone behavior.

■ *Purposeful discussion*—Discussion is used as a means of planning, of enlightening and guiding, of solving problems and answering questions, of arriving at decisions, and of evaluating group and individual enterprises. Discussion which is designed to serve a purpose calls for clear interplay of ideas and real thinking together. Speakers need to make their meaning clear and listeners need to give thoughtful attention so that the purpose of the discussion may be achieved. A speaker may find his contribution challenged and be required to defend his point or modify it to help reach a conclusion that is satisfactory to the group. If he feels he cannot modify his stand any further, he must decide what adjustment he can make to group needs and still hold his dissenting opinion.

Children can gradually evolve their own standards for participation, similar to those which follow:

Have something to say
Say it clearly so others will understand what you mean
Speak in a clear, pleasant voice
Make your speech (usage) acceptable
Back your points with evidence from authorities where necessary
Listen with an open mind to the opinions of others
Think through and weigh the opinions of others
Be willing to change your mind if you are convinced another idea is better
Be courteous at all times, even when you disagree
Give thought to the needs of the group as well as your own needs and interests (34)

Sharing of experiences may be the purpose of a group discussion or it may be a factor in it. Children, as well as adults, are dependent upon their own experiences for the kind and quality of contribution which they make to any group enterprise. There is evidence that "a selective process underlies the contributions to any discussion. The children who take part actively select from their total recalls the facts, the incidents, the ideas which seem fitting to the subject matter" (34, p. 80). With younger children and less mature children, any discussion resembles an "experience meeting" rather than a discussion which revolves about an accepted point. Even older children frequently wander off onto various subthemes which are suggested by the main theme or which enable the children to recount experiences which have been brought to mind. When the purpose is sharing experiences, the monologues dealing with the experiences of individuals will predominate. "Lone-star" performances have less place in types of discussion which are to result in decisions or action unless an individual child happens to have had experience in the area being considered.

A great deal is being written about the need for developing in all citizens an understanding of group processes. Some understanding can be developed in the elementary school. Children nine to twelve years of age can begin to learn how to serve as discussion leaders both of small groups and of the whole class. They can learn how to draw out the ideas of others, how to keep the discussion moving, how to summarize and draw material together at the end of a discussion, and how to plan for group action. They can have the experience of serving as group recorder. They can also learn to draw upon the knowledge and experience of those in the group who know most about the subject and use them as resources to supplement the thinking of the group as a whole. All such experience begins simply; the teacher serves as leader and guide, turning over to individuals bits of responsibility they appear ready to handle. She stands by to give suggestions, guide from within the group as a participant, or take over the leadership when she is needed. Children need to stop from time to time to evaluate the progress they are making in carrying on group discussion and the effectiveness of the discussion in serving its purpose.

Baker studied the contributions of children to general class discussion in Grades Two, Four, and Six in three schools of varying socioeconomic level in New York (3). Growth in maturity was shown in the types of topics selected for discussion: animals, games and play, and home and family life in Grade Two; trips, books, and moving pictures as well as current happenings in Grade Four; whereas children of Grade Six discussed national and world events as well as current happenings in their metropolitan area. There were clear evidences of growth in (1) increased use of material from various sources, (2) greater reliance on the results of the children's own thinking, (3) greater concern for the remote as contrasted with the immediate in both time and place, and (4) increased evidence of association of ideas in a real "meeting of minds."

Many teachers find, as Baker did, that one of the most difficult problems to deal with in group discussion is the tendency of a few children to do a large portion of the talking, often with little real knowledge and with little, actually, to say. Some will even strive to divert the discussion into areas with which they are familiar. Developing a sense of responsibility to the common goal and common good in place of overdesire for "stage center" and ego satisfaction requires individual guidance.

The use of discussion for purposes of planning, solving problems, arriving at decisions, and evaluating enterprises calls for several steps. There is, first of all, the proposing of possibilities. These have to be weighed and their implications, methods of operation, difficulties, and opportunities examined. Those of less practical value are eliminated until the children agree upon the plan, solution, or decision that best satisfies the need and the group interest. Voting is sometimes resorted to in making a final decision if there is persistent difference of opinion. When discussion can be carried through to the point where consensus of opinion is evident, the result is usually more satisfactory. Children need to learn the place and function of voting in a democratic organization, but there is danger that a vote may be called for too soon with the result that an articulate majority drags along an unwilling and unconvinced minority. Mutual understanding which results in consensus of opinion is of greater educational value.

■ *Utilizing parliamentary procedures*—There is difference of opinion as to when children are ready for class organization with class officers and meetings which call for parliamentary procedure. Some teachers hold that, since children of nine years of age are interested in clubs and organizations outside of school, such classroom organization can begin at fourth grade level. Other teachers are convinced that very little of such emphasis is needed before sixth grade or junior high school. In any case, there are some learnings which are a part of parliamentary procedure which children need and can use in the elementary school. The most important of these are the following:

1. Knowing when to speak
2. Presiding over a group discussion
3. Performing duties and carrying out responsibilities of class officers [or chairmen]
4. Making decisions by means of voting
5. Making and seconding a motion
6. Abiding by the will of the majority yet understanding the point of view of the minority

Some of these concepts and skills can be learned through group and committee work. There are many points at which children function best in groups that center about common needs or common interests. Again, no assignment of learning responsibilities to definite grades is possible. The maturity of the children and the needs of the situation will determine organization and procedure.

■ *Asking and answering questions*—So much of the learning of children and adults is the direct result of questioning that this merits special attention. Children should become increasingly skillful in determining just what information is needed and in wording questions clearly and concisely as well as courteously. The person to whom the question is addressed needs to listen to find just what is called for and to word his answer so that the information is clearly given. The questioner must be alert to the response and should learn how to interrupt and set the answerer on the right track if the question is misinterpreted. He should learn how to follow through, courteously but persistently, to see that the information he needs is forthcoming. Watts mentions at many points the need for training children to say what they mean clearly and directly. In the matter of asking and answering questions children can be taught to see the value in clear-cut, concise statements which do not wander from the point. They must learn that insincere or embarrassing questions are not permissible at any time but that sincere and courteous questions deserve thoughtful and sincere answers.

■ *Giving and following directions*—The matter of giving and following directions requires the development of both speaking and listening abilities. Children need to learn to listen intently and make sure that they understand a direction before translating it into action. They need to give attention to the steps in directions and the sequence into which they fall.

In order to give directions, children need to consider the points at which guidance will be needed and the most effective sequence of points. They need to learn to express the directions clearly and concisely in words that cannot be easily misinterpreted. Where examples are needed to clarify meaning, they need to learn to select pointed examples and express them clearly. This is another type of situation which gives the children practice in saying exactly what they mean in clear and definite words and sentences.

■ *Giving oral reports*—In making reports, the selection of ideas and their arrangement need at least as much attention as the spoken word and its delivery. A fundamental principle in all oral work is that the teacher "is concerned with speech as a medium of communication rather than an interpretative art, so that the attention of the child, from the first taken up with what he intends to say, only at length comes to include how best to say it" (29, p. 64). Certainly, the selection of pertinent material is the first need. Children in the intermediate grades can learn to outline and organize their ideas and thoughts. They can understand the responsibility of the reporter to present his material accurately. They can see the need for giving the report in a clear and interesting manner, using examples where they will add interest and clarity to the presentation.

Detailed outlining undoubtedly belongs in the secondary school, but children of the intermediate grades can learn to make lists of topics and subtopics which throw the points into a simple outline of sequence and relative importance. This can be learned through note-taking in connection with reading and also in the preparation of talks and reports.

While the content of the report is of greatest importance, the children need to give attention, both individually and as a group, to evaluation of their techniques of reporting and the effectiveness of their presentation. Standards here will not differ greatly from those suggested for general discussion on page 192.

■ *Some social skills*—Learning to introduce people and to serve as host or hostess, guest, or audience will be taken care of in actual social situations. The enrollment of a new child in the group provides opportunity for the practice of introductions as the children are guided in introducing the newcomer to other children, the music and art teachers, the principal and others in the school organization. Inviting a parent to tell of his trip to Mexico; asking an overseas veteran to tell of a country he has visited; requesting the school health officer to tell the children how to avoid and how to care for colds—many such opportunities provide more formal situations in which children can learn to introduce a speaker.

Occasions on which parents or other grades are invited into the classroom to see and hear reports of the children's work provide situations in which children can practice the courtesies and responsibilities of host and hostess and social participants. Planning will be called for, careful carrying through of plans, and evaluation at the end. Classroom dramatizations, reports, and sharing as well as invitations to assembly programs and programs in other classrooms serve to develop understanding of audience responsibility.

Social understanding and skill in social participation develop best in real social experience. Reading and talking about them cannot provide the same values. Knowledge of what one should do, without opportunity to practice it, tends to result in self-consciousness rather than poise and confidence in social situations. Many experiences are necessary before confidence can be attained.

■ *Broadcasting and listening to the radio and television*—Some schools use their public address system to give children experience in broadcasting. The local radio stations in some communities set aside regular times for school broadcasts and others encourage occasional broadcasts by school children. Television stations may allow time for occasional short programs.

Opportunity to broadcast can be used as motivation for speech improvement. Children can study the broadcasts of experts to note styles of speaking, voice, enunciation, pronunciation, rhythm, and oral punctuation. Listening to study certain clearly understood points should prove interesting and enjoyable homework. Older children can give special attention to vocabulary and to methods of catching and holding interest. Such study might be followed by preparation and the putting on of imaginary broadcasts at school, if the interest warrants it.

Equipment for recording children's voices is particularly valuable in speech improvement. All schools should be equipped with wire or tape recorders or other speech-recording machines. If children can hear their own speeches, reports, or oral reading played back to them it is a relatively simple matter to stimulate and guide improvement. Often, a child's failure to work upon his problem is the result of lack of clear understanding of just what the problem is and how to go about improving it. To record and play back material at periodic intervals gives the child something to work for.

Radio and television can be used as sources of material for classroom contributions: human interest stories and anecdotes, current affairs, literature, and dramatizations. Through the utilization of these media, standards of taste can be developed for judging the validity of informational programs and the artistic and literary quality of dramatic and literary programs.

The use of films and other visual aids can be made to serve the purposes of enrichment and the building of standards, also. Television, with its combination of some of the values of both radio and motion pictures, is used in many schools for basic lessons as well as for enrichment.

There is serious danger that these methods of passive intake will make of us a nation of absorbers, not a nation of active doers. For this reason, if for no other, dramatic play and dramatization are very important to education because they call for initiative and active, productive effort. Since Chapter 17 is devoted to this matter, no detailed presentation is needed here.

☐ ORAL LANGUAGE COMES FIRST

Spoken language precedes written language in all areas of language development. Before children can write good sentences they must be able to hear and sense the difference between word groups that are sentences and those that are not sentences. Before they can improve poor or unacceptable usage in either oral or written work they must be able to recognize the difference between the better form and the poorer and select the better. This will be given further attention in Chapter 14. Man developed a useable spoken language long before he developed a written one. The evidence appears clear that adequate opportunity to use and to refine oral language is essential for all children in the elementary school if they are to develop concepts and standards which will form a solid foundation for further growth and learning in more advanced school work and in life itself.

This is the era of the spoken word, and children need to learn to speak and listen in order to gain the values from life which they are capable of gaining. There is some little truth in the statement made by an English educator that the ability to speak and to listen is more important for successful, happy living in today's world than the ability to read. Children who learn to look realistically at life outside the school will see the need for all of the language skills. The language arts develop together in the elementary schools and the work in oral communication is basic to all the rest.

☐ SELECTED REFERENCES ☐

1. Anderson, V. D. et al, "Communication: A Guide to the Teaching of Speaking and Writing." *Readings in the Language Arts.* New York: Macmillan Company, 1964.
2. Association for Childhood Education International, *Basic Human Values for Childhood Education.* Washington, D.C.: Association for Childhood Education International, 1963.
3. Baker, Harold V., *Children's Contributions in Elementary School General Discussion.* Child Development Monographs, No. 29. New York: Bureau of Publications, Teachers College, Columbia University, 1942.
4. Blair, Arthur Witt, and Burton, William H., *Growth and Development of the Preadolescent.* New York: Appleton-Century-Crofts, Inc., 1951.
5. Blough, Glen O., and Huggett, A. J., *Elementary Science and How to Teach It.* New York: Dryden Press, 1958.
6. Brogan, Peggy, and Fox, Lorene K., *Helping Children Learn.* Yonkers-on-Hudson, N. Y.: World Book Co., 1955.
7. Burrows, Alvina T., *Teaching Children in the Middle Grades.* Boston: D. C. Heath and Co., 1952.
8. Craig, Gerald S., *Science in Childhood Education.* Practical

Suggestions for Teaching, No. 8. New York: Bureau of Publications, Teachers College, Columbia University, 1944.

9. ———, "Science in the Elementary School." *What Research Says to the Teacher,* No. 12. Washington, D.C.: Department of Classroom Teachers, American Education Research Association of the N.E.A., 1957.
10. Cunningham, Ruth, and Associates, *Understanding Group Behavior of Boys and Girls.* New York: Bureau of Publications, Teachers College, Columbia University, 1951.
11. Davis, Allison, and Havighurst, Robert, *Father of the Man.* New York: Houghton Mifflin Co., 1947.
12. Department of Elementary School Principals, National Education Association, *Language Arts in the Elementary School.* Twentieth Yearbook. Washington, D.C.: National Education Association, 1941.
13. Evertts, Eldonna L., *An Investigation of the Structure of Children's Oral Language Compared with Silent Reading, Oral Reading, and Listening Comprehension.* Unpublished dissertation. Bloomington: Indiana University, 1961.
14. Foshay, Arthur, and Wann, Kenneth D., *Children's Social Values.* New York: Bureau of Publications, Teachers College, Columbia University, 1954.
15. Gesell, Arnold, and Ilg, Frances L., *The Child from Five to Ten.* New York: Harper and Brothers, 1946.
16. Gesell, Arnold; Ilg, Frances L.; and Ames, Louise B., *Youth: The Years from Ten to Sixteen.* New York: Harper and Brothers, 1956.
17. Greene, Harry A., and Petty, Walter T., *Developing Language Skills in the Elementary Schools* (2nd Ed.). Boston: Allyn and Bacon, Inc., 1963.
18. Hilliard, Pauline, *Improving Social Learning in the Elementary School.* New York: Bureau of Publications, Teachers College, Columbia University, 1954.
19. Hurlock, Elizabeth B., *Modern Ways with Children.* New York: Whittlesey House, 1943.
20. Jenkins, Gladys G.; Shacter, Helen; and Bauer, William W., *These Are Your Children.* (Expanded Ed.). Chicago: Scott, Foresman and Co., 1953.
21. Jersild, Arthur T., *Child Psychology* (Fifth Ed.). New York: Prentice-Hall, Inc., 1960.
22. La Brant, Lou, "The Relations of Language and Speech Acquisitions to Personality Development." *Mental Hygiene in Modern Education.* Paul Witty and Charles E. Skinner (Eds.). New York: Farrar and Rinehart, Inc., 1939. Chap. XII, pp. 324-352.

23. Loban, Walter D., *The Language of Elementary School Children*. Research Report No. 1, Champaign, Ill.: National Council of Teachers of English, 1963.
24. Mackintosh, Helen, Chairman, *Children and Oral Language*. Washington, D. C.: Association for Childhood Education International, 1964.
25. Michaelis, John U., *Social Studies for Children in a Democracy* (3rd Ed.). New York: Prentice-Hall, Inc., 1963.
26. Mulgrave, Dorothy I., *Speech for the Classroom Teacher* (3rd Ed.). New York: Prentice-Hall, Inc., 1955.
27. National Society for the Study of Education, *Teaching Language in the Elementary School*. The Forty-third Yearbook, Part II, Chicago: University of Chicago Press, 1944.
28. Olson, Willard C., *Child Development* (2nd Ed.). Boston: D. C. Heath and Co., 1959.
29. Pinto, Vivian De Sola (Ed.), *The Teaching of English in Schools: A Symposium*. London: Macmillan and Co., Ltd., 1946.
30. Postman, Neil, and Associates, *Television and the Teaching of English*. New York: Appleton-Century-Crofts, Inc., 1961.
31. Preston, Ralph C., *Teaching Social Studies in the Elementary School* (Rev. Ed.). New York: Rinehart and Co., 1958.
32. Schonell, Fred J., *Backwardness in the Basic Subjects*. Edinburgh: Oliver and Boyd, 1942.
33. Shane, Harold G.; Mulry, June Grant; Reddin, Mary E.; and Gillespie, Margaret C., *Improving Language Arts Instruction in the Elementary School*. Columbus, Ohio: Charles E. Merrill Books, Inc., 1962.
34. Smith, Dora V., "Growth in Language Power as Related to Child Development." *Teaching Language in the Elementary School*. The Forty-Third Yearbook, Part II, of the National Society for the Study of Education. Chicago: University of Chicago Press, 1944, Chap. IV, pp. 52-97.
35. Strickland, Ruth G., *The Language of Elementary School Children: Its Relationship to the Language of Reading Textbooks and the Quality of Reading of Selected Children*. Bulletin of the School of Education, Vol. 38, No. 4. Bloomington: Indiana University, July, 1962.
36. Watts, A. F., *The Language and Mental Development of Children*. London: George G. Harrap and Co., Ltd., 1944. Boston: D. C. Heath and Co., 1947.
37. Witty, Paul, and Kinsella, Paul, "Televiewing: Some Observations from Studies, 1949-1962." *Elementary English* 39:772-779, December, 1962.

individual differences in language needs.

Language differences show up clearly as children enter school. At no other point are our various regional and social dialects more evident. The range of proficiency in the use of language is equally clear. At one end of the range are children whose language is as good as or better than that of the average adult in the community, while at the other end are children who are severely limited or actually handicapped in language. The classroom teacher must be a sensitive diagnostician and analyst as well as a student of the local culture and community language behavior. Then she must adapt her teaching methods and expectations to all degrees and types of difference. The extent to which teachers can do this adapting and differentiating sympathetically yet objectively will determine in large measure the command of language the children will demonstrate at the end of six or seven years in the elementary school.

There are many types of language experience which all children need to have in the schools and under the guidance of skillful teachers. A large portion of the curriculum experience which involves language can be common experience, but individuals have special needs of varying sorts which must be met through individual guidance and teaching. Some types of individual guidance can be cared for unobtrusively through what appears to be purely incidental teaching if the teacher is sensitive to each child's needs and alert to opportunities to help him. Other types of individual help will need to be provided through various types of group work or in brief periods which the teacher sets aside for concentration on work with a single child. At times, speech specialists may take over the program of therapy for a child with a serious disability. This will probably involve taking him from the classroom for a brief period of work daily or two or three times a week.

Good speech for everyone is a major goal of all language teaching in the elementary school. Effort is directed toward helping each individual to develop his speech so that it is increasingly acceptable among the educated people of his community, and so that he speaks with poise and sensitivity to the demands and opportunities of communication in any type of situation.

Good speech calls for a clear and pleasing voice, clear articulation and enunciation, correct pronunciation, and good diction.

Teachers at all grade levels need to provide opportunities to talk freely and naturally with each child who is new to the room in order to become acquainted with his speech and locate any problems which need to be considered in guiding him. A program of speech improvement should start in the kindergarten and continue without interruption throughout the child's school experience. Children's speech problems are largely individual problems and need to be studied and cared for individually, though group work will help with refining and improving the speech quality where no serious problems exist calling for specialized treatment.

Most of the more serious speech problems which children bring to school are deeply ingrained and too persistent to be cared for during a single school year. Work must be carried on consistently and persistently, year after year, until the child has made as great gain as he is capable of making. The kindergarten and primary teachers bear the responsibility for locating children who need special help and seeing to it that problems are diagnosed and a program of treatment planned and instituted. Teachers who have these children in later grades are responsible for carrying on the program which has been instituted for the children until the needs are met or until as much has been accomplished as the nature of the case permits. Children who require special help need careful watching.

☐ SPEECH IMPROVEMENT FOR ALL CHILDREN

Almost all children profit from some types of help with speech. An occasional child from a highly favored home has had good models to listen to and copy during his early years and has had enough attention to his speech needs so that he speaks clearly and well. Other children, even from homes where the parents' speech is satisfactory, need help with voice, enunciation, or other elements that make up good speech. They have no serious handicaps but some emphasis on good speech will help them to improve the quality of their utterance. There are entire neighborhoods or large areas where speech tends to be slurred or voices are poorly used.

When there are no serious speech problems but merely careless habits or a low standard of speech production, improvement can be brought about through attention to speech in any or all of the situations which call for spoken language. Children can be encouraged to give thought to their speech in discussion groups, conferences and interviews, the giving of talks, reports, and announcements. Activities such as choral speaking, dramatization, radio work, and oral reading before an audience provide motivation for a high quality of vocal production. Children can be brought to understand the quality of speech that is needed for any presentation before an audience and can work toward a high standard of excellence. Even children who are too timid to volunteer in discussion and conversation will blend their voices with others in choral speaking or possibly lose their self-consciousness in playing a part in dramatization and thus not only improve their speech but add to their confidence and poise in facing people. Oral reading is of value only when it is real audience reading which gives the child a feeling of responsibility for interesting and holding his audience. Oral reading has little value for speech improvement, or any other purpose probably, when each child holds an identical copy of the material the reader is reading; there is no incentive to make one's reading clear and interesting when everyone else is looking at identical text.

☐ THE SPEECH OF THE TEACHER

In speech work, as in everything else, it is impossible to overemphasize the importance of the teacher's example. When a young child tells a story he has heard the teacher tell or repeats a poem he has learned through listening or chiming in as the teacher read it, he invariably includes in his presentation the voice, inflection, and intonation used by the teacher. As has been said of the preschool level, the quality of the teacher's voice determines the pitch and volume that will be used by the children in their responses to each other as well as to her, and sets the emotional tone of the classroom.

In order to bring about speech improvement that will carry over into the out-of-school experience of the child and stand up against the influence of the examples he finds there, the child must have a great deal of experience with using good speech. Acceptable forms of speech must sound right and feel right to him so that his ears are trained to accept the sound of the better form and so that saying it will seem natural to him. Such help may come from the example of the teacher's speech.

☐ CHILDREN WHOSE LANGUAGE DEVELOPMENT WILL DEVIATE

In any group of children there are some who deviate from the usual pattern in their development. Deviations are of many sorts but perhaps the most common are: the linguistically precocious child; the child who is a slow starter in language but who progresses once he is started; the mentally retarded child; the child from a foreign background; the physically handicapped child with speech, hearing, vision, or other physical impairment; and the child handicapped by poor environment and experience. While care for children who deviate adds materially to the teacher's burden of responsibility, it also adds to the challenge of teaching and to the deep sense of satisfaction which any good teacher feels when she sees boys and girls facing their handicaps and conquering them or learning to live with them and above them. Children learn a great deal from each other. One takes for granted that the presence in the class of the linquistically precocious child is good for other children, but the handicapped child can be an asset to the other children, also. It was heart warming to the principal of a school when mothers of children of above average ability remarked that their own children were learning thoughtfulness and consideration through their interest in the speech-handicapped children who had come to the school from a near-by clinic. The presence of children who deviate can be used to help all the children learn to recognize the fact that there is worth in everyone, regardless of the points at which he may differ. The respect children gain for personality and for human dignity and worth is far more important than the additional effort the teacher must put forth to care for the growth of these deviants.

☐ THE LINGUISTICALLY GIFTED CHILD

One is less likely to think of the child who is precocious in language as a child in need of special care, yet he may need the guidance and protection of the teacher as much as does the handicapped child. Such a child has a vocabulary far in advance of the other children. His language usage and the quality of his expression may be almost as mature as those of the teacher, yet he may lack understanding of how to communicate with children less mature in language than he. Since his advanced attainment in language is probably the result of a great deal of contact with adults, he stands in special need of social experience with children, yet his advanced language and the more mature interests that accompany it tend to cut him off from close association with other children.

The social problems of these children appear at various age levels. When Daniel, in the first grade, mentioned a disk he was using in a building project the other children responded with derisive laughter saying, "Daniel says 'disk'! He can't say 'dish.' He means a dish." Five-year-old Dickie turned on the two boys who were pushing for a turn on the slide with, "You'll see what the result of that will be. That's always the result." The extra violent push he received was not so much resentment of his words of caution as of the fact that they did not know what he was talking about. Keith, in the sixth grade, unwittingly developed great resentment in the other boys in the class because his responses in all group work were so clear, mature, and convincing—and always stated before the other boys had opportunity to think out a response—that he gained more than his share of the attention and approval of an immature student teacher who was leading the group. In the cases of Dickie and Daniel, the teachers watched for points at which they could help the boys interpret their meaning to the children and help the children see that they needed to be sure they understood what was meant. Because Keith was older and more mature, his teacher talked the problem through with him and helped him to see his need for giving the other boys a fair chance to contribute their ideas. She also guided him to see that he could be helpful to the boys by drawing out their ideas and finding ways to use them instead of thrusting their ideas aside and substituting his own. Keith had extraordinary mental ability but needed to learn how to use it in working with people in varying situations.

It is difficult for teachers as well as parents to remember that the child who is advanced in vocabulary development and facile in his use of language is not necessarily advanced in every way and to avoid pushing him into work with the academic skills before he is ready for them. Command of words for oral use does not insure general maturity and stability sufficient for the task of learning to read, nor does it insure well-developed eyes for the purpose. Facility in the use of language does not guarantee the ability to understand even so basic a mathematical concept as $2 + 2 = 4$. A child gifted in language may be immature emotionally and physically, may be highly dependent upon adults, and may even lack many types of concrete firsthand experience. His readiness for the development of skills needs to be studied just as carefully as that of slower children.

The precocious child can be encouraged to gather material for the enrichment of interests being carried on in the classroom, to tell stories to the children, and to dictate stories and accounts of experiences for the teacher to write down. If his motor skill is sufficiently advanced he can be encouraged to do his own writing. It is often true, however, that the motor skill of such a child is not at all advanced, and it is sometimes actually very slow to develop. He should not be pushed into writing until his muscular strength and co-ordination are ready for it. If a typewriter is available he may take great interest in typing bits of material by the "hunt and peck" method if someone will provide the spelling he needs or write copy for him to use.

Occasionally, such a child is precocious in reading as well as speech. If that is the case, he can be encouraged to read to the class or to a smaller group of children, for various purposes—for pleasure or to answer questions. Again, care needs to be exercised to see to it that his other needs are met as well as his reading needs. Pat, who could read before his entrance into kindergarten, was felt by both mother and teacher to be in far greater need of social contacts than of reading. Even at this early age Pat was using reading to avoid playing with children. If he was invited to join a play group or to help build with the blocks he would stand watching the other children for a few moments rather wistfully, then return to hide himself in his book rather than put forth the effort to enter into the play. Since he lacked techniques for entering into group experiences rather than interest, the teacher's efforts were directed toward helping him to become a social participant rather than a resigned isolate.

Usually, the child who is advanced in one or more areas needs the normal types of classroom experience which are good for other children, with opportunities to continue developing in his areas of strength. All types of enriching curriculum experiences are good for him. He will probably gain more from these experiences than other children because of his advancement in language. When he has learned to read and write he can forge ahead more independently. He can assume responsibility for wide reading and making reports to the group, for interviews and other means of gathering information to further group interests. He needs to develop individual interests, also, and to be encouraged to set high standards for himself in carrying them out. Acceleration which puts him with older children rarely meets his needs. It is usually better to keep him with his age group and guide him into expanding and deepening his interests and improving his skills and techniques, and to give him many opportunities to work with his peers, both as leader and as follower. If he has special talents in the creative arts these should be encouraged and developed.

☐ THE CHILD WHO IS A SLOW STARTER

There is great variation in the age at which babies begin to talk. One baby may be using three or more intelligible words by his first birthday while another may not attempt a word for a few more months. By two years of age some children are using a number of words and speaking very clearly, while others are still using jargon or scarcely talking at all. The child who is making average progess is using simple declarative and interrogative sentences with ease, and adding also some complex and compound sentences of considerable length by the end of his fourth year, while slower children are still using a meager vocabulary and fragmentary sentences.

While parents are gratified if their child talks at an early age they take for granted variations of several months, at least, just as they do in the matter of the eruption of the child's teeth, or the first step in crawling or walking. The fact that a child is slow in developing speech does not necessarily mean that the child is below average in mentality, even though there is a fairly high correlation between mental ability and ability in language. Some children who are late in starting to talk make good progress and are doing about as well as others of their age when they enter school; it is often impossible to tell them from the earlier starters. This is particularly true of children whose delayed speech was due to prolonged illness or lack of physical strength and stamina in their early years.

It is not unreasonable to suggest that the child who was slow in developing speech may also prove to be slow in developing skill in reading and writing the symbols of language. He may be a little older than other children before he manifests readiness to learn to read and before he makes much progress. Slow starters frequently move very slowly for quite a time without much evidence of progress, then accelerate the rate of growth once they have made a good beginning. Certainly it is true that the progress these children make depends upon the skill of the teacher in keeping them free from discouragement, embarrassment, or frustration during this growing period. There is little doubt that they will achieve up to their capacity if they are permitted to progress at their own rate with encouragement and guidance but without any forcing or crowding.

Children who are retarded in speech but have no speech defects should be given many experiences that are vitally interesting to them and should be encouraged to enter into many language situations. They should be recognized and approved when they put forth effort to express themselves and to contribute to the group. They should be given opportunities to work and play with children who talk freely, and should be put in close contact with children who will respond to them and respect their tempo, because these children are often slow to respond, though the response is adequate if the listener will be patient enough to wait for it. They may put forth extra effort if the teacher expresses interest in their wishes or ideas but waits to respond until they have really tried to express themselves clearly. The slow learner needs to be kept happy and secure in the classroom, but he must be given the motivation of vital interests and friendly encouragement to speed him on his way.

☐ THE HANDICAP OF POOR ENVIRONMENT AND EXPERIENCE

Children handicapped by poor environment and meager experience need a great deal of experience in exploring the opportunities the school can provide and in doing the things they have not been privileged to do. They need a great deal of time and help to build readiness for learning to read and for the other academic work of the school. Reading and other aspects of skill development should be delayed until they have at least partially made up for the deficiencies in their environment through many types of experience.

If the environmental handicap shows itself mainly in meager vocabulary of words and meanings, the child needs many experiences of all sorts. Some of them will be simple neighborhood experiences that are commonplace to other children. He will need picture books and stories and opportunity to talk about them with an adult so that he learns words for what he is seeing and learns to talk about what he hears, using the appropriate vocabulary. Every effort to enrich his experience will have to include talk so that he learns to express his thinking and talk about his observations with ease and with accuracy. The talk helps to strengthen and clarify his concepts of word meanings.

If the child's handicap shows itself mainly in poor grammatical usage he will need sympathetic and prolonged help. The poor language usage a child acquires in his home and community is not easily overcome. Once the structures of his language are set they can be changed only slowly. If his family is content with the language he uses and the sole motivation for improvement must come from the school, little permanent gain can be expected unless the child can be made to want improvement himself. The child's security resides in the home folk who feed him and care for him and love him more than does anyone else. At times a child will cling tenaciously to his poor usage because he feels, consciously or otherwise, that he cannot afford to be different from those who love him. The school can tune his ear to correctness and motivate him in various ways to practice it at school but it will not carry over outside the teacher's immediate influence until he can be led to want something better for himself than his home has given him.

As is true of all other children with handicaps which affect language, these children need trips for firsthand study, dramatic play, stories and simple poems to listen to, attractive books to look at and later to read, and a quantity of materials for expression through drawing, painting, construction, and other media. They need a great deal of time to talk about what they are doing and to build new interests and enrich old ones. Choral reading, group dramatization, opportunities to make announcements, deliver messages, make telephone calls (after help with preparation for them) motivate the child to practice his school speech and raise its standards. Encouraging the child to join Sunday School, playground, scouting, or other organized boy or girl groups where the leader uses English that is better than the child's own may make it possible for him to hear correct usage a larger proportion of the time. Suggesting programs for him to listen to on the radio or view on television, or motion pictures for him to see may also provide him with added hours of listening to good speech. Every possible resource should be utilized to help him use correct speech in situations which demand it until what is correct not only sounds right but feels right to him as he says it. The more he practices good speech the more likely he is to carry it outside the school.

Only strong personal desire to improve can spur children to enough effort to prevent their relapsing into the standards of the home and community during out-of-school hours, and the total number of these language hours far exceeds the number under the guidance of the school. Children who come from unfavorable language backgrounds do not require specialized methods but more guided experience of many common types and more time to absorb it. They need guidance that is consistent but at the same time patient and sympathetic.

☐ OUR LATEST CONCERN—THE CULTURALLY DEPRIVED

The children whose problems society is most aware of at this time are the children from culturally disadvantaged backgrounds. Cultural deprivation almost always includes language deprivation. The needs of many preschool children are being met as far as possible in Head Start classes. Some schools have followed federal suggestions and have instituted follow-up measures to make sure that the gains children have made in the preschool experience are not undone by rigid, prescriptive and restrictive programs in first grade. But these efforts do not take care of all of the children who need help. Wider Horizons programs and Upward Bound programs have been set up in some places for junior and senior high school students, but there is no help for the elementary school child unless the school provides it. The great majority of these culturally disadvantaged children bring to school a language which has met their needs in the home environment but which differs greatly from the language of the school. Theirs may be a Negro dialect from an isolated or segregated environment in the South; it may be language picked up on the streets because the home speaks a foreign language; it may be of Spanish origin; or it may be just the "Me and him ain't got none" kind of English which the child has learned from adults who speak that way. In any case, the language of the teacher and the school may be so different from what the child knows outside of school that he is uncomfortable with it.

Whatever the child's language is, it tells his teacher three things: his speech tells her the quality and kind of language he hears at home; his vocabulary gives her insight into his background of experience—nouns tell what things and people he has encountered actually or vicariously, while his verbs tell her something about his activities; the way he uses language gives her a fairly clear picture of his self-image—confident, adequate, perhaps even aggressive, or timid, fearful, lacking in self-confidence and self-respect. What the language cannot tell her is how bright he is—only that he has had an opportunity to learn.

A study by Loban of the language of children in Oakland, California and studies by Bernstein of cockney-speaking children in London cause both men to arrive at the same generalization—that a child from a poor language environment uses only a small portion of the potential of his language. He has not learned to think with it, to reason from cause to effect, hypothesize or to use it imaginatively. Loban suggests that, for these children, teachers should ask fewer "what" questions, "What does it say? What happened?" and many more "If then" questions, "If this were true, then what—?" "Why do you suppose—?" They need consistent help to use their language for all kinds of thinking and reasoning. They need this help to expand their use of *their own* language more than they need constant correction of their substandard or nonstandard usage. Loban suggests that later, when children reach perhaps sixth grade, they can be guided to take note of the language used in different vocations—that of the doctor, the minister, news analysts and others on television and radio—to find the kind of language needed for such opportunities. He feels that they might then be mature enough to want to *add* that type of language to their repertoire. Meanwhile, teachers can use many opportunities to call attention to differences in the way English is spoken in various parts of the United States and in other English-speaking areas so that the children's ears and minds are kept tuned to differences and their vocal organs are kept flexible enough to reproduce sounds and patterns that differ from their home ones.

While inner city children are claiming much of public attention, many rural children have similar needs. Their experiences differ from those of the city child but may be just as meager and their need for help with language fully as great.

By no means do all culturally disadvantaged children come

from the homes of the poor. Some are not economically handicapped but handicapped by neglect and rejection. Such children may be physically well cared for and have all that they need of what money can buy but be sadly deprived of contact with adults who are interested in them and really care for them. The language of these children may be the language of the servants, not their parents, or there may be lack of language because no one talks to them or in any way provides them with language. Nowadays, such children may have television sets of their own and may have more acquaintance with the shadowy people on the screen and their ideas than with flesh and blood people who talk with them. The needs of these children may be quite similar to those of other disadvantaged children but for different reasons. Sometimes the home can be encouraged to give children opportunities to grow through firsthand experience, hopefully with someone who will also provide talk, since even the most vivid sensory experiences do little or nothing for language development unless they are accompanied by personal interaction and communication.

□ OUR MIGRANT CHILDREN

Many of the increasing numbers of children who follow the crops from one part of the United States to another from season to season come to school for very short periods and are on their way again. Some of them, like Billie Davis, the subject of the National Education Association's film, *A Desk for Billie,* are children hungry for a chance to settle down, to have a home, and to live like other children. Janie, in Doris Gates' story, *Blue Willow,* was another such child. All too often, schools and teachers tend merely to tolerate them today knowing that they will be gone tomorrow.

Fresno, California has taken a very different point of view. In an unusually impressive little book, *Teaching Children Who Follow the Crops,*[1] teachers are reminded that every day in school for these children is utterly precious. Teachers are asked to have a vacant desk or space ready and an extra pile of the books the children are using so that when a new child appears he can be welcomed with, "Come. We have a place all ready for you. This is your desk and here are your books. Look them through

[1] Published by Fresno County Superintendent of Schools, Fresno, California, 1955.

and find something we can read and talk about together." The child is given materials of several levels so he can find a point in difficulty and in content where he can fit in and begin work. His language experience begins with being assigned a Buddy who will show him the building, introduce him to teachers and children, and be his first friend.

Most of these children are academically behind others of their age. They have had experience in travel and different environments but often without much help with language. They are a special group of the culturally deprived which is growing in size through the years.

☐ THE MENTALLY RETARDED CHILD

The child who is mentally retarded will, almost of necessity, be retarded also in speech. He tends to enter school at approximately the same chronological age as children of normal mentality, but he enters with the handicap of a smaller vocabulary and immature patterns of speech. His usage may be poor and his articulation somewhat infantile, depending upon the extent of his mental retardation and the dialect of his home. Since his mental age is lower than his chronological age it is safe to assume that his language development will be closely related to his mental age. If there is no impairment of his speech mechanism, it is possible for his speech development to follow the sequential pattern of normal children but at a slower rate. Thus, a child with an intelligence quotient of 80 may be eight years in chronological age and six-plus years in mental age, in which case his speech and language development would be assumed to be approximately that of a six-year-old child. Actually, the language development may be even more retarded if the child has suffered neglect or over-protection because of his mental deficiency; also, it may be more highly developed if parental concern has caused him to be given the advantage of skillfully and carefully directed guidance.

The problem of the mentally retarded child is not a remedial one but rather one of additional time to learn and develop. His best sources of help are children who speak better than he and the good example of the teacher. He gains nothing from attempts to force or crowd him and he can develop a sense of inadequacy and inability that will thwart even his best efforts to grow and learn. No matter what his attitude and effort may be, he can progress only so fast as nature has made possible for him.

The best motivation for the slow-learning child is found in natural social situations that call for speech. His desire to participate in the activities of the group keeps him pressing forward. He should be safeguarded from embarrassment and a sense of failure through adjusting what is expected of him to what he is capable of achieving. Children more advanced than he can be taught to accept him as he is and give him sympathetic consideration and help when he needs it, rather than ridicule, avoidance, or ostracism. Through his presence in the group, other children can be taught consideration and thoughtfulness.

The mentally retarded child needs many firsthand experiences. He learns less from books and other forms of vicarious experience than do normal children. Firsthand experiences through school trips and contacts with things and people will help him to build vocabulary of words and meanings, particularly if the words that go with the experiences are used over and over again in many related ways. After having visited a farm with his class he can study pictures of farm life and reinforce his learning through reliving it, whereas the pictures may have been of little learning value to him previous to the experience. The retarded child will learn in the same general manner as normal children but he will reach each stage at a later chronological age, will remain in each stage longer, and will require more experience and more repetitions for learning. He will need a great deal of sympathetic guidance and encouragement to keep him working up to his capacity. Efforts to push him into more rapid learning will only add to his problem because they will destroy his sense of security and undermine his faith in his ability to learn. Without that faith and the self-respect that goes with it, he can achieve very little.

☐ THE CHILD WITH DEFECTIVE SPEECH

The difficulties of children with speech defects are of many sorts: physical, mental, emotional, and social. Many children with speech defects have some physical or physiological problems which cause or contribute to their handicaps. Since speech is the chief avenue of social communication, these children tend to show more psychological and emotional conflicts than any other type of handicapped children. Not only is the child with a speech defect handicapped in normal social intercourse or partially cut off from it, but since his handicap is not obvious like blindness, deafness, or a crippling condition, he tends to receive less sympathy and consideration and may even be blamed for his condition. Actually, the speech defective is no more responsible for his condition than are the others whose handicaps are more apt to excite compassion (1, p. 125).

Every primary grade group is almost certain to include a few children who have retained some infantile forms of speech. That a child continues to use these forms may be due to parental fondness for the last remnants of baby expression, or it may be the result of the fact that the child, as he began to learn to talk, said the forms incorrectly because he did not perceive them accurately and continues to say them because he hears no difference between what he says and what others say. In any case, he has practiced his form for a long time and it is not an easy matter for him to correct it, though he can do so with motivation and guidance. The child who still says "*tat*" for *cat,* "*durl*" for *girl,* and "*yittuh*" for *little* may be perfectly capable of forming the correct sounds if he is given help with perceiving the correct sounds and shown how to manage his speech apparatus to form the sounds. Thereafter his major needs are practice in using the correct sounds wherever they fit and encouragement to put attention and effort into the practice. He needs to be protected from ridicule and encouraged to participate in all types of social contacts with other children.

Simple problems of lisping can usually be taken care of by the classroom teacher through helping the child, perhaps with the aid of a mirror, to understand how to place his tongue and then guiding him in practice. Indistinct and careless speech can be improved through the type of program suggested for all children, though those whose speech is most unsatisfactory may need additional help and practice. Stuttering and stammering are more difficult to deal with because they involve psychological and neurological problems. The services of a speech specialist are needed for diagnosis and therapy. The teacher's co-operation is essential to provide the child the kind of relaxed, unhurried, and happy working conditions and wholesome relationships, both with other children and with the teacher, which are essential to build the sense of security needed by children with these afflictions.

The child who is hard of hearing is almost certain to have

difficulty with speech. There are certain sounds, especially the voiceless consonants such as *s*, *f*, and *h*, that he is most likely to miss or find difficult. Any child who is inattentive, who turns his head as if to hear better, who uses an unusually soft or loud voice, or who does poor work in school should have his hearing checked. Some states, Indiana among them, require periodic hearing tests to locate and measure hearing loss. Children found in need of help should be referred to physicians for medical care if improvement is possible, or taught to read lips, or provided with hearing aids.

Physiological defects such as malformations of the tongue, teeth, lips, palate, roof of the mouth, or vocal cords or nasal obstructions require diagnosis and treatment by a medical specialist. Surgery may be required to put the child's speech mechanism in the best possible working order. Thereafter, treatment by a speech specialist will probably be needed to help the child make the necessary speech adjustments and to re-educate him in speech.

There are many causes of speech defects. Some of these are psychological and some are neurological as well as physical. The services of physicians, surgeons, orthodontists, psychologists, and psychiatrists are needed as well as those of speech experts in order to care for all kinds of cases. Unfortunately a child's problem rarely has a single cause. Physical problems give rise to social and emotional problems, and all together influence mental development.

Neurologists and speech experts call attention to the problem of eye and hand dominance and its relation to speech and reading. There are a number of theories regarding handedness and the proper treatment of the left-handed child. Emotional disturbances are found among children who have been forced to change their hand preference and in some cases this appears to bear a definite relationship to stuttering, awkwardness, and general behavior maladjustments as well as reading disabilities.

Some experts believe that a child has a natural lateral dominance and others that the child is born with no preference but learns to favor and to use one hand more than the other very early in life. Those who hold to the latter theory appear convinced that a child can be taught to use his right hand if training is consistent, carried on in a friendly, helpful manner and without strain, and done before the child has developed habits which must later be broken (8). Orton believes that there are two periods in the life of a child when his natural hand preference must be accepted and in no way tampered with; one is the period when the child is acquiring spoken language, from two to four years of age, and the other the period when the child is learning to read and write at school, probably from six to eight years of age (16).

As opinion stands at the present time, the school is probably wise to permit the child to use the hand he has learned to use in his home and to help him make all the necessary adjustments to learn to write and read from left to right, which is the reverse of the natural process for the left-handed child.

Turner found that among adolescents, those who were emotionally unstable tended to show less clear preference for the use of eye, hand, and foot than did the more stable young people. It is conceded that the language function is tied up in one hemisphere of the brain of each individual and that is the hemisphere opposite the dominant hand. Children without distinct dominance may therefore be confused at many points and find many types of learning somewhat more difficult.

The intelligence level of many children who have speech defects falls below average, though by no means all speech defect cases are cases of low intelligence. The factors that influence a child's growth are so interrelated and interwoven that anything which causes retardation at one point may cause retardation at others also. For this reason, many children with physical or developmental handicaps of any sort tend to have problems with educational achievement, both because attention must be divided between their many conflicting needs and because the handicap limits their range of experience.

Children with speech handicaps frequently develop personality problems which are in themselves handicaps. The defeat and frustration they experience in their desire to communicate may result in seriously withdrawn behavior or, at the other extreme, in highly aggressive behavior. In either case, improvement in ability to communicate may help to solve behavior problems. This was true in the case of Howie, a well-developed and fine appearing boy who was enrolled in the kindergarten of a demonstration school in order to have special speech training. Physicians found his hearing loss so great that it was impossible for him to learn speech through the usual process of imitation and his vision problem so serious that he was fitted with very thick lenses. During his early weeks in the kindergarten Howie required constant watching because his inability to communicate caused him to respond like an enraged animal when other children reached for blocks he considered his property or got in the way of his interests. Through daily work with a speech teacher, Howie learned to speak well enough to make his wishes and feelings known; and when a hearing device was used, his progress was very rapid. Since he was to return at the end of the year to his home in a small town where there was no available speech clinician, it was deemed wise to attempt to teach some reading, even though Howie was not yet quite old enough for first grade. His progress in learning to read was very rapid from the moment his alert and hungry mind sensed that here was another means of communication through which he could make contacts and expand his knowledge and interests. His problems of behavior smoothed out as his skill in speech and lip reading grew until his aggressiveness became limited very largely to a drive to experience and to learn.

Since the area of speech has many facets and the literature dealing with speech improvement is extensive and valuable, several references are included at the end of the chapter. It is impossible to do more than touch upon some of the aspects of speech within the limitations of this book.

☐ OTHER PHYSICAL HANDICAPS AND THEIR EFFECT UPON LANGUAGE DEVELOPMENT

The problems of the child with a hearing loss have been touched upon in the preceding section. Such a child needs physical diagnosis and treatment, if he can profit by it. Since he is cut off from normal social intercourse, he needs help with making social contacts and finding a place in a social group. He needs firsthand experience, wherever that is possible, and every opportunity to enrich his stock of words and meanings. He will need special consideration from both teacher and children in order to achieve the language development he needs. He should be placed in a favorable position for hearing, at all times, and both children and teacher will need to give thought to him so that he is given opportunity to hear, where that is possible, or to read the lips of speakers. Children and teacher will need to learn to talk directly to him and to speak clearly and distinctly. The child, through his training in lip reading and also his work in the class, needs to learn to give attention to facial expression and gestures as well as the movement of lips, in order to gain meaning. He needs to learn to make his vision compensate in part for his lack of hearing. Visual methods can be used in many instances in teaching him.

The child who has poor vision finds the world a confusing place filled with dim, blurred images. He needs skilled medical diagnosis and treatment as well as skilled educational treatment. As is the case with the child who has poor hearing, he needs help with making social contacts and learning how to participate in social groups. He can be taught where to sit in order to see as well as possible, how to adjust materials and learning situations to his needs, and how to protect the very precious vision which he has. Through the use of well-adjusted lighting and sight-saving materials, if he needs them, he can be taught to read and write without endangering his vision.

Again, training in compensation is necessary. A child with poor vision can be taught to compensate for a portion of his loss through development of the senses of hearing and touch. He should be permitted to handle materials and learn through tactile sense impressions whenever that is possible. Other children can be taught to explain and demonstrate and help the child learn through means other than vision. Oral teaching should be used wherever possible.

Children who are restricted as to locomotion or suffer other muscular or movement restrictions will need to be taught to make adjustments as well as have adjustments made for them in the carrying on of the school program. This will be true also of children with low physical vitality and of those whose health is precarious for any reason. Any physical handicap which keeps a child from playing and working freely with other children and prevents his exploring and experiencing in the countless ways children employ, limits the child's opportunity to develop language because the experience background essential to language growth is missing. Whenever this is true, the child may be immature in his responses and interests and may be operating below the level of his mental capacity. If his physical condition warrants his being in school, adjustments can be made to take care of his need for rest and for protection from overstimulation and overexertion so that he can participate in the learning experiences he needs.

These children may have no serious speech problem but only

the retarded development that has resulted from their need for special physical care and protection. In school, as well as at home, the physical needs come first and the learning experiences can be made as valuable as possible without endangering the child's health.

All children who are physically handicapped need, more than anything else, to be encouraged to live as normally as their handicaps permit. They should be helped to recognize their limitations, accept them, and co-operate with the teacher to gain the greatest possible value from learning situations in the school. If morale can be kept high and self-confidence developed and maintained, they can find happiness in growing and learning.

During the last decade, educators and others have become aware of the existence in the schools of brain-damaged children. With this recognition is the need for meeting the individual needs of these children through better program planning. There have always been some of these children in the schools but until recently they have not been studied in depth. Usually, for lack of recognition, they have been relegated to special education classes where they have been complete misfits.

A review of the present literature relative to the identification and rehabilitation of the brain-damaged child brings to light a massive quantity of material – more than 20,000 articles. These have been written by people studying the problem from various points of view, particularly medicine, psychiatry, and education, and using different terminology, all of which is confusing but points the way toward solutions of some of the problems.

The diagnosing of brain damage is a complicated process because it must take into account such factors as clinical behavior, history, neurological signs and findings. These factors must be evaluated in the light of the child's background, environment, and inter-personal behavior.

A basic characteristic of these children is retardation in learning to read. Behaviorally, they are usually hyperactive, have a short attention span, tend to perseverate – to repeat an action or idea through inability to shift readily from one activity to another – and they are easily distracted. Educators, psychiatrists, pediatricians, and ophthalmologists are becoming involved in studying and evaluating the brain-damaged child, noting all pertinent information before estimating the child's potentialities for development and charting a plan for rehabilitation.

☐ THE PROBLEM OF A FOREIGN LANGUAGE

In the early period of life in this country, English was the language used in most American homes. During the past hundred years the immigration has been largely from northern and then southern Europe, from areas where other languages are spoken. The end of World War II brought to the United States many European immigrants who knew little or no English. There continues to be heavy migration of people from Puerto Rico, Cuba, Mexico, and other Latin American countries into our urban and industrial areas. In many school systems, the proportion of children from homes where a foreign language is used almost exclusively or where children are exposed to two languages has increased. See pp. 470–472 in Chapter 19.

Learning one language is a difficult developmental task for any child, but learning two languages during the first few years is more than twice as difficult. The child who has learned only a foreign language in his home or has learned two languages starts school with at least a temporary language handicap. If he has learned only a foreign language, he stands out as different from the other children and is unable to communicate with them. Unless there are children who speak his language in his home or neighborhood for him to play with, he has probably had almost no contacts with children and is shy and lacking in ability to play with children at all. His language has been a barrier to social contact and he may already have encountered enough ostracism or teasing and ridicule to feel self-conscious and inferior, or at least different from other children. Such weapons do not depend entirely upon language; a child can sense their import even though he cannot understand any of the words through which they are expressed. The foreign-speaking child needs to learn as rapidly as he can enough English to enable him to enter into the life of the classroom and to be ready to begin work on the symbol forms of the language used in reading and writing. If he has natural aptitude for language he will learn the language of his school environment rapidly because the children as well as the teacher will be his resources for learning.

A child who has used a foreign language in his home but has

learned some English outside it will present a different type of problem. If he has been so fortunate as to live in a community where his neighbors speak English well, he will have made a good beginning in learning English. For economic or social reasons or both, foreign families tend to live in less favored neighborhoods, especially when they first come to this country. The probability is that the English the child has learned is poor in usage and he has much to unlearn as well as more to learn. He may be confusing the two languages unless he has learned to associate one with certain individuals and situations and the other with other people and situations. Using more than one language with the same individual appears to be confusing to a child until he has attained some mastery of both languages. Both this child and the one who has learned only the foreign language need many social experiences, good language example, and a great deal of time and patience while they learn to speak the language of the school.

These children need many firsthand experiences with all sorts of common situations in order to learn the vocabulary associated with them. They need to play house, visit grocery stores, cook, have tea parties, visit American homes, go to see a farm, watch construction projects, and do any and all of the common things which are dealt with in children's early readers and other textbooks. They need to hear over and over again the words associated with these activities, to associate them with pictures, hear them in stories, and use them in countless ways. Dramatic play is one of the child's best methods of learning if talking accompanies it at many points. Pictures of familiar activities can be used as talking material; often the pictures in preprimers and other introductory books can be used for this purpose without emphasis on reading. The child needs a great many opportunities to hear English spoken in situations where the meaning and usage are clear. Usually speaking the language should precede attempts to learn to read or write it. Children who speak acceptable English can be taught to include the child in their activities and to help him at every opportunity.

While, ideally, learning to speak the English language should precede learning to read and write it, this is not always possible. The great influx of Cubans into the Miami and Dade County area of Florida has made it necessary for the schools to devise ways of teaching children to read and write English who are now learning to speak it. New York City has a similar problem with its Puerto Rican children, and there is a sprinkling of the problem in other cities.

Where there are a number of children in a classroom who speak the same foreign language it is sometimes difficult to get them to make enough use of the English they are learning in school to master it. A teacher of Mexican children once exclaimed in frustration, "How are we going to make these children stop using Mexican on the playground and everywhere else outside of school and make them practice their English!" It is impossible to force such children to practice outside of school what they see little use for, or use too poorly to enjoy using. The teacher's problem is to find as many uses as possible for their English so that they gain power and satisfaction in the use of it. She must also, at all times, respect the language of the child's home.

Sometimes a way to motivate interest in the new language of the school is to express real interest in the child's home language. Letting him teach other children a song in his language or tell them how certain things are said in that language helps him to understand the sincere respect the teacher and the group feel for this other language. This, in itself, is often motivation for increased effort to add the school language to his repertoire so that he can use both as they serve his purposes. For further discussion, see Chapter 19.

☐ SELECTED REFERENCES ☐

1. Barbe, Walter B., *The Exceptional Child.* The Center for Applied Research in Education, Inc., Washington, D.C.: 1963, pp. 78-85.
2. Black, Millard H., "Characteristics of the Culturally Disadvantaged," *The Reading Teacher* 18:465-470, March, 1965.
3. Bower, E. M., *Early Identification of Emotionally Handicapped Children in School.* Springfield, Illinois: Charles C. Thomas, 1960.
4. Crosby, Muriel, "Living Language," *Childhood Education,* Vol. 42, November, 1965.
5. Davis, Allison, "Teaching Language and Reading to Disadvantaged Negro Children," *Elementary English* 42:791-7, November, 1965.
6. Delacato, Carl H., *The Diagnosis and Treatment of Speech*

and Reading Problems. Springfield, Illinois: Charles C. Thomas, 1963.
7. Deutsch, Martin, "The Role of Social Class in Language Development and Cognition," *American Journal of Orthopsychiatry* 35:78-87, January, 1965.
8. Dunn, Lloyd M., Editor, *Exceptional Children in the Schools.* New York: Holt, Rinehart and Winston, Inc., 1963.
9. Eisenson, Jon, and Ogilvie, Mardel, *Speech Correction in the Schools.* New York: Macmillan Company, 1957.
10. Heck, Arch O., *The Education of Exceptional Children: Its Challenge to Teachers, Parents, Laymen.* New York: McGraw-Hill Book Company, Inc., 1953.
11. Hildreth, Gertrude H., and others, *Educating Gifted Children.* New York: Harper and Brothers, 1952.
12. Jensen, J. Vernon, "Effects of Childhood Bilingualism" *Elementary English* 39:132-143, February, 1962, and 39:358-366, April, 1962.
13. Kirk, Samuel A., and Johnson, G. O., *Educating the Retarded Child.* Boston: Houghton Mifflin Co., 1951.
14. La Brant, Lou, "The Relations of Language and Speech Acquisitions to Personality Development." *Mental Hygiene in Modern Education.* Paul Witty and Charles E. Skinner (Eds.). New York: Farrar & Rinehart, Ind., 1939, Chap. XII, pp. 324-352.
15. Loban, Walter, "What Language Reveals," in *Language and Meaning,* pp. 63-73, Association for Supervision and Curriculum Development, N.E.A., 1966.
16. Mulgrave, Dorothy I., *Speech for the Classroom Teacher* (Rev.). (3rd Ed.). New York: Prentice-Hall, Inc., 1955.
17. National Society for the Study of Education, *The Education of Exceptional Children.* The Forty-Ninth Yearbook, Part II. Chicago: University of Chicago Press, 1950.
18. Newton, Eunice, "The Culturally Deprived Child in our Verbal Schools," *Journal of Negro Education* 31:184-7, Spring, 1962.
19. Orton, Samuel Torrey, *Reading, Writing, and Speech Problems in Children.* New York: W. W. Norton and Co., Inc., 1961.
20. Smith, Madorah, "Progress in the Use of English after Twenty-Two Years by Children of Chinese Ancestry in Honolulu." *The Journal of Genetic Psychology* 9:255-258, June, 1957.
21. Stevens, Godfrey, and Birch, Jack W., "A Proposal for the Classification of the Terminology Used to Describe Brain-Injured Children." In *The Exceptional Child,* edited by James F. Mogary and John H. Eichorn. New York: Holt, Rinehart and Winston, 1960, p. 148.
22. Strickland, Ruth G., *English Is Our Language: Guide for*

Teaching Grades I and II. Boston: D. C. Heath and Co., 1950.

23. Werry, J. S., and Weiss, G. and Douglass, V., "Studies on the Hyperactive Child, I. Some Preliminary Findings" *Canadian Psychiatric Association Journal*. 9:120-130, April, 1964.
24. Witty, Paul (Chrm.), *Mental Health in the Classroom*. Thirteenth Yearbook of the Department of Supervisors and Directors of Instruction, National Education Association. Washington, D.C.: The Association, 1941.
25. Zintz, Miles V., "Problems of Classroom Adjustment of Indian Children in Public Elementary Schools in the Southwest," *Science Education* 46:261-9, April, 1962.

Vocabulary

Since Shakespeare's time, the number of words in the English language has increased from 140,000 to somewhere between 700,000 and 800,000. While English has borrowed many words in the past and is still borrowing, most of this addition has come from the natural growth of the language and the rearrangement and adaptation of elements already in it (5, p. 5). The rapid expansion of knowledge and experience will continue to require the invention of new words and the adaptation of old ones. Evans says,

> If a contemporary Rip Van Winkle had slept for 40 years and awakened today, he would have to go back to school before he could read a daily paper or a magazine. He would never have heard of atomic bombs or babysitters, of coffee breaks, contact lenses or flying saucers – nor of eggheads, mambo or microfilm, nylons, neptunium, parking meters or smog.

All of these words and far more have been added in the lifetime of great numbers of present-day adults but added so gradually and naturally that people are unaware of the total numerical extent of the accumulation. Many a newly coined word fits a need so admirably that it is easily absorbed into the language of its users to be spoken and written at will. The adult who has a variety of interests continuously adds to his vocabulary.

Children amass an amazing number of words during their preschool years. These are words to which they can attach meaning; they are a part of the listening and understanding vocabulary though the child may not use anywhere nearly all of them in his speech. Many words and meanings that are strikingly new to adults are as at home in the vocabularies of children as the commonest words of the language. The word "capsule" has a new and discrete meaning for adults as the vehicle of the astronauts, but this may be the only concept for the word in the minds of many children. Such words as "auxiliary" and "orbit" would, until recently, have been considered far beyond the range of children's vocabulary, yet both words are meaningful to all children who watched the space flights, saw the action of the auxiliary rockets, and listened to the anxious discussion of the number of orbits accomplished. Our present word lists, valuable as they are for basic vocabulary of words, do not include many words that are freely used by children.

A study by Evans presents interesting proof of this fact. She tested 225 sixth grade children to determine how many they knew of a ten percent sample of the 4000 addends in the 1959 reprint of the second edition of Webster's New International Dictionary of the English Language. Of the words in her sample, 63.6 percent were new words, 32 percent were words with new meanings, and 4.25 percent were acronyms. The sixth grade population as a whole recognized and comprehended slightly more than half of the sample of 400 words added to the dictionary between 1934 and 1959.[1] How much better a similar population of adults might have done is a question. This is indeed evidence that new words are a part of the experience of today's children.

Every individual has not one but several vocabularies. They merge, of course, and are used in a variety of ways, but just as a bilingual child learns to put forth, almost automatically, only the language that is called for by the situation, so all mature individuals learn to fit the use of their vocabulary to their concept of situation and need. Pooley calls attention to the fact that ceremonial distinctions in language are found in even the most primitive societies where the language of the council fire or religious ceremony differs in vocabulary and tone from that of the hunt or the harvest (18). In our society, we distinguish three or more levels of language usage which we employ almost unconsciously. There is the informal speech of the more intimate life of the home and the hours of recreation with people whom we feel no need to impress. There is the somewhat more restrained speech of conversation with strangers or of public occasions and professional relationships. And there is also the deliberate, carefully chosen language of address used on formal occasions. Parallel types are found in writing in the informal letters to one's family and intimate friends; in the report or business letter which requires more precise and ordered expression; and in the formal paper prepared for publication, particularly in a scholarly journal. It is also true, as Pooley points out, that business and professional people tend to employ a technical or specialized vocabulary in communicating with colleagues of like background and interests which would not be

[1] Mildred W. Evans. An Investigation of Sixth Grade Pupils' Comprehension of a Sample of the Four Thousand Addends to the 1959 Printing of the Second Edition of Webster's New International Dictionary of the English Language. Unpublished paper. Indiana University, 1967.

easily understood by people less well acquainted with the field.

☐ VARIOUS TYPES OF VOCABULARIES

Every individual who is literate has several overlapping and somewhat interwoven vocabularies. The commonest words of the language appear in all of them. Some words are used informally in some settings and more formally in others, while other words are restricted to certain types of situations. The number of words an individual recognizes and comprehends is undoubtedly greater than the number he has occasion to use in any form other than perhaps in reading. The types of vocabulary which need to be considered in educating a child can be discussed under four headings:

1. Understanding vocabulary
   - Listening: the words recognized and comprehended through listening
   - Reading: the words recognized and comprehended through reading
2. Speaking vocabulary
   - Informal: the words used in the process of everyday living
   - Formal: the reservoir of words the individual understands and can draw upon when the occasion calls for them
3. Writing vocabulary
   - Informal: the words used in personal correspondence, notes and memoranda, and personal diaries
   - Formal: the words used in more formal correspondence, business and professional material, and for publication
4. Potential, or marginal, vocabulary
   - Context: words which could be interpreted from context
   - Analysis: words which could be interpreted because of knowledge of word form (prefixes, suffixes, roots) and because of knowledge of other languages

■ *Understanding vocabulary*—One understands a large number of words which he encounters through the eye in reading or through the ear in listening. An individual's reading vocabulary is the vocabulary he can respond to in reading through recognition of the word and comprehension of its meaning. Reading is not only recognition of words but it involves also getting meaning from the recognized pattern of symbols on a page. One can gain meaning from symbols only if he can bring meaning to the recognition of those symbols. The meaning lies in the mind of the reader. It is likewise true that one recognizes and understands words he hears spoken. Those also carry meaning for him if there is meaning in his own mind which can be attached to or associated with the sounds he hears uttered. In both reading and listening, some word meanings can be gained from the context in which they appear even though the reader or listener has never encountered them before and might not know them otherwise. There are also words which can be interpreted because their form is similar to known words or involves new combinations of known forms. Seegers calls this vocabulary which has not been learned but could be interpreted through content or form *potential* or *marginal* vocabulary. It will not need to be taught or learned in order to be recognized in situations of use (27).

An individual's reading and understanding vocabulary usually is larger than his writing vocabulary. Only a portion of the words one may later write are included in the spelling vocabulary taught in the schools. Everyone learns some spelling through reading but the amount learned through associations built up in reading differs greatly with individuals. An occasional person files away a mental image of the words he has read and can spell each of them thereafter. The majority of people lack such clear visual imagery and some gain relatively little spelling without more concentration on the form of a word and the elements that make it up than they give to it in the course of reading. The inability to spell words needed only occasionally is compensated for by the development of skill in use of a dictionary, though the greater one's independence of the reference book the greater his ease and fluency in writing. There are undoubtedly words which are needed more frequently in writing than in reading, but these would be relatively few in number.

The extent of the vocabulary one responds to through listening is also large. With children it undoubtedly exceeds the size of the reading vocabulary and forms the basis for the reading vocabulary. Unless the child has at least heard a word and learned to associate meaning with it he finds difficulty in learning to read it. This accounts in part for the difficulty children have in learning to recognize certain types of abstract and unpicturable words in learning to read. A child learns to recognize such words as *dog, car, train, little,* and *pretty* fairly easily. He can respond to the first three with mental images and emotionalized reaction; he likes a car, a dog, and a train. He can also respond to the words *little* and *pretty* because, while they have in each instance to be associated with some object they describe, at least he has feeling and meaning reactions to them in any situation in which they appear. Words like *what, which,* and *once,* on the other hand, are difficult for many children to learn to read. It is true that they have heard the sounds many times in various contexts but when the word is pulled out of context for recognition purposes there is no mental or emotional image upon which to tie it. A child cannot think a *what* or a *which* or a *once.* Those are among the links that hold sentences together and shape them into a pattern, but they have little individuality in the mind of a child.

Words dealing with abstractions are among the last that a child learns to recognize and speak because the concepts that go with them require a degree of maturity which is attained slowly. A child can at least partially understand words like *love, punctuality,* and *friendship* before he can understand the word *patriotism,* because the former can be associated with concrete persons and situations while the latter must remain more nearly a purely intellectual concept.

In any case, the learning of words and word meanings tends to be done on the oral level at first. Only after one has learned to read and has read a good deal can he begin to gain new concepts and new words directly from print without having had other experience with them first.

■ *Speaking vocabulary*—The average individual's speaking vocabulary tends to be quite different from his reading vocabulary. It is informal and utilizes a good many words seldom found in reading material. This informal vocabulary includes many contractions such as *won't* and *couldn't* and also the whole vocabulary of homely words used in the process of daily living. It includes the family modes of expression and the family words and idioms with their peculiar meaning. Children learn to distinguish between family expressions and those used outside the family. Many expressions are only used within a family group.

The child's oral vocabulary is of first importance in the elementary school because it forms the basis for the development of the reading and writing vocabularies. Children need guidance to add new words to their vocabularies but also need experience, in quantity, to deepen and enrich the meaning values of the words they have partially learned. The more numerous the experiences the richer will be the meaning values of these words.

As children grow and develop, they add to their potential speaking vocabulary words which they seldom use but which they can use if occasion demands them. The mature, well-educated adult can use in his formal speech any vocabulary he can respond to in reading. On formal occasions he is not limited to the speech of daily living but goes beyond it to any type of specialized vocabulary—scientific, literary, or otherwise—which the occasion demands. Not only does the educated person draw upon a wide vocabulary for more formal occasions but he also refines his usage to fit the more imposing occasion. The person of lesser ability who operates on a lower linguistic level would find it impossible to enter into some types of language situations because his language has not developed beyond the informal home-and-family-living level.

■ *Writing vocabulary*—The writing vocabulary of an adult may include, at least potentially, all of the words he knows in reading as well as all of the words he uses in speech. If he is a capable and experienced writer he spells most words automatically, and for any that he is less sure of he has techniques for using the dictionary and other guides economically and resourcefully. Most individuals, however, use a comparatively small proportion of this potential in their actual writing even though studies have shown that adults use different words in writing from the ones they use in speaking. Children, on the other hand, use fewer words in writing than in speaking.

The words children use in their writing depend entirely upon the stimulus. They will attempt to write and spell many words they have not been taught, if there is adequate motivation. They may be able to write some which they do not speak. Because this is true, it is impossible to get an accurate count of the number of words a child can write. The child writing to thank a relative for a gift may work out his own phonetic spelling of unlearned words which he wants to use. Probably one important caution to teachers is to avoid making spelling a clear-cut matter of right and wrong at first. A young child attempting to spell a word may start the word correctly, or may spell some portions of it correctly, and be stimulated to further effort by commendation for a good try but discouraged by the arbitrariness of the teacher's red-penciled markings which condemn the whole effort because a portion of it is wrong. An individual's writing vocabulary, as well as other aspects of his vocabulary, tends to grow throughout life. The school does not serve as the child's only teacher, though it is responsible for both motivation and a good foundation.

■ *Potential or marginal vocabulary*—The potential vocabulary of an individual includes all the words he could interpret because of his background of knowledge and experience with other words. Some of the potential vocabulary can be interpreted because of the context in which it is used. If one has studied prefixes, suffixes, and roots, the potential area includes a good many words. Knowledge of other languages, particularly Latin, enlarges the potential vocabulary. Some studies have thrown a little light on this aspect, though it is impossible to actually measure potential vocabulary (26).

□ STUDIES OF SIZE OF VOCABULARY AT DIFFERENT AGES

The extent of a child's vocabulary at any age depends upon a number of factors. Obviously, the quicker the mind the more words the child will learn. The majority of intelligence tests tend to be largely language tests. They test both native intelligence and learned responses. A child is dependent upon opportunity and experience in the learning of language. Harry, the son of parents of low mentality, had an exceptionally meager vocabulary on entrance into school, but the speed with which he acquired new concepts and new vocabulary indicated ability to learn. The child had acquired all the vocabulary that was available to him in his meager environment and all that his preschool experience afforded. When more was available he absorbed it readily. An intelligence test, administered when Harry entered school, would have shown an exceedingly low mental age. A few months of enriched experiences and careful attention to the growth of vocabulary through those experiences brought about rapid mental development. Native capacity and environmental experience both play a part in vocabulary development but the child is dependent upon opportunity and experience, regardless of his capacity. In this realm, environment and experience appear to have the greater influence, since a child with a slow-learning mind may gain proportionately more vocabulary in a privileged environment than can the child of good ability in a seriously restricted environment.

Many people have studied the growth of vocabulary in comparatively recent years. Parents have recorded the early vocabulary growth of their own children, and a number of researchers have made studies of the vocabulary of various groups of children in order to determine the extent of vocabulary at different age levels and the rate at which children acquire vocabulary. All research in vocabulary development encounters certain practical difficulties. It is not too difficult for an adult living in constant contact with a small child to record each new word the child uses. Serious difficulties arise when the vocabulary total becomes unwieldy, especially when the child begins to spend a portion of his life apart from the adult and is subject to influences the adult cannot follow or control. Studies of the vocabulary of children beyond the home years are based on samples of vocabulary. Here the conclusions reached depend upon:

1. The group selected for study. There is evidence that socio-economic level, background of experience, the place of the child in the family constellation, and a variety of other factors influence the findings with regard to vocabulary.
2. The methods used for determining whether or not a child *knows* a word. Should the criterion be ability to define the word, or is it sufficient for him to demonstrate some knowledge of the word by pointing to a picture or selecting one item from a multiple choice list? Should he know various shades of meaning and be able to use the word in a variety of types of sentences, or is success at one point satisfactory?
3. The way in which the examiner defines a *word* as a unit of measurement. Shall all the forms of the word *walk* be counted as one word or shall *walk, walked, walking*

be counted as three words? Is the word *spring* a single word or shall *spring* meaning the season, *spring* meaning to leap up, *spring* meaning a bubbling fountain of water coming from the earth, and *spring* meaning the mechanical device used in the upholstering of a chair or a car be counted as four separate words? Certainly, from the teaching point of view, *bear* meaning an animal, *bear* meaning carry, and *bear* meaning tolerate are three distinctly different words. Thorndike, in his *Teacher's Word Book*, treated each of these words with its various forms and meanings as one word (36). More recent studies have considered the matter of semantics and counted each separate meaning as a separate word.

4. Whether the vocabulary studied is a vocabulary of use or of understanding. Some studies record the words actually used under certain circumstances or in a certain setting, while other studies sample a wide vocabulary to test children's understanding of it.
5. The method of selecting the sample of words for a vocabulary test. Samples taken from word lists or from the dictionary have been selected by a systematic sampling method – the first word on alternate pages, or some such plan. It appears true that the larger the dictionary used for the selecting of a sample the greater the proportion of commonly used words and words which have a variety of meanings. Smaller dictionaries allot relatively less space to these words. The sampling method used by Seashore and his co-workers which utilized an unabridged dictionary probably gives a more accurate estimate of vocabulary size than studies which drew their sample from a smaller total list.

☐ STUDIES OF THE VOCABULARY OF PRESCHOOL CHILDREN

There have been many studies of the language growth of preschool children. Since this is the period during which the child acquires a working command of the common words needed in everyday living, any study of language development is in a sense a study of vocabulary. Probably the best known and most important studies which have been made are these:

Mary M. Shirley (30) studied the language growth of twenty-five babies from birth to two years of age. Observations were made at frequent intervals during the early weeks and less frequently during succeeding weeks. The most important points from her study are presented in Chapter 4.

Madorah E. Smith (31) studied the total vocabulary of children from one to six years of age by recording sentences spoken and by testing through the use of objects, pictures, and questions. Her figures have been quoted by many writers and appear on page 78 in Chapter 4. This study, made in 1926, was the first serious attempt to devise a vocabulary test for young children.

Madeline Darrough Horn and the Child Study Committee of the International Kindergarten Union (11) studied the vocabulary of normal children before entering first grade. The words listed were obtained from three sources: words used by children in kindergarten, words children used when stimulated by pictures, and words children used in the home. This study, reported in 1928, has been used in various ways by teachers, textbook writers, makers of tests, and mothers in the home guidance of their children during forty years since its publication. It lists 2,596 words in the order of frequency of use in the records gathered from the three sources. This study is still valuable though there is little doubt that in the intervening years children of this age have added many other words to their use vocabularies through contact with radio, motion pictures, television, and other more recent sources of stimulation and experience.

Clifford J. Kolson utilized techniques similar to Horn's in his 1960 study of the vocabulary of kindergarten children. He found the vocabulary of the children in his study to be 3,728 words in contrast to Horn's 2,596 words. In both studies, these were words actually used by the children under certain circumstances and in certain home and school settings. It was interesting to note that 97 per cent of the vocabulary of the schools' beginning basal readers appeared in this sample of the words used by the children (11, 13).

These studies deal with extent of vocabulary in relation to age. Other studies have dealt with proportion of the various parts of speech found in children's vocabularies, with the relationships of vocabulary to the child's loquacity, and with the length of the verbal responses children use and the evidence of language growth found in these factors. An interesting study made by Shirley in 1938 dealt with the concepts known to children from two to five years of age. Verbatim records were made for 336 children during play periods of 30 to 45 minutes. It was found that the most common concepts dealt with mother, home, father, and siblings. At least half the concepts recorded seemed to arise out of the common needs of children. The study calls attention to the importance of the function of language to express wants, desires, and feelings (29).

☐ STUDIES OF THE VOCABULARY OF SCHOOL CHILDREN

Some of the more recent studies have indicated vocabularies, at all grade levels, far greater than the earlier estimates. The most significant of the studies are the two which follow.

> Rinsland (19) studied children's writing vocabularies. He analyzed over 100,000 papers written by school children in grades one through eight, a total of more than 6,000,000 running words, and found the writing vocabularies at the various grade levels to yield the following totals:

GRADES							
1	2	3	4	5	6	7	8
DIFFERENT WORDS							
5,099	5,821	8,976	9,976	11,449	11,304	14,820	17,930

(19, p. 12)

> In this study, roots, derived forms, abbreviations, and contractions were all listed as separate words. Only baby talk, slang, provincialisms, colloquial expressions, trade names, and proper names, except very well-known terms, were deleted. Letters, expositions, original stories, poems, examination papers, and other materials were sent in from schools all over the United States, supplemented by records of conversations of first grade children.

> Mary Katherine Smith (32) used a test devised by Seashore

and Eckerson, administering the test to the first twelve grades. The test used a systematic sample taken from an unabridged dictionary, in this case the third word down from the top of the left-hand column of every eighth page. This gave a total of 331 basic words. The results of the test are given in terms of basic words and derivative words (22, p. 4).

TABLE TWO

Vocabulary figures taken by Seashore from the study of the vocabularies of public school children by Mary Katherine Smith

Grade	Basic	Derived	Total
1	16,900	7,100	24,000
2	22,000	12,000	34,000
3	26,000	18,000	44,000
4	26,200	18,800	45,000
5	28,500	22,500	51,000
6	31,500	18,000	49,500
7	35,000	20,000	55,000
8	36,000	20,000	56,000
9	38,500	24,000	62,500
10	40,200	27,300	67,500
11	43,500	29,500	73,000
12	46,500	33,500	80,000

The average growth in total is approximately 5000 words per year from the first through the twelfth grades. The proportion of derivative words in the entire vocabulary increases greatly through the years, from about 30 per cent in first grade to about 60 per cent in college. Seashore and Eckerson carried the study on to the college level and found in three universities an average vocabulary on the part of students of 61,000 basic words, plus 96,000 derivative words, or a total of 157,000 words (22).

Burleigh H. Shibles repeated in 1959 the tests used by Smith and found the total understanding vocabulary of first graders even higher, 18,924 basic words, 7,438 derived words, and a total of 26,363 words (28).

The studies by Smith and Shibles were studies of understanding vocabulary and Rinsland's study was of writing vocabulary. At the first grade level, these figures far exceed those of Kolson at the kindergarten level, depending presumably on sampling and other experimental techniques.

These studies give much larger and probably much more accurate estimates of the vocabulary children understand and can use than any of the earlier studies or than that of Kolson. Writing vocabularies are much smaller than understanding vocabularies but they, too, are far larger than earlier estimates. Too much of the writing done by children in the traditional school is limited to assignment and prescription which give children little or no opportunity to indicate what words they might like to write or might be able to write if they were encouraged to write what they chose upon topics which really interested them. The restrictions placed about the writing were often similar to the one imposed by an inexperienced student teacher in a second grade who told the group to use, in the letters they were eager to write, only words they were sure they could spell. The children's vocabulary of words they were sure they could spell was so limited that the entire group was reduced in a very few minutes to using their pencils for chewing rather than writing. When they were offered help with spelling words they did not know, they returned to the writing with evidence of great relief. There was no lack of words to express their ideas but the teacher-imposed restriction cut off the flow of words.

□ WORD LISTS USEFUL TO ELEMENTARY TEACHERS

There are several word lists which are useful to elementary teachers even though they are not, for the most part, studies of the actual vocabulary of elementary school children. They are useful as check lists in the teaching of spelling and in the selection of basic reading vocabulary. The most valuable of these are listed by Russell (20, pp. 192, 193).

Buckingham and Dolch (1), in *A Combined Word List,* combine and show the overlapping of eleven word-count studies. This is one of the most useful of the lists of frequently used words.

Dolch (3) in the chapter on "Sight Vocabulary" in his book, *Teaching Primary Reading,* gives two word lists. One is a list of 220 words, omitting nouns, that are highly useful as a basic sight vocabulary; the other is a list of

95 commonly used nouns. This is a useful check list for remedial work and for work with slow-learning children.

Fitzgerald (7), in an article in *Elementary School Journal*, "The Vocabulary of Children's Letters Written in Life Outside the School," gives a list that may serve as a guide in the teaching of spelling.

Gates (8) studied the hard spots in common words. His book, *A List of Spelling Difficulties in 3876 Words*, indicates also the grade level at which various percentages of children knew the meaning of the words on a multiple-choice test.

Gates (9), in his *A Reading Vocabulary for the Primary Grades*, lists approximately 1800 words which should ordinarily appear in the basic reading vocabulary of the primary grades. This has been widely used as a check list in the preparation of textbooks for the primary grades.

Horn (10) was a pioneer in the preparation of word lists. *A Basic Writing Vocabulary*, while it was published in 1926, is still valuable. It contains 10,000 words commonly written by adults and would therefore be more valuable for older children.

Rinsland's study (19) has been mentioned earlier. His publication, *A Basic Vocabulary of Elementary School Children*, lists over 25,000 words and gives, by grade levels, the frequency of occurrence of each in children's writing.

Stone's Graded Vocabulary for Primary Reading (33) lists 2164 words selected from those appearing most frequently in twenty-one each of pre-primers, primers, first readers, second readers, and third readers published between 1931 and 1941. The words are graded into ten reading levels.

Thorndike and Lorge (35) in *The Teacher's Word Book of 30,000 Words* extend the well-known word lists from the 10,000 published in 1921 and the 20,000 published in 1932 to 30,000 words. This volume lists words in terms of their frequency as found in 1,000,000 running words and in 4,000,000 running words. Thorndike studied a wide sampling of adult writing including juvenile books. One needs to remember in using this list that these words were not actually used by children. The list does not include derivatives and it treats such a word as *bear* or *spring* as a single word without any reference to differences in meaning.

It is worth while to note what word lists do *not* tell us as well as the uses to which they can be put. They tell us the frequency of use of words but give no evidence of degree of difficulty for children to learn, understand, and use. Lists cannot tell us what words children *should use.* Children should learn and use the words they need in their situation. The tasks of teaching are to provide children with a rich variety of learning experiences and help them acquire the words they need to use in connection with those learning experiences. It will probably never be possible to prescribe the order in which children shall learn the words of the English language.

☐ SEMANTICS

The term *semantics* has come into common use among students of language in fairly recent years. It deals with meanings and their evolution in language. Interest in semantics grows out of the realization that a large number of words have many meanings and that meanings change with the evolution of thinking. Children come upon new meanings for words they recognize and find it impossible to make sense of what is heard or read because they cannot fit the meanings they know for the word into the context in which the children find it. Children must learn that *fair* does not always mean "just," the meaning they have probably learned first. They must also attach meaning to it in such word patterns as "a fair-haired child," "a fair day," "going to a fair," and "a fair piece of work"—meanings only moderately clear.

The number of concepts children are expected to acquire is far greater than the number of separate words they need to learn to read, write, understand, and speak.

In addition to the problem of the meanings found in a dictionary for a single word, words have special meanings for individuals as a result of their own experiences. Almost everyone can list certain names he likes or dislikes for people. One person likes the name Jane or Harold because he has liked all the Janes and Harolds he has chanced to know; another person dislikes the names because he associates them, consciously or unconsciously, with people he has not liked. The word "red" applied to people has a sinister meaning in many parts of the world. The words "progressive" and "conservative" mean different things to different people and create different emotional reactions. An American and a Russian using the word "democracy" mean something quite different.

All of this means that words cannot be defined exactly because each person reads into them the meaning they have for him as the result of his experience. Teachers need, therefore, to be as sure as possible that children understand what is said to them and what they read. Also we need as teachers to listen carefully for the meanings the child uses. Children need plenty of opportunity to talk about what they read in their own words so that the teacher may know what they are thinking as they read, and to what extent they understand the meaning that is there. Anything that involves abstract language will always be a source of difficulty to a child because concepts of abstractions develop late and require many contacts in different settings. Figurative language is always troublesome and requires explanation and use in a variety of situations before it takes on any meaning.

Children cannot tell an adult, in many instances, which meanings they lack in dealing with a topic or reading a selection. They are in the position of the child with poor vision who is asked whether he can see an object well. Since this vision is all he has and all he has ever known, he cannot tell whether he sees the object adequately; only as corrective measures are applied through glasses or treatment can he look back on his previous condition and realize how handicapped he was. It is the task of the teacher to work with the child closely enough and give him sufficient opportunities for expression through informal discussion, art expression, dramatization, and every other available and suitable avenue so that she detects vagueness and lack of clear understanding and can set the child on the right track.

□ A LANGUAGE GROWS AND CHANGES

A language is not a static thing. It lives and grows. Its forms are not fixed but developing. Teachers need to realize this and teach it to children as the occasion arises. Even primary school children encounter this concept from time to time. An example of this occurred when a blind college student was invited to bring her Seeing-Eye dog to show the first grade children how he guided her about. She called attention to the recently coined descriptive term *Seeing-Eye,* and explained its meaning. She also explained how she took notes in class and showed the children how she wrote and read braille. She explained, meanwhile, that this form of writing was devised for the blind by a Frenchman whose name was Braille. She said the writing was first called Braille writing but now is just called braille and people have come to know that the word means a form of writing.

Older children are greatly interested in exploring a subject of recent development to see what new words it is adding to common use. Aviation has not only added new words like *aileron* and *fuselage* but has added new forms for old words. We have come to accept the word *contact* as a verb as well as a noun. To say that we "contact a friend" has become accepted usage. *Sonic* and *supersonic* are words that were unused by most people until the production of jet-propelled airplanes. World War II added words that will probably remain a part of the language. Any surprise attack of any sort may be labeled "blitzkrieg." Words are borrowed, or used in new forms, as well as new ones created to fit new needs. Children in the middle and upper grades can find great pleasure in tracking down sources of words that interest them, in studying their derivation, or the history of the uses to which the word has been put.

Children of all ages would be interested in watching for newly coined words. The explosion of knowledge in science and other realms is so great that a list of new words appearing for the first time within a school year would be both interesting and impressive to children. Most of these new words are made of old parts. The chemist coins a name for his new compound by utilizing parts of the names of elements that make up the compound. The word "telstar," applied to the orb sent into the ether to deflect sound waves, serves as a good example. Children can glean the meaning of the syllable "tel" from its meaning in such words as "telephone" and "telegraph" and the reason for the addition of "star" is apparent. Becoming vocabulary sleuths would not only interest children but reinforce their emerging concept of the growth of a language.

Older children can become interested in the endless possibilities for adaptation and change of existing words. There is the telescoping of words: *motel* for motor hotel, *smog* for smoke and fog; the cutting of words: *gas* for gasoline, *auto* for automobile; the building words of initial letters: *CARE* for Committee for American Relief in Europe, *radar* for radio detecting and ranging. There are also the endless additions through the use of the prefixes "pre," "re," "un," "im," "dis," or the suffixes "less," "ness," "ism," and the turning of nouns or adjectives into verbs through the addition of "ize"; *circularize* and *randomize;* the use of the same word as both noun and verb: *stone, paper, run, stack,* and the like.

☐ THE DEVELOPMENT OF VOCABULARY IN CHILDREN

Vocabulary development appears to take place quite slowly at first, then very rapidly through the preschool period. A number of people have called attention to the fact that the child remains on a plateau in language development while he is putting his energy and attention into learning to walk. After such a plateau, there is apt to be rapid progress in vocabulary development.

Both preschool and school-age children are dependent upon experience for vocabulary development. Drever is quoted as saying that in the growth of children's vocabularies, "environment affects the nouns, interest affects the verbs, and mental grip is shown by pronouns, adverbs, prepositions, and conjunctions" (4, p. 20). Watts interprets Drever to mean that "if you want to increase the number of nouns which a child can use the best way to do it is through an enrichment of his material environment, while the surest way of enlarging his stock of verbs is by extending his practical interests" (37, p. 40). He assumes, of course, that there is someone at hand to supply the language that a child needs in each new experience.

Direct emphasis on vocabulary building begins with the child's first year in school. In nursery school all experiences add new vocabulary because the child at this age is acquiring the basic vocabulary of everyday experience. In kindergarten, careful attention is given to learning the vocabulary of school living and of group co-operation. All of the types of vocabulary building experience found in the elementary school begin in a simple form in the kindergarten. Attention is given to the new

In the growth of children's vocabularies, "environment affects the nouns, interest affects the verbs . . . ." Firsthand experiences reinforce words and meanings.

words in all types of work and play experience, in songs, stories, and poems, and in excursions and sharing situations. As the children build a train, the teacher may turn their attention to pictures showing the various parts of a train – engine, Pullman coaches, passenger coaches, dining car, flatcar, refrigerator car, caboose, and all the other units. They talk of the conductor, the engineer, the brakeman, the maintenance crews, and the passengers. Firsthand experiences through a visit to a train, photographs, picture books and perhaps a film, stories, poetry, songs, block construction, dramatic play, and conversation all serve to build and reinforce words and meanings. An advanced group may even build a picture glossary, allotting a page or a space on a chart to each new word and illustrating it with a drawing or a picture cut from an old magazine.

Teachers in the primary school have devised ways of calling attention to new words and giving them the emphasis and use that make them a part of the children's equipment. A child announced to his first grade teacher one morning, "My mother's back! She's been to a convention." Another child asked, "What's a convention?" At sharing time the teacher suggested that the child repeat his news to the group. They talked about the word *convention,* wrote it on the board, and used it in a variety of ways. Then the teacher recorded it on a chart headed, "New Words We Have Learned." A second grade group keeps a file for new words. Big index cards are filed alphabetically in a box. As new words are encountered, each is written on a separate card or sheet and the word *pasture* is filed by Pat, who has charge of the *p* words, and the word *silo* by Susan, who has charge of the *s* file. The children may illustrate the word on the card if it is a picturable word. Children needing these words in their writing may refer to the cards.

Picture dictionaries are now available in quantity so that copies of several may be added to the classroom library. If a new word does not appear in the picture dictionaries, the teacher may look it up in the junior dictionary on her desk and read or translate to the children the meaning that is given. Children can be introduced in many ways to the services rendered by a dictionary so that when they reach the middle grades and are mature enough to begin the more concentrated work leading to mastery of dictionary use, the motivation for learning has been built.

A number of means of developing vocabulary are summarized in the list which follows. The last two suggestions serve to make children aware that a language is a growing, changing medium, not a fixed and static one.

1. Informal conversation and discussion, stopping to give attention to words when the situation and the interest make it advisable
2. Reading aloud to children material which they can understand and enjoy and which enriches and supplements their own reading as well as adds to their appreciation of their cultural heritage
3. Reading textbook material with the children when it is difficult—reading and talking, talking and reading—to make vague and unfamiliar ideas clear ones through association and application to the children's own experience
4. Taking field trips to gain firsthand experience. Both careful planning and the follow-up activities are essential for the complete experience
5. Using films and other types of auditory and visual aids which fit the study and add to its values
6. Expressing new meanings graphically through various art mediums
7. Dramatizing words very simply, as in the old game of charades or through a more elaborate play
8. Encouraging children to keep individual records of new vocabulary
9. Keeping group records of the new vocabulary found in various experiences
10. Giving attention to shades of meaning, to colorful words, to action words, to words that are especially vivid and effective
11. Encouraging children to discover meaning from context and perhaps to check their meaning with the dictionary, at times, to determine their success in deducing meaning
12. Working various types of exercises which meet the need of the group or individual; there are many kinds:
    a. Working with prefixes and suffixes
    b. Searching for synonyms and antonyms
    c. Checking in a list all words of like derivation

d. Completing sentences by adding suitable words or word groups
e. Matching words and definitions
f. Fitting words into categories: animals, things to eat or drink, words describing people, words dealing with measuring
Keeping lists of these in the classroom to help with writing
g. Word-meaning tests
rapid—happy slow fast race

13. Carrying on dictionary activities
14. Reading, reading, reading. The more the children read the more meanings they learn.
Reading things one is interested in
Reading easy things for fun
Reading anything and everything that adds to the values of the things one is doing or studying
Reading to build new interests
Reading newspapers, magazines, books, catalogs—anything that adds interest to living
15. Keeping a record of newly coined words, noting the old parts from which they are made and the situation or need that called them into being
16. Noting old words that are taking on new meanings and speculating as to the reason for the change or addition.

Words and meanings comprise much of the stuff of which life is made. The higher the level of civilization the more important they become. If children are to live richly and to lay hold on their intellectual inheritance they need vast resources in words and meanings to draw upon.

☐ SELECTED REFERENCES ☐

1. Buckingham, B. R., and Dolch, E. W., *A Combined Word List.* Boston: Ginn and Company, 1936.
2. Dale, Edgar, and Razik, Taher, *Bibliography of Vocabulary Studies.* Columbus: Bureau of Educational Research and Service, The Ohio State University, 1963.
3. Dolch, Edward W., *Teaching Primary Reading.* Champaign, Illinois: Garrard Press, 1941.
4. Drever, James, "A Study of Children's Vocabularies." *Journal*

of Experimental Psychology 3:34-43, 96-103, 182-188, March, June, December, 1915.

5. Evans, Bergen, "Your Speech is Changing." Chapter I. *Readings in the Language Arts* by Verna Dieckman Anderson, et al. New York: The Macmillan Company, 1964.
6. Ferguson, Charles W., *Abecedarian Book.* Boston: Little, Brown & Company, 1964.
7. Fitzgerald, James A., *A Basic Life Spelling Vocabulary.* Milwaukee: The Bruce Publishing Co., 1951.
8. Gates, Arthur I., *A List of Spelling Difficulties in 3876 Words.* New York: Bureau of Publications, Teachers College, Columbia University, 1937.
9. ———, *A Reading Vocabulary for the Primary Grades* (Rev. & Enl.). New York: Bureau of Publications, Teachers College, Columbia University, 1935.
10. Horn, Ernest, *A Basic Writing Vocabulary.* University of Iowa Monographs in Education, No. 4. Iowa City: University of Iowa Press, 1926.
11. International Kindergarten Union, *A Study of the Vocabulary of Children before Entering the First Grade.* Washington, D. C.: International Kindergarten Union, 1928.
12. Kennedy, Arthur G., *English Usage.* National Council of Teachers of English. English Monograph No. 15. New York: D. Appleton-Century Co., Inc., 1942.
13. Kolson, Clifford John, *The Vocabulary of Kindergarten Children.* Unpublished doctoral thesis. Pittsburgh: University of Pittsburgh, 1960.
14. McCarthy, Dorothea A., "Language Development." *A Handbook of Child Psychology* (Rev.). Carl Murchison (Ed.). Worcester: Clark University Press, 1933. Chap. VIII.
15. ———, "Language Development in Children," *Manual of Child Psychology.* Leonard Carmichael (Ed.). New York: John Wiley and Sons, Inc., 1954
16. McCarthy, Dorothea A., *The Language Development of the Preschool Child.* Institute of Child Welfare Monograph Series, No. 4. Minneapolis: University of Minnesota Press, 1930.
17. National Conference on Research in English, *Interpreting Language: An Essential of Understanding.* J. Conrad Seegers, Chairman. Chicago: National Council of Teachers of English, 1951.
18. Pooley, Robert C., *Teaching English Usage.* National Council of Teachers of English. English Monograph No. 16. New York: D. Appleton-Century Co., Inc., 1946.
19. Rinsland, Henry D., *A Basic Vocabulary of Elementary School Children.* New York: The Macmillan Co., 1945.

20. Russell, David H., *Children Learn to Read.* Boston: Ginn and Co., 1961.
21. ———, *Dimensions of Children's Vocabularies in Grades Four Through Twelve.* Berkeley: University of California Press, 1954, pp. 315-414.
22. Seashore, Robert H., "The Importance of Vocabulary in Learning Language Skills." *Elementary English* 25: 137-152, March, 1948.
23. ———, "How Many Words Do Children Know?" *The Packet.* (D. C. Heath and Co.'s Service Bulletin for Elementary Teachers), Vol. II, No. 2, Nov., 1947, pp. 3-17.
24. Seegers, J. Conrad, "Language in Relation to Experience, Thinking and Learning." *Teaching Language in the Elementary School.* The Forty-Third Yearbook, Part II, of the National Society for the Study of Education. Chicago: University of Chicago Press, 1944, Chap. III, pp. 36-51.
25. Seegers, J. Conrad, and others, "Special Tools That Facilitate Expression." *Teaching Language in the Elementary School.* The Forty-Third Yearbook, Part II, of the National Society for the Study of Education. Chicago: University of Chicago Press, 1944, Chap. VIII, pp. 148-193.
26. ———, *Vocabulary Problems in the Elementary School.* National Conference on Research in English. Research Bulletin No. 7. Chicago: Scott, Foresman and Co., 1939.
27. Seegers, J. Conrad, and Seashore, Robert H., "How Large Are Children's Vocabularies?" *Elementary English* 26:181-194, April, 1949.
28. Shibles, Burleigh H., "How Many Words Does a First Grade Child Know?" *Elementary English* 41:42-47, January, 1959.
29. Shirley, Mary M., "Common Content in the Speech of Preschool Children." *Child Development* 9:333-346, Dec., 1938.
30. ———, *The First Two Years: A Study of Twenty-five Babies.* (Intellectual Development, Vol. 2.) University of Minnesota Press, 1933.
31. Smith, Madorah E., *An Investigation of the Development of the Sentence and the Extent of Vocabulary in Young Children.* (Studies in Child Welfare, Vol. 3, No. 5.) Iowa City: State University of Iowa, 1926.
32. Smith, Mary Katherine, "Measurement of the Size of General English Vocabulary through the Elementary Grades and High School." *Genetic Psychology Monographs* 24:311-345, Nov., 1941.
33. Stone, Clarence R., *Stone's Graded Vocabulary for Primary Reading.* St. Louis: Webster Publishing Co., 1941.

34. Templin, Mildred C., *Certain Language Skills in Children*. Minneapolis: The University of Minnesota Press, 1957.
35. Thorndike, Edward L., and Lorge, Irving, *The Teacher's Word Book of 30,000 Words*. New York: Bureau of Publications, Teachers College, Columbia University, 1944.
36. Thorndike, Edward L., *A Teacher's Word Book of the Twenty Thousand Words Found Most Frequently and Widely in General Reading for Children and Young People* (Rev.). New York: Bureau of Publications, Teachers College, Columbia University, 1932.
37. Watts, A. F., *The Language and Mental Development of Children*. London: George C. Harrap and Co., Ltd., 1944. Boston: D. C. Heath and Co., 1947.

TEACHING
CHILDREN
TO
READ

Reading has become an absolute necessity for any kind of satisfactory or even safe living in our society. To drive a car or even to go from place to place on foot in a modern city requires reading. There are practically no jobs left that can be carried on successfully without reading. Even the ditch diggers must manage expensive power machinery which calls for careful following of directions. Television was once thought of as a threat to reading but it seems instead to have increased the demand for at least some kinds of reading.

Parents are deeply concerned that their child learn to read. Some of them and a few professional educators would like to have reading taught earlier than is customary because there is so much to learn today, and children need reading as a tool to get on with the learning. Articles have appeared in popular magazines suggesting that parents begin to teach their child to read before his first birthday, or at least before he comes to school. In some communities the schools are being challenged to justify their time schedule for the teaching of reading as well as their materials and methods.

□ WHEN SHALL READING BE TAUGHT?

In the United States, six years of age or first grade is the accepted time for the teaching of reading. The same is true of many of the schools in England, though some of them and all of the Scottish schools begin at age five. In the Scandinavian countries and in Russia reading is taught to children at the age of seven. A Norwegian scholar studying in a midwestern university on a Fulbright grant asked to visit schools and was sent into a variety of city and county schools. He came back from his visitation asking, "Why is a wealthy nation in such a hurry to push its children into reading? If yours were a poor nation I could understand it." Norwegian schools, he felt, had fewer reading problems than schools in this country because children were more mature when they started reading. The matter of learning to read is now recognized as one of the most important and most difficult of all the developmental tasks the child is called upon to achieve. It is a task imposed by the culture and not one for which a child has a natural yearning, as he has for growing big and strong so that he can hold his own with the people about him, and learning to talk so that he can communicate with them and gain help in meeting his own personal needs and desires. The fact that reading developed relatively late in the history of mankind is proof that it is not an inherent growth need but rather a need that has emerged within the culture into which the child is born. If he had been born a few generations earlier, or even today in a part of the world in which the culture remains primitive, he might not need to learn to read in order to live a satisfying life. Now, in our culture, he must not only learn to read but learn to *want* to read if he is to live at all richly or even adequately.

Reading is a complex mental process that involves the doing of several things simultaneously. The reader must recognize the symbols which represent speech and must bring meaning to what he recognizes. There is no meaning in the marks one reads – the meaning is in the mind of the reader. Little children are just in the process of learning words and meanings. To be able to decipher symbols if one could not infuse meaning into them would be completely useless. In addition, the reader must relate what he is gleaning to what he knows if there is to be any real understanding. Lastly, but actually concurrently, he must integrate what he is reading into perspective.

The process of listening is a very similar process to reading but there are major differences. A speaker helps a listener by his use of pitch, stress, and pauses. He clots together the words in his sentences that belong together and pauses slightly before going on to other clusters of words. Also, he pitches a little higher and emphasizes a little more strongly the key meaning-bearing words in his sentences. He says, perhaps, "The boy ate the candy," placing heavy emphasis on "boy" and "candy" and slight emphasis on "ate," letting the structure word "the" fall into a trough of sound. The reader has no such help. He must turn the stimulus of marks that move along in even rows into speech and thence into meaning. He has the advantage that he can set his own pace and reread if he wishes but he must, himself, put words into perspective in sentences, and ideas and sentences into perspective in paragraphs and pages of material.

Since when one reads he reads language, it is difficult to see what a child could do with reading before he has had enough experience with language to understand how it operates and to have ready a wide repertoire of words and meanings. Children from two to five years of age spend an immense amount of energy in the task of mastering a language. This comes first with the child as it did with the race. Man achieved a spoken language countless generations before he achieved a scheme for the graphic representation of that language.

☐ THE BACKGROUND FOR SUCCESS IN LEARNING TO READ

Since the 1920's a great deal has been said and written about readiness for reading. For a time, a mental age of 6.6 was widely accepted as requisite to success in learning to read. Then research made it clear that mental age was not the only determining factor. If a child was to be helped to grow into reading in ways naturally suited to him and his needs, he might succeed at a younger age than if he were to be put into a rigid skill-drill type of program. How the child was to be taught to read was as important as his level of maturity.

Language development is the first and most important element in readiness for reading. Children the world over learn the sound system of their language by the age of three or four so that they say words just as they are said by people around them. They learn the grammar of their language by the age of eight so that they put words together in strings and sentences, just as they hear other people doing it. They learn their vocabulary by imitation, of course, accepting the words for objects and ideas just as other people use them. But, looking back to the findings cited in Chapter 4 on how children learn their language, children do not learn a language as an endless series of single discrete items. They begin very early to be aware of patterns and to sense intuitively some of the rules for the operation of their language. By the time they enter school at the age of five or six, children are using all of the kinds of sentences adults use. Children from average American homes come to school using a vocabulary of at least 2500 words and with an understanding vocabulary probably 10 times as large. They have mastered a language, though they will in succeeding years, in school and out, greatly expand and refine their use of it.

Reading requires fine powers of visual and auditory discrimination. Children must distinguish instantly and accurately symbols that look very much alike: *m* and *n*; *u* and *n*; *b*, *d*, *p*, and *q*; *s* and *z*; *m* and *w*; *e*, *o*, and *c*. They must be aware of the difference in sound between *f* and *v*; *m* and *n*; *s* and *z*; *ch* and *sh*. They must be aware of directional orientation, as in *on* and *no*; *was* and *saw*; *spot* and *stop*. Parents can do a thousand things with little children to help them become aware of likenesses and differences—at home, as they ride in the car, at the supermarket—anywhere. Teachers must go on with the work of developing auditory and visual discrimination in children who lack it.

Another prime requisite for success in learning to read is interest in books and stories. The parents who read to their child and enjoy stories and poems with him are giving him a priceless gift. The child who comes from a home where reading is nonexistent or of little importance must be helped to find enjoyment in listening to stories and looking at books before he can bring much motivation to the task of learning to read.

The ability to give concentrated attention is also important. Enjoying stories and books, playing games, observing things in nature, and losing himself in play activities all help to extend the child's span of attention and his ability to concentrate.

Recent evidence indicates that the child who learns to recognize and name the letters before he comes to first grade has a distinct advantage over the child who does not. Alphabet blocks and attractive ABC books are fun for any child if parents will name the letters for him and play little recognition games with them.

Naturally, the child who is physically well can more easily put effort into reading than can a child who has physical problems, whether these be vision or hearing problems, nutrition, general lack of physical stamina or any other handicap. The child who is accustomed to playing with groups of children can more easily turn his attention from children to what the teacher is teaching than can the child who is socially insecure. General emotional stability is an asset also, since learning to read is a relatively slow process, requiring patience and persistence.

☐ CHILDREN WHO READ EARLY

Every kindergarten or first grade teacher encounters an occasional child who has learned to read before coming to first grade. Durkin found 49 of them among 5100 children she tested in California and a little larger proportion in a similar study in New York (6). These were children she described as "pencil and paper kids"—children who wanted to write their names and went on to other writing, often before they attempted any reading. A child who watches others reading and realizes that the good food his mother puts on the table, the exciting things his older siblings talk about, and the news that distresses his father are all related to mysterious little black marks on paper wants to know about them. Perhaps he asks to turn the pages while his mother reads a familiar story because he remembers what happens last on a page. Trips to the supermarket to select packaged goods from the shelves, the traffic signals, and signs along the way all excite his curiosity. Parents of such children often insist that they have not taught the child to read but have answered his questions and given him all the help he asked for.

□ SHALL THE KINDERGARTEN TEACH READING?

Because there are children who learn to read before the age of six, some schools are being urged to teach reading in the kindergarten. The answer of many teachers is that there is a great deal else the child needs to do and learn at the age of five which will build background for success in reading a little later. An occasional child may be eager for help with learning to read and he should be given all the help he asks for or needs. If he is already reading, he can be encouraged now and then to select a story from the library table to read to the children at story time. But *he* should be encouraged to take the initiative in selecting the material, time, and duration of his reading. This is vastly different from sitting every five-year-old down to the task of a formal program of reading instruction. It is better for most of them to be increasing their power with language, developing auditory and visual discrimination, enjoying listening to and perhaps dramatizing stories and poems, building vocabulary, enriching experience and in many ways developing their ability to attend to and to concentrate on a variety of kinds of interest.

There are opportunities during the kindergarten year to introduce the children to written language. Perhaps they compose a note to the mothers telling of a special event, an invitation to another class to come in for a dramatization, or a note to a child who is ill. Possibly the teacher writes a story dictated by a child. One kindergarten teacher prepared a large scrapbook with a camera snapshot of each child at the top of a page that was all his own. From time to time, she encouraged the child to dictate a story for his page, or wrote on it something he contributed at sharing time. There is need in any kindergarten for signs on buildings built of blocks and for some kinds of dramatic play. The teacher uses every opportunity to help children understand what reading and writing are and their usefulness. If the children take note of similarities in sounds and graphic patterns, so much the better, but these are not formally taught.

Kindergarten children differ from community to community. Some have had a rich background of preschool experience, some a pitifully meager one. All children should be challenged and aided to grow toward reading but not necessarily in reading itself during the kindergarten year. Children who come from or attend Head Start programs need an immense amount of language and experience enrichment before they can succeed in reading.

□ HOW TO TEACH BEGINNING READING: AN UNENDING DEBATE

Since the publication of a highly controversial book, Rudolf Flesch's *Why Johnny Can't Read,* in 1955, more people have given more attention to the teaching of reading than at any time in history (8). Teachers and reading specialists have sought to make clear to parents and the public how reading is taught in the schools and why. Increased effort has been put into diagnosing and remedying reading difficulties when they occur.

One method of teaching reading has dominated the American scene for forty or more years, what has come to be called the basal reading method. In recent years, other possibilities have been developed, almost entirely by dissatisfied people outside the circle of reading specialists—linguists, curriculum specialists, and specialists in the general language arts field. Studies have indicated values in each of these methods but no clear consensus regarding the worth of any of them as compared with basal reading programs. Each method has ardent proponents and each has been tested in some schools. Space permits only a brief sketch of the major tenets of a few of them.

□ BASAL READING PROGRAMS

Perhaps the best available statement of what basal reading programs are designed to do is that of Sheldon in the report

Perspectives in Reading, a contribution of the International Reading Association. He says,

> Basal reading instruction is concerned with the development of those fundamental habits, attitudes and skills essential to effective silent and oral reading.
>
> The program rests on the assumption that a set of essential and fundamental skills are generally known and that these are of such a nature that a series of books, workbooks and manuals which present these skills in a sequential order are essential to their development.
>
> Proponents of the use of basal readers suggest that an adequate basal reading program provides the essential prerequisites to successful growth in word comprehension, interpretation and all aspects of mature reading. However, it is recognized that the basic skills are brought to full use when children are lead to utilize these skills in reading of library books and the texts used in the various content areas (11, p. 28).

In general, reading specialists support the following statement which appeared in *Learning to Read,* the report of a conference on reading called by Conant in connection with his studies of American education.

> By and large, the child learns precisely what he is led to learn in response to the content and structure of the teaching materials. As applied to the teaching of reading, this means that effective teaching depends upon the careful programming of reading materials in terms of (a) the sound values of letters and letter combinations, (b) practice in recognition of words as wholes, (c) the apprehension of meaning both of single words and large units such as phrases, sentences, and paragraphs, and (d) the development of suitable habits of adjusting one's approach to reading in the light of one's purpose for reading (11, p. 28).

The overall program of basal reader series is eclectic in the sense that it is designed to develop readiness, vocabulary, word recognition and word perception, comprehension skills, and a love of literature—all worthy and important aims. The endless debate regarding the teaching of reading results from the fact that for too many children these aims are not achieved. The need for reading is so well recognized that some schools are testing other approaches to reading in the search for some way to help more children learn to read more easily and effectively. Many schools are convinced that nothing better has been suggested than a basal reading program and some of these are adding to their staffs specially trained people whose tasks are to help teachers do better what they are doing and to diagnose and set up remedial programs for children who are not succeeding in the basal reading programs.

The basal reading approach places emphasis from the beginning on reading for meaning. Critics of the method are convinced that the first emphasis should be placed on breaking the code. Three methods now in use are designed to do this, the phonics method—of which there are many varieties—a revised alphabet method, and a linguistically based method. Chall's study points to these as the methods favored by research (4).

☐ PHONICS—WHEN AND HOW MUCH?

Whenever critics speak disapprovingly of the teaching of reading they can be depended upon to lay most of the blame for poor reading on the "sight-word" method. The notion is abroad that schools, or at least some of them, attempt to teach the child to recognize words as "wholes" by their total shape and configuration. Schools are accused of teaching each word separately and relying mainly on visual perception and memory for recognition of all the words taught in reading. Actually, this has never been true. Basal reader systems tend to start with a few sight words but teach children, quite gradually, phonic clues to recognition as well. It is doubtful that there has ever been a reading program based on sight recognition alone because it is so much more logical and economical to help children distinguish between "was" and "saw," "them" and "then," "these" and "those," by calling attention to the sounds of the distinguishing letters. Conversely, there probably is no system for teaching reading that does not give attention to other methods of recognizing and remembering words than just symbol-sound correspondences. One cannot pronounce "bow" nor spell the word "right" and "write" without knowing its meaning. It would be absurd to try to teach the *ough* words through phonics because there are no rules one can apply to "though," "through," "thought," "enough," "bough," and "thorough" to help with pronunciation.

All systems of teaching reading give attention to phonics or its equivalent. The question is not whether phonics shall be taught but rather *when* and *how much*. Basal reader systems all carry on a program of phonics which is carefully and systematically woven into the entire reading program, particularly in the primary grades after children have acquired a small sight vocabulary. The work starts with consonant and vowel sounds and covers all of the basic sound and spelling patterns of English. Attention is given to structural analysis where it fits: inflections—"look," "looks," "looked," "looking"; affixes—"hook," "unhook," "agree," "disagree," "disagreeable"; and compounds—"something," "without," "grandfather." Part of this is taught in the intermediate grades rather than the primary.

Some special phonics textbooks place heavy emphasis on phonics in the first grade, even preceding any emphasis on reading as thought-getting. Many specialists in reading are committed to the gradual teaching of phonics rather than the heavy initial emphasis on deciphering. They maintain that heavy emphasis on phonics at the beginning results in slow, laborious deciphering which children continue to use when they should be learning to react to larger units than letters. A further problem cited by some is the difficulty of teaching children to read for meaning when their first contacts with reading have been centered mainly on letters.

☐ A LINGUISTIC APPROACH

Charles C. Fries, an outstanding proponent of a linguistic approach to reading, states his thesis very plainly. "Learning to read is not learning to *know* something, it is learning to *do* something." That something is high-speed recognition of letters and sequences of letters in words so that recognition may result in the gathering of meaning from what is read. His plan and that of Barnhart and others begins with recognition of upper and lower case letters of the alphabet, then of common regular spellings using groups of those letters. Because the consonant-vowel-consonant pattern is the commonest spelling pattern in English—"cut," "hat," "pin," "met," "not"—it is the starting point for pattern recognition. Blends of consonants come next, "spin," "slam," "stand," and the like, followed by words with the signal *e*—"cute," "hate," "pine," "note," and then other sequentially planned modifications. There are no illustrations in the children's books. They are to rely on the print alone for meaning.

☐ THE ALPHABET PROBLEM AND ITA

A major problem in teaching children to read English is the fact that the language is written with 26 letters which must be used to represent more than that number of sounds. Since the 15th century, as a result of shifts in pronunciation which occurred between the times of Chaucer and of Shakespeare, the spelling of many English words and their pronunciation has lacked clear-cut correspondence. Consequently, many intelligent people during the intervening centuries have felt that anything that will improve the coding system, even temporarily, for beginning readers should have careful consideration by educators. A number of people, beginning in 1517, have had a try at it.

The scheme that has created widest interest is the Initial Teaching Alphabet, widely known as ITA, which is a product of Sir James Pitman, a member of Parliament and head of a publishing firm. The alphabet consists of 44 characters which represent the 44 basic sounds of English. It uses 24 of the traditionally used letters (omitting X and Q) and adds characters which are related in shape to the letters or letter combinations which they replace.

ITA has been tried by individual teachers in a number of first grades in the United States and in one entire school system, that of Bethlehem, Pennsylvania. It is used in scattered schools and communities in England, numbering approximately 60,000 children in 1964-65.

ITA is what its name implies, an alphabet for initial teaching. Children are encouraged to transfer their skill to materials written in traditional orthography as soon as they have learned to read – some in first grade and the rest, hopefully, in second or third grade. ITA is also being used in remedial work with older boys and girls who have failed in the usual reading programs on the theory that these children profit from a fresh approach to reading and are encouraged by the thought that, when they learn to recognize 44 letters they can then read a variety of simple books.

The value of ITA lies in the one-to-one relationship of symbol and sound. Once children have learned the relationship for the 44 symbols, they can read a variety of books printed in this system. Another value claimed for ITA is that children write it with sufficient ease to write prolifically. No evidence has been offered of the time required to learn to write in the traditional orthography of 26 letters.

INITIAL TEACHING ALPHABET
(i/t/a)

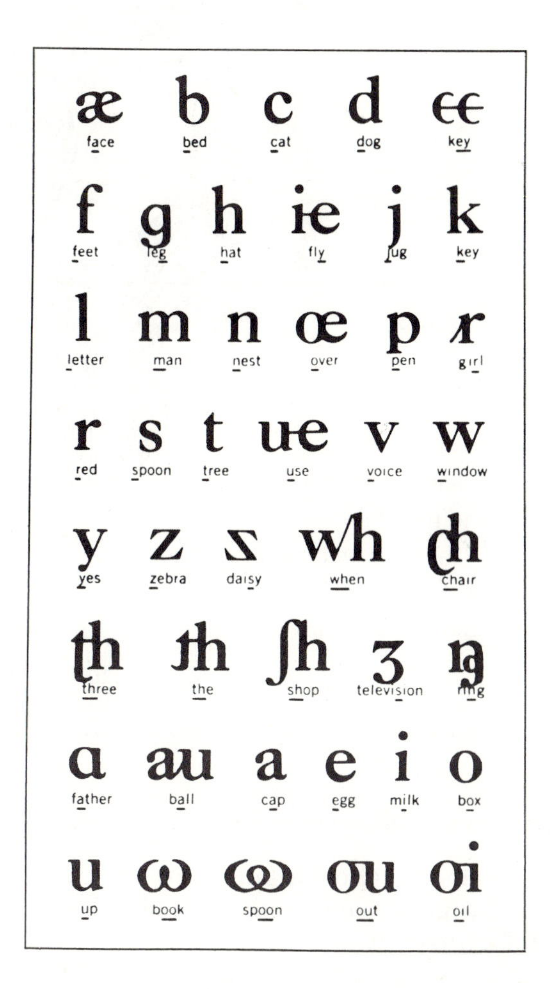

This chart and the illustration on the next page are reprinted by permission of Initial Teaching Publications, New York.

sum birdz in a tree sau them. thæ had tω laf.

the turtl wonted tω tauk tω the birdz about hiz trip, but hee nue hee cωd not œpen hiz mouth.

5

☐ LANGUAGE EXPERIENCE APPROACH TO READING

Every child brings to school a language. He can listen and he can talk. The language approach to reading begins with this language and utilizes it as the material for reading. Children are encouraged to draw and paint pictures and talk about their in-school and out-of-school interests. In the case of a picture, the teacher writes under the picture the child's story of it. If he says, "This is my Dad. He is washing the car," that is what the teacher writes for him. Stories and accounts may be composed and dictated by an individual, a group, or the whole class. The children are placed so that they can watch the teacher write. She calls attention to what she is doing. "I have to start here with a big capital letter, don't I! We'll put a mark like this at the end of the sentence. Now what else shall we say? Can anyone help me spell that word? Here it is, up here." Should a child say, "My sister saw some, too," or "My mother made me a doll dress," the teacher might say, "Listen to the sound of those words—*sister, saw, some.* They all start with the same sound, don't they, so I'll have to start all of them with the same letter, *s.*" Or, "Do you hear the *m* sound in all of those first words, 'My mother made me.' I'll have to start all of them with the letter *m* because they all start with the *m* sound."

Some teachers in England believe that no child should be given a printed book to read until he has made at least one little book of his own, and a late developer should probably make five or six such little books. Children delight in doing it and learn through the experience something about what writing is and the nature of books and reading. They learn that the ideas for books start in the heads of people, are put into words, then into graphic symbols on a page. When the words are read back they say just what their composer wanted them to say. They can be read again tomorrow or next week and the words are there to stay because they have been recorded.

The major proponent of the language-experience approach to reading is R. Van Allen. He suggests that the concepts a child develops as he composes, dictates, and later writes are these:

> What he thinks about he can talk about.
> What he can talk about can be expressed in painting, writing, or some other form.
> Anything he writes (or is written for him) can be read.
> He can read what he writes and what other people write.
> As he represents the speech sounds he makes in written symbols, he uses the same symbols over and over again in different groupings.

Teachers who work with the plan have found ingenious ways to help children with spelling when they begin to write their own stories: picture dictionaries; card files on desks; lists of frequently needed words arranged according to category—food words, game words, and the like. Always, a child who is writing is encouraged to ask for the words he needs by bringing a pencil and a scrap of paper from a box, whispering to the teacher the word he wants her to write for him, then returning to his place and incorporating it into his sentence.

As children become aware of words, the letters that compose them in written form, and symbol-sound correspondences, they are ready to try the reading of beginning books which may or may not be reading textbooks. A language approach to reading takes children logically from the known—spoken language—to the unknown—reading and writing. Reading and writing are taught together as two faces of the same coin.

☐ DEVELOPING WORD RECOGNITION SKILLS

All good modern reader series and the teacher's guides that go with them offer help in planning a systematic program of word-recognition skills. Such programs have to be adapted to the needs of groups and individuals but many types of suggestions are offered. *The work need not all be done in readers*—it can fit into any reading or language situation in which it would be profitable if it does not interfere with emphasis on other values more important at the moment.

In basal reader programs the bulk of the systematic attention to word recognition techniques, particularly phonic and structural analysis falls in late first, second and third grades, or at least after children have gained a clear concept of reading as thought-getting and have a fund of words they recognize with ease. Some children learn quite rapidly to use what they know of phonic elements to decipher unfamiliar words. For other children phonics seems almost impossible to learn and apply until more maturity is gained through a variety of kinds of language and reading experiences. Too much emphasis on phonics or too early emphasis, can result in slow, letter by letter "sounding out" which decreases interest in learning to read and is highly detrimental to emphasis on the thinking aspects of reading.

Authorities on reading agree that knowledge of symbol-sound correspondence is essential in deciphering unfamiliar words. The consonant sounds in English are fairly dependable and most children learn to recognize these sounds without difficulty. Vowels present a different problem. The sound of long *a* is spelled in fourteen ways in words commonly used in English. Some vowels and combinations of vowels are phonetically undependable. The words containing *ough* carry too many sounds to be taught phonetically. And there are no rules that will help children to pronounce accurately *sew* and *few*, *break* and *freak*, *done*, *gone*, and *lone* and many other combinations that look alike but are sounded differently.

Most teachers teach children to use a combination of methods in learning to recognize words. A phonic method or its equivalent is used where it fits; a word is learned as a sight word if that is the most helpful and economical method of learning it.

It is well known that the number of different alphabetic characters in the written language does not equal the number of different sounds in the spoken language. Since English does not have a one-to-one correspondence between sound and letters, and some letters must represent more than one sound, and a single sound may be represented by different letters or combinations of letters, children need to learn more than one way to recognize words. They should be taught to use phonetic analysis wherever it is helpful and to utilize other cues whenever they are more serviceable. In most reading situations analysis of entire words is seldom necessary particularly if pupils have been taught to use configuration, picture clues and context meaning clues along with structural and phonic analysis.

☐ ORAL READING IN THE PRIMARY GRADES

The process of learning to read should not be a steady upward climb with no opportunities to stop to enjoy one's gains. Children, during this period, need quantities of *easy, interesting* reading material. They need to read and read so that they encounter many times, in many types of stories, all of the common words of English that hold together our sentences whether one is reading a letter from a friend or a treatise on atomic energy. Those common "glue" words should be read many times in all sorts of material until they are recognized instantly and accurately and the child can give his major attention to the key words that furnish the unique content of the piece he is reading.

Oral reading is enjoyed by primary children and should have a distinct place in the daily program. This does not mean that children should be asked to read aloud material that everyone else has also read. The best motivation for good oral reading is an opportunity to make a real contribution—to read to others material that is new to them and will therefore have interest and value for them.

Being able to recognize words does not always result in good oral reading. Oral reading is good when the reader has the meaning and the mental pictures it calls up so clearly in mind that his words cause others to conjure up similar mental pictures and to think similar meaning. A child who rarely uses complete sentences in his talk, or who rarely, if ever, speaks in complex or compound sentences, will find it difficult to read such sentences aloud. Rarely, at this stage, will a child be able to read aloud better than he talks.

Oral reading is a complex process for young readers. This means that for most school purposes, silent reading should precede oral reading. The child usually needs an opportunity to make sure that he can recognize and comprehend the words and the ideas which the author has written into the story before he attempts to interpret them for others.

Difficulties of many types may be encountered in the silent and oral reading experiences provided in any single class period. The reader may have difficulty identifying a new word or recognizing an old one. He may have difficulty comprehending an idea because he lacks certain concepts. His problems may instead be a lack of confidence in his oral reading or a problem of voice control and pronunciation or enunciation. In order to provide for the instructional needs of all the children in the class, teachers place them in various reading groups.

□ GROUPING AND CARE FOR INDIVIDUAL DIFFERENCES

Grouping for reading can be of many sorts and organized on several bases. Sometimes, reading groups will be based on similar learning rates or similar levels of reading skill. Sometimes children will be drawn into groups for special help with techniques which they need to develop. At other times interest in story content draws children together—those who want to read about penguins join one group and those interested in cowboy or farm stories join other groups. For oral reading children can get together in pairs or in small clusters to share stories that interest them. They can read alone to the tape recorder in order to hear how they sound in reading aloud. The key to grouping success, *flexibility*, adds interest and challenge. Through flexible grouping, teachers find many ways to care for individual differences in needs and interests.

☐ LEARNING TO READ BY READING

The success which children attain in learning to read is closely related to the satisfaction they find in their experience with reading. It is true that children must encounter words many times in the process of learning to read before they react instantly and accurately with the meaning that fits each symbol pattern. This obvious need for repetition has caused many teachers to put children through endless hours of wearying, boresome drill in order to gain rapid recognition of words. Other teachers have found that children learn better when they are provided with fresh contacts with words in new content and in varying context. They find that repetition can come through contacts of many sorts, not just over and over again in the same context or in isolation on flash cards and chalkboard, or in workbooks. The interest and challenge children find in their learning experiences colors their progress at all points.

The initial stage of independent reading is the stage in which a child begins to recognize, from context or from their similarity to known words, and to use independently, some of the phonic clues he has been taught to recognize. At this time he should have access to a quantity of material which will catch his interest and which is of a level of reading difficulty which will allow him to gain meaning from his reading. A child at this stage takes great delight in his growing power and will give it an immense amount of exercise if the material at hand is suitable for his level of skill and of sufficient variety so that he can find material that interests him. With sensible and consistent guidance, children make rapid progress during this period. It is a critical period, because too difficult materials, poor teaching techniques, or pushing a child too hard may have disastrous results.

Mere reading of textbooks is not enough reading to make a child a real reader. Children must read far more material than that to become rapid and skillful readers and gain satisfaction from reading. Recognition of this fact is found in the appearance of central libraries in modern elementary school buildings as well as classroom libraries in all classrooms from kindergarten through the sixth grade. Children are encouraged to read widely in material which fits their interests and level of reading ability. Through this wide reading they gain practice, grow in satisfaction and enjoyment in reading itself, and come to think of reading as an essential element in good living.

A good reading program for the primary grades will include: (1) emphasis upon helping children with techniques which make them independent readers; (2) opportunity to read widely in material which interests them; (3) opportunity to share their reading with others; and (4) opportunity to listen to the teacher's reading aloud of stories that stretch their interest and imagination to higher levels and encourage them to read material of better and better quality and provide them with an example of good reading to strive toward.

It is clear that for such a program no one set of reading materials is sufficient. Children enter the reading situation possessing a wide variety of interests, backgrounds and personal goals. To expect one set of materials to meet all of the needs of all of the children is not realistic. Many teachers have wondered whether the kind of material in basal readers for young children may not be partly responsible for the number of boys who do poorly with reading. For many bright and capable little boys the simple stories of home life and play with toys have no appeal. To children whose life is centered in crowded housing and sidewalk play space there is nothing they can identify with and nothing to sharpen their interest in reading. If it is necessary in the primary grades to teach children how to read through using a highly controlled vocabulary of these basal books, then they should be freed from the restriction for at least a portion of their reading and encouraged to read material of their own choice, guided only as to level of reading but given freedom in the choice of subject matter.

From the very beginning, the teacher must be alert to diagnose the problems of each individual child and to find ways to remedy them. Children need not become "remedial" reading problems if their needs are met as they arise. Children who learn rapidly need challenge and opportunity to make rapid progress, lest they lose interest and become content with a lower level of performance than they are capable of. Slow-learning children need to be protected from undue pressures and from experiences that undermine their self-respect and confidence in their ability to learn. Children with special vision and hearing problems need teaching techniques adjusted to

their needs so that their unimpaired senses can be made to compensate for the senses that do not function adequately. They can learn to read, but guidance should be tailored to their individual needs. *All children would learn to read if they could.* It is the task of the school to study each child and find the best possible ways to help him achieve up to the level of his capacity to learn.

☐ LACK OF CONCLUSIVE RESEARCH

A large number of research studies have been recorded comparing one method with another but without conclusive results. The major battery of such studies were those carried on in the schools of 27 cities under United States Office of Education financing. In many instances, the experimental plan being studied brought better or as good results as established methods. Two major conclusions seem to stand out. Good teachers who are keenly interested in what they are teaching get good results regardless of method; and overall, methods which give major emphasis to code-breaking techniques—phonics or a linguistic approach—seem to do a little better than methods which put their major emphasis at the beginning on reading for meaning.

☐ AN ECLECTIC METHOD

Few approaches to the teaching of reading follow a single pattern exclusively. Some of them combine a number of worthwhile possibilities. Since children tend to learn better in any area if they understand the process they are learning and how it operates, many teachers begin their program with at least some emphasis on a language-experience approach. After all, children come to school with a well-developed language. They know it, as Horace Mann said in 1835, by ear, tongue, and mind. Now they must learn to respond to its representation in print which they must respond to by eye and mind, or by tongue too, if reading orally. There is logic in the linguistic approach which gives attention in systematic fashion first to the regular spellings of English, then gradually to its less regular spellings. There is virtue too, in the one-to-one sound and symbol relationship as presented with ITA. Many teachers are striving to use the best of several possibilities in order to help children to reach as soon as possible a point at which they can select from the classroom and school library the books they want to read and have the teacher's help and guidance in reading those books. Individualized reading, described in greater detail in the next chapter, can begin as soon as a child can read even a little material independently. Since the goal of all teaching of reading should be personal satisfaction and enjoyment, the sooner the child can experience it the better.

□ FOLLOW-UP PROGRAMS AND HELP FOR THE CULTURALLY DISADVANTAGED

It is well known that many children from culturally disadvantaged homes fail to master reading or at least learn more slowly than more favored children. One reason is obviously the fact that they have a language deficiency. Another is lack of motivation. Reading is not a part of life in their homes. No one has ever read to them; in short, no one reads. Many people are convinced that there is nothing in the average reading textbook that can be used to entice such children to read. In the main, the stories deal with homes and life quite different from the children's own.

Head Start programs and kindergarten programs that meet the needs of these children are designed to build the children's language and experience backgrounds in a great variety of ways. A good primary grade program must painstakingly follow-up and expand these gains.

For children who know little or nothing about reading, a language-experience approach seems almost the only sensible possibility. Teachers provide children with experiences which they then talk about and convert into brief and simple story material. Since many of these children may speak a dialect which differs from the teacher's language and the language of books, teachers have to make an important decision. Should they write for a child exactly what he says or should they transpose it into conventional standard English? Some teachers are convinced that, if a child is to identify with the material and become aware of what reading is, they must write the child's own language. After a time they can say to a child, "That is one way to say it and I understand just what you mean. In books it is usually said this way. I'll write it both ways for you." Still later the teacher may say, "Can you tell it to me the way it usually is said in books so I can write it that way?" Whether this brings better results than writing only in standard English is not yet known, but it seems psychologically sensible and perhaps even more humane, if one's goal is to build a child's confidence and self-respect as well as teach him to read.

These children need many gay picture books, much listening to stories they can understand, opportunities for dramatization, and choral reading as soon as they are ready for it. Special efforts will have to be put forth to help them learn to love books and stories and to build reading into their lives. There may be little help from the children's homes but great satisfaction for the teacher when reading begins to mean something to these children.

☐ READING IN ENGLISH PRIMARY SCHOOLS

The contrast between the teaching of reading in many of our schools and what is now being advocated in England merits careful attention. While in some of our first grades, and especially for some children, learning to read is a happy experience, in other first grades and for all too many children the experience is grim indeed. English children learn to read, as do most children in this country, but the close adherence to a single method with graded readers commonly found here is absent from the schools Featherstone saw in an intensive program of school visitation. A portion of his report is presented here. The author of this book made the same observations in her own visit to more than thirty schools in England.

> How they learn reading offers a clear example of the kind of individual learning and teaching going on in these classrooms, even in quite large ones. . . . Reading is not particularly emphasized, and my purpose in singling it out is purely illustrative, though the contrast between English classes and most American ones, where reading is a formidable matter, is vivid and depressing.
>
> At first it is hard to say just how they do learn reading, since there are no separate subjects. A part of the answer slowly becomes clear, and it surprises American visitors used to thinking of the teacher as the generating force of education: children learn from each other. They hang around the library corners long before they can read, handling the books, looking at pictures, trying to find words they do know, listening and watching as the teacher

> hears other children's reading. It is common to see nonreaders studying people as they read, and then imitating them, monkey doing what monkey sees. Nobody makes fun of their grave parodies, and for good reasons.
>
> Teachers use a range of reading schemes, sight reading, phonics, and so forth, whatever seems to work with a child. . . . Increasingly in the good infant schools, there are no textbooks and no class readers. There are just books, in profusion. Instead of spending their scanty book money on 40 sets of everything, wise schools have purchased different sets of reading series, as well as a great many single books, at all levels of difficulty. Teachers arrange their classroom libraries so they can direct students of different abilities to appropriate books, but in most classes a child can tackle anything he wants. As a check, cautious teachers ask them to go on their own through a graded reading series—which one doesn't matter.
>
> However a child picks up reading, it will involve learning to write at the same time, and some write before they can read; there is an attempt to break down the mental barrier between the spoken, the written and the printed word. . . .
>
> . . . Gradually as a child amasses a reading and writing vocabulary, he reaches a fluent stage and you see six-year-olds writing stories, free-verse poems, accounts of things done in class, for an audience that includes other children as well as the teacher.[1]

In his preface to this report, Featherstone says, ". . . I do want to note that there are few reading problems in the good British schools; and the heads of the schools predict that the few remaining problems will disappear when the informal methods of the infant schools are extended for another year." The goal of all good American schools is also to meet the needs of all children as they learn to read. Perhaps greater informality and more concern for individual differences will meet the needs of our children also. Through this more relaxed, informal program, rapid learners forge ahead at their own rate, reading books that interest them and reading aloud to the teacher now and then. Slower learners move ahead comfortably without any sense of inadequacy or any evidence of adult disapproval. When the individual needs of children are met as they appear, there is no need for remedial work. Remedial work implies that something has gone amiss which needs to be remedied. If needs are

[1] Joseph Featherstone, "The Primary School Revolution in Britain." *The New Republic*, August 10, 1967.

met throughout the process of learning to read because the methods used with a given child are those that seem to work best for him, there is nothing to remedy. Whatever a child's rate of progress, it is still progress without the discouragement bred by failure.

The objective of the reading program in the primary grades is to help children learn to recognize the symbols, turn the visual stimulus into speech and thence into meaning, a symbol → sound → meaning sequence. Beyond that, it is to guide them into increasing depth of comprehension, and above all, into enjoyment of reading.

☐ SELECTED REFERENCES ☐

1. Austin, Mary C. et al, *The First R: The Harvard Report on Reading in the Elementary Schools.* New York: The Macmillan Company, 1963.
2. Bloomfield, Leonard and Barnhart, Clarence, *Let's Read,* Detroit: Wayne University Press, 19
3. Bond, Guy L. and Wagner, Eva Bond, *Teaching the Child to Read,* 4th Edition. New York: The Macmillan Company, 1966.
4. Chall, Jeanne S., *Learning to Read: The Great Debate.* New York: McGraw-Hill Co., 1967.
5. Conant, James B., *Learning to Read,* A Report of a Conference of Reading Experts. Princeton, New Jersey, Educational Testing Service, 1962.
6. Durkin, Dolores, *Children Who Read Early.* New York: Teachers College Press, 1966.
7. Featherstone, Joseph, "The Primary School Revolution in Britain." *The New Republic.* August 10, September 2, and September 9, 1967.
8. Flesch, Rudolf, *Why Johnny Can't Read.* New York: Harper & Brothers, Publishers, 1955.
9. Fries, Charles C., *Linguistics and Reading.* New York: Holt, Rinehart and Winston Company, 1963.
10. Gray, William S. *The Teaching of Reading and Writing.* Monographs in Fundamental Education, No. 10, Paris: UNESCO, 1961.
11. Kerfoot, James F., Editor, *First Grade Reading Programs.* Perspectives in Reading, No. 5. Newark, Delaware: International Reading Association, 1965.
12. Lee, Dorris May and Allen R. Van Allen, *Learning to Read Through Experience.* New York: Appleton-Century-Crofts, 1963.

13. Monroe, Marion, *Growing Into Reading.* Chicago: Scott, Foresman & Company, 1951.
14. Russell, David H., *Children Learn to Read.* Boston: Ginn and Company, 1961.
15. Smith, Nila Banton, *Reading Instruction for Today's Children.* Englewood Cliffs, New Jersey: Prentice-Hall, Inc., 1963.
16. Stauffer, Russell G., Editor, *The First Grade Reading Studies: Findings of Individual Investigations.* Newark, Delaware: International Reading Association, 1967.

MAKING READERS OF CHILDREN

A reader is a person who reads. Teaching children how to read is not the same thing as making readers of children. There has been a system of compulsory basic education in this country for many years and teaching children how to read has been a fundamental point of emphasis in that system; yet ours is not, even today, a nation of readers. A reader is not a person who *can* read; a reader is a person who *does* read. There is evidence to indicate that the time devoted to reading activities by some of the products of our schools is very little indeed. One investigator concluded that among many of our population book reading may average less than four minutes a day (7, p. 41). In many of our schools, emphasis has been placed almost exclusively on teaching children how to read; there has been little emphasis on teaching them what to read and what to read for. Perhaps this is one of the reasons why the out-of-school reading of many children and adults is pitifully meager. The great tragedy is that these people appear to recognize no shortage in their personal lives as the result of this restricted and insignificant intake. If children are to regard reading as an essential part of the pattern of satisfactory living, they must learn to use it as a method of solving their problems, of adding the understanding and knowledge they need to attain desired ends, and of increasing the enjoyment, depth, and significance of life itself. Therefore, both the process of reading and the product must be satisfying.

A look about his home community is all that is necessary to convince even the most casual observer that there is a relationship between the level of reading interests an individual develops and the kind of life he leads. A person who reads widely and well can enter into personal and vocational enterprises where success is dependent upon the ability to learn from printed material. A person who must depend upon direct, personal experience or upon listening to the experience of others from their own lips or from verbal recordings will be limited to the interests, skills, and knowledge he has opportunity to acquire through these means. His choice of vocation, the friends he draws about him, his leisure time pursuits, and even the neighborhood in which he makes his home may be determined in part by his intellectual and social interests which grow out of reading.

The child who comes to think of reading as pleasurable experience enjoys reading and wants to read. The more he reads, the more easily he reacts to the content of his reading and the more satisfaction he gains from the process. If the material is suitable in difficulty and the content within the range of his comprehension and interest, he finds pleasure in constructing the ideas it presents. Because this is true his interest expands and deepens and leads him on to further experience, deeper appreciation, and greater ease in reading. His progress is a spiral, constantly climbing upward. The child who lacks interest tends to be a slow, laborious reader. Consequently, he dislikes reading and avoids it whenever he can. Since he reads only what is required of him, he has relatively little practice and therefore his reading remains slow, laborious, and lacking in interest. He spins in a vicious circle; interest, ease, quantity and quality of experience, appreciation, and progress remain on approximately the same low level. Add to this the fact that his general morale is lowered because he comes to feel that his achievement is less than that of other children, and he is in a difficult state indeed. The vicious circle must be cut into to stop its spinning before he can make any real progress. Development of interest, adjustment of material and expectation to possible achievement, and individual encouragement and help are needed if he is to succeed. Interest and a measure of successful and satisfying experience are essential to growth.

Occasionally, one finds a child or an adult who has reached a stage of introversion in which he takes refuge in reading to avoid social contact and the wear and tear of actual experience. In his case, the meanings he attaches to the page are products of his own fancy, a part of the fabric of his own private world, not the everyday world of reality. Such an individual needs to be guided and enticed into real experience and encouraged to enter into social contacts, both for his own mental health and to enable him to paint the mental pictures of his book world in realistic forms and colors.

A truly well-conceived developmental program in reading should make success possible for all children, within their own capacities and limitations, so that they can enjoy both the process of reading and the experience they gain through reading. They must grow both in reading power and in power and insight through reading. Children cannot be highly motivated by intangible or long-deferred goals. They live and think largely in the present because they have not yet had the experience nor developed the maturity which are necessary to comprehend a distant goal and the long-term program of action which is required to reach it. They must find some satisfaction in reading at each step in the learning process. Their growing skill must be a means to increasingly satisfying ends—ends which they can recognize and understand, or they will not covet further skill for further experience.

☐ THE TRANSITION PERIOD IN LEARNING TO READ

In the primary grades most of what the child reads is story material. Toward the end of the third or certainly by the fourth grade the child is called upon to read an increasing variety of types of material. This is a critical stage in the child's learning to read. It is almost inevitable that many children at some time during this period become impatient with their skill because they cannot keep up with their interests or the work required of them. There is also danger that a child may become satisfied with his own immature reading and not advance to more mature forms. Guidance which helps a child to learn to read many types of material for many purposes causes him to leave behind his primary grade habits and develop ways of reading that are more mature. Growth does not take care of itself but requires careful guidance and teaching.

It is sadly true that there is still an occasional teacher who begins at this stage to assign material in readers and other textbooks, provide time for the children to "study their lesson" and then "hear" the children read or recite what they have worked out through their own inadequate methods. Such a procedure is *not teaching* and does little or nothing to improve a child's methods or his comprehension. Many children read little better after a year of such work than they did at the beginning of the year. All children need help with mechanics and with thought-getting if there is to be real gain. They need help in relating what they read to what they already know and in reacting thoughtfully and analytically to what they read. And they need help in making material come to life so that they can enter into it with understanding and enjoyment.

This is especially true as children are called upon to read increasing amounts and kinds of material in the various subject matter areas of the curriculum. There are basic skills that must be acquired and fundamental kinds of thinking that must be learned, as is true in every area of human endeavor. The task of learning to read cannot be assigned to the primary grades, nor even to the elementary school, alone. It is really a lifetime task. The elementary school program helps the child to recognize and interpret the common material of the English language as it appears in stories and in the content of social studies and science material, arithmetic problems, and other types of written material with which the child is called upon to deal during these years. He cannot learn to read chemistry, higher mathematics, psychology, economics, or all the other intellectual matter into which he may be drawn in later years. To learn to deal with the vocabulary and methodology of these areas would do him no good until he has occasion to use them and has developed the background and the maturity for understanding them. All individuals who are real readers continue to learn to read as long as they live and continue to read. They expand and deepen their vocabulary of words and meanings and polish and refine their skill through continuous experience with reading.

Teachers of intermediate grades are responsible for helping the children recognize the importance of reading. Along with helping them expand and refine their reading skill and adapt it to varying purposes they must also be concerned with higher level reading abilities. If children are to become active readers, they must learn to be critical and creative readers. They must learn to look beneath the surface of words to recognize overtones and undertones that add significance to meaning. Many pupils are intellectually capable of reaching out beyond the demands of the elementary school classroom. The reading tool is in their hands and they can use it. Their need now is to further sharpen it and make it serve a variety of purposes.

□ SHARPENING THE READING TOOL

Adults use reading in a variety of ways and to serve many purposes. Directions for carrying through a process are read carefully, step by step. A housewife reads recipes this way; an amateur "do-it-yourself" carpenter or mechanic reads the directions for the basement tool bench he is assembling or the chair he is refinishing; a business executive or a contractor checks his plans and contracts in this manner. Each of them reads the daily newspaper more rapidly, skimming here, reading more carefully there. Technical articles and books are read carefully with attention to details, while magazine stories, murder mysteries, and novels are read more rapidly for general impressions and story content. Every adult who uses reading to serve his daily needs and interests does a number of types of reading.

Children in the elementary school also have need for many types of reading. A verbal arithmetic problem must be read carefully, step by step, with attention to every detail. Directions for performing a science experiment call for the same type of reading. Reading social studies material calls for weighing points, noting the main points in paragraphs and the supporting details and putting them into perspective in one's thinking. Skimming may be called for in locating content for reports or to answer questions. Reading stories for pleasure is a different sort of reading. The mind follows the thread of the story and frequently gives little attention to descriptions and details except as they paint a background for thinking the main thread.

Children need help throughout the elementary school years in learning to recognize the requirements of varying types of reading situations and guidance in adapting their reading techniques to those requirements. Intermediate grade children need constant guidance in the development of study skills. How to locate material, how to take notes as they read, how to organize their material for oral or written reports—all this must be learned. Children need to learn to locate and to evaluate sources, weigh and check the reliability of their material, and analyze it for value. All of this requires careful guidance and teaching. It calls for reading *with* children and helping them to do the kinds of thinking that are necessary until they are capable individually of doing it independently with effectiveness and economy of effort.

Vocabulary presents problems for many children. Each new subject and each area of content add new words, many of which are completely unfamiliar. Old words take on new meanings. More and more of the new terms a child encounters are abstract and outside the realm of personal experience. Children need to be given help with meanings and encouragement to talk new meanings until the concepts come clear so that they can integrate them into their growing mass of experience and understanding.

Probably the best and most important way for children to

expand their understanding of language and also to expand and refine their own use of it is through reading. The more a child reads, the more accustomed he becomes to the many ways in which people express ideas and the many purposes language serves. The scientist or mathematician in stating a problem or presenting the results of his work chooses words with great care in order to express his precise meaning and to make it clear and understandable to the audience for whom he is writing, whether it is a scholar in his own field, a layman with general interest in his field, or even a child. There is no extraneous or irrelevant material, no excess verbiage. The social scientist tries to make basic principles shine through his delineation of facts and processes. The literary scholar and creative writer use language with artistry to gain the effects they seek. Skillful writers in each field try to use language so that it serves the needs of their specialized subject. The more a child reads the more he expands his vocabulary of words and meanings and his repertoire of techniques for getting across the shades of meaning he wants to express. The more he reads the more easily he interprets what the author is striving to express and the more skillfully he senses undertones and overtones and their effect on his own thinking.

The middle grades are especially important for the development of skill in differentiating and adapting reading to varying materials and purposes. Guidance for teachers is available in books on the teaching of reading and in the teachers' manuals of children's reader series (3, 6, 8, 10, 12, 13, 14). The skills of interpretation, and of note-taking, outlining, gathering bibliographic data for reports, skimming to locate material, and the like should be taught to all children. They can be taught in any suitable material that children have occasion to use; they need not be taught from a reading or language textbook. They can be taught in social studies, science, or any other content material just as well. *But they must be taught.* Any pupil who goes to junior high school without the basic study skills the middle grades should teach is a sadly handicapped person.

☐ INDIVIDUALIZED READING

More and more teachers are working toward highly individualized programs of reading with opportunity for the teacher to work individually with each child. In this plan the children select the materials they wish to read from the school or classroom library. Self-selection takes care of the matter of interest and the teacher then helps the child to read the material of his choice (17).

An individual conference with the teacher at frequent intervals is an integral part of any individualized reading program. Children come to her individually for brief periods of help with the materials they are reading. Some people fear that children will not make progress unless the teacher reads with each child each day. Yet individual help for even five minutes on alternate days is often more help in the course of a week than each child is given when he is a member of a group of ten children. The factor of self-selection of material holds the interest at a high level and results in greater gains for many children than group teaching could possibly bring. The teacher, as a result of her individual work with the children, keeps a simple running record of each child's progress. She can call together, for periods of special help, those children who have similar needs for more phonics, more help with structural analysis, or with study techniques. She can follow each child's progress and see that he gets the help he needs when he needs it.

Periods are set aside now and then for children to share what they are reading. A child may wish to select a particularly interesting or exciting part of a book to read to the group. Or he may use the opportunity to advertise the book to encourage others to read it. Sometimes, children who have read the same book will prepare a skit depicting episodes in the book that have particular dramatic possibilities. Occasionally, a child may draw a picture or construct a model that represents a point of special interest in the book.

To help children with selection of material to read, teachers sometimes do what the headmaster of a school in England delights in doing (2). He may appear at a classroom door at any time with an armful of books he wants to introduce to the children, markers protruding from each one. His children say when they see him, "Oh goody! Tasters today!" He reads from one book perhaps an exciting incident, from another a beautiful description, from another a bit of humor, or perhaps an exciting build-up for a mystery or a special event. Then he places the books on the library table saying, "I'll leave them in case you care to read them." One can be sure that children scramble for them and have to sign up for turns to read them. Thus he introduces children to books of high quality which they might easily miss. Sometimes a book starts slowly or fails to catch a child's interest yet he would happily continue reading it if he knew more about it. Many children need encouragement to plunge into the really fine books when there are so many lesser books that appear easier to read.

It is not necessary that a teacher check each child's comprehension of each book he reads in an individualized program. The brief conference periods in which a child reads aloud to the teacher some of what he is reading to show her how he handles it, with perhaps a discussion of an item of meaning, is all that is necessary. Children select their reading material in terms of interest as well as difficulty. If a child is deeply interested in a subject he will be able to read material on that subject even though it is more difficult than his usual reading material. Conversely, if he is not interested in the subject, even material of a level he is capable of handling will be read poorly or laid aside as too difficult or too uninteresting to struggle with. Interest and background of experience may be more important in the selection of reading material than a carefully controlled vocabulary.

Teachers in the United States are fortunate indeed in the quantity and quality of material available for middle grade children to read. Federal funds have been available for several years to build good library collections for the elementary schools but the schools must give them top priority. There are books on so many subjects and at so many levels of difficulty that every child can find some he is interested in and at his own level of reading skill. The problem of teachers is to know the pupils well enough to help them find books to fit their interests and needs.

☐ BOOKS OF ALL SORTS

Textbook reading alone is not enough reading to make a child a reader. He must read more than that and reach the point where he reads of his own free will, because he wants to read, and in his own undirected time. Textbooks in various subjects have value in a basic, developmental program but they cannot serve as the whole program. Wisely used textbooks, selected to fit the needs of individuals and small groups, are valuable in developing the foundation upon which the structure of self-education can be built. Guidance in reading should take the child into all sorts of materials; simple, informational materials, poetry, and many types of stories. In his independent reading, the child should have opportunity to sample a wide variety of material, including science, historical material, content dealing with other lands and peoples, stories that are true as well as the many good "could-be-true" stories. Humor has a place, as has adventure and mystery that is wholesome and on the child's level of understanding and maturity.

Not all of the books that children read will fall into the category of literature. But all of the material they read should be well written, consistent, accurate, and suitable for its purpose. Children sense sincerity, integrity, and consistency in books and respond to it favorably. Since children are in the process of building taste and judgment with regard to books, they need to be provided with many pleasurable experiences with material chosen to fit their moods and immediate interests. The teacher who has the ability to provide the right book at the right time will go far toward making children enthusiastic consumers of good books.

Children, like adults, read for experience, for expansion, and for enjoyment. When they reach the stage at which reading skill makes it possible for them to read independently to further their interests, one finds that their purposes do not differ in kind from those of adults. They read for experience which they can enjoy and appreciate through the words of others. They read for personal expansion and growth, to add to their knowledge, answer their questions, and solve their problems. Such reading helps to provide the depth and fullness of life, the emotional, social and spiritual security which all people, young and old, are constantly seeking.

Children at this age need to use reading in many types of situations and for many purposes so that they become increasingly aware of the possibilities and the values of reading. They can explore the local resources for reading materials and begin to develop independence in finding the materials they need to serve their purposes and feed their interests.

☐ THE NEED FOR WIDE READING

Children of elementary school age should dip into many subjects and explore a wide range of types and styles of writing. This is a period in which interests are being built and tastes formed. Some children show definite preferences at an early age and read quantities of the type of material they like. This is not always good material. A child may run to series books for a time, reading book after book of similar material—often harmless but also of little literary or intellectual value. Some children live through a period of nothing but comic books or books of doubtful quality and content. There are children who enjoy material of good quality and read quantities of it, but all of one general kind or on one topic.

It is important that children be allowed to select their own material for wide reading but there is need for guidance and the opening up of new possibilities. A child cannot know what he may like until he has some experience with it. Teachers can introduce new topics and new styles of writing to children through reading aloud books that the children might otherwise pass by. Perhaps a bood should be read to children in its entirety. Sometimes, merely reading an introductory chapter and calling attention to interesting content which follows will sharpen children's interest. At times, telling a bit of the story, or giving children the setting for it, will send them off to read it.

It is important to arrange with children means of recording the books they read. One teacher keeps a file of five-by-eight-inch cards in a box on her desk. As each child finishes reading a book, he and the teacher together record the book on his card. This gives the teacher opportunity to talk with the child informally about the book, to discuss an interesting character, to compare their reactions to parts of the story, or to chuckle together over an amusing episode. It is not a quiz session but a sharing of experience, yet it gives the teacher opportunity to learn whether the child really read the book and what it meant to him. This plan also affords the teacher opportunity to help the child make his next selection. Perhaps they go to the shelves together to look for possibilities or the teacher may suggest books for the child to sample. A boy in a fourth grade had read many books dealing with science. The teacher called his attention to the fact that all of his choices were valuable but of one kind. She took him to the shelves and pulled out books of a variety of kinds, suggesting that he lay aside his interest in science for a time while he looked into other fields. The books she suggested included a humorous tale, a gripping story, some material dealing with history—a wide variety. The boy willingly made his selections for a time in other fields before returning to his much-enjoyed science.

☐ LATER STAGES OF READING

During the intermediate or low-maturity stage the child reaches the point where he can read much of the common material read by adults. Newspapers and magazines, fiction, and informational material become available to him. If the child has had adequate guidance during his earlier experience, he is now beginning to read silently more rapidly than he can read orally and he is able to pick up more material at a single glance. He can unlock unfamiliar words through syllabication and other more mature word techniques. The child can begin to suit his reading to his purpose; he can skim and can read more analytically. His skills are becoming specialized and he is learning to use them effectively. The world of reading is opening up for him but he needs encouragement and guidance in reaching out for it. It is particularly important to remember that during these intermediate grade years the child needs a great deal of reading beyond mere school and textbook reading if he is to become a mature and accomplished reader.

The advanced stages of reading which follow the development of the elementary school years are the stages for the polishing and refining of skills and the broadening and diversification of interests. These are important years for reading growth and development. This latter period never comes to an end. The individual who enjoys and uses reading is forever adding to the effectiveness of his techniques as he utilizes them. He adds more and more of knowledge and experience as well as more resourcefulness in gaining knowledge. His ability to interpret what he reads grows more mature as he matures in judgment and power.

It is the responsibility of the elementary school teacher to teach children how to read, to guide them in learning what to read and what to read for. The wealth of material available makes it possible for teachers to meet the needs of all children. There is plenty of material of all sorts to help the gifted child expand his experience and his knowledge to the limits of his capacity. There is also carefully written material of high interest level but low level of difficulty for the child who learns slowly. There is material to feed special intellectual interests and material to develop emotional maturity. For both teacher and children, the reading experience can be highly satisfying.

☐ UTILIZING RESOURCES FOR LEARNING

Throughout the years of the elementary school, children should become increasingly aware of the resources for learning and for enjoyment that are available through reading. All children need to be introduced to the library at an early age and helped to find and utilize its resources with increasing skill and satisfaction. Library experience begins with the classroom library, expands to the school library, then to the public library. Eight- and nine-year-olds can begin to use a simple card catalogue as soon as they have learned to follow an alphabetical system. Other resources for library reference are introduced as the children are ready for them.

Dictionary use begins with picture dictionaries and simple alphabetical files in the primary grades. In the fourth grade, children are given special help with the use of a junior dictionary and begin to develop the dictionary techniques they will continue to use throughout life. Children are taught to use encyclopedias, an atlas, almanac, and resource material of many sorts through carefully planned lessons and a follow-up of consistent guidance until the resources can be used easily and effectively. All of this requires careful planning and systematic teaching. Skills do not develop of themselves.

The rate of learning will vary greatly from child to child during these years. Gifted children will achieve independence early and slow-learning children will require patient, consistent guidance over a period of years which extends on up into the secondary school. Part of the work children do with resource material will be individual work and part group work. Children can learn to help each other. It is good for able children who are potential leaders to learn to help and guide others who learn more slowly. Every child who has abilities which can be used in leadership needs to learn how to be an acceptable leader. He needs to learn how to guide and help others so thoughtfully and sympathetically, without domination, impatience, or intolerance, that he brings out the best in others and causes them to reach a higher level than they could without his help. These abilities and attitudes the gifted child must acquire under guidance and helping other children use resources for learning affords valuable opportunities for such growth. Slow-learning children need experiences which build up their interest in learning and their confidence in their own powers, not experiences so far beyond them that they lose interest and faith in their ability to learn.

☐ GUIDANCE THROUGH READING

A teacher who knows well the children in her class, knows their strengths and weaknesses, their conflicts and problems, can often guide them through reading into self-understanding and new attitudes toward themselves and others. Reading Eleanor Estes' *The Hundred Dresses* will help children to understand the feelings of the child rejected by her group because she dresses poorly. Doris Gates' *Blue Willow* and Marguerite De Angeli's *Bright April* will help them understand the migrant child and the child who differs in color. There are books to help children who have no experience with stable homes and loving parents to understand and appreciate what home can be so that they will want something better for themselves and their children when they grow up. There is an increasing number of books written to help the adopted child, the child placed by the welfare department in a temporary foster home, the child who is blind, and other children whose lives differ from the usual pattern, adjust to life as they find it. Teachers need to know both children and books in order to help children learn to understand themselves and other people and to face up to the conditions life imposes.

Other suggestions for the use of books are found in Chapter 17. Following the selected references at the end of this chapter are sources to which teachers can turn for an annotated list of children's books. These lists are revised by their publishers from time to time and kept up to date.

☐ PRIMARY GRADE METHODS AND INTERMEDIATE GRADE ACHIEVEMENT

There is a great deal of research comparing children's achievement at the end of first grade as the result of using one method or another to teach beginning reading. There is an incredible lack of longitudinal studies which indicate how children taught by various methods achieve later in the middle grades. The

27-cities study of beginning reading financed by the United States Office of Education in 1965 was designed as a one-year study with no follow-up. Some of the 27 programs were extended through the second year and a few through the third year. These will constitute an important longitudinal picture but far more of such research is needed.

The book by Jeanne Chall, *Learning to Read: The Great Debate*, which was her report of an intensive three-year study of reading financed by the Carnegie Foundation, is the target of much controversy among reading specialists though it is happily received by some of the public. After studying earlier research and present textbooks and visiting schools in the United States, England, Scotland and Canada, she concluded that the evidence indicated to her that a reading program which involved extensive attention at an early stage to the code of English reading brought better results by the fourth grade in overall reading achievement. She granted that children taught with a code emphasis might progress more slowly at first than children taught by a method which emphasized meaning, but that by third or fourth grade the former children equaled the latter in rate and also read more accurately (4). Chall did not emphasize any single code emphasis, i/t/a, phonic, or a linguistic method, but created consternation among the proponents of the current basal reader methods.

The fact that this controversy could exist, after so much research has been done of a variety of kinds, makes clear the need for better planned research, particularly of a longitudinal nature, to determine under what kind of early teaching children become interested, self-motivated readers who consider reading an integral part of all good living. No one has yet tackled the very important problem of children's feelings as they learn to read and the effect of those feelings on their success in learning and their future consumption of reading material. Clearly, there is much work to be done here.

☐ DIAGNOSIS OF SPECIAL READING PROBLEMS

Regardless of the method used to teach reading and the care with which it is adapted to individual differences, there will always be some children for whom learning to read presents special problems. At long last neurologists, psychologists, psychiatrists, and pediatricians are beginning to consider with teachers the problems of these children and suggest ways to help them. Not all children who do poorly in reading fall into this group. Some children do poorly because they are bored and find little to interest them in the materials presented and in what is expected of them. Teachers have always been aware of the needs of children with vision and hearing problems. Now attention is being called to children who have problems of perception and to minimally brain-damaged children. Elementary teachers are being called upon increasingly to study the research and guidance that is available to them. Reading is too important and the potentials of these children too valuable to fail to meet their needs. They can learn to read with proper help. It is possible for these children as well as the many culturally disadvantaged children to attain the reading skill which will make available to them the vocational, social, and cultural opportunities which they need and can use. This society owes them but teachers must take the initiative and assume the responsibility for making available to each child the resources of help and guidance which he individually needs.

□ SELECTED REFERENCES □

1. Austin, Mary C. et al., *The First R.: The Harvard Report on Reading in the Elementary School.* New York: The Macmillan Company, 1963.
2. Bell, Vicars, *On Learning the English Tongue.* London: Faber and Faber, 1947.
3. Bond, Guy L. and Wagner, Eva Bond, *Teaching the Child to Read.* Third Edition. New York: The Macmillan Company, 1966.
4. Chall, Jeanne S., *Learning to Read: The Great Debate.* New York: McGraw-Hill Company, 1967.
5. Conant, James B., *Learning to Read: A Report of a Conference of Reading Experts.* Princeton, New Jersey: Educational Testing Service, 1962.
6. De Boer, John T. and Dallman, Martha, *The Teaching of Reading.* Revised Edition. New York: Holt, Rinehart and Winston, Inc., 1964.
7. Fries, Charles C., *Linguistics and Reading.* New York: Holt, Rinehart and Winston, Inc., 1964.
8. Gans, Roma, *Common Sense in Teaching Reading.* Indianapolis: Bobbs-Merrill Company, 1963.

9. Gray, W. S. and Rogers, Bernice, *Maturity in Reading: Its Nature and Appraisal.* Chicago: University of Chicago Press, 1956.
10. Harris, Albert J., *How to Increase Reading Ability.* Fourth Edition. New York: Longmans Green and Company, 1962.
11. Jennings, Frank, *This Is Reading.* New York: Bureau of Publications, Teachers College, Columbia University, 1965.
12. Russell, David H., *Children Learn to Read.* Second Edition. Boston: Ginn and Company, 1961.
13. Smith, Nila Banton, *Reading Instruction for Today's Children.* Englewood Cliffs, New Jersey: Prentice-Hall, 1963.
14. Staiger, Ralph, and Sohn, David A., Editors, *New Direction in Reading.* New York: Bantom Books, 1967.
15. Strang, Ruth; McCullough, Constance M.; and Traxler, Arthur E., *The Improvement of Reading.* Fourth Edition. New York: McGraw-Hill Book Company, 1967.
16. Strickland, Ruth G., *The Language of Elementary School Children: Its Relationship to the Language of Reading Textbooks and the Quality of Reading of Selected Children.* Indiana University, Bloomington: Bulletin of the School of Education, Vol. 38, No. 4, July, 1962.
17. Veatch, Jeannette, *Reading in the Elementary School.* New York: The Ronald Press Company, 1966.

□ BOOK LISTS FOR TEACHERS, PARENTS, AND LIBRARIANS □

(These are revised about every five years.)

American Council on Education (ACE)
1785 Massachusetts Avenue N.W., Washington, D.C.
Reading Ladders for Human Relations, compiled by Muriel Crosby and Committee

American Library Association (ALA)
50 East Huron Street, Chicago, Illinois
A Basic Book Collection for Elementary Grades

Association for Childhood Education International
3615 Wisconsin Avenue N.W., Washington, D.C.
Bibliography of Books for Children, compiled by Evelyn C. Thornton and Committee

R. R. Bowker Company
1180 Avenue of the Americas, New York, N.Y.
Best Books for Children, compiled by Joan (revised annually)

Eakin, Mary K.
Good Books for Children
Chicago: University of Chicago Press
New York: Pocket Books

Larrick, Nancy
A Parent's Guide to Children's Reading
New York: Pocket Books

National Council of Teachers of English (NCTE)
508 South Sixth Street
Champaign, Illinois

Adventuring with Books: A Book List for Elementary Schools
New York: Signet Books

Books for Beginning Readers, compiled by
Elizabeth Guilfoile
Champaign: The Council

learning to write

The most difficult to acquire of all of man's language skills is writing. It is the only basic skill that the college feels obligated to teach. In spite of the fact that college English departments chafe under the burden of Freshman Composition classes, most of them accept the responsibility, insisting the while that the work ought to be done by the schools before the students come to college. Many people who speak well and read with ease are not good writers, and some people who can write reasonably well do not enjoy writing and do no more of it than they are obligated to do.

Why is this? The spoken language has, in the course of man's history, long preceded his development of a written language. Writing involves a synthesis of a number of separate, discrete skills which the writer utilizes in orderly sequence yet almost simultaneously. He must:

1. make up his mind what to write and arrange his ideas in the sequence he wants to produce
2. put the ideas into words and the words into sentences that say what he wants to say yet are conventional and clear enough so that the reader can interpret his thought
3. come to terms with a sentence before he starts to write it. One cannot edit amid ships as he does in speech when he says, "All of us, three to be exact, thought that—we definitely concluded that—." Everyone does some of this editing in speech yet it cannot be done in writing
4. write horizontally across a page in left to right direction
5. select from among the 26 letters of the alphabet the ones needed to spell the words he wants and arrange them in proper sequence
6. make his hand do what his mind wants it to do in forming the letters so that they are legible (or strike the right keys on a typewriter)
7. use appropriate starting, stopping, and other punctuation—the traffic signals along the way to guide the reader.

The young child, as he begins to write, must learn to do all of these things in order to turn his thought or his speech into graphic representation.

Learning to write is not easy in any case, yet teachers frequently make it harder than it needs to be by insisting on careful, even writing, neat papers, perfect spelling, and proper punctuation to the extent that the child cannot possibly give the attention he needs and wants to give to what he is attempting to say. Unrealistic requirements and failure to arrange the steps in learning so that children can comfortably climb them, may be the basic reasons for poor writing in the schools and, of course, out of them.

In fact, concern with "correct" writing has completely overshadowed and crowded out all else in the writing experience of many children. Applegate, in *Helping Children Write*[1], said, "If the climate of the room is such that correctness is paramount to discovery and exploration in word use, a teacher or parent will kill the very thing for which he seeks." Children have been taught how to write when they had nothing to write, no need for writing other than the teacher's assignment, and no desire for it except the desire to conform to school requirements for the comfort and satisfaction that such conformity may yield.

Ability to express oneself either orally or in writing grows with the growth of interests one is eager to express. The child whose background of experience is meager and who lacks keen and absorbing interests may learn to write material that is mechanically correct in form but will probably contain nothing that is worth reading. Interesting the child in a variety of activities and providing enriching social experiences produces better results than emphasis on writing skills. The ability to express grows out of a sense of power and personal worth, a sense of having something to offer that will be of interest to others. It requires also sufficient sense of security and of being accepted and wanted by others to give the child the confidence to put forth effort to express himself.

Burrows and her co-writers distinguish between practical writing and personal writing in guiding children in written language (7). Practical utilitarian writing is done in any situation in which there is need for it. It includes the writing of invitations, notes to parents and others for various purposes, business letters, orders, memoranda, reports, any type of writing that serves a purpose in the work the children are doing. Practical writing is usually to be read by people other than the writer and therefore must be written so that it can be read easily. Per-

[1]Mauree Applegate, *Helping Children Write*. Scranton: International Textbook Company, 1949, p. 31.

sonal writing is for the individual who writes it, primarily, though it is often shared with others. Creative, imaginative writing of stories, poems, or plays would fall into this group—anything the child wishes to express. In the practical writing, the teacher furnishes whatever guidance she feels the child is ready for and can use. The personal writing is the child's own and is accounted satisfactory when it is satisfactory to him, when it says what he wants it to say. Here the emphasis is placed upon getting his ideas down. Spelling, penmanship, neatness, punctuation, and such external items are not considered unless they interfere with the expression of ideas. The child is trying to catch his own ideas and get them down on paper so that they represent him and the quality and flavor of his thinking.

Though the two aspects of writing develop separately, in a sense, and serve different purposes, the child carries over, gradually, what he has learned of techniques in the practical writing and applies it where it fits and serves his purpose in the personal writing.

Throughout all good teaching of writing, the emphasis is first and always upon saying something that is worth saying and saying it effectively.

☐ FIRST EXPERIENCES WITH WRITTEN LANGUAGE

A child's first experience with written language may come in his home through dictating to his mother a message to be put into a letter to his grandmother or his father. Or the child may insist on a pencil and paper and scribble a bit, saying, "Put this in Daddy's letter. It says, 'I love you, Daddy. Come home soon.'" Written language usually begins with the writing down by an adult of the child's spontaneous expression. The earliest letters to Santa Claus are written that way. Some mothers are interested in preserving a child's spontaneous remarks as part of a record of his growth.

In nursery school, the teacher may occasionally encourage the children to tell her what to write in a note to a child who is ill. Four-year-olds would be interested in such a project and some three-year-olds might care to enter in. The teacher may take down a child's remarks about something he has created in order to include them when he shows his creation to his mother. Other bits of recording may be in order from time to time. The child becomes aware of the process and its purpose and may enter into it spontaneously if it interests him.

Kindergarten children find frequent opportunities to dictate their ideas for the teacher to write. A child may wish to tell a story about the picture he has made and have it written beneath or on the back of the sheet. Some children may be interested in having the teacher write down the stories they tell about Christmas or other interest or occasion and put them into their own book for the library table. The absence of a child from the group may be the occasion for composing a letter, or there may be need to gain permission of the principal and the parents for a proposed trip. Dictating a note of thanks to a neighbor after visiting her flower garden or to a mother who has helped with a cooking project not only gives children a concept of how to write notes but also of when to write them.

Normal development in learning to write does not begin with putting a writing instrument into a child's hands and copy material before his eyes. Writing is a means to a variety of ends, not an end in itself. Written expression has value in terms of what is expressed and the purpose it serves. Children need to approach written expression first of all from the point of view of something to say and the need for saying it in written form.

□ STEPS IN GROWTH IN WRITTEN LANGUAGE

There are clearly distinguishable steps in developing the ability to express one's thinking in written form. Some children will have many ideas but little notion of how to get them transferred to paper, while others have a noticeable lack of ideas and therefore, no concern for the mechanics of writing. Some children will be able to compose and write with a fair degree of ease and there are others who will be successful in a practical job of writing if the teacher will help with spelling, guide placement on the paper, and help with checking or proofreading. Such a sequence of steps as the one which follows cannot be alloted to age or grade levels because each child needs to live each stage until he is ready to move on to the next. (20).

■ *Dictation*

Spontaneous expression of ideas. The teacher takes the material down exactly as the child gives it or assumes responsibility for arranging it into readable units.

Expressing ideas in thought units or sentences in such form that the teacher can put them down.

Dictating sentence units more skillfully and purposefully, with attention to the writing process and the purpose to be served.

Learning suitable expression for various purposes: modifications of form and tone for an invitation, a "thank-you" note, a business request, a note of congratulation or sympathy.

Developing individual style. Learning to express one's thinking in writing as colorfully and individually as in speaking.

■ *Dictation with copying*

Dictating material for a purpose, but the child writing in the greeting, signature, or a sentence or two to make the material his own.

Dictating, but the child making his own copy, not using the teacher's or a duplicated copy.

■ *Writing with all the help he needs*

Doing own writing, turning to the teacher for help with spelling, letter form, spacing, and other such matters. The content and expression are the child's own, but the teacher gives careful guidance in the matter of form to make it suit its purpose.

Doing own writing with less dependence upon the teacher, fewer requests for help. The teacher and the child check the first draft of the material together. The child then copies the material if the use to which it is to be put warrants it.

■ *Writing with increasing independence*

Writing with occasional help, and learning to use self-help materials in doing practical writing, such as a dictionary and a handbook of writing style showing forms for letter headings and other accepted patterns. Checking the first draft with the teacher and making a final copy, if need be. This stage is more apt to be found in the intermediate than in the primary grades.

Writing, independent reading for errors and points lacking

in clarity, then checking the material with the teacher before completing the final copy.

In all of these steps, the emphasis is placed first and all the time upon content and purpose. It is important that children approach any writing project with interest and complete it with a sense of satisfaction in fulfilling their purpose. "Ever since we began expecting children to write only when they had a genuine interest or the earnest desire to do so, we have found them eager to write well." So say the Bronxville teachers, and the record of their experience proves their point (6).

What is true of oral language is true also of writing: that it develops best in a wholesome atmosphere in which children feel free to express their real thoughts and feel assured of genuinely friendly and sympathetic interest. When a child is relaxed and himself, he is much more able to express his thoughts.

☐ DICTATION: THE TEACHER SERVING AS SCRIBE

Since emphasis on content of expression and purpose must precede emphasis on form, dictation is the essential first step in the program of written language. In the kindergarten and much of the primary school period the teacher may need to serve as scribe for both practical and personal writing. Individual children begin to do their own writing as they are able to do so, but the teacher stands ready to take the child's dictation when it meets his needs, even after the stage of self-writing has begun.

Often, much of the early dictation is of imaginative stories or personal experiences the children wish to record. Sometimes it is a matter of group composition, with various children chiming in with thoughts they think appropriate and wish to have included. More often it is a matter of individual stories with the storyteller being accorded whatever time he needs to round out his story and bring it to conclusion. In the dictating of stories or poems the teacher takes down what the child says just as he says it, then reads it back for the child to listen to and make sure that it is just as he wants it. There is no attempt at teaching. This is the child's own material and it is recorded as he wishes it. Only when it does not make clear sense will the teacher offer to change it.

In the writing of practical material, the teacher may call attention to the form into which she is putting the material. If the purpose is a group invitation to another class to come for rhythms or a play, she may ask, "How shall we start our invitation? I'll put 'Dear Kindergarten Boys and Girls,' here at the beginning so they will know at once that the letter is written to them." The group may be guided in checking very carefully to see that all the necessary information is given – day, time, place, purpose – so that there may be no mistakes. Then the teacher asks, "Now, how shall we end our invitation so that the children will know who sent it?" Throughout such writing the children's attention is called to the steps in thinking and procedure as the writing progresses. They are developing concepts of form and the purpose served by the elements of form, even though they cannot yet write it down for themselves.

Sentence sense is developed in this way, and the children are introduced to punctuation. Perhaps the teacher asks, after the greeting is written, "What shall we say first? Who will tell us a good first sentence?" If the words flow from the group too rapidly for the teacher to get them all down, she may call attention to the problem. "I can't write so fast. Let me finish this sentence first," and she reads it back to the children. "Now I am ready for your next sentence, Carol."

Punctuation is introduced in similar manner. "That is the end of the sentence so I'll mark it with a period. It is like a traffic signal. It means, 'This is the end of this part.' " Or, "He is asking a question, isn't he? I'll put a question mark here." Or, when a direct quotation is included, "Mr. Brown is talking in this part. I'll put these marks here at the beginning and the end of the talking part so people will know just what Mr. Brown said." The children are not expected to remember these details or when and how to use them. The frequent mention of them introduces the child to the concept of signs and signals along the way to help the reader to make easy progress and to understand clearly what is meant. Learning the forms will come later, but understanding and motivation for the learning begin early and develop through many experiences. In all cases, the teacher reads the material back to the children so that they may hear what they have produced and make changes if they wish to do so.

This is the procedure for the language approach to reading described in Chapter 11 on page 269. The material the child dictates and his own early writing are used as his introduction to reading. The child learns what writing and reading are and how each operates. Again, the teacher must accept the child's offering in his own dialect, guiding him as suggested earlier, into recognition of the dialect in his books and the spoken dialect of the school.

The combining of reading and writing was what Featherstone saw in his study of English schools and what this author saw in a semester of school visiting in England. Featherstone says,

> When a child starts school, he gets a large unlined notebook; this is his book for free writing, and he can put what he wants in it. On his own, he may draw a picture in it with crayon or pencil, discuss the picture with the teacher, and dictate a caption to her, which she then writes down for him: "This is my Dad." He copies the caption, writing just underneath. In this way he learns to memorize the look and sound of his dictated words and phrases, until he reaches a point where, with help, he can write sentences. Often his notebook serves as his own first reading book.
>
> He also gets a smaller notebook, his private dictionary, in which he enters words as he learns them . . . you see six-year-olds writing stories, free-verse poems, accounts of things done in class, for an audience that includes other children as well as the teacher.
>
> As a rule, teachers don't pay much attention to accuracy or neatness until a child is well on in his writing. . . . Under these methods, where the children choose the content of their writing, there seems in fact to be more attention paid to content than externals, such as punctuation, spelling and grammar. In the good schools, these are presented as what they are, living ways to get a meaning across, to be understood.

Dictation has a legitimate place in the language program as long as any child has need for it. Most children will be ready to try the writing of brief notes and other forms of practical material before they are ready to put down on paper their own creative, imaginative writing. In writing practical material, the purpose serves as a point of reference. If a child becomes lost in putting down a sentence or forgets what he planned to say, he can go back to his purpose and its needs and be set on the track again. If a child has thought through a story or conceived a plan for one, he may be unable to hold on to his sequence of thought while he laboriously uses a pencil, struggling to spell the words he wants, and trying to remember how to form a letter he has forgotten. When he has told his story, so that his thinking has been captured, he is quite willing to put forth the effort to make his own copy of it. The words, the spelling, the form are all there in the teacher's copy, and he can give his full attention to reproducing it.

Some children will start out bravely and enthusiastically with independent writing, but become discouraged because they are unable to spell many of the words they want to use. They lose the thread of thought while they try to figure out a possible spelling or wait for their turn for the teacher's help. Other children become seriously fatigued with the combination of mental and physical endeavor and are ready to lay aside the material or to taper it off, omitting part of what they meant to say and ending weakly. If the teacher will serve as scribe for the last few lines, the whole story can be rounded out to the child's satisfaction. Or the teacher may jot down the ideas the child plans to use next for his later writing.

Original poetry calls for dictation even after the children have reached a point at which they can write their own stories. Perhaps it is because it lacks plot and sequence and is thought of as a whole, that it is harder for the child to write. Perhaps it is because it is a unit and he cannot think it clearly in a pattern of lines. At any rate, dictating is some children's choice for poetry thoughts long after they have taken over the writing of their own stories.

In the dictating of practical material, there is no problem with regard to the final form of the production because the teacher takes care of that as she writes it down. In writing children's stories, and poetry also, the teacher assumes the responsibility for getting the material onto the page in readable form. When the child takes over the writing, his product may discourage him unless the teacher is alert to furnish all the guidance and help he needs in order to develop a feeling of satisfaction in his growing independence.

□ DICTATION WITH COPYING

Children can begin to make their own copies of dictated material as soon as they have reached a level of muscular control and eye-hand-mind co-ordination which makes it possible. The introduction to practical writing is a gradual one. The children first learn to write their names in order to care for their properties. The next step may be the writing of memoranda to take home, copying the words "lunch money," "banking," or "gym shoes" on a slip to remind them to tell mother of their need. The earlier notes of invitation or asking for permission which are prepared in first grade may be group composition which is then duplicated so that each child can sign his name and take home his copy. Later, he can insert the greeting, "Dear Mother," as well as his signature. Still later, a portion or all of the letter may be dictated by each child individually, so that each will copy his own original letter.

The use of a felt pen designed for sign and chart writing has advantages over the use of the chalkboard for taking down material children are to copy. The writing can be spaced on the newsprint sheet as children will space it on their paper. The distinct black-on-white is easier to see from a distance, or the sheet can be hung near the children who are copying it. The sheet can be put aside for later use, if need be, leaving the chalkboard for material of less permanent value which can be erased as needed. Better still, each child may have a duplicate copy on his desk to follow, rather than one at a great distance.

Teachers of young children become sensitive to the possibilities for writing in the activities children engage in and find a number of real uses for writing that do not overtax the children nor make writing distasteful to them. Young children should not be expected to write very frequently or very much. A great deal of time has been wasted in the past in trying to force immature minds and undeveloped hands to acquire writing skill. Children differ in the age at which they are ready to undertake writing just as they do in learning to walk and to talk. Given encouragement to learn in their own good time, as they are ready for it, they learn to write successfully without strain and with real enjoyment of writing.

□ WRITING WITH ALL THE HELP HE NEEDS

When the child is ready to try his hand at independent writing, he needs a great deal of help, help which is given freely and promptly, if he is to continue to write happily and to keep working toward higher standards. This is a critical stage in the process of learning to write. It is here that many children lose all interest in writing and seem never to regain it. Help which makes it possible for the child to achieve a satisfying product sharpens his interest in writing. Discouragement and frustration because too much is expected with too little help is devastating to his interest and his whole attitude toward writing. Because of the many points which must be kept in mind, a child's first stories which he writes for himself may be shorter and of poorer quality than the material he previously dictated. Teachers have devised different ways to get around to all the children in a group to give them adequate help at this stage. One method is to work with a relatively small group while the rest of the class carries on other activities. The teacher then brings these children together in a corner of the room or around a table. As each child asks for a word he needs but cannot spell, the teacher writes it quickly on a slip of paper so that he can use it and go on immediately with his writing. Some teachers have tried writing the words called for, on the chalkboard, but this is less satisfactory. The fact that words have to be asked for in louder tones, since the teacher is stationed farther away, is in itself distracting. If the board has many words on it, the child may become lost, or his word erased before he has finished with it. Also, it is a much more difficult task to copy from the chalkboard at a distance than to copy from a slip of paper on one's desk. Some teachers suggest that a child write what he thinks are the first letters of a word he needs and leave space until the teacher can help him – a short space for a short word, longer for a long word – but rely on his best guess at initial letters to help him remember the word he planned to use. Thus a child can continue his writing without waiting for help. If a larger group is writing so that the teacher cannot have them all close about her, she may group together those who will need the most time and help, and slip to the others at their places as soon as she can when a hand has been raised.

The problem in the early stages of independent writing is to give the child the help he needs and to set up no restrictions which hamper him. Reference was made in another chapter to the unhappy experience of a group of second grade children who were about to write letters of appreciation to a poultry farmer whose farm they had just visited. They were eager to begin when the inexperienced teacher guiding them said, "Be careful to use only words you are sure you can spell." The children started work bravely but each child found himself, almost immediately, in the midst of a sentence calling for a word not in his limited spelling vocabulary. Erasers were used vigorously as the children wiped out the sentences and tried again. Soon more pencils were being chewed than being used for writing. When the supervisor suggested that the teacher offer to spell the words they needed, the writing went on in earnest. Subjecting beginners to trying and frustrating experiences as they struggle to develop independence serves only to decrease their interest in writing and arrest the development of quality of writing and hold it at a very immature level. Satisfying experiences, on the other hand, add to the child's sense of power and achievement and encourage him to go on working.

A few schools about the country still cling to the habit of insisting that the children learn to do cursive writing in the second grade. It is just at this time that the children have reached the point where manuscript writing has become a tool which they can use with some degree of ease and confidence. Adding another form of handwriting at this time seems tragically wasteful, from the point of view of overall learning. It is based upon the insistent conviction of some administrators, teachers, and parents that a child is not writing until he is using cursive writing. Actually, manuscript writing plays an increasing role in adult life and in various types of occupations so that some individuals use only manuscript writing from choice. Experience and research have proven it to be a far better vehicle for the writing of children from six to nine years of age than is cursive writing.

With many children, enthusiasm for writing their own stories begins in the second grade. In one school, a seven-year-old announced shortly before Christmas that she had written a Christmas story at home. The group was enthusiastic when she shared it with them and, spurred on by her success, she exclaimed, "But this is only the first chapter. There will be lots more because I am writing a book." New installments were written both at home and at school; some contained only a few sentences, others a page or more. Interest grew to the point that a number of children gave up plans they had made for gifts for their mothers to write her a "book" instead. Much of the spelling was phonetic and the sentences were not always clear but the enthusiasm was great enough so that the epidemic of writing continued unabated after the holidays.

Writing may be combined with interest in drawing and the children may fit together stories and picture sequences as did Joanna in her story of "The Flea and the Girl," reproduced in the Guide for Teaching Grades One and Two of *English Is Our Language* (20), pp. 89-98). Not all seven-year-olds show the feeling for a well-knit plot that is found in Joanna's story, but many are interested in a sequence of events. The quality of the handwriting is less important than that interest in writing be encouraged.

A third grade group had spent several very delightful weeks in a study of the heavens. They had visited the planetarium and had enticed their parents into evening expeditions to a near-by hill or at least into the front yard to locate the easily identified constellations. Their writing took two forms: brief summary statements of facts that had impressed them, and poetry. The factual reports the children wrote themselves, then helped to duplicate them, each in the child's own writing, so that everyone could have a copy to bind into a booklet. The poems they dictated.

The teacher had read a variety of poems dealing with the heavens. One day, toward the end of the study, the children gathered together the books that contained their favorite poems and the teacher reread all of them. Then she remarked that she would be glad to write down any thoughts they might have for poems of their own. Those who were not interested might return to other writing or to art work of any sort. Only a half dozen children left the group and they moved with consideration for the children who were deep in thought. A little girl said, "I have a good start for a poem: 'Lady Moon, Lady Moon, You are like a gold, gold spoon–." As she hesitated, another child added, almost instantly, "In the dish of the dark blue air." There was a murmur of approval from almost everyone in the room. It was a delightfully intriguing word picture. They were off to a good start and more than half the children volunteered word pictures or poetic thoughts before they were willing to stop and go on to other things. Some children went about other work for a portion of the time and came back to hover over the group and listen when something they overheard caught their fancy. The teacher wrote each contribution as it was given and read it back so that its author and the others could savor it a second time. Later in the day, as they had time, the children made their own copies of their poems from the teacher's hastily written copy. The interest in dictating poems continued for several days. A child might bring pencil and paper to the teacher at the lunch table, or at any other uncrowded moment, and ask that a poem be written.

POETRY WRITTEN BY A THIRD GRADE GROUP

Lady Moon, Lady Moon,
You are like a gold, gold spoon
In the dish of the dark blue air.

Martha and Ruth

Over the hills and far away
The moon is shining up in the sky.

David

The moon is hanging up in the air,
The moon is shining among the stars,
The moon is shining with all his might
And he sails across the sky so bright.

Sandy

The Eclipse

The moon came to the sun to play
He did because he came that way!

Mary

When there is an eclipse
The moon comes to visit the sun.
It must be fun
To visit the sun!
If I could go up and visit the sun
It would be fun!
It would be fun!

Ruth W.

☐ THE BEGINNING OF INDEPENDENT WRITING

The degree of independence in writing which can be attained by eight-year-olds in the third grade differs materially from child to child. Schonell found the level of writing done by English children to be greatly influenced by the emotional life of the child, his level of social interaction with both children and adults, and his background of experience, interest, and knowledge (17). These played a larger role than intelligence, in many instances. The child whose experience has built in him a sense of adequacy and of personal worth will progress faster, regardless of intelligence, than will the child who thinks less well of himself and his capacity to contribute something of worth.

Children who lack confidence and lag behind in expression activities need a variety of kinds of help. They need guidance and encouragement to play with children, to forget themselves and enter into all kinds of play experiences. If parents understand the problem they may find ways to enrich the child's experience through trips, library books, home conversations, the gathering of materials, the encouragement of hobbies, and through welcoming other children into the home. The school can add to the child's experience in many ways and can help to build up the child's sense of personal worth.

□ CREATIVE EXPRESSION THROUGH LANGUAGE

Creative expression is an essential part of wholesome all-round growth and development. School children do not add to the imaginative literature of the world anything of lasting value but they add materially to their own mental and emotional health through the production of even the crudest products. It is not for the product that creative expression is important but for the expansion of the child's own inner powers and the deepening of his sense of his personal worth and integrity.

Expression has come to be recognized as a valuable form of therapy. The armed services utilized a variety of forms of expression, during the war period and after it, for the purpose of reclaiming shocked and confused minds and helping them to find in themselves the balance and power to think and achieve that are essential to mental health and personal well-being. Men and women who cannot stand up to life, who turn inward to avoid it or become warped by life's pressures, have been found to be helped by the therapy of manipulation of materials which respond to their touch and will. Such creative manipulation helps to release them from the bondage of fears, frustrations, and sense of inadequacy which has reduced their mental and emotional powers below the level of their personal control.

Psychologists and psychiatrists are using opportunities for play with toys and work with plastic materials as means of studying the problems of disturbed and poorly adjusted children. They are finding that, through expression, children portray their inner conflicts and sometimes succeed in relieving them. Teachers in England found, during the worst of the bombing in World War II, that children needed opportunities for expression more than anything else. Through such opportunities they released tensions and fears which could be released in no other way.

Classroom teachers interested in studying the imaginative expression of children frequently find a theme that is highly revealing repeated over and over in a child's writing. The timid child, in his story, is big and brave; the neglected child is protected and loved; the child who is hungry for possessions has them in quantity. The child who is afraid of his father is triumphing over adults in his imaginative creations. There is evidence, in the writing of many children, of the need for release and for compensation for reality as they find it.

The task of education is that of building in individuals strength and inner resources to protect them from stress and to develop them to the point of highest usefulness. Teachers will find few child geniuses in the course of a lifetime of teaching. There will be relatively few children who show promise of producing material for public consumption. All children need help to respect the resources of their own minds and to improve both the quality of their thinking and feeling and their skill in expressing them.

☐ THE CLIMATE FOR CREATIVE EXPRESSION

The first requisite for any program which includes creative expression is, of course, a relaxed and happy teacher-child relationship and wholesome, friendly relationships among children. Children are so highly sensitive to the emotional and social climate of a classroom that few of them can be persuaded to bring forth their inner thoughts and feelings unless they feel reasonably sure of sympathetic response. Children need assurance that their effort will not be laughed at, criticized, or made the subject of too much attention either from the teacher or from their peers. James A. Smith, in his book *Setting Conditions for Creative Teaching in the Elementary School* (19), points out that the role of the teacher in establishing such a relationship is vital. "Children will not be relaxed nor will they feel free to contribute their ideas in an autocratic situation where the structure of the classroom is dependent on leadership of the teacher alone." He is convinced that the formal schoolroom quickly destroys individuality and the joy of creating because it is "wrong" to be different from the standards set by the teacher. Although the drive to create is as strong within children as the drive for status, the drive to be approved is stronger and is a more basic need.

The second requisite is flexibility and freedom from pressures. A working environment which permits freedom of action and flexibility in the use of time and learning materials is far more conducive to independent initiative and original thinking than one which has a rigid time schedule and course of study.

The third requisite is a wealth of experience. Children need the knowledge and insight that come from firsthand experience through trips out into the environment, when that is the best method of learning. They need constant contact with real life experiences in the classroom and an abundance of all sorts of interests and materials.

The fourth requisite is an obvious one, but one which teachers cannot afford to forget: experience with literature suited to the interests and needs of children. Children would have little interest in telling or writing original stories unless they found stories interesting and enjoyable. No child would think of creating a poem who had not heard and enjoyed poetry. Children cannot create in a vacuum. Creation grows out of fullness of experience and the urge to share that experience.

An extensive and much publicized curriculum project carried on in the schools of Nebraska is one in which children's literature is used as the inspiration and springboard for writing. This is mentioned in Chapter 17 on page 425.

A fifth requisite often forgotten in the demands of daily activities is a physical setting that offers interesting and varied visual stimuli. A change of pictures in the room can be obtained for little more than a few minutes effort. Libraries frequently have framed pictures to loan; the art department may have student works they would be happy to have displayed; and should these sources fail, outstanding prints can be obtained at very little cost. An attractive science corner, or plants displayed in an artistic manner can add greatly to the physical environment. Bulletin boards can display stimulating and provocative material. A sixth requisite might be mentioned, though perhaps it should come first: an alert and interested teacher.

> The teacher should cultivate continuously in herself an awareness of the meanings and wonders of everyday life. By being a vivid, colorful person, she stimulates children's vigorous curiosity and joy in exploring new interests. This is the starting place for the accumulation of many meaningful experiences which are so interesting and vital to children that they want to talk about them. It is here that the teacher, watching very carefully for manifestations of the individual spirit, gives enthusiastic appreciation to any evidences of original and unique expression. Thus children are *moved* to tell their thoughts in a way that is truly their own (7), pp. 7, 9).

☐ MOTIVATION FOR IMAGINATIVE WRITING

Children derive motivation for imaginative writing from many sources and many types of experience. Some children enjoy stories and books so much that they want to produce some of their own. Other children are motivated by a particular experience with an exciting or meaningful story or a poem that especially pleases. Still others respond to a vivid personal experience such as a tramp along a trail in the fog; the rhythmic motion induced by a windy day; or the beauty of color in a scene, a flower, or a sunset. Other children respond to the sound of music or the physical exhilaration of a race through crackling leaves or crunching snow. The spark that kindles the desire to write is unpredictable, and also, from the point of view of teacher planning, somewhat undependable. Often, enthusiasm starts with a few children who have facility in writing and the strong desire for self-expression that leads to spontaneous writing. Others are intrigued by the process and pleased with its outcome and are stimulated to test its possibilities. These children will need more help and encouragement than those whose interests set the pace.

Any efforts to force children into creative writing not only defeat their purpose but build emotional barriers against other types of writing as well. Giving children the necessary time, encouragement and guidance to grow into interest in self-expression through writing, produces more genuine and lasting interest.

☐ FORMS OF CREATIVE EXPRESSION

Children differ greatly in the form of their creative interests. One child may bring in poem after poem, while another child may prefer to take a few facts out of a history story and embroider them into an extended tale. Children who enjoy expression with crayons and paints can be encouraged to tell in writing the story of their pictures.

Actually, any expression which is the individual's own is for him creative expression. This includes diaries, personal letters, and some types of reports. Elementary teachers have fallen into the habit of thinking of stories, poems, and plays when they think of the creative writing of children. Story writing predominates, though the expression of poetic thought comes naturally and easily for some children. Plays are written by individuals occasionally, though frequently they are written as group projects, participated in by several children or by the entire class.

Writing personal letters to family and friends and "putting something of themselves into them," is a form of creative, personal writing children enjoy at many points in the elementary school. There are opportunities for announcements and reports which stimulate the individual or group to consider original and interesting methods of presenting the necessary material. Children like to combine illustration with text. Primary children, especially, enjoy decorating their letters, announcements, stories, and poems with illuminated letters, borders of design and color, or realistic sketches that illustrate the text. The interest is similar to that which operated in the Middle Ages when monks produced hand-illuminated manuscripts in the monasteries, though the quality of the children's decoration is often crude and primitive.

□ EXAMPLES OF EXPERIENCES THAT STIMULATE EXPRESSION

A first grade teacher took her class to look out of the windows of the auditorium balcony on a morning when there was a fresh fall of snow on the mountains in the distance, though the grass on the school lawn was still very green. As the children moved from window to window, looking and talking about the beauty of the new snow on the rocky peaks and the color contrasts, the teacher took note of the interesting descriptive expressions used by the children in their chatter. When they returned to the classroom, she said, "I was very much interested in some of the things you said as you looked at the mountains. Some of them sounded almost like poetry. Would any of you care to have me take down poems you think of as you think of the mountains with their fresh coat of snow?" The response was enthusiastic and the poems which resulted came from a number of different children. Some are scarcely poetic thoughts at all, while some have real beauty of imagery. Those which follow are samples which range from the least interesting to the most interesting of the group. Those who tried to find rhymes or to play with words produced little of value. Those who were concerned with word pictures or feelings were closer to real poetic thought, as is always true of children. Rhyme gets in the way of all except the most accomplished poets.

When winter comes
And the snow falls on the mountains
It makes them all white
And covers the trees
And falls on the town
And all around.

Leonard

It's hailing
It's snowing
All over the town.

Nancy

The mountains are so high
I'd like to know why?

Doran

Mountains look like castles.
They are funny castles
Because they are all covered with snow.
Below them are little men
All running around.
They are the town.

Betty

The same group of children had a large school garden in the spring. The interest in poetic expression grew out of the teacher's comment on a chant that had started spontaneously on the way to the garden one day. The child who was pulling the wagon loaded with tools chanted happily, "I'm pulling the wa - gon! I'm pulling the wa - gon!" Soon the entire group of thirty-eight was chanting with him. When they returned to the classroom the teacher remarked that the fun of the chant had made the trip to the garden especially pleasant. A little girl said, "I can sing what we did today," and she sang "We pulled the weeds, and planted the seeds!" to an uphill and downhill tune. This led to a variety of song and poem ideas, offered from time to time for several days and taken down by the teacher whenever they were offered. Again, most of them are word pictures.

I like my velvet pretty pansies
Because they have such long, long stems.

Jean

Bend, little flowers, bend!
You are pretty when you bend.
Call the wind to make you bow
Like kings and queens at court.

Isabel

Grass green!
Grass green!
I like to play in the grass so green.
I wish the grass were green every day
Then I could play in the grass every day.

Isabel

Frank Dempster Sherman's poem "Daisies," stimulated a brief outburst of interest in dictating poems. One child said, "I thought of a poem that is almost like that." Two other poems followed in fairly rapid succession.

In the morning the sun is bright,
And she is dressed in yellow
  And a yellow hat and coat
  And some little yellow shoes.
In the night she covers her head up
  So it will be dark.
Then in the morning
She kicks the covers off
  And looks to see if it is a nice day.
If it rains,
  She pulls the covers up again.

Isabel

At night when I go to bed
The stars are in the sky.
The moon is the mother.
She puts them all to bed.
Then in the morning I know
I know where they are.

Isabel

The stars are daisies.
The moon is a lady
Who comes and picks them every night.
The flowers are white,
The centers are round and yellow.

Doris

Some third grade poems which grew out of interest in a study of astronomy and the reading of a variety of "sky poems," as the children called them, were given earlier in the chapter.

□ SOME TYPICAL PRIMARY GRADE STORIES

Stories appear at almost any time. If the children understand that the teacher is interested in taking down stories that children wish to tell, they will come to her with them before school, at recess time, and at any time when she is not too busy to pause a moment and write for the child. The stories which follow are characteristic of these levels.

AN AFRICAN BOY'S ADVENTURES

Chapter I – In Africa

Once there lived a boy and his father. They lived in Africa. Once his father told him that they had no food in the hut. Then his father told him that he would have to stay and watch while he went hunting. While his father was hunting he heard a tom-tom beating. Then he saw warriors surrounding the hut.

Chapter II – In the Jungle

While his father was hunting in the jungle he heard his son tom-toming to him to come and save him from the warriors.

After his father got the message he began to run. After he ran a long time he sat down. After a little rest he got up and began to run again.

Chapter III – His Son is Missing

His father ran and ran. Soon he saw the hut. It wasn't surrounded by warriors. Then he looked inside the hut. He did not see his son. Then he saw footprints and he followed the footprints. Soon he saw the tribe. He saw his son.

Chapter IV – The Tribes Fight

After his father looked a long time he decided he would have war on the tribe. Then he went back to his hut. He got his tribe ready to fight the other tribe.

Chapter V – His Son Returned

Then the father got his tribe ready to fight the other tribe. Then his tribe made a sudden attack. The other tribe lost the fight and his father got his son back and they lived happy ever after.

Bernard

THE CALVES ON THE FARM WHERE BONNIE LIVES

Grandad has some calves.
He has them out in the country.
He takes them out of the barn so they can eat grass.
The calves drink milk out of a bucket.
One calf runs and kicks up his heels.

Bonnie

☐ GOALS FOR WRITTEN EXPRESSION IN THE PRIMARY SCHOOL

Because of the nature of children and their real life needs for written language, goals in the primary school must, of necessity, place attitude, interest, and individual aptitude first. This marks the beginning of a long period of growth. It is far more important that young children sense possibilities, develop interests, and make a good start with growth than that they meet prescribed standards. The really important objectives for that growth are the following:

- Interest in the use of writing to serve various purposes
- Interest in self-expression through language
- Increasing interest in thoughtfully conceived material, whether for practical or personal use
- Increasing skill in dictating or writing clear and interesting thoughts
- A developing concept of a sentence as a unit of thought
- Increasing realization of the function of capitalization and punctuation and some beginning in ability to use them appropriately
- A growing sense of responsibility to use valid content where facts are called for, and interesting content whether fact or fancy
- Growing sensitivity to colorful, vivid, and moving language
- Interest in developing suitable personal style which expresses one's own thinking
- Constantly expanding interest in writing in its many forms.

It would be absurd to try to set standards for the writing of children. Ability and interests will cover a wide range. Interest is more important than anything else, and interest begins with content and use, never with the mechanics of form. With guidance, encouragement, and examples, children begin to develop their own standards.

☐ SELECTED REFERENCES ☐

1. Applegate, Mauree, *Easy in English.* Evanston: Row, Peterson and Company, 1960.
2. ———, *Freeing Children to Write.* New York: Harper and Row, Publishers, 1963.
3. Baxter, Bernice T., *Teacher-Pupil Relationships.* New York: The Macmillan Company, 1941.

4. Bell, Vicars, *On Learning the English Tongue.* London: Faber and Faber, 1947.
5. Biber, Barbara; Murphy, Lois B.; Woodcock, Louise P.; and Black, Irma S., *Child Life in School: A Study of a Seven-Year-Old Group.* New York: E. P. Dutton and Co., Inc., 1942.
6. Board of Education, City of New York, *Developing Children's Power of Self-Expression through Writing.* Curriculum Bulletin, 1952-3 Series, Number 2. New York: Board of Education of the City of New York, 1953.
7. Burrows, Alvina Treut; Jackson, Doris C.; Saunders, Dorothy O., *They All Want to Write.* Englewood Cliffs, N.J.: Prentice-Hall, Inc., 1962. Third Edition.
8. Chukovsky, Kornei, *From Two to Five.* Translated by Miriam Morton. Berkeley: University of California Press, 1963.
9. Cole, Natalie R., *The Arts in the Classroom.* New York: John Day Co., 1940.
10. ———, *Children's Art from Deep Down Inside.* New York: John Day Co., 1963.
11. Cutforth, John A., *English in the Primary School.* Oxford: Basil Blackwell, 1954.
12. Dixon, John, *Growth through English.* Reading, England: National Association for the Teaching of English, 1967.
13. Loban, Walter D., *The Language of Elementary School Children.* Champaign: National Council of Teachers of English, 1963.
14. Marshall, Sybil, *An Experiment in Education.* Cambridge, England: The University Press, 1966.
15. Muller, Herbert, *The Uses of English.* New York: Holt, Rinehart and Winston, Inc., 1967.
16. National Council of Teachers of English, *Children's Writing: Research in Composition and Related Subjects.* Champaign: The Council, 1961.
17. Schonell, Fred J., *Backwardness in Basic School Subjects.* Edinburgh: Oliver and Boyd, 1942.
18. Smith, Dora V., "Growth in Language Power as Related to Child Development." *Teaching Language in the Elementary School.* The Forty-Third Yearbook, Part II of the National Society for the Study of Education. Chicago: University of Chicago Press, 1944.
19. Smith, James A., *Setting Conditions for Creative Teaching in the Elementary School.* Boston: Allyn & Bacon, 1966.
20. Strickland, Ruth G., *English Is Our Language: Guide for Teaching Grades I and II.* Boston: D. C. Heath and Company, 1950.
21. Watts, A. F., *The Language and Mental Development of Children.* Boston: D. C. Heath and Company, 1947.

WRITING IN THE INTER-MEDIATE GRADES

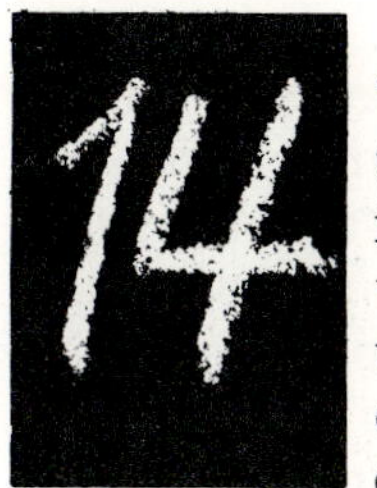

"I would give them enough patterns, but not in the form of exercises. I would give them patterns in speech, in books, in poetry, and in plays. I would not subject my pupils to ten minutes a day under the ultraviolet lamp of intense grammatical exercises, but would instead seek out every patch of literary sunshine and see to it that the pupils worked and played in its warmth and light until grammatical usage and good style, the balance and cadence of sentences, and the happy choice of the most significant words soaked into them through every one of their senses. . . . It is much more important, surely, to be bursting with things to write about and not know precisely how to write them, than to know all the rules and not have anything to write."[1]

Such methods remind one of what was once called progressive education in this country, but the emphasis is strictly English—the fundamentals of reading, writing, talking, and listening—learning to use language better.

Children who have experienced the kind of beginning with written language which is described in the preceding chapter will go on smoothly and easily to expansion of interest and greater independence in the intermediate grades. If they have not had such experience, there is no better time to start it than the present. The same principles apply in written language at any grade level. With wholesome primary school experience as a background, many children will be developing independence in writing and showing great pride in their independence. There may still be a few reluctant writers who lack the personal and experience background for interest. There will be some children whose work is still immature in quality, while others will be thinking and writing more maturely.

Richness and breadth of experience are as essential for this age level as for younger children. All kinds of educative experience in social studies, science, literature and reading, art, music, hobbies and individual recreational interests—all provide the essential structure and working material for oral and written language. Normally developing children from nine to twelve years of age have a wide range of interests, eager intellectual curiosity, tremendous energy, and a vital and insistent urge to be doing all sorts of things.

[1] Sybil Marshall, "An Experiment in Education." Quoted in *The Uses of English*, p. 42.

Interest in language can be keen in the intermediate grades and because of children's many interests it has much to feed on. Whether oral and written language continue to flower depends entirely on the teacher's attitude toward it and on what she values. The results in these grades are all too often exceedingly disappointing. A number of reasons are easily identified. Dora V. Smith stated the problem clearly in her article several years ago in the Forty-third Yearbook:

> The further the child progresses in the elementary school, the greater is the danger that his language period may degenerate into one of exercise-doing, learning words in columns out of context, or studying language forms divorced from the use he is making of language during the rest of the day. Special care, therefore, needs to be exercised to continue the kind of rich program of well-motivated enterprises common in the lower grades in order that the growth of language may continue in relationship to the development of meaning and that the challenge of a social purpose may motivate expression. Then the needed remedial drill and positive instruction in word knowledge and linguistic forms may be related directly to the problems which confront the pupil in his daily use of language (21, p. 59).

Authorities in this country and in England are in agreement that English cannot be taught divorced from content and from actual need. The tremendous emphasis one finds upon textbook teaching in the intermediate grades is largely responsible for the problem of poor writing.

> The emphasis is still on spelling, punctuation, margins, and a composition-a-day, to the exclusion of writing for pleasure and for the opportunity it affords for personal development. We all know too well the methods which built in us the horror and fear of writing. No well-punctuated sentence, no correctly spelled composition was worth the price (8, p. 7).

Older language textbooks and, unfortunately, some of the newest ones, separate language teaching from the needs for language in other types of learning situations in the school and from the life needs of the children, and attempt development through isolated drill lessons. Good teaching draws the skills for emphasis from the daily needs and experiences of the children themselves and whatever practice is called for grows out of and fits back into the actual language needs and experiences of the children.

The problem of the opportunities and needs for oral language experience in the intermediate grades is discussed at length in Chapter 7. Practically all of the points discussed with regard to oral language apply to written language as well, and many of the opportunities for oral work can provide excellent motivation for written work when the circumstances or projects call for it.

☐ SITUATIONS CALLING FOR WRITING

The day-by-day experiences in any modern classroom present endless opportunities for writing if the teacher is alert to recognize them. Since they are a logical part of other experiences, sometimes meeting basic needs, sometimes adding enrichment or pleasant social experience, children have opportunity to learn the service that writing can render as well as how to write for different purposes. Some of the classroom situations which may lead to writing are:

1. Situations requiring direct communications through writing
   - A. Social notes of thanks, sympathy, invitation, etc.
   - B. Business letters, orders for materials, preparations for a trip, or requests for information
   - C. Friendly letters to pen pals or foreign friends
   - D. Gift tags and greeting cards
2. Situations needing a record
   - A. The making of plans
   - B. Class activities, events, sports, excursions, or science discoveries
   - C. Minutes for clubs
   - D. Class histories, diaries, or logs
3. Situations requiring filling out forms
   - A. Registration slips, examination blanks, applications for admission to Red Cross swimming classes, checks, and receipts
   - B. Telegrams or cablegrams
4. Situations requiring written work materials
   - A. Reports by individuals or groups
   - B. Panel discussions
   - C. Directions and recipes
   - D. Lists of materials—properties needed for a play or similar activity
   - E. Dictation or copying of information or directions

        F. Bibliographies
    5. Situations needing publicity
        A. Advertisements, notices, or announcements
        B. Articles for school or local newspaper
        C. Headlines for newspaper articles
        D. Legends for bulletin boards and exhibits
        E. Room duties to be posted
    6. Situations stimulating the writing of
        A. Original arithmetic problems
        B. Riddles, puzzles, jokes
        C. Word pictures of people and places
        D. Editorials, news stories
        E. Stunts, skits, plays
        F. Songs, dramatizations, original choral readings
        G. Poems, stories, myths, fables

The situations which can lead to written expression are legion and during the course of a year can provide a vast amount of practical experience for each child. Both in school and out, boys and girls of these ages do best when the job to be done is a real one with real social implications.

☐ RANGE IN ABILITY IN THE INTERMEDIATE GRADES

The higher one goes in the grades, the wider the range in abilities one is apt to find in a single classroom. From the fourth through the sixth grades, any class is almost certain to contain children who are becoming highly skillful and independent in writing and some who still need to dictate their ideas, then copy them, in carrying out some purposes. The age at which children become able to keep thoughts in mind while they transfer them to paper differs materially from child to child. Most children can manage the handwriting part of the task. Their muscles and co-ordinations have developed to the point where they can do as much writing as most tasks would require without undue physical strain. For some children, however, the physical act of writing is slow and for them time limitation may be a serious detriment to good writing. Lack of ability in spelling, and also in reading, may retard the written expression of some children, and lack of mental capacity is always a retarding influence.

The actual experiences of children influence both the ability and the interest they show in writing. Research from a variety of sources indicates that in all school performance the child who has a large repertoire of expressions to draw upon and the ability to conceptualize abstract phenomena has distinct advantages.

Early success in writing has a positive influence on a child's attitude toward future related activities. The competitive type of assignment where the "best" letter is sent, the "best" papers are posted on the bulletin board, the "best" stories are read to the class, leaves some children out before the writing is started. Such assignments serve only to discourage those who most need motivation, inspiration, and help.

In no area of the individual's maturing is arrested development more common than in the area of communication. This early leveling off and failure to mature shows especially clearly in written language. The child whose early efforts have resulted in personal satisfaction and a sense of achievement will go on growing with reasonable motivation. The child who has tried but felt himself unsuccessful or has felt that the end results scarcely justified the effort will be a difficult child to motivate. As motivation for growth and improvement in written language, nothing serves as well as real needs for writing which can be met by the child with a reasonable amount of effort and adequate adult guidance.

☐ SETTING STANDARDS THAT ARE REALISTIC

John Steinbeck says in his book *Travels with Charley,*

> When I face the desolate impossibility of writing five hundred pages a sick sense of failure falls on me and I know I can never do it. . . . Then gradually I write one page and then another. One day's work is all I can permit myself to contemplate and I eliminate the possibility of ever finishing.[2]

Many students meet the next writing assignment with a "sick sense of failure." It may not be the assignment that frightens them but rather the unattainable standards that have been set for them. The notion that papers written by elementary school children should be neat, error-free, idea-laden products is simply not realistic.

[2] John Steinbeck, *Travels with Charley in Search of America.* New York: The Viking Press, 1962, p. 23.

The teacher's first responsibility in all practical writing that is designed to serve a purpose is to see that the child understands the purpose and the obligations that need to be assumed in meeting it. If the motivation inherent in the situation is such that the child takes over the purpose and makes it his own, he will proceed largely under his own power even though he may still need a great deal of guidance in carrying through his purpose. If a child shows no interest in the purpose which motivates the other group members, it is often better to guide him into another kind of writing rather than to force him to do something that holds little meaning for him. Children rarely turn out work of high quality solely for the purpose of meeting an assignment. And since the rate at which they work covers a wide range, a flexible time schedule is an absolute necessity.

Since adults vary their standards to suit their concept of a situation and need, children not only should be permitted the same privilege but should be guided in the development of sensitivity to the demands of a situation. If the writing situation is one which calls for a memorandum for personal use, the children should be encouraged to do the writing in such form that it will meet their personal need. Group discussion may precede any writing situation and a variety of methods may be suggested and evaluated. Then each child is free to do the task in his own way, the requirement being the meeting of the need. If the writing which the situation demands is for a social purpose, to be read or used by others, then the needs of others must be considered as well as those of the individual doing the writing. Children need to learn the points at which conformity to accepted procedure is necessary as well as points at which they may feel free to meet the need in their own way. Guidance is necessary in any case, since children need help to see the possibilities that exist in a personal situation as well as help to learn the accepted procedure in a social situation which calls for conformity to an accepted pattern of writing.

☐ THE WRITING OF LETTERS

All adults who received even a few years of elementary schooling as children were given some instruction in letter writing as part of the course of study in English. There is ample evidence that much of the teaching was poorly conceived or inadequate; at any rate it failed to "take" with many children, particularly with those who live on an economic and social level which demands relatively little letter writing. Many business concerns are put to an immense amount of effort and expense as the result of poorly written letters that cannot be handled efficiently because of lack of clarity or lack of essential information. A great mail-order house maintains a large staff whose sole task is to decipher, track down, and read between the lines of inadequate letters so that the correct merchandise can be mailed to the hard-working people who have sent money for it.

Letter writing means nothing to children as an exercise in a drill book but it means a great deal when they have real occasion to write a letter. Children need to learn two things: *when* to write a letter and *how* to do it. Concentration on the *how* is of value only as the other point is taught also.

A mature adult who is thoughtful of others in his business and social contacts finds occasion to write many types of letters. He knows how to adapt the form, style, and content of his letters to his own needs and those of the persons to whom he writes. He has learned also the psychological principles which underlie good human relationships and how to apply them sincerely and purposefully. He understands the real function of each portion of standard letter form and adheres to the form accurately, not in the spirit of meeting an arbitrary requirement but in the spirit of consideration and thoughtfulness for the time and convenience of others.

Letter writing, like almost everything else one attempts to teach children, is learned readily and effectively if the thinking, understanding, and feeling parts of the matter are taken care of first: if the children appreciate and understand the significance of the thing they are doing and enter into it emotionally as well as intellectually. Form, in human behavior, has come about for reasons which children can learn to understand. To teach a child that he must always write his address here, the date there, put a comma here, and a semicolon there has little meaning. If he understands that the heading is orientation for the person to whom he is writing, the address is insurance of receiving a response, the salutation is a greeting to establish contact with the thinking and attention of the person to whom he is writing, it makes sense to a child and he learns it.

The socially mature adult finds occasion to write at least the following types of personal and business letters. Opportunities for similar types of letters are available in any school year if the teacher watches for them. Study situations and social situations call for a variety of letters.

BUSINESS LETTERS

Requests for materials, help, advice, or information
Orders for materials
Letters of acknowledgment
Letters of complaint
Letters of explanation
Letters of apology
Letters of appreciation
Furnishing information
Answering requests

PERSONAL LETTERS

Letters to share experiences and to maintain contact
Letters of thanks and appreciation
Letters of invitation
Letters of acknowledgment
Expressions of sympathy
Extending of congratulations
Letters of explanation
Letters of apology
Expression of praise and commendation
Requests for services
Offers of services

It is not difficult to find opportunity for practically all of these kinds of writing in the course of a year's experience with a group of children. Discussing and thinking through the situation and the need would be the first step. Deciding on content to suit the need would come next, and consideration of form would come last of all.

■ *Business letters*—In many studies which children carry on in the classroom, there are important values in encouraging them to utilize written communication to enrich their study. Letters to the appropriate agencies requesting information and materials not only provide an opportunity to use writing skills but the anticipation of return mail helps to keep interest high. The class may wish to visit a business, factory, airport, or museum. Letters requesting permission to make the trip and letters of arrangement accompany the wish. Letters of appreciation follow logically at the end of the trip, or there may be need for more information or for clarification of time, costs, or similar matters.

When discussion has made the purpose clear, the children are ready to consider, and perhaps to outline, the content for the letter. If it is an order for materials and prices are known, the content of the letter must include a statement of what is wanted, presented with clearness and with enough information and detail to make the order easy to fill. The amount of money to be included and the form in which it is to be sent are both important, and also where and to whom it should be sent and a clear statement of the name and address of the sender. The reason for each point and the function it serves will be made clear to the children. Then they are ready to consider the form of the letter itself.

A model, presented on the chalkboard or in a textbook or handbook, helps children to visualize the form they are working for. Some textbooks give a clear statement of the function of each part of a letter, but it is wise to talk about it from time to time to make sure that the child acquires the thinking that is basic to conscientious performance. The heading tells the reader where one is and on what day he writes the letter. That serves as orientation for the reader and also tells him where to send his reply. Since there are many offices in a building or many people in a business establishment, so that a letter might be misplaced even after it is opened, it is necessary to repeat the name and address on the envelope within the letter itself. Then comes the greeting. One usually greets a person he calls upon with, "Hello, John!" or "How do you do, Mr. Smith?" before he begins giving his message; so a letter contains a greeting, both for the sake of courtesy and to catch the attention of the reader. When the complete message has been stated, one is ready to conclude his written interview. In dealing with people face to face, one might say, "Good-by," but that is less suitable in a letter. Other forms of formal and informal closings have come to take the place of the face-to-face type of leavetaking. Signing one's own name very plainly at the end not only makes it clear who is the writer of the letter but helps to insure getting a response.

Punctuation comes in for discussion as the letter form is reviewed. "How do you say your address in giving it orally?" "141 South Tenth Street, Greenville, Indiana." "Notice where the stops are as he says it. He stopped after *Street,* didn't he; so that calls for a warning sign, a partial stop, or a comma, as we call it. Greenville, Indiana. He stopped after the name of the town; so a partial stop, or comma, goes there. Are there any stops in the date? January 17, 1951. Yes, one stops after the number of the day; so we need a comma there also." Punctuation is arbitrary only where it is essential for clarity. Children who learn to think of it as signs along the way, to help the reader to read the material as the writer thought it when he wrote it, will have little difficulty with punctuation.

A letter which a child is to mail when he has finished writing it probably requires a rough draft which is to be checked with the teacher before the final copy is written. Teachers have found that children are not averse to copying what they have written when the final copy must serve a social purpose (8). Copying for its own sake can be boring and irksome, but copying for the sake of consideration and courtesy to someone else, and to make a good impression in the eyes of others, is something which a child can understand and accept willingly.

There are so many kinds of writing to do in carrying through the many interests of an alert class that there is no justification for having all children write letters when only one can be sent. Class participation may be important in planning the letter and considering its form; then one child can be selected to do the writing. Obviously, since this is a learning experience, the child who can do it best is probably *not* the child to select, because he does not need the practice as others do, though he might be asked to help a less capable child turn out a usable product. In the case of letters of appreciation to someone who has been helpful, each child may wish to write his own letter and all can be sent.

■ *Personal letters*—In the intermediate grades, personal letters are probably individual letters, though there may be occasions which call for a composite letter formulated by the group. As in the case of business letters, the three steps are important: understanding of purpose, determining of content, and consideration for form; and they fall into the order listed.

In considering the purpose to be served by a personal letter, the children may need to give attention to their own attitudes which they wish to portray clearly and also to the feelings and attitudes they wish to engender in others. Children from nine to twelve years of age are growing rapidly in ability to put themselves in the place of another and to think how he would feel and react under certain circumstances. A young child lacks the ability to enter into the feelings of someone else; he can react only to his own feelings, interests, and needs. The ability to sense the feelings of others, to comprehend their attitudes, and to recognize their needs is a product of maturity. Children develop it gradually but wholesomely if they grow up in contact with adults who are thoughtful and understanding in their reactions to others, and emotionally well-balanced.

If the letter is one for the purpose of maintaining contact and sharing experience, the child needs to learn to project his thinking to consider the interests of the person to whom he is writing: "What would interest Jim most? What experiences would he enjoy sharing with me?" or "What would Grandmother want to hear about? What news is she hungry for?" In the case of writing to a child overseas as a "pen pal," through the Junior Red Cross, perhaps: "What would give him a clear picture of the way we live? What will help him to feel that he knows me as a friend?"

A letter of congratulation is a generous outpouring of happiness for the good fortune or achievement of another, while a letter of praise or commendation may contain a little more of appraisal and analysis. This will be too fine a distinction for some children, but in real situations they can begin to sense it. Children are taught to say, "Thank you," from an early age; so letters of thanks and appreciation are easier for a child to compose. A letter of sympathy calls upon the child to say in words, very simply and sincerely, the sympathy he feels for someone who has met with misfortune or loss. One does not expect or try to obtain depth of thought and feeling at this upper childhood and preadolescent level, but understanding is growing and feelings can be guided into wholesome expression.

Children have occasion to write letters of explanation or apology because of situations which arise, and they need help to learn to understand their obligation and accept the responsibility which is theirs. Rice tells of the experience of a group of eighth grade boys and girls in learning to write letters of complaint and letters of apology.[3] The children were surprised to learn that a complaint could be entered in a courteous manner and interested to consider the psychological effect on the reader of a courteously worded complaint which assumed right motives and high standards of fairness on the part of the offender rather than offering condemnation. All of them recognized the need to learn how to explain, apologize, or make amends in such manner that the offended person would accept the apology or explanation in the spirit in which it was given. One girl told of her predicament when her dog killed the much-

[3]Mable F. Rice, "Letter of Complaint." *Elementary English Review* 21:20-23, January, 1944.

loved cat of a neighbor who was away at the time. A boy's baseball had broken a window while the owner was away and he wanted to be the first to tell the man and to make amends.

Learning to write letters when they are needed and so that they arouse the desired emotional reaction takes time, but it is a kind of learning that is far more important than mere memorization of letter form. Form is important and children can learn to take pride in turning out a product that does them credit. But form without intellectual integrity, depth of insight, and understanding and without emotional balance is of little value. It is the content that makes the letter serve its purpose in the last analysis. In the writing of all types of personal letters, children need to be encouraged to be themselves, to put something of themselves, sincerely and freely, into what they write so that the letter speaks of them and for them. This is exceedingly important.

In the writing of personal as well as business letters the teacher will need to check the first draft with the individual child. If corrections are needed she can suggest ways of making them and see to it that the corrections are made. The last step may need to be the making of a new copy so that the child will feel pride and satisfaction in his achievement and so that the letter may speak well for him. In this connection, children can be taught that personal letters are private and not to be shared by other children unless the writer wishes to do so. The child does things correctly under the teacher's guidance so that he gradually develops high standards that are not laid aside when teacher guidance is no longer present because they are developed from within and are his own.

☐ OTHER FORMS OF PRACTICAL WRITING

The exact form which practical writing takes depends upon the activities going on in the classroom and the points at which writing functions in them. There are functional applications of writing at many points in social studies, science, literary, and other types of activities. There are also many points at which writing is used to make the various aspects of daily living run smoothly. Labels and posters help with the organization of materials; captions add value to bulletin board exhibits. Records and notices keep the *Lost and Found* department running smoothly as well as school banking, lunch money, the activities of the Junior Red Cross, the athletic program, and the School Council. These needs arise occasionally or intermittently and are handled as the situation demands.

■ *Record keeping*—Recording events for an individual or class diary, yearbook, or newspaper provides excellent opportunity for learning how to pull out the significant points in a situation and portray them in clear-cut sentences. An occasional child may wish to keep an individual diary or yearbook, but too constant concentration on such recording may become so time-consuming and tiresome as to decrease interest rather than advance it. A group record can be contributed to by different children so that the burden on any one is slight. Each can volunteer to record the thing that interests him and the variety in presentation adds to the interest of the class book.

Note taking is an essential part of gathering material for a report, a discussion, an article for the school newspaper, or perhaps as a record of ideas one wishes to include in creative writing. Fourth grade children can learn to list essential points, preparatory to learning to outline. Fifth grade children can begin to distinguish between main and subordinate points and put their material in simple outline form; while in the sixth grade, many children are ready to do a more detailed form of outlining.

Children may find it necessary to take notes as they carry on science experiments, take trips, or follow through with individual hobbies and interests. Often these are very sketchy notes which are organized and put into better form when the activity is completed. Such work should be done under teacher guidance so that the child learns the value and function of correct form and understands it clearly enough so that he can gradually become independent in the use of it.

Children may decide to keep different kinds of records as group projects. Perhaps one group keeps a science notebook, recording the experiments that have been carried out. Another group may keep a detailed record of trips, interviews, or the contributions of speakers whom they have invited to visit the class. Reading records are kept by many classes. Here again, care must be taken that required reports on books read do not become so burdensome that they detract from the enjoyment of reading. A simple record of what has been read probably suffices, with the encouragement of more detail if children are interested in adding it. If the class is organized for class or club meetings, there will be need for secretary's minutes of meetings and other forms of records. Committee reports may need to be written for the record.

Middle and upper grade children can begin to record the bibliographies of references they use in preparing a report or in getting ready for a discussion. Author, title, and the pages used may be sufficient to record, though sixth grade children may be ready to use complete bibliographical data: author, title, place of publication, publisher, and copyright date.

■ *Reports* – Reports of individual and group study form a part of almost every major interest in which children engage. The material for the report may be drawn from reading, from interviews, from experimentation, from firsthand study and observation, and from concrete experience. The child or group is called upon to give attention to selecting points, arranging them in logical sequence, fitting them into the proper pattern of emphasis and perspective, and presenting them so that they will be interesting and valuable for others. Recording may be an individual matter, but reporting is always a social one, and children need to learn to consider the social aspects of the task. This is important training.

Committee work usually culminates in a report of one sort or another. It may be a written report or it may be an oral one made from prepared notes. Committees may function as a unit of the class or as a part of club activity. Assembly programs and Student Council may furnish other occasions for reports.

The necessary teaching and guidance accompany the preparation of the report. Children can be made aware of the needs of the situation and helped to find ways of meeting them. The learning experience is worth more to a child if he can have the help he needs in the preparation of his work so that the result of his efforts brings satisfaction. Learning of one's mistakes when it is too late to correct them is of little practical value and it undermines the child's security and his interest in trying again.

If children are to write well they should live with the material they are studying or experiencing until it becomes truly their own before they attempt to write about it.

> . . . a child needs time to assimilate thoroughly an experience, be it study, excursion, reading, or observation, before the ideas

> gained can become a part of his own mechanism. In our experience writing about yesterday's trip to the museum has been sadly unsuccessful. . . . Time for experience to ripen is as important a phase of the ideas-into-writing cycle as the actual putting pen to paper. Reflecting, talking, thinking about what one has done become a necessary precursor to that condition of clear perception that makes clear writing possible (8, pp. 73-74).

When children are gathering material for a report they need opportunity to talk over the ideas they are gleaning, to mull them over, toss them about, sort and resort them until it is possible to fit them into logical arrangement. Vague impressions are drawn out of the twilight between ignorance and clear understanding and take on clear outline and tangible form as they are looked at and lived with in broad daylight. Gradually, the children learn to organize the material they have gathered through "bundling" like materials together and fitting them into something like a logical sequence so that one idea feeds into and prepares for the next. The development of a sense of order in thinking and writing takes time and cannot be hurried.

Occasionally, a group has opportunity to prepare a radio or television script for an actual broadcast. It may be a broadcast for use over the public address system of the school. Study, planning, writing, classroom tryout, and rehearsal all have language values as one more source of motivation which stems from a real life situation.

Some schools or classes publish a newspaper, magazine, or yearbook which stimulates not only imaginative writing but informational writing as well. In one school, a magazine is published twice a year with the sixth grade serving as editorial staff for the publication. Setting up plans and policies, visiting classrooms as reporters, writing news items and editorials, studying magazines for organization, format, style of writing, and interests appealed to, is from beginning to end a language project. Preparing articles, editing, proofreading, and planning promotion and distribution are all valuable experiences.

All-school newspapers are sometimes fairly elaborate publications but very simple class newspapers also have value. Some classes write a single copy which is posted on the bulletin board for reading; others mimeograph, ditto, or hectograph the publication so that all the children may have copies. In one school, the children's newspaper was used as an instrument for public relations in the community. The children not only took home their own copies but delivered copies to all homes in the neighborhood where there were no children.

☐ TEACHING AND EVALUATION

The teaching of correct writing procedure and the development of standards should be taken care of in the practical writing which the children have occasion to do. Here the teacher, working with the children, develops understanding of the proper form for the writing problem they are dealing with. She guides their learning of procedure and techniques, develops attitudes of pride in effort and work that is well done, and fosters the sense of social obligation which is essential in communication. Even though the problem may be the same for the entire group, the level on which each child deals with it depends upon his maturity and his previous experience. Thus, the teaching and guidance are of necessity highly individualized.

The modern school has not discarded direct attack on learning problems but it does insist that teaching bear close relationship to use. New skills and techniques are taught when there is need for them, need which the children consciously face. Teachers can foresee needs for new skills or for the refining and polishing of partially acquired ones and can develop in children awareness of those needs through careful planning of incidental experiences. Incidental experience may occasionally be accidental but usually it is planned rather than unplanned experience as far as the teacher is concerned. Drill has a place but it tends to be successful only when it is purposeful practice in a skill which the child understands and for which he sees some practical need. Superimposed drill with the motivation stemming from teacher requirement is rarely fruitful of secure and permanent learning regardless of the number of repetitions involved. Practice, in which the motivation stems largely from the child's desire to acquire the skill to serve his purposes, may be highly valuable. The stronger the child's inner motivation the fewer repetitions he will require for mastery. Repetition can be gained in two ways: either the child can repeat the performance over and over again in the same drill situation or he can repeat it many times in new situations. In the former instance, drill may reach the point of diminishing returns through sheer boredom, while in the latter instance interest is kept high through new content and new experiences.

Throughout the course of incidental writing and in every sort of activity and enterprise, the teacher is on the alert to discover weaknesses that need direct attack. Perhaps the entire class needs work on direct and indirect quotations, on recognizing incomplete sentences, on the use of the apostrophe in contractions, or on the topic sentence of a paragraph. Time is set aside for this study and several types of material may be used as study guides for children of differing levels of maturity. Various types of self-help material can be employed and children encouraged to develop independence in the use of them. Models, guide sheets, textbooks with the handbook material they include, real handbooks, alphabetized spelling lists, and the dictionary all have a place in such study. Practice materials are devised within the situation to give each child the amount and kind of practice he needs. There may be only a small group within the class who need direct attack on a problem. They can be given the help and practice they need while the rest of the class goes on with reading for enrichment, creative writing, or other stimulating work. It is poor teaching practice to insist that a child who knows the material being studied participate with the class; such participation cannot avoid boredom, and boring situations develop more bad habits than good ones in any case. If the teacher is a student of educational research and educational literature she knows which problems need most attention because of their functional value in modern living. She knows which problems the child will learn to handle through later experience and which need attention at this age level. Both direct and indirect attack are used in systematic manner but the basis for the systematic planning is the needs of the children. The sequence of material in textbook and course of study will serve as a guide in many instances, but the needs of the children determine the actual sequence in teaching.

Teaching is not a matter of presenting new material, drilling on it for a time, and thereafter giving assignments and marking the child's work. Teaching is constant guidance of thinking as well as operation. It is *working with the child all the way* and helping him to do the task to the best of his ability. It is building attitudes as well as skills: a sense of social and personal responsibility, pride in achievement, and increasingly high standards that become the child's own.

☐ EVALUATION

Evaluation, then, is in terms of growth and is a co-operative undertaking of teacher and child. Children are forever evaluating themselves. A child says, "That's the best outline I have made. I know how to do it now," or "I know what I want to say but my writing isn't very good," or "That doesn't sound the way I mean it. I'll have to fix it." Teachers have spent vast numbers of profitless hours grading children's compositions, marking all the errors with red pencil and returning the papers to the children. Children, and college students as well, profit very little from such evaluation of their work. They look for the mark on the paper and feel either satisfaction or dissatisfaction but they rarely look at the corrections or turn to reference material or to the teacher to learn what is wrong and how it should be corrected. Still less do they study the correct forms so that they can avoid similar errors thereafter. The material is cold and the interest is gone. Since no use is to be made of the material, correcting it seems unimportant. Correcting the child's material *with him*, as soon as he has done what he can with it, means co-operative analysis and evaluation while the material is still warm and vital to the child. He helps to locate and analyze his mistakes and corrects them under the teacher's guidance. He learns why they are wrong and what to do next time to avoid error. The analysis and evaluation are a part of the learning process itself, not an arbitrary anticlimax to it.

Since no definite and rigid requirements are set for each grade level, there are no hurdles which must be leaped by all children. Each child starts where he is and grows from one level to another as his abilities permit. If interest, sense of responsibility, insight, and effort to achieve are progressing satisfactorily the child's work must be accounted satisfactory for him, regardless of the level of maturity which it demonstrates. For the child who appears not to be achieving up to capacity, careful diagnosis is needed. Perhaps he has had little experience with written language in his previous years in school and has to build interest, attitudes, and a sense of adequacy before he can achieve up to his mental capacity. It may be that meager personal experience or lack of social security in the group is basic to his problem. As researchers have indicated, emphasis on skills is not very helpful to him until the underlying causes of his problem are recognized and remedied. Each child's problem is different and requires individual study and guidance.

☐ CREATIVE WRITING

It is as true in the intermediate grades as in the primary that creative writing differs from practical writing in emphasis and teaching techniques as well as in the content and form which it employs. The development of skills and the teaching of written form are taken care of in practical writing, while creative writing is free writing, with the emphasis on originality of content and style. A creative product is the child's own and is satisfactory when he is satisfied with it. Gradually, as skills become well developed and knowledge well assimilated, what is learned in practical writing is carried over and applied in imaginative and creative writing.

Children who have been fortunate enough to have in the primary grades the kind of free writing experience described in the preceding chapter will go on with creative expression in the intermediate grades as a matter of course. Children who have been deprived of such experience may require time and a great deal of background work and encouragement before they are ready to participate freely in creative work.

The essential steps in providing the background work have been described in the previous chapter. Children will write when they have something to say and when they have the vocabulary necessary to say it. One way to help them have something to say is to provide an environment that is alive and full of ideas. A teacher can invite ideas to grow by providing challenging experiences throughout the entire day, not just during a creative writing period. Along with the experiences must come suitable periods of time to discuss what has taken place. Children need time to live with an idea, to mull it over, to fit it into the context of their own thinking and make it truly their own before they can write about it.

Teach the children to learn by observing what goes on around them, to notice colors, details, moods, and emotions. Help them to make use of sounds they hear as a source of inspiration. These real experiences coupled with the vicarious experiences of reading and listening to stories, poems and books can provide children with a wealth of ideas to talk about, to dramatize or to write about. Encouragement to select the "right" words, the vivid, clear, telling words for the writing can result in delightful products, both prose and poetry.

Even with suitable preparation some children may still be unable or unwilling to write. Growing into enjoyment of written expression may take time and a good deal of encouragement, but forcing is almost certainly doomed to failure in the end. Since the content of creative writing and much of the inspiration for it must come from the child himself, there can be no real production until he is ready for it. He may do fairly satisfactory practical writing where the content can be drawn from the situation, from experience, or from books and still find it impossible to let his imagination take wings or to express his imaginings for others to share. In such cases the teacher must be willing to accept stiff and meager productions until the child has reached a stage of emotional security and mental expansion at which he can create something of interest to himself and dare to put it forth for others to see.

A fourth grade teacher took advantage of the children's interest in the Charley Brown comic strip and Charley Brown's Christmas which appeared on television to get some delightful expressions of what happiness meant to them. Called "A Page Full of Happiness," these are some of the exclamations which resulted:

Happiness is ten mini dresses.
Happiness is when somebody punches you and misses.
Happiness is when the teacher thinks you're one of the best children in the class.
Happiness is learning how to read.
Happiness is Saturday, Sunday and holidays.
Happiness is admitting it when you do something wrong.

After enjoying the beauty of October while traveling to and from school, another fourth grade teacher raised a question about how the various forms of life prepared for winter. The following lyrical expressions resulted.

In the fall there will be a party, a party of trees that is.
Although they are just a bunch of trees they look like ladies to me.
A party of beautiful ladies with their yellow and gold and even red gowns.
One tree has a pretty yellow gown with a big red bow.
But soon the party will have to end because it soon begin to snow.

Elisa

My close our changing colers now. Soon it will be time to go to bed. The snow will cover me like a white blanket. All summer long the angels over flode there flower garden just for me. The sun over flode his heart just for me. Now its' time to say my prayers and thank God, for His blessing. I am bare, and I will be back.

Sarah

Fall is the beginning of football, but the ends fore trees, poor trees!
The trees lose there leaves and, like, hibarnate in a way.

The fish a common creature of the sea doesn't really hibarnate, for every so often get out there homes.

By now the birds should be down south.

But what I really like about fall is football!

I'd better stop talking about fall it's snowing out there.

Steve

☐ POETIC EXPRESSION

The experiences from which poetry is made are readily available to pupil and teacher alike. They are life itself—with all of the feelings and responses that each individual makes to it. It remains for the elementary teacher to help children translate these experiences into the magic of verse. The word *translate* means, among other things, to change to another form and certainly that definition describes accurately the task of a poet. To describe the "solid commonplaces on which all living is based" with words that lift the reader out of the commonplace is a skill which deserves to be cultivated. This poem written by a fifth grader is an example of a child's translation.

October Trees

October trees are dressed in red,
They sleep on beds of gold,
They comb their hair
With the windy air,
And undress again in the cold.

Mary Ann

The form of the poem makes very little difference. The young writer learns first to see with feeling and then to translate the feeling into words. At first an uneasiness may accompany efforts and any attempt on the part of the teacher to change or correct the draft or even to acknowledge it as poetry may cause the writer to abandon the operation. To encourage further writing of poetry the teacher must provide time for reading poetry to the children. Both the teacher's reading and recordings of poems read by professional artists should be a consistent form of motivation. But the teacher should avoid reading to children only poems which rhyme. Much of the finest of poetry does not. Rhyme can interfere with poetic thinking when children create poems of their own. All too much creative writing is doggerel, not poetry, if children distort sentence structure and meaning to produce rhymed verses. Without rhyme, they can often create material of fine poetic quality and rhythmic flow.

In her delightful book *An Experiment in Education,* Sybil Marshall of England writes her agreement with this point, "Attempts to rhyme were never forbidden, though I was always chary of them, because of the feeling that the use of both rhythm and rhyme would result in a kind of forced cleverness, or else degenerate into sheer doggerel" [17, p. 165].

A group of eight- and nine-year-olds had been listening to and dramatizing some stories of China from various books. Their interest in China started when a little girl brought a Chinese doll she had just received. They had tied strings around the neck and wrists of the doll and used her as a puppet in dramatizing some of the stories. The interest in stories of China lasted for a number of days and included interest in modes of behavior and expression among the Chinese. The teacher read aloud several short word pictures from the ancient Chinese Book of Odes, compiled in 500 B.C., which are quoted in *Anthology of World Poetry* by Mark Van Doren. The children were keenly interested in the mental pictures and moods which the selections created, and talked freely about them.

At the end of the reading the teacher inquired whether the class would care to attempt some word pictures of their own. She offered to write down any the children cared to express. The first contribution volunteered came from Bernard, the boy who was the best athlete in the class. He gave the poem with thoughtful absorption, hesitating as he approached the end of his picture. The final line was offered almost instantly by a very sensitive little girl in the group; Bernard nodded his approval and added it to the rest to round out his picture.

Early in the morning all the world is still;
People coming and going through the country road
And the soft wind blowing
And the trees swaying their weepy heads
And the sun is just about to come over the mountainside;
The world is waking up for a new day.

Bernard

The children appeared highly appreciative, and other word pictures were offered as fast as the teacher could take them down. In each case, the poem was read back to the child to make sure that it was as he wished it. The children of this class had long been writing their own stories but dictation was the preferred method for poems. The examples which follow were liked especially well by the children.

Just a hilltop and large trees swaying.
It is morning. The sun is coming up
and there is dew on the ground.
The flowers are awakening
And raise their heads to the sun.

Ruth

The wind blows over the hilltops
And sets the flowers waving.
The sun comes over the hilltops
And sets the water shining.
Little ducks are swimming
And little frogs on land.

Sandy

When the sun sets the valley a glistening glow of evening
Little kittens tumbling and playing in the dust;
Yet over the sounds of the desert little sand foxes playing;
It is their evening play time
When the sun sets the valley with its evening glow.

Martha

Most children enjoy putting their thoughts into words, though the results vary in literary merit. Occasionally, one finds a child whose expression stands out in the group, a gifted child who needs only opportunity, encouragement, and the sincere respect of the group to produce material that shows promise. Such a child was Martha. For some time after the period in which the class concentrated on the appreciation and expression of word pictures that had poetic quality, Martha came to the teacher now and then asking, "Do you have time to write a poem for me?" The accepted plan in this fourth grade was that the teacher would write from a child's dictation at any time when she could spare a moment from her responsibility to group enterprises being carried on at that time. One of the poems followed the reading of "The White Seal" in Kipling's *Jungle Book* and another was inspired by stories of Holland. "The Wind" was dictated when she came in on a stormy morning.

Softly now the light of day is bathed with white mists;
Cool raindrops fall and patter the leaves' and
flowers' faces.
Flickers of lightning dash across the sky
And when I see the lightning
I repeat to myself this verse—
Fishes of the dark north sea
And animals of the north icy grounds
Tell me where that flicker ran!

In the long swell of the Pacific
Baby seals are playing with their mothers,
Playing all through the drowsy day
And at night tucking their flippers under them
For the long rocking swell of the Pacific

The wind, he flies
Across the skies
And swoops and cries
And swells and dies
And brings the lapse.
The shutters snap
And wake the baby
From his nap.

In the ways of Holland
In evening or at dawn
The geese go a-swimming
Paddling in the pond,
All through the husky day
Drowsing in their lazy way.
The sunset's rays are golden light
Windmills make the whirl
In Holland, . . . in Holland.[4]

The fourth grade class had been discussing various kinds of power in connection with their science work. One child told of the figure of Prometheus over the fountain at Radio City and the teacher read the story of Prometheus' theft of fire from the gods. The children decided to put into a poem the effect of fire on human life and use the poem at a parents' meeting as part of their summary of their study of power. The poem was a group composition, starting with the idea of Prometheus presented in the Radio City bas relief, "Prometheus brought the fire to man, which proved a means to mighty ends." All of the children participated in the composition of the poem, suggesting lines, evaluating and revising them until they had caught in words the spirit and thought they wanted to convey. They liked the rhythmic swing of it and gave no thought to rhyme but centered their attention on meaning.

Prometheus brought the fire to man;
From Mount Olympus came the fire.
It proved to be man's greatest gift
Unlocking secrets from the earth.

Man found that fire gave him light.
The forest beasts, they feared the fire.
It melted metal from the stone;
It cooked his food and kept him warm.

Now comes the age of iron and steel;
Skyscrapers towering everywhere,
The whirring buzz of great machines,
Run by steam and coal and oil.

[4]Poems from the Third Grade and the Fourth Grade Oak Lane Country Day School of Temple University

Electric current traveling fast
Through the air without a sound
Links together many lands
Making brothers of all men.

Prometheus brought the fire to man;
From Mount Olympus came the fire.
It proved to be man's greatest gift;
It proved a means to mighty ends.[5]

☐ INTEREST, EXPERIENCE, AND GROWTH

Some children write a great deal in their spare time as well as during periods devoted to the purpose; others rise to that level of enthusiasm only occasionally during the course of a school year. The teacher's interest in creative writing is in itself a potent factor in children's response. The teacher who sees value in children's creative writing and enjoys watching children develop will find time for children to write. Interest often goes in waves. Children may spend all available time on it when they are full of ideas and then do relatively little with it for a period. A good lead by a child or new experience and tactful stimulation by the teacher, and they go at it again with renewed enthusiasm. Occasionally, there is a wave of interest in a certain form of writing and everyone works on it enthusiastically for a time. An epidemic of gangster stories or mysteries may strike a group and almost everyone turns his attention to writing lurid tales stimulated by comic strip, TV, or motion picture plots. The teacher's guidance problem here is the same as in the guidance of reading. It does little good to attack the problem through direct disapproval, through forbidding the writing or taking away the books. Opening up other interests, reading stimulating and colorful material of a more wholesome nature, or turning the children's attention to dramatics or other forms of expression brings them through to new interests and enthusiasms without decreasing the zest for writing itself.

The studies conducted by Edmund (12) provide similar findings about the types of experiences which seem to form the preferred basis for children's stories. For both fifth and seventh grade pupils the experiences acquired through books, radio,

[5] Co-operating group poem, Fourth Grade, Oak Lane Country Day School of Temple University

television, films and other vicarious means resulted in longer stories with more descriptive words than did firsthand experiences. These findings lend themselves to a variety of interpretations, not the least significant of which is the possibility that fifth and seventh grade pupils have not had enough opportunities to use firsthand experiences as the basis for writing. Of course, it may well be that young people of these ages do not always choose to have their real and personal experiences displayed before their peers. It takes a great deal of courage to offer one's experiences and writing skills for evaluation by adults and still more for fellow authors.

In the intermediate grades as well as in the primary grades, the real values in creative writing lie in what is happening to the child, not in the story, poem, or play he has produced. If the child is growing in depth of thinking, in imaginative creation, in respect for the worth of his own ideas, and in ability to be himself, then the work is good regardless of the quality of what is written. But it stands to reason that a child cannot grow in those ways without improving the quality of his output. The mere fact that other children who are his peers are willing to listen to and comment on what he has written causes him to put more and more of himself and his best thinking into it. As he sees how much clearer his material is to the reader when he uses the writing techniques he is learning in his practical writing, he gives more thought to punctuation and matters of form.

No clear distinction can be made between what is creative in writing and what is purely practical. A personal letter to a friend or the report of an experience can be creative writing, in a sense. The distinction that is needed lies between the writing in which emphasis is placed on learning how to do things and on practicing to gain skill, and the writing in which the emphasis is on expression of one's own imaginative and original thinking for the pleasure that can be derived from such expression.

Children grow and improve in their creative writing as well as in the practical writing. In *They All Want to Write,* the authors tell of children's efforts to catch and hold the attention of the class through their stories and their growing awareness of what it takes to "catch" an audience. A child confides to his teacher, after watching the audience reaction to his story, "You know that last story wasn't so good. . . . It was too long and nothing happened really" (8, p. 106). The action of a story, a particularly intriguing and rapid "take-off," a novel or suitable closing, an element of surprise or clever building up of suspense, a character who becomes a real personality, all these and many other elements, commented upon by children or teacher, help young writers to see ways to improve.

The contrasts between the two forms of writing lie in the nature of the writing itself and in the purposes each serves in the growth of the child. One is concerned with artistic self-expression, the other with functional communication. "One is personal, individual, imaginative, and highly perishable. The other is more utilitarian, realistic, or intellectual, and needs the discipline of correct mechanics to be socially acceptable" (8, p. 184).

☐ EVALUATION

All evaluation can be constructive with emphasis on what is good. In every case there is something on which to build. Perhaps the idea is good though the presentation of it is less so. Calling attention to a well-chosen word, a clear sentence, a vivid picture, or an interesting glimpse of a character helps the writer to see in what direction to work.

A physics professor from Massachusetts Institute of Technology remarked in a committee conference, "Everyone knows that writing has to be taught individually." Teachers can find time and ways to give a moment of individual attention to each child's writing if they recognize the value to the individual child of even a small amount of personal interest in what he is striving to express.

☐ GOALS FOR WRITTEN EXPRESSION IN THE INTERMEDIATE SCHOOL

In order to stimulate and guide the growth of children, teachers need to be clear as to the types of growth they are striving to attain. In the pamphlet *Children Learn to Write*, Ragland lists these working goals for the growth of the child as an individual:

Sensitiveness to occasions for writing.
Desire to write when there is need.
Inclination to write for pleasure.

Tendency to put more and more of himself into what he writes.
Ability to get his ideas on paper so that the reader will understand.
Power to revise what he has written so that it will serve his purpose.
Recognition and appreciation of good writing.
Desire to improve and belief that he can (20, p. 77).

She thinks of teachers as needing goals for their own attitudes and achievements so that they can be sure they are putting first things first. What is needed first depends upon the situation and the children. Teachers who are growing in their own ability to analyze the needs of their children and determine ways and means of meeting them are growing themselves as they work with children. These are the goals suggested:

Think of writing as an inseparable and essential part of living and learning in and out of school.
Accept as a major responsibility—helping children grow as persons.
Consider writing a by-product of thinking.
Recognize that learning to put ideas on paper is a complex task.
Set the goal for each child—improvement consistent with ability.
Grow as they study children and help each move toward the goal which represents maximum growth for him.
Make writing a vital part of their own living. (20, p. 77)

Though the details of objectives and methods will vary with groups of children and with schools and teachers, the basic philosophy of real teaching is the same and is concerned with meeting the needs of each individual child through experience and guidance that is suitable for him. The good teacher considers each child worthy of the best effort she can expend.

□ SELECTED REFERENCES □

1. Applegate, Mauree, *Easy in English*. Evanston: Row, Peterson and Company, 1960.
2. ______, *Freeing Children to Write*. New York: Harper and Row, 1963.

3. ______, *When the Teacher Says, "Write a Story."* Evanston: Harper and Row, 1965.
4. ______, *When the Teacher Says, "Write a Poem."* Evanston: Harper and Row, 1965.
5. Arnstein, Flora, *Adventures into Poetry.* Palo Alto: Stanford University Press, 1951.
6. Bell, Vicars, *On Learning the English Tongue.* London: Faber and Faber, 1947.
7. Braddock, Richard R., et al, *Research in Written Composition.* Champaign, Illinois: National Council of Teachers of English, 1963.
8. Burrows, Alvina T., Jackson, Doris C. and Saunders, Dorothy O, *They All Want To Write.* Englewood Cliffs: Prentice Hall, Inc.
9. Clegg, A. B., editor, *The Excitement of Writing.* London: Chatto and Windus, 1965.
10. Corbin, Richard, *The Teaching of Writing in Our Schools.* New York: The Macmillan Company, 1966.
11. Dixon, John, *Growth Through English.* Reading, England: National Association for the Teaching of English, 1967.
12. Edmund, Neal R., "Do Intermediate Grade Pupils Write about Their Problems?" *Elementary English,* 1960, 37:242-43.
13. ______, "Writing in the Intermediate Grades." *Elementary English,* 1959. 35:491-501.
14. Hopkins, Lee Bennett, "From 'Trudeau's Garden' ". *Elementary English,* 1967; 44:613-616.
15. Loban, Walter D., *The Language of Elementary School Children.* Champaign, Illinois: National Council of Teachers of English, 1963.
16. Leavett, Hart and John David, *Stop, Look, and Write.* New York: Bantam Editors, 1964.
17. Marshall, Sybil, *An Experiment in Education.* Cambridge, England: The University Press, 1966.
18. Muller, Herbert, *The Uses of English.* New York: Holt, Rinehart and Winston, Inc., 1967.
19. National Council of Teachers of English, *Children's Writing: Research in Composition and Related Skills.* Champaign, Illinois: The Council, 1961.
20. Ragland, Fannie J., *Children Learn to Write.* Pamphlet Publication No. 7. Chicago: National Council of Teachers of English, 1944.
21. Smith, Dora V., "Growth in Language Power as Related to Child Development." *Teaching Language in the Elementary School.* The Forty-Third Yearbook, Part II of the National Society for the Study of Education. Chicago: University of Chicago Press, 1944. Chapter IV.

22. Squire, James R., "The Teaching of Writing and Composition in Today's Schools." *Elementary English*, January, 1964, 41:3-14.
23. Walter, Nina Willis, *Let Them Write Poetry*. New York: Holt, Rinehart and Winston, 1962.
24. Wittick, Mildred L., "Improving Written Composition." *National Elementary Principal*, November, 1965, 45:14-18.
25. Wilson, Grace E., *Composition Situations*. Champaign, Illinois: National Council of Teachers of English, 1966.

GRAMMAR
AND
USAGE

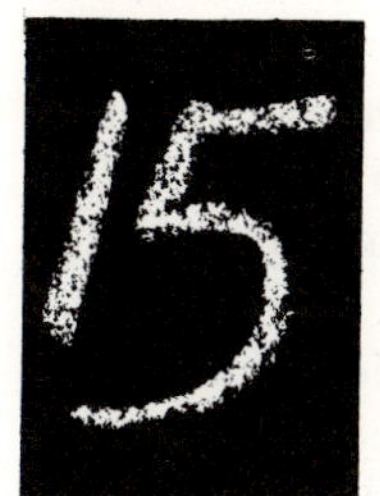

The point of view hopefully held for this chapter is expressed by Davies, a British scholar and teacher at Cambridge, in his little book *Grammar Without Tears.* He states as the purpose of his book, ". . . to help the reader use English grammar more effectively, with less pain to himself and more pleasure to others, and in such a manner as to avoid damaging a major national asset." What he says of the English and their schools is equally true of Americans and theirs:

> Each succeeding generation, as it moves into middle age, complains that the young have no idea of grammar, and that their English is deplorable. New books on English grammar are written and published, schoolmasters are exhorted to pay more attention to the subject, and things go on much as before. The grammarless young in their turn grow older, and renew the same complaints and the same fruitless remedies (9, pp. 9-10).

In their report on *Basic Issues in the Teaching of English,* representatives of four scholarly organizations in our own country stated in 1959:

> A knowledge of traditional grammar is sometimes considered an intellectual discipline and a social necessity. Accordingly, over the past century, grammar has been taught in thousands of classrooms, but with little apparent effect upon the written or spoken language of many pupils. Perhaps it was naive to expect it, in terms of what we know today about the language learning process; but in any event, new approaches to this problem may be worth considering (7, p. 9).

Since the publication of this report, a good many teachers as well as scholars in linguistics have been looking critically at the present teaching of grammar and its failure to achieve its assumed goal for even a majority of our students.

In his book *The Power of Words,* Stuart Chase says, "Grammar as I learned it in school rolled off me without leaving a perceptible trace, except that uneasy feeling for 'correctness.' The only conscious grammatical efforts I now make are (1) not to split infinitives—and why shouldn't I?— (2) not to displace 'whom' by 'who'—but again why not? 'Shalls' and 'wills' can go climb trees. I take my grammar from the deep, unconscious wells of the culture, and so far it has served me to say what I want to say with reasonable economy . . . . it is to those wells that the writer should repair, rather than to his grammar books" (5, p. 98).

Bell, writing in England, expresses his conviction that only after children have acquired correct usage are they ready for any work in systematic grammar. He feels that good English is founded, "not upon formal teaching but upon the gradual practice of expression." This means that there is little room for systematic grammar before the secondary school (2, p. 98).

Studies of the effect of learning grammar on children's speech and writing indicate little or no gain. Even gifted children from highly privileged language environments who have responded well to the systematic teaching of grammar fail to show gain in their personal use of language when compared with children of similar background who have had no formal instruction in grammar at all. Children's attitudes toward grammar may affect the problem.

☐ GRAMMAR VERSUS USAGE

One must at the outset distinguish clearly between usage and grammar, for they are not the same. Usage is defined in a recent dictionary as "the customary way of using words, sounds, and grammatical forms in a language." Usage is concerned with what people actually do with language. Grammar, on the other hand, is defined as the system of a language, its phonology, morphology, and syntax. A grammarian is a scientist who studies language systems—and every language is an arbitrary man-made system.

What the three practitioners, Davies, Chase, and Bell are saying in the preceding quotations is that one's usage may meet the prevailing standards for language output even though his knowledge of grammar as a system may be negligible.

The linguist Martin Joos is making the same point in the quotation with which he begins an article on "Language and the School Child." In it, a winner of two Pulitzer prizes, reminiscing about his boyhood schooling, says,

> The trouble was arithmetic and grammar. My thick skull for mathematics was a source of humiliation. . . . So, in the end, I just gave up mathematics.

> Grammar I wasn't obliged to give up, not having paid it any mind to begin with. I had no intention of doing so now. My position on grammar was that it served no useful purpose. This business of learning which words were verbs and which words nouns; what was the subject of the sentence and what the predicate; and that mumbojumbo about moods and tenses—there seemed no more sense to it than learning the alphabet backward (which one teacher required her kids to do). My teachers and my parents said grammar was necessary, to know how to read and write properly. *Bushwa.* As often as any other kid I was asked to read my compositions before the class.[1]

What the twelve-year-old did not know was that he had learned a grammar by ear as he learned his language and that he was closely bound to that grammar even though he was unwilling to look at it as a grammatical system. Because his usage was satisfactory he felt no need to study grammar.

It is not what one knows about grammar that makes the difference in his choice of vocation and the social realm in which he can operate. His usage, however, makes an immense difference. If he uses his language in ways that offend the ears and sensibilities of educated people, he will not be accepted into either the vocational fields that demand standard English or the society of people who use it and consider it important.

Joos maintains that the child has learned the grammar of his language by the age of eight and that "the books are closed on it" at that time (15). This would be a discouraging concept for teachers who consider knowledge of grammar important if it were not possible to give attention intellectually at a later date to what one has learned intuitively and through a sort of language osmosis earlier.

Usage, then, is concerned with the way in which people actually speak, with those accepted practices which make understanding possible between hearers and speakers and between readers and writers. Even young children can see how impossible it would be to communicate if people did not abide by certain common ways of saying and writing things so that radio and television programs could be understood by listeners all over the country, and so that people carrying on telephone conversations, miles apart, could understand each other. The magazines and newspapers delivered to homes everywhere would provide only material for confusion and misunderstand-

[1] Marquis James, *The Cherokee Strip.* New York: Viking, 1945, p. 120 f.

ing if there were not commonly accepted ways of writing things which made them understandable to all who read them.

Children can be taught that it is a matter of common courtesy to speak and write in accepted form so that others will not be inconvenienced, confused, or misled by their unfortunate choice of words, poor handwriting, unfamiliar spelling, or misleading punctuation. Just as care in the use of speech avoids misunderstanding and hurt feelings, so courtesy and consideration in written language help to keep human relationships on a smooth and comfortable working basis.

It is important that children acquire information about several areas of usage in order to learn to conform to the accepted practices which make the use of language successful. Usage is concerned with grammar, pronunciation, spelling, handwriting, punctuation, and choice of words in bringing about mutual understanding. Present-day usage is the important criterion: teachers are concerned with *the facts of usage today,* not with the materials of yesterday's textbooks.

There are certain rules regarding usage to which an educated person must give attention whether he wishes to or not. In both his speech and his writing he must live up to certain basic standards.

1. Grammatical usage must meet the informal standard of his place and time.
2. The words chosen must express the meaning clearly.
3. The structure of sentences must be in accord with prevailing patterns.

Three additional rules are essential in writing:

4. Spelling must be in accord with the accepted usage of the time.
5. Punctuation and the use of capital letters must follow the prevailing custom.
6. Paragraphs must be well constructed for the purpose and the material written down in conventional form.

Few rules for the use of the language can be absolute. They change from period to period of human development. Most of present-day adults, for example, were taught not to end a sentence with a preposition. But in some instances a preposition is a good word to end a sentence with. When Winston Churchill, a master of the English language, chooses to do so deliberately, it is certainly permissible for others to do so. The present adult generation was taught never to begin a sentence with *and*. But some of the finest writing in the English language—Shakespeare and the King James version of the Bible—use the form and many writers nowadays are using it increasingly in books, magazines, and newspapers.

It is not important that elementary school children understand the reasons for the forms that they use. It is important that they do the correct thing often enough, have enough real experience in doing it, so that it becomes automatic. The more automatic good speech and good writing become, the more completely the producer can give his attention to the content of what he is saying or writing. The form, after all, is only the vehicle for the content.

Usage problems of children vary from one language community to another and also with the age of the child. Five- and six-year-olds may still be using past tense forms which are regular and in accord with the child's grammatical scheme but not with the irregularities or the customary patterns of the language. Examples heard by many kindergarten and first grade teachers are *brang, gived, buyed, breaked,* and *tooked.* The probability is that these forms are the child's own and not forms used by the adults in his family. Most of them are cleared up by the age of seven if the teacher calls attention to the correct form through her own use of it. If, however, the incorrect form of the verb is in common use in the home, the problem will probably continue on into later grades. The forms of the verbs *see, do, come,* and *go* are among the most difficult to correct—"I seen it," "He done it," "It don't," and the like. Problems of agreement of subject and verb will take time. Pronouns are difficult for some children also. Pooley offers a list in his book, *Teaching English Usage,* which will be helpful to teachers who have to decide which problems to work on and in what order to deal with them (25, pp. 180-181).

The wise teacher will not attempt to work on all of the problems she finds imbedded in the speech of her class. She will select for intensive work those items which carry the greatest social penalty—those which grate most harshly on the ears of educated people—and those which the children need to use most frequently. And, certainly, she will select only a few to work on at a time—two or three—until the children are making satisfactory progress in substituting the new and better for the old forms.

The level of English toward which the elementary schools and even the secondary schools should strive with all children is informal standard English. While children should learn in their experience with literature to understand and appreciate literary English and English that is suitable for certain formal occasions, their own needs are well met if they use freely and easily English that meets the informal standard used by educated people in their comfortable, ordinary intercourse. It is basically correct yet it is flexible enough and broad enough in its possibilities to meet all communication needs. It is, in fact, the English language as it is today.

This chapter will concern itself mainly with grammatical usage, diction, handwriting, and punctuation. Spelling is dealt with in a separate chapter because of the concern that teachers and the public feel for spelling and because of the volume of research available in this field.

☐ HELPING CHILDREN IMPROVE USAGE

In order to improve the usage which children employ in their speech, it is necessary, first of all, to diagnose their strengths and weaknesses. Teachers do this in a variety of ways. Primary teachers try to provide many opportunities for children to talk among themselves, freely and informally, in work periods in which they are free to choose the materials and activities they prefer. There are also periods in which children may share their out-of-school experiences through showing or telling about the things in which they are interested. Intermediate grade teachers provide time for informal conversation among individuals and groups, listen to the children's talk in sharing, planning, and discussion sessions and may also construct tests or employ objective tests of usage. One good method employed by some teachers is to keep at hand a record blank, during the first few weeks of school, and jot down the usage errors they hear or find in writing, indicating the name or initials of the child who used the unsuitable form. The teacher then has a record of the usage problems of this group of children, the frequency of occurrence, and the children who need help. If objective tests are used, it is always wise to confirm the findings through free discussions of topics which interest the children or through the writing of stories. Short autobiographies of previous school experience have been suggested for written evidence also, to check the validity of the test. No textbook or course of study can tell the teacher the needs of her group. Her own study of her class will do that.

Following diagnosis of the weaknesses children show, the next step is to decide which problems to work upon. Obviously, not all children's examples of poor usage need concern the teacher at any one grade level. In any list of difficulties there will be some that represent more extreme departure from accepted usage than others, that grate more harshly on the ears of educated people. These will be given first attention and the most concentrated effort. The level of usage which the elementary school seeks to attain is that of good colloquial speech. Distinctions between *who* and *whom, shall* and *will,* "It is *I*" rather than "It is *me*" are not problems for the elementary grades. They belong to the stage of later polishing for those students who aspire to use formal or literary English.

■ *Helping young children*—Some children come to school using good colloquial speech because their parents speak well and have given the children adequate guidance and motivation to produce good speech. Young children sometimes bring to school immature forms of speech which are their own simplifications of speech patterns. These may be due to the child's efforts to be consistent where the language is inconsistent, or they may result from failure to note the way other people use certain forms of expression. Every kindergarten and first grade teacher knows the child who says gaily as he comes into the classroom, "Look what I brang you!" or informs her, "This is a boughten dress. My mother buyed it for me!" All that is needed in most cases is for the teacher to say, "I am glad you brought it. You bring us so many things! You brought something yesterday too," or "That is a pretty dress your mother bought for you." Using the correct form in her answer as she expresses appreciation of the child's contribution may be all that is necessary to help him catch the right form. If, later, he still has not caught it the teacher may say, "It sounds better to say it this way"—but only after she has expressed her appreciation of the thought or the act. Young children who are fond of their teacher absorb a tremendous amount from her example without being conscious of doing so.

One's speech is an intimate part of himself. To change it is to change himself. As was indicated earlier, a child's security is tied up with the people from whom he learned his language. If he feels, consciously or unconsciously, that changing his language separates him from the close embrace of that relationship he may be unable to change or fearful of doing so. Not until he feels secure in himself and sees value in speech which differs from that of his home is he likely to put forth effort to add a new dialect.

■ *Helping older children*—There are always some children, particularly in the upper grades, who know good speech but do not practice it, and there are others who have had no experience with good speech outside of the school and have little motivation to acquire it. These children need help to see value in improvement, but it must be given in such manner that it does not cast a humiliating reflection on their family and neighborhood backgrounds. A suggested approach to the problem is "from the viewpoint of helping young people acquire a varied and serviceable wardrobe in language" so that they will find themselves at ease and effective in language situations other than those of intimate personal acquaintance (16, p. 8). These children need many types of social experience and a highly functional approach to language improvement. Their attention can be called to the fact that everyone uses more than one dialect. One does not talk to a three-year-old the way he talks to an adult. Nor does he talk on the playground the way he talks when he meets an important visitor. Children can be reminded that everyone talks in his home and among his close friends the "homey" talk that is customary or comfortable there. But everyone also has need for the kind of talk called for on important occasions with important people. Through practice on this kind of language at school, children can become comfortable and confident in their use of it. If their own home language is substandard, they can be motivated to *add* the new level of language as an asset. This approach is psychologically far more sound than criticism of the home language.

Selected television and radio programs, recordings, and appropriate talking pictures give children models for good speech and tune their ears to the sound of it. Opportunity to participate in audience situations stimulates them to put forth real effort to meet the standards they associate with such situations.

Writing intelligent letters of appreciation and evaluation to artist stars of stage, television, and screen who depend upon fan mail for evidence of popularity, catches the interest of many older children. They can be encouraged also to carry on correspondence with children in schools in other parts of the country and to write to "pen pals" in other countries. Interviews to gather material for classroom work, the presenting of talks or reports on their reading or firsthand explorations in the community, newscasts, and dramatizations of all sorts provide good opportunities to enlarge their "wardrobe of language" and smooth out the imperfections.

Improving children's usage calls for both individual and group work. The methods used depend upon the type of usage to be corrected and the proportion of children within the group who have difficulty with it. If it is a problem of only a few children, there is no justification for making it a matter for class work; guidance and help can be given to individuals as occasion arises. If the difficulty is experienced by the majority of the children, it may be called to the attention of the class, the unsuitable form discussed, and the suitable one emphasized. Opportunities can then be provided for use of the preferred form, and individuals recognized and commended as they put forth effort at self-improvement.

Interrupting a child when he is speaking to correct an error is usually ineffective and may be actually harmful. The child's thought is centered on the ideas he is expressing, not on his words, and this is as it should be. Unless the content of what he is saying has some value, the form in which he says it is of little consequence. Primary school children, especially, are too immature to keep both content and form in mind. When the child has finished speaking, the teacher's first response should be to content only: "That was very interesting! You must have been quite excited when it happened. Perhaps you can watch for more news for us." Only after the teacher and the group have responded to the subject matter of the child's contribution, so that he feels comfortable about it or feels a glow of satisfaction or pride in their response, is he ready for any correction or guidance as to the form of it. If he is a retiring, sensitive child, the teacher will wait for a moment with the child in private when she can reiterate her appreciation of his contribution and then call his attention to a better way of saying what he tried to express, and give him an oral pattern to go by: "It sounds better to say, 'The fire truck came back *slowly*.' Try to say it that way next time. Thank you for telling us about the fire truck and the firemen you saw." Correction should always follow reaction to the worth of the child's contribution and be kept subordinate to it.

The question is frequently raised as to whether it is good to encourage or to permit children to correct each other. Probably this is poor practice in many situations and for many groups of children. If, however, a group reaches the point of friendly, wholesome relationships and motivation where children are genuinely concerned to help each other, it may have value. The teacher would then be concerned to see to it that there was mutual give and take so that there was no danger of decreasing the confidence of some children while others were becoming overaggressive.

There are many opportunities to help a child prepare the contribution he wishes to make to the group so that he can feel confidence in his presentation. Such thinking through of a contribution can be kept reasonably spontaneous and informal, yet it motivates the child to give thought to his audience and to consider means of making his contribution most fruitful for them.

Occasionally it is possible to provide practice exercises which give the child or the group opportunity to concentrate upon a form they are seeking to improve. If the sentences used for practice are the children's own or sentences such as they might use in their own speech and writing, then some directed practice may be valuable. Children cannot develop independence through reworking *other* people's language. They must work on their own.

In order to help children gain lasting value from corrective work, teachers need to analyze any textbooks or workbooks they feel called upon to use to determine whether it is best to omit certain exercises, to have only selected children who need the prescribed practice do the exercises, or to make up their own skill-practice materials and situations to fit the immediate needs of their children without regard to textbooks and workbooks. Very rarely will all children in a class need any type of specific correction.

A. E. Smith, writing to teachers in England, says this:

> To the many teachers who will most probably continue to work from a textbook of English exercises, in spite of anything that

> may yet be said here, we would extend one plea, begging them that, before setting children to work from such a book, they do ask themselves these questions: *Is there any real point in setting my class to do this in writing? Would it not be more sensible to do it orally? Is there, in fact, actually any real advantage in doing it at all?* (28, p. 110).

His suggestion to English teachers is valuable for American teachers as well!

Pooley in this country, writing under the banner of the National Council of Teachers of English, speaks equally strongly:

> The great majority of language work-books and seat-work practice pads are educationally unsound in both material and method. In material they are indiscriminate in selection of content and are far too inclusive for the ordinary needs of children. Side by side with fundamental corrections . . . appear rules and strictures of refinements beyond the needs of children, or rules based on ignorance and prejudice. Even were the type of practice given in such books the best aid to learning usage, there is in general insufficient practice on the fundamental items and far too much practice on unnecessary corrections (25, p. 184).

Some children will need a great deal of guided practice in situations of practical value to correct the poor usage they have thoroughly learned before coming to school. But there are other children who employ good usage automatically and have never done anything else. To have these latter children fill in blanks with correct forms of expression, or look at both correct and incorrect forms and mark the correct one is to leave them worse than one found them! Previously these children used the correct form unconsciously. Now they have to think which is right and which is wrong. The true goal of all good teaching is the *automatic, unconscious use of good English.* That has now been undermined!

In any case, there is no assurance that those who fill in the practice pages of workbooks will thereafter use the practiced form in their speech and writing. Only practice in good English in speech and in meaningful writing such as they will use in life outside the school can bring this result.

The geographic expanse of the United States and the diversity of the components which make up its population result inevitably in a wide range of regional and social dialects. There are homogeneous school districts in which all children learn a good quality of English in their homes and are ready at school for help with refining their language and expanding its usefulness. There are also homogeneous districts in which children hear only a nonstandard dialect, a mixture of English with a foreign language, or only a foreign language. In fact, in many homes of low socio-economic level children may hear very little language at all because people at this level tend to use language sparingly and only to meet immediate concrete needs. Probably the majority of teachers have heterogeneous classes with a wide range of language problems and needs which call for careful study and conscientious attention to individual differences.

For the first time in history, the nation as a whole has been giving thought and financial aid to schools which enroll children from culturally disadvantaged homes to help these children compensate in school for some of their early disadvantage. A major emphasis in such compensatory education must be on language.

Loban, in his intensive study of children's language in Oakland, California, and Bernstein, in his study of the cockney speech of London, found that individuals of lower socio-economic level use basically the same grammar as other speakers of English but their usage and vocabulary are different and they are limited in the uses to which they put language (19, 3). These people do not use devices for expressing tentativeness; there is no expression of supposition or hypothesis. They do not use language to express subjective reactions of feeling or emotion nor to explore the nuances of ideas. Their lives are focused in the present, the practical, the concrete. They use short sentences or partial sentences and lack the repertoire possessed by more skillful users of language of ways to extend and amplify sentences.

The need of these children is for oral language, quantities of it, and encouragement to use language in many ways and to explore its possibilities. It is *not* grammar they need but help with manipulating sentences. Teachers' questions should not call for simple *what* and *when* answers. They should be questions that begin with *Suppose that–*, *What if–*, *Why*? These should be followed by, "How do you think–? Has someone else another idea? How else could we say (or do) it?" Continuous effort needs to be made to link language with thinking.

Since this development will have to take place in children's own language, Loban strongly recommends that teachers ignore children's problems of usage while they learn to use their language in new ways and find satisfaction in their growing power to say what they want to say. It is certain to be true that, as self-image improves, these children become increasingly able to imitate the language patterns they find in use in the school.

☐ GRAMMAR—WHAT DO WE MEAN?

The problem of distinguishing between grammar and usage can be attributed to the fact that the word "grammar" is commonly used to carry three different meanings, as Francis has pointed out:

> The first thing we mean by "grammar" is "the set of formal patterns in which the words of a language are arranged in order to convey larger meanings." It is not necessary that we be able to discuss these patterns self-consciously in order to be able to use them. In fact, all speakers of a language above the age of five or six know how to use its complex forms of organization with considerable skill; in this sense of the word—call it "Grammar 1"—they are thoroughly familiar with its grammar.
>
> The second meaning of "grammar"—call it "Grammar 2"—is "the branch of linguistic science which is concerned with the description, analysis, and formulization of formal language patterns." Just as gravity was in full operation before Newton's apple fell, so grammar in the first sense was in full operation before anyone formulated the first rule that began the history of grammar as a study.
>
> The third sense in which people use the word "grammar" is "linguistic etiquette." This we may call "Grammar 3." The word in this sense is often coupled with a derogatory adjective: we say that the expression "he ain't here" is "bad grammar." What we mean is that such an expression is bad linguistic manners in certain circles (12, p. 70).

Children master intuitively and by imitation the set of formal patterns in which the words of their language are arranged in order to convey the meanings they wish to express; they have this pretty well taken care of by the time they come to school. Grammar conceived of as "linguistic etiquette" is handled by the school through helping children with usage. That leaves grammar as a field of study which is approached in highly scientific manner by the linguistic scientist but from the point of view of practical utilitarian values in the elementary school.

□ A NEW APPROACH TO GRAMMAR: WHY?

In the report on "The Basic Issues in the Teaching of English" referred to on page 357, this group of scholars stated ". . . over the past century, grammar has been taught in thousands of classrooms, but with little apparent effect upon the written or spoken language of many of the pupils." They concluded, therefore, that "new approaches to the problem are worth considering." These scholars were aware, as are all teachers acquainted with the typical program in elementary English, that most language textbook series begin the teaching of formal grammar in the third or fourth grade and repeat the same material with a little more each year until the end of high school. Yet college teachers complain bitterly that many students who have been exposed to the same grammar year after year still do not know it.

In preparation for a conference of linguists a few years ago, the grammar in five series of commonly used elementary school textbooks in English was charted showing where each element was first mentioned, where defined, and how followed up. The response of these distinguished linguists was, "Why do you make grammar so hard for children? Why teach definitions when they only make trouble? Why make it all so abstract? Why not teach children how their language operates?"

A number of American linguists have in the last quarter century developed new ways of looking at English which seem far more fruitful than the schoolbook grammar of past generations. The traditional grammar was quite adequate for describing Greek and Latin but not so adaptable to an analysis of English. English is a Germanic language, even though it employs many words of Latin or Greek origin. The linguists have attempted to achieve scientific precision by concentrating on the patterns of form and arrangement characteristic of the structure of English.

Transformational or generative grammar is the latest and most promising contribution. It stems from the work of Noam Chomsky of the Massachusetts Institute of Technology, which has come to be recognized by many linguists and educators as one of the most significant developments in the study of language in this generation (6). Students of his theory have attempted to take his "scientific grammar" and adapt what seems most valuable and applicable in it to classroom teaching. Material is becoming available for high school and college teachers, but relatively little that is useful has been written for elementary teachers. Yet within Chomsky's theories are ideas and a point of view which can be readily applied to help elementary school children understand their language and use it more effectively. Teachers, however, must take care to distinguish between what is suitable for the linguistic scientist and what is valuable and useful for the child.

☐ AN APPLICATION OF GENERATIVE GRAMMAR

Extensive studies of the language of elementary school children done in California by Loban and in Indiana by Strickland and others point to one clear-cut conclusion: the best measure of the maturity of a child's language is his ability to expand and elaborate sentences (19, 29). If this conclusion is accepted, the program in language in the schools should give children all the help they need to build effective sentences that fit the pattern of English.

While English has an enormous vocabulary and therefore the potential for the creation of sentences is unlimited, the patterning of English sentences is relatively simple. Borgh's definition of a sentence is helpful: "The basic English sentence seems to be the simple declaration, having as its immediate constituents a subject and a predicate" (18). Always to be avoided are definitions which state that a sentence "conveys a complete thought." The most basic definitions suggest that a sentence combines a noun phrase and a verb phrase as in this commonly used formula: Sentence → Noun Phrase + Verb Phrase (S → NP + VP). It is often diagrammed thus:

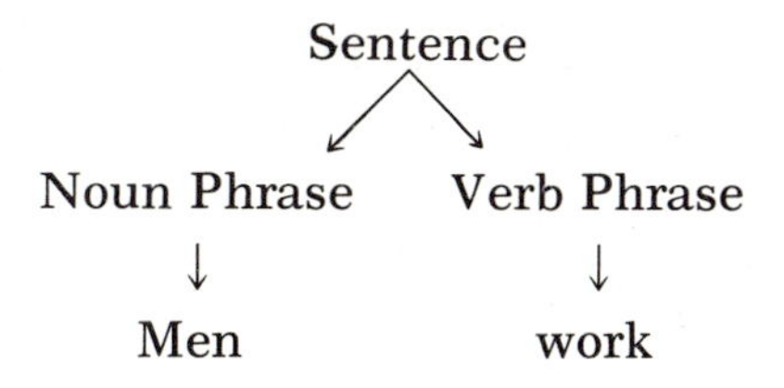

Grammarians vary in the number of kinds of basic sentence types they list in describing the structure of English sentences.

The number seems to vary from three to ten. For the purpose of the elementary school these three are basic:

1. The transitive-verb sentence
   The boy bought a pizza.
2. The intransitive-verb sentence
   He hurried home.
3. The linking-verb sentence
   The pizza was hot.
   The pizza tasted good.

The linking-verb group includes the forms of the verb *be* and the verbs sometimes called copulative verbs which express simply the relationship between subject and whatever follows the verb.

☐ UTILIZING AN INHERENT INTEREST OF CHILDREN

Children like to manipulate language. The evidence lies in the labor the child from two to five puts into learning his language. Four-year-olds talk endlessly; six-year-olds grasp every new word that comes their way and use it on all possible occasions; middle-grade children enjoy any spicy new term that they encounter; high school young people invent their own language to fit their moods and enterprises. This interest in language and in doing things with it can be utilized in helping children to build sentences and to understand how the structure of sentences operates.

Children are aware by the time they come to school of sentences versus nonsentences. The sentence in a child's storybook, "Pa threw the cow over the fence some hay," always elicits chuckles as the children say, "He didn't throw the cow over the fence. It was the hay he threw." They understand the meaning of this Pennsylvania Dutch sentence but recognize that in their own language this is not the way to say it. In the following strings of words, children can invariably select the sentence:

Man a mistake the made.
The man made a mistake.
Mistake a made man the.

They consider the nonsentences amusing but certainly not

sentences. Through dictating captions, stories, or other material in the first grade for the teacher to write, children become aware of a sentence as a unit of talk which they watch take shape as a unit of writing. They are ready, consequently, to begin to look at sentences to see how they are built. This can well begin rather systematically in second or third grade.

☐ LEARNING TO EXPAND SENTENCES

Children enjoy taking a basic sentence like any of the preceding list and finding ways to expand it. Take the sentence, "The man bought a pizza." It already contains a *what*; it was a pizza that he bought. They can add a *when*. "Last evening the man bought a pizza." It is easy for the children to see that the time words could just as well be put at the end of the sentence, depending on whether the speaker wished to emphasize them or let them tag as incidental information. Then they could add words indicating *where*: "Last evening the man bought a pizza at a delicatessen"; words indicating *why*: "Because his wife was away, the man bought a pizza at a delicatessen last evening"; and even a *how* if it is needed: "Last evening, because his wife was too busy to cook, the man hurriedly bought a pizza at a delicatessen." This suffices to illustrate the process that can be used in expanding sentences. The children can add elements of *what, when, where, why,* and *how* to basic kernel sentences, as they are needed to expand and elaborate the message carried by the kernel sentence.

Leaders in England as well as in the United States suggest that children need to take care of problems of usage before they begin a systematic study of grammar as a subject. It may also be said, and fully as wisely, that they need a great deal of experience with building sentences before they study grammar as a science. Children are highly motivated to *play* with language to learn what one can do with it. They are not motivated to study it abstractly.

The Indiana University study of the language of children brought to light the fact that children of seven and eight years of age tend to use a great many "run-on" sentences composed of a number of coordinate parts held together by "ands." Teachers often tell these children to stop using "ands" but give them little or no help with how to say what they want to say without using "and" as a connector. The result very often is the choppy sentences one finds in primers, which do not do what the child wants them to do. Good speech is rhythmic and flowing, not choppy. Children would enjoy remodeling a run-on sentence if the teacher would put the parts of it on the chalkboard and challenge them to find other, perhaps more grown-up ways of saying it. Such a sentence as, "Saturday we went downtown and we saw some friends and we had lunch and then we went to a show," might be structured to say, "Saturday, while we were downtown, we met some friends who had lunch with us and then we all went to a show." Children like to play with language, to toss ideas into different molds and find which are most effective. Certainly, this would lose interest if it were overdone, but some such experience would help children learn to weld clear, tightly knit sentences to carry their meaning.

☐ THE TERMINOLOGY OF GRAMMAR

Children like to know the names for things and certainly today's children who talk glibly about space exploration and supersonic flight do not need to have vocabulary watered down. The terminology of grammar is both interesting and useful to children if they are introduced to it incidentally in situations in which its meaning is clear.

Suppose a child has used a dull sentence where a more vivid, colorful one would better meet the need. The teacher responds to the sentence, "He went home from school," by saying, "Yes, we understand what you mean. But what other verb could we use in place of *went* to paint the picture more vividly?" Perhaps they will try the verbs, *strolled, raced, hurried, rushed, sauntered,* and the like, to see how the picture changes. Or the children might modify the picture through changing the subject or adding descriptive modifiers—adjectives, adverbs—to come out with, "The unhappy boy dragged his feet reluctantly toward home."

Or, the teacher might encourage children to notice the subjects of sentences. A subject might be a determiner and noun, "The boy," the pronoun, "He," or "The boy who just moved into the house across the street and who is very friendly. . . ." Teachers can find many opportunities to use the terminology of grammar where it fits and the meaning is clear without abstract definitions which, as the linguists said, only get in the way.

The terms "noun phrase" and "verb phrase" are easy for children to learn. "Determiner" may mean more to children than "article." Teachers should use what they like of the newer terminology of the linguists but not lay aside their old terminology if they care to use it. Names of parts of speech and grammatical rules have no place in the elementary school unless they are useful in helping children build better sentences to express their meaning. Anything beyond that should wait for the junior high school.

☐ TRANSFORMING SENTENCES

If children are keenly interested in how language works, they may take note of what one does to change a statement into a question. Their attention can be called to the addition of an auxiliary or helping verb, the change in the main verb, and the fact that noun *John* no longer leads.

> John bought the new book.
> Did John buy the new book?

Children make little or no use of the passive form of sentences, but there might be occasion in the later grades to look at this transform:

> John bought the new book.
> The new book was bought by John.

Here the subject is transferred to the end of the sentence following the word *by*, and again an addition is made to the verb.

What teachers do with transforms would necessarily depend upon the children's mastery of the language and their interest in manipulating it.

☐ SUMMARIZING A POINT OF VIEW

Help with usage is a prime need of many elementary school children who have learned a language which is substandard and which may close doors to social and vocational opportunity. This is not a matter of condemning the child's language and forcing him to change it but rather of helping him *add* what he needs of the accepted or prestige dialect of his geographic area for the value it will add to his life and experience.

Grammar as a formal study is suspect in the elementary

school. Many educators are convinced that this belongs in the junior and senior high school. The elementary school can and should use every opportunity to help children learn to speak and write better sentences through experience in constructing sentences. Much of this can and should be playing with sentences, trying a variety of ways to express an idea, and evaluating their output in terms of clarity first, and vividness and interest as well.

☐ AMERICAN ENGLISH DIALECTS

American speech lacks uniformity in pronunciation and usage, a fact which adds considerably to the interest of travelers within our country as well as those from outside it. We should be sorry to have teachers train Maine children so that they no longer add an *r* to the word *idea.* We should lose much of interest if the people of Georgia and the people of Kansas learned to speak exactly alike. We are interested in the "wait on me" which one hears in Indiana, whereas the rest of the country says "wait for me." (20, 26) Something of interest would be lost if people from the Pennsylvania Dutch areas ceased to reverse "leave" and "let," even though the reversal is obviously not correct. Americans like the diversity within their English-speaking country and take pride in the ease with which communication is carried on in spite of the diversity.

Good speech for both children and adults is inconspicuous speech and speech which is easily understood. Children tend to acquire the pronunciation patterns of their parents and others with whom they are closely associated, unless their speech apparatus is defective or their learning impaired. If the adults speak clearly and pronounce words in accepted conventional manner, the children will have no difficulty with pronunciation unless they permit their speech to be slovenly, with insufficient movement of the vocal apparatus, particularly the tongue and lips, to make the speech distinct.

Pronunciation of words differs, even in the standard dictionaries. Dictionaries, like grammars, record the best current practice, and often there is great diversity in practice. There is variability in the use of accent and in the pronunciation of vowels, but consonant sounds are not highly variable.

Children are not called upon to determine which are preferred or acceptable pronunciations. Teachers and language experts do that. The teacher's problem in the elementary school is to listen to the speech of each child and try to correct it if there is any conspicuous deviation from the speech that is commonly accepted as good in that particular geographic area. She may need to work on the child's speech also, if it is sufficiently different from standard usage to cause difficulty in reading or spelling. Much of the work of improving pronunciation is related to the teaching of spelling and will be discussed in the following chapter.

□ HANDWRITING

Handwriting has an interesting history in the schools of the United States. Three or four generations ago handwriting was an art which was executed slowly, painstakingly, and very beautifully by most of the people who could write. By the turn of the century or shortly thereafter, the majority of people could write, and speed became important in handwriting in order to take care of the many uses to which writing was put. Systems were devised in which legibility and speed could be attained through emphasis on arm rather than hand and finger movement and perfect uniformity in style became a major goal. Many present-day adults practiced long and diligently to attain awards in the form of badges and certificates for making perfect copies of model handwriting and doing so within prescribed time limits. Daily drill periods for all children were the rule throughout the country and the good writers spent as much school time in practice as did the poor writers. The aim was to make every child's handwriting exactly like every other child's handwriting. Originality of style was outlawed.

It is true in handwriting as in all other basic language skills that a certain amount of uniformity is essential to effective utilization of the skill for communication purposes. But complete uniformity, if it were actually attainable, would call for a number of changes in legal customs. One's signature on bank checks and legal documents is important because, theoretically, it is distinctly one's own and attempts to reproduce it are considered forgery. Handwriting is accepted in evidence in court cases and has been used as major evidence in bringing about convictions for crime. The fact that the schools have never succeeded in making all children's writing exactly alike makes this possible.

Individuality in handwriting is the result of several factors. The muscular behavior of individuals differs. Some people move slowly while others do everything at a more rapid tempo. This is as true of walking and talking as it is of doing things with the hands. Some people find fine, delicate movements easy to make, others do better with larger, bolder strokes and movements. Some find rhythmic, flowing movement easy to attain; for others, movement is more choppy, more staccato. The quality and speed of an individual's handwriting are influenced by his health and energy as well as by the quality of eye-hand-mind coordination he has been able to develop. Also, some people enjoy developing a highly individual, more artistic handwriting while others are content to produce a practical, utilitarian product and care less for artistry. For whatever reason or combination of reasons, young adults write as they wish to write or as they find it convenient to write, regardless of the emphases on form and style through which they labored as children, and their handwriting will change still further as they grow to old age.

But everyone would agree that enough uniformity to meet standards of legibility in handwriting is important. Courtesy demands sufficient uniformity to prevent inconvenience, frustration, or misunderstanding on the part of readers. *Legibility is the first essential* in all writing and each individual finds it necessary to develop *speed and ease of writing sufficient to meet all of his writing needs.*

A major development in handwriting took place during the 1920's with the introduction of manuscript writing into the elementary schools. It was not a new form of writing but a revival, in simplified form, of the handwriting of the monks in the monasteries of the Middle Ages, the handwriting used in the hand-illuminated manuscripts which now fill the cases of the great museums. Manuscript writing had been used in England for some time before its introduction into the United States; the new form was adopted rapidly by private and experimental schools, though its introduction into the public schools required another ten years or more.

Manuscript writing can be learned very quickly and can be used for purposes of communication while it is being learned. The simple letter forms, composed of circles and straight lines, can be copied fairly easily by young children. They can turn out a legible product almost from the first attempt. The fact that

each stroke of a letter can be drawn separately and that the letters are not joined in the forming of words makes writing simple and easy to copy. The wrist of the young child still has cartilage where bone will form later, and his finger muscles are still undeveloped at the age at which he needs to begin writing, so a simplified form is a great boon to teacher and child alike.

Most schools now add cursive script to the child's writing equipment in the third grade, others add it in the fourth grade, while a few schools permit children to use manuscript writing exclusively, unless they choose to learn the cursive form. A survey by Freeman, reported in 1946, indicated that 84.3 per cent of the 727 cities responding were teaching manuscript writing at least in the first grade and had found that the advantages in so doing far outweighed any possible disadvantage (14).

A few schools add cursive writing at second grade. Second grade appears to many people to be too early to add cursive writing for two main reasons: (1) Children still have not developed enough muscular skill to make cursive writing easy, and the time spent in learning it at this level is excessive. (2) Children have only just reached the stage at which they can enjoy manuscript writing as a tool, and they are beginning to be prolific writers because they enjoy doing imaginative and other types of writing. Adding a new form of handwriting at this time cuts off the interest in creative writing just as it is beginning to flower and makes the whole problem of writing more difficult than it has any need to be. By late third grade or fourth grade, children can swing into cursive writing with greater ease and still retain their interest in writing.

If handwriting is learned as a tool and used as a tool in many types of work, the legibility and speed which children need to acquire can be attained without the daily drills so commonly found even in Grades Five and Six a few years ago. There is little justification for daily drill, especially beyond the stage at which the child achieves a legible hand. Emphasis on good handwriting on the final draft of letters, reports, compositions, and the like gives children practice in careful writing. Genuine purposes for writing will take care of the problem of speed, since it must, in the last analysis, be an individual matter. Some children will need to isolate letter forms and practice to improve them from time to time but the majority of children need little if any of such drill. Children who need help can be worked with individually or in small groups if their needs are similar.

A great deal of time has been wasted on class drill in the past which might better have been spent on more library reading or other enriching experiences. Proof of this lies in the fact that the quality of writing done by high school and college students who had daily drill periods for handwriting in the elementary school is little or no better than the quality of writing of those who did not have such drill.

□ PUNCTUATION

On the adult level, punctuation is the most personal of all phases of usage, primarily because it is used to increase clarity and emphasis in the written expression of thought. Good writers range from almost complete disuse of punctuation marks to the use of so many that a sentence is broken into many little fragments. It is impossible to establish uniform practice, even if that were ideal. Editors differ so much in their use of punctuation that some writers leave part of that task for the editor to care for. Completely consistent uniformity in the use of punctuation would be inconsistent with fine, discriminating writing.

Marks of punctuation are traffic signals along the way to tell the reader how the writer wishes him to proceed. There are capital letters to signal beginnings of sentences and periods, question marks, or marks of exclamation to signal ends of sentences. Commas are partial stops, suggesting that the reader slow his pace here because of a slight change of thought. Semicolons indicate a more decided change and colons indicate that a procession of somewhat parallel points is to follow.

Children can be taught to see the value to the reader of marks of punctuation. Nystrom tells of a little boy who attempted to read a composition written by another child, and his indignant exclamation, "How do you expect me to read that, no starters and no stoppers!" (28, p. 66) As the teacher writes from the child's dictation, she inserts the necessary punctuation. She may call attention to it, saying, "That is a question, isn't it? I'll put a question mark here at the end," or "I'll have to mark the part that John said so we'll know that he was talking."

Most of the teaching regarding punctuation must be done in the children's own writing. It was recommended in Chapter (13) that the teacher work with young children as they write, answering all questions and giving help wherever needed. The teacher may ask a child to read to her what he has written and may put in the "traffic signals," telling him why each one is needed to make the material clear to the reader. In the intermediate grades, children will be using some punctuation correctly as the result of the individual and group help they have received earlier. Now the teacher proofreads with each child the material he has written (if the material is to be read by others) and helps the child to put in the marks that are needed. This is individualized teaching of the kind that bears fruit. (See Chapter 14.)

Mastery of the use of forms of punctuation comes about gradually and not all children attain it during the same time interval. Consequently, it would be impossible to set definite standards of achievement for each grade. Teachers will work on the placement of capitals and periods from the beginning of experience with writing. Question marks will find their way into early writing also. The use of the comma in the date and between the name of the city and state may come fairly early. It is important for teachers to remember at all times that the best learning comes through having the child read his own composition with the teacher and find the places where traffic signals are needed for clarity.

□ CHOICE OF WORDS

Diction, or choice of words, is also a matter of usage. This has been considered at a number of points in this book. It is important to remember that the extent and quality of the vocabulary an individual possesses determines in large measure the words he will choose to use. Choice of words is dependent in part upon extent and richness of personal experience. People who overuse a few dull words are probably people whose first-hand experience and vicarious book experience are sadly limited. Broad experiences, the development of many interests, and appreciation of good literature and good speech are essential to good diction. An individual whose ear is tuned to catch interesting words and who is sensitive to shades of meaning and feeling is likely to use vivid and interesting words in his own speech and writing.

Adults, as well as children, may fall into a habit of using the same word to serve many purposes. Often, on rereading a personal letter that one has written, he finds that he has sadly overworked certain words when other, more colorful and even more suitable words could have been put to use. Many children are prone to use "omnibus" words. Everything is "wonderful" "cute," "keen," or "cool."

Children can find real enjoyment in searching for exactly the right word to fit a purpose that interests them. A class of ten-year-old girls in an English Junior School were setting about the task of writing a composition or story which would include conversation between two characters. They had agreed upon this method of checking on their use of quotation marks or "inverted commas" as they called them. The teacher suggested that each girl, before she started to write, make a list in her rough notebook, of all the words she could think of to use in place of the word "said." The notebook lists were long and varied and included such words as *explained, remarked, retorted, offered, protested,* and even *exhorted,* and *simpered.* A soft chuckle could be heard now and then as a girl thought of a good possibility. The written compositions served the purpose for which they were planned and also brought forth some colorful, interesting writing. Teachers need to remember that reasonably "correct" writing which is flat and dull and expresses no exactness of meaning is poor writing. It may present evidence of some learning regarding correctness of form but it represents poor English usage.

From early childhood on, children enjoy playing with words. The avidness with which they lay hold on spicy, new expressions and even vulgar slang proves their interest in words. Many children would find pleasure in discovering the history of words—their origin and the differing uses to which they have been put through the years. Holiday names, Christmas, Easter, Hallowe'en, and place names from various national and racial origins would interest them. A map of the United States or of any single state reveals names from a large number of original sources. The source and meaning of their own names, both the family name and the child's given name can be found in unabridged dictionaries and in special dictionaries of names. If teachers take time to discuss interesting words found in reading and spelling, children can become keenly interested in words and in working toward clear, exact, and colorful expression.

SELECTED REFERENCES

1. Allen, Harold B. (Ed.), *Readings in Applied Linguistics*. 2nd. Ed. New York: Appleton-Century-Crofts, Inc., 1958.
2. Bell, Vicars, *On Learning the English Tongue*. London: Faber and Faber, 1953.
3. Bernstein, Basil, "Language and Social Class," *British Journal of Sociology*. II, 1960:271-276.
4. Carroll, John B., *The Study of Language*. Cambridge: Harvard University Press, 1959.
5. Chase, Stuart, *Power of Words*. New York: Harcourt, Brace and Company, 1954.
6. Chomsky, Noam, *Syntactic Structures*. New York: Gregory Lounz Book, 1957.
7. Conference Report, *Basic Issues in the Teaching of English. Supplement to Elementary English*. Champaign: National Council of Teachers of English, October, 1959.
8. Cook, Luella B., "Teaching Grammar and Usage in Relation to Speech and Writing." *Elementary English Review* 23:193-198, 213, May, 1946.
9. Davies, Hugh Sykes, *Grammar Without Tears*. New York: The John Day Company, 1953.
10. DeBoer, John J., "Grammar in Language Teaching." *Children's Writing: Research in Composition and Related Skills*. Champaign: National Council of Teachers of English, 1961.
11. Evertts, Eldonna L., *An Investigation of the Structure of Children's Oral Language Compared with Silent Reading, Oral Reading, and Listening Comprehension*. Doctoral Dissertation. Bloomington: Indiana University, 1962.
12. Francis, W. Nelson, "Revolution in Grammar," *Readings in Applied English Linguistics*. Edited by Harold B. Allen. New York: Appleton-Century-Crofts, Inc., 1964.
13. Freeman, Frank N., "Survey of Manuscript Writing in the Public Schools." *Elementary School Journal* 46:375-380, March, 1946.
14. Fries, Charles C., *American English Grammar*. National Council of Teachers of English. English Monograph No. 10. New York: D. Appleton-Century-Co., Inc., 1940.
15. Joos, Martin, "Language and the School Child." *Harvard Educational Review*. Vol. 34, No. 2, 1964, pp. 203-210.
16. Kaulfers, Walter V., "Grammar for the Millions." *Elementary English*. 26:1-11, 65-74, 107, January and February, 1949.
17. Laird, Charlton, *The Miracle of Language*. Cleveland: The World Publishing Company, 1953.
18. Lamb, Pose, *Linguistics in Proper Perspective*. Columbus, Ohio: Charles E. Merrill Publishing Company, 1967.

19. Loban, Walter D., *The Language and Meaning of Elementary School Children.* Research Report No. 1. Champaign: National Council of Teachers of English, 1963.
20. ———, *Problems in Oral English.* Research Report No. 5. Champaign: National Council of Teachers of English, 1966.
21. Malmstrom, Jean, and Ashley, Annabel, *Dialects – U.S.A.* Champaign: National Council of Teachers of English, 1963.
22. Marckwardt, Albert H., and Walcott, Fred G., *Facts about Current English Usage.* National Council of Teachers of English. English Monograph No. 7. New York: D. Appleton-Century Co., Inc., 1938.
23. Mencken, H. L., *The American Language.* (4th Ed. Rev. and Enl.) New York: Alfred A. Knopf, Inc., 1936, Supplement One, 1945.
24. National Council of Teachers of English, Commission on the English Curriculum, *The English Language Arts,* Vol. 1. New York: Appleton-Century-Crofts, Inc., 1952.
25. Nystrom, Ellen C., "Improving Handwriting in Use." *Children Learn to Write.* Pamphlet Publication No. 7. Fannie T. Ragland (Comp.).
26. Pooley, Robert C., *Teaching English Usage.* National Council of Teachers of English, English Monograph No. 16, New York: D. Appleton-Century Co., Inc., 1946.
27. Reed, Carroll E., *Dialects of American English.* New York: The World Publishing Company, 1967.
28. Schonell, Fred J., *Backwardness in Basic Subjects.* Edinburgh: Oliver and Boyd, 1942.
29. Shane, Harold G., *Linguistics and the Classroom Teacher.* Washington, D.C.: Association for Supervision and Curriculum Development, 1967.
30. Smith, A. E., *English in the Modern School.* London: Methuen and Co., Ltd., 1954, pp. 130-134.
31. Strickland, Ruth G., *The Language of Elementary School Children: Its Relationship to the Language of Reading Textbooks and the Quality of Reading of Selected Children.* Bulletin 38, No. 4. Bloomington: School of Education, Indiana University, 1962.
32. ———, *The Contribution of Structural Linguistics to the Teaching of Reading, Writing, and Grammar in the Elementary School.* Bulletin 40, No. 1., Bloomington: School of Education, Indiana University, 1964.
33. Thomas, Owen, *Transformational Grammar and the Teacher of English.* New York: Holt, Rinehart and Winston, Inc., 1965.

SPELLING

16

The English language is written with only 26 letters, though the entries in Webster's Third International Dictionary published in 1961 number over 450,000. Children are amazed to realize the immense number of combinations which can be achieved with only 26 letter units. Actually, no one would consider trying to master all of the words in an unabridged dictionary because the lifetime needs of even the most erudite scholar would not include all of them. The writing needs of most people are met with only a few thousand words. Ernest Horn, who has probably produced more research on spelling than any other American educator, doubts the value of teaching in school more than 3000 or 4000 of the massive number of available words. These are the words almost everyone would have occasion to use. Beyond that, for anyone who goes far beyond elementary school, is some of the vocabulary of special areas of scholarship that is needed in the more advanced fields of study: chemistry, physics, biology, advanced mathematics, history, economics, government, and the like in the high school; higher levels of these subjects and anthropology, philosophy and many other fields at the college level. Professions have their own highly specialized vocabularies: medicine, pharmacy, law, social work—almost any vocation one can think of. Not all of these words are in even so complete a listing as the Webster's Third International Dictionary. The total might be nearer 800,000 words if they were. Some professions publish their own dictionaries of terms to supplement the more general dictionaries. Students and adults beyond school age pick up the spelling of the words they need as they need them. It is the basic spelling that is the responsibility of the elementary school.

Spelling has only one purpose—to enable readers to gain meaning from what is written. If one had no need to write for anyone but himself, any type of code might serve his purpose. But since most writing exists to be read by others than those who wrote it, it is essential that there be a conventional system for translating meanings and oral symbols into graphic symbols. Spelling can scarcely be called one of the language arts, but it is an essential element in literacy. Stowing away a certain amount of knowledge of spelling is a basic task of children in any school.

☐ ENGLISH SPELLING

English spelling has been a severe trial to schoolteachers and a good many other people ever since Samuel Johnson assembled his concept of it in "A Dictionary of the English Language" in 1755. Previous to that time literate English-speaking people spelled pretty much as they wished. In the sixteenth century a word like *guest* might appear in print as "gest," "geste," "gueste," "ghest," or "gheste" (25, p. 115). The printers wanted some sort of regularity about the way words were spelled but found it hard to agree, and for centuries some words fluctuated. As people accepted the spelling recorded for them in the early English dictionaries these forms came to be considered standard or correct and all other spellings were considered wrong.

The next great lexicographer after Johnson was an American, Noah Webster, who published a book, later known as "Webster's Spelling Book," in 1783. This famous "blue-backed speller" was memorized from cover to cover in many log cabin schools and "little red schoolhouses." The "spelling bees" in these early schoolhouses are mentioned in many stories of pioneer life. To have gone through the whole speller (and sometimes more than once) was almost the measure of one's education. As a result, Americans became perhaps even more conscious of correct spelling than the English and more arbitrary in their adherence to standards. But even at the present time people who write English do not always agree upon spelling. Americans write *labor, check, fulfill, mold* and *learned* where the British prefer *labour, cheque, fulfil, mould* and *learnt*.

The reason English spelling is a trial is clear to anyone who attempts to match sounds and letters in some of the most commonly used words. There are nine common ways to spell the long sound of *a* and Americans use five other less common ones, some of which are borrowed from French.

Common Spellings of $\bar{a}$
a–as in aerial or aorta
a followed by silent *e*–as in mate, cane
ay–as in play
ey–as in they
ei–as in veil
ea–as in great
ai–as in chain
eig–as in reign
eigh–as in neighbor

Less Common or Borrowed Spellings
eh—as in eh?
ee—as in entree, matinee, fiancée
é—as in fiancé
et—as in croquet
au—as in gauge

Likewise, the long *o* sound is found in many different combinations of letters. It appears in *no, low, owe, sew, beau, dough, chauffeur.* Or suppose one tries to spell the word *cinnamon.* The sounds of the first syllable might be spelled

sin—as in sincere
syn—as in syntax
cin—as in cinder
cyn—as in cynic or Cynthia

Any language that develops an alphabet begins by coming as near as possible to spelling a word the way it sounds. A perfect alphabet is one in which each sound is represented by a single letter—one phoneme for one grapheme, a one-to-one relationship. English has only 26 graphic shapes with which to represent all of the sounds of the language and, obviously, English utilizes more than 26 sounds. Some English spelling is highly regular and some, especially words borrowed from other languages, appears irregular. Sound and spelling correspond at the beginning but, unfortunately, pronunciations differ from time to time and from place to place. When Anglo-Saxon was spoken in England many words were spelled phonetically that are unphonetic as we now pronounce them. The word *knight* was pronounced *k-n-ĭ-h-t.* Eventually people dropped the pronunciation of the *k* and the *h* and drawled out the *i* so that it had the long sound of *i* in *nine* instead of the short sound of *i* in *it.* People continue to write *knight* though they have pronounced it *n-ī-t* for nearly a thousand years (25, p. 114). The pronunciations of many common words differed in Shakespeare's time from their pronunciations today. Certainly a language used as mother language by a quarter of a billion people from Melbourne to London to Chicago will not be pronounced in exactly the same manner by everyone. The Australians pronounce *Australia, gray, lace* and *veil* with the long *i* sound where English and American speakers would use the long *a* sound. The pronunciation of the letter *r* in the United States varies from the *uh* sound of the Georgian in "fathuh" to the harsh, drawn-out *r-r-r* of the Middle West, "fatherrr." Speakers in Maine add the *r* sound to the end of the word *idea*, although they add no *r* to its spelling.

Should spelling change with pronunciation? If so, English might soon become a language of such diverse regional spellings as to be almost unintelligible to people from other regions. The answer has always been a compromise. Pronunciation has changed and will continue to change. Spelling reformers encounter resistance to their proposals even though some of their logic is perfectly clear. *Professors cud rite buks on speling refawm* and children could learn to write *Meri had a litl lam* (4). But the immense literature now available in English would become difficult to read unless it was all reprinted in the prevailing phonetic pattern. Many people, among them the playwright George Bernard Shaw, have been convinced that English spelling should be simplified to the point where letters coincide with sounds but it has not been done because of the many regional differences in English pronunciation. So the compromise continues – English speech changes slightly from place to place from generation to generation, but English spelling tends to cling to the standards set by Johnson and Webster. Children and foreigners will probably always have to learn to spell *bough, through, enough, though, thought* and all the other words that are illogically spelled from the viewpoint of simple phonetics. Perhaps in time radio and television may standardize the use of the language to such an extent as to make systematic simplification of spelling profitable. Meanwhile, to avoid the modern equivalent of a Tower of Babel, people the world over write English words using the same letters whether they pronounce the words similarly or not.

☐ PATTERNS IN ENGLISH SPELLING

In spite of all of the irregularities in English spelling which are the result of borrowing words from other languages and evolutionary changes in the pronunciation of words, the language is written with an alphabet which is phonemically based. A phoneme is a basic unit of speech sound and is represented by a grapheme – a basic written unit. Linguists disagree regarding the number of phonemes in the English language, the numbers claimed ranging from 38 to 47 or more. The suprasegmentals of levels of pitch, stress, and pauses are often fitted into the phoneme classification also.

In writing English, word patterns are represented by spelling patterns which consist of sequences of letters. These spelling patterns represent the word patterns even though the individual letters in the sequence do not always represent the sequence of phonemes in the spoken words. In many English words the symbol-sound correspondence is perfectly regular but in many others there are the major or minor irregularities which have just been called to the reader's attention.

The commonest spelling pattern in English is the consonant-vowel-consonant pattern (C-V-C), with the vowel representing a short vowel sound. A great many one-syllable words and syllables in polysyllabic words follow this pattern, as in "pin," "cut," "hat" or each of the syllables in "velvet." A number of other words such as "chap," "shed" and "then" begin with a digraph or end with one, as do "dash," "with" and "such." Here two letters are required to write the digraph sound. Some such as "bell" use a double consonant to represent one phoneme or two different letters to form the one sound, as in "back." The next modification is the use of two or more consonant sounds and letters to precede or follow the vowel, as in "spot," "past," or "strand." Add to this list the words ending in silent "e" which signals a long vowel sound, and the C-V-C pattern with its variations account for the spelling of hundreds of words and syllables.

Fries advocates teaching many words through attention to significant contrasts. Though he is dealing with contrasts in reading, what he offers has values for spelling as well (5, p. 178 ff). The silent "e" signal takes care of a number of words. But there is also double "ee" in contrast to single "e" in "red"–"reed," "met"–"meet"; "ai" in contrast to "a" in "pad"–"paid," "plan"–"plain"; "oa" in contrast to "o" as in "got"–"goat," "sock"–"soak"; "ou" in contrast to "o" as in "bond"–"bound" and "shot"–"shout." While the emphasis on contrasts may prove of greater value in teaching reading, the idea is worthy of study in teaching spelling.

Another regularity is the consistency of the spelling of the two phoneme syllable or suffix "ing." It can be preceded by one, two or three consonants, "sing," "bring," "string" or can be reduplicated as in "singing," "bringing," and "stringing." Even words beginning with silent "k" or "g" are alphabetic except for the one silent letter, as witness, "knack," "knife," "knot" and "gnat," "gnome," or "gnostic."

Several researchers are studying intensively the patterning

of English spelling and finding far more regularity than has been previously recognized (4, 15, 19). This can and must fairly soon change the selection and grouping of words for the teaching of spelling and perhaps the entire approach to the methodology of teaching. The values in such grouping may prove to be of two sorts: (1) grouping similar words will help children see that much of English spelling is patterned and dependable, and (2) it will help children develop a sense of power in spelling and thus add to their motivation to achieve the perfection they need in spelling.

The pages which follow sketch what appears to be rather general practice at the present time in teaching spelling in the schools. Suggestions are made on p. 409 for modifications of procedure to utilize grouping of words by patterns to facilitate learning spelling.

☐ TWO IMPORTANT OBJECTIVES FOR TEACHERS

Learning to spell the words one needs is a never-ending task. Any literate adult who gives attention to the inventions and the new areas of skill and interest which concern mankind is forever learning to spell new words. No present day adult learned as a child in school to spell *supersonic, atomic fission, penicillin, antibiotic* or any one of scores of newly used words. Some of the words adults use glibly did not exist when they were children and many others did not carry the meaning they carry today. It is possible that every individual learns far more spelling after he leaves the last class in which it is taught him than he ever learns in school. So objective number one for the teaching of spelling must be: *Help each child develop an effective method of learning spelling.* This must be a method that he can use by himself as he has occasion to learn new words. It must be one that is economical of effort and as thoroughly effective as possible.

Studies by Horn, Thorndike, Gates, Rinsland, Fitzgerald, and others present ample evidence regarding the common words of English—those that are used more frequently in all types of writing whether formal or informal, dealing with ordinary everyday ideas or highly specialized ones. We have evidence regarding the most-needed words. Objective number two then must be: *Help each child learn to spell accurately and confidently as many as he can of the common words of English.*

☐ PREPARATION FOR SPELLING

A child's first awareness of the fact that words are made up of separate elements may come through listening to the reading of his alphabet rhyme book as he points to the letters. Or it may come as he watches his mother print his name in big block letters and tries to copy it for himself. Four-year-old Betty leaned on the arm of the chair as her mother jotted down the last items of the grocery list before they started for the supermarket. When her mother wrote the word *Beets,* Betty said, "I have one of those in my name, but only one of those and two of those" pointing to the B, E, and T of the word her mother had written. Probably many children are learning to spell T-i-d-e, *Tide* and D-u-z, *Duz* and a score of other words at a very early age because of television commercials.

Perhaps most children are first aware of the need to arrange letters correctly when they try to write an identifying name on a picture they have drawn or a piece of wood from the scrapbox that they are fashioning into a boat or other object of personal importance. Six-year-olds recognize the need for identifying their property in the midst of so many children and work hard to copy the name cards the teacher has given them. As five-year-olds they may have asked the teacher for a sign for their block firehouse or a name for the railroad station they built for their dramatic play. Now they are ready to do simple writing for themselves. Some children learn to recognize letters and spell a number of words before they enter first grade.

Work with drawing, painting, scissors, and clay have helped to build eye-hand coordination. Putting together picture puzzles and other work with materials has helped to build visual discrimination for sizes and shapes. Singing, listening to music, saying rhymes and jingles have helped to build sound discrimination. Talking with individuals and the group and listening to the teacher's clear speech as she reads stories and poems and sings the words of songs have helped the child to hear and to articulate sounds correctly and to enunciate words and syllables clearly. All this is background for his task of learning to spell.

The first words a child learns to spell after he has mastered the writing of his name may be *dear* and *mother* for the notes that must go home carrying special messages or asking permission for school excursions. At first the teacher duplicates the body of the note, but later the child can copy the message the class has agreed upon. Still later, he will want to write his own note.

Many children become aware of initial consonant sounds early in the first grade. If Mary says, "That word starts the way my name does!" the teacher takes time to help the children play with the sound, to find other names in the group that begin with the same sound and to name all of the appropriate words they can think of. Some children notice sounds early, some much later. Spelling begins slowly and incidentally in the first grade so that children who are ready for it can pick up new spellings as they need them and those who are not ready are provided by the teacher with the spellings they need.

☐ SPELLING IN THE SCHOOL PROGRAM

Spelling is an essential element in any writing experience. Beginning in the primary grades, children need spelling in order to write of their personal experiences and to do creative writing of fanciful or realistic material. They need spelling as they write of science interests and interests that fall into the social studies realm and even in some of their work in mathematics. Any material that is to be read by others must follow conventional patterns of spelling if others are to glean the proper meaning. Spellings are arbitrary and all too often illogical from the child's point of view. Probably one of the reasons it is difficult to motivate some children to really work on spelling is that its arbitrariness is to them incomprehensible.

■ *Spelling and oral language*—A child who is learning to put his own ideas down on paper writes as he would talk. His word usage and sentence structure are those he uses in his speech. Many poor spellers have difficulty because they try to spell what they say. The seven-year-old who asks his teacher how to spell "smorning" because he wants to write "I got up late 'smorning'" needs help with speech and perception if he is to spell accurately. The college student who writes *reconize* and *enviorment* for *recognize* and *environment* is writing what he habitually says.

Children who come to school articulating certain sounds incorrectly need a great deal of help with speech before they do much with spelling. Those children who articulate sounds accurately, enunciate syllables and word endings clearly, and pronounce words correctly find spelling easier than do children with poor speech. Some children need help with listening in order to hear sounds accurately, to catch all of the syllables in a word, and to reproduce the word correctly. Here the pronunciation of educated people in the region is the accepted pronunciation.

If children have had opportunity to talk about the material they are to write, they will spell better than if they approach it without oral preparation. If the writer has an abundance of ideas and has heard them expressed and thought of them in sentences, he can more easily put them down on paper. If his ideas flow with ease he can give more attention to spelling as he puts them down than he can if he has to struggle with ideas, sentence structure, and spelling all at once.

■ *Spelling and reading*—Schonell maintains, as do others in England and the United States, that most children can read many words a year or more before they can spell them (28). Primary teachers in this country tend to agree that some children learn a good deal of spelling through their reading, though some learn very little. People who work with children who need remedial help with reading often find these poor readers to be even poorer spellers. Russell found that, at the end of the second grade, spelling ability was closely associated with ability to recognize words in reading and to blend the word meanings into the larger meaning of the paragraph (27). Recognition of letters of the alphabet and skill in visual discrimination of words were also closely related to readiness for spelling. Reading helps children expand and deepen their meanings for words and add new meanings. Reading words in context helps them to see that words which look alike may carry very different meanings.

In her studies of children who learned to read before coming to school, Durkin found a number who were what she called "pencil and paper kids," children who wanted to write and perhaps wrote before they read. Of course, the spelling they needed was supplied them as they asked for it. Also, evidence is clear that children who come to school able to recognize the letters of the alphabet have a distinct advantage in learning to read and write over those who do not. Some kindergarten teachers call attention to letters as they write the signs or labels children want for their creations or their dramatic play and as they write the stories children dictate. All of this is good preparation for spelling.

Both in reading and in spelling, words which carry concrete meaning are easier to learn to recognize and to spell. The words *play, fun, dog,* and *movie* are far easier to learn than *what, once, because,* and *these* because the child can picture the former words concretely or respond emotionally to them, whereas *what* and *because* are indefinite and intangible. A difficult word like *Christmas* or *bicycle* will be easily learned if it means a great deal to a child.

It is sometimes suggested that the new words a child learns in his reading he should also learn to spell. Adults as well as children read and understand many words they have no occasion to write. If a word learned in reading is needed also in writing, the one learning situation will reinforce the other. Word lists which can be used when writing, picture dictionaries, and later more mature dictionaries are a necessary part of a good spelling program.

■ *Spelling and writing*—Young children like to tell about the pictures they have made and may soon be copying captions or stories about them. The group composes notes to absent children or to mothers and soon some of them can make their own copies.

Spelling is not taught systematically as a skill in the first grade. The children may give attention to a frequently used word as, for example, the word "Dear" at the beginning of a note or letter, and some children will become sufficiently interested to learn to spell a number of words. This is particularly true in some of the primary schools of England where children are encouraged to do a good deal of writing, beginning at the six-year-old level (7). If a word is used frequently in material the teacher writes for the children or material they dictate for her to write, she may ask, "Could anyone help me spell this word? How does it start? Yes, *Monday* starts the same way as *mother, make,* and *March*. There are many words that start that way." Calling the children's attention to spelling and giving them clues as to how to go about learning it, forms an introduction to later work and gives children a sense of its importance. Children should be encouraged to go as far as they can in spelling a word, and the teacher then helps them to finish it. Some teachers feel that emphasis on spelling should wait until the children have made a good beginning with reading, because the habits to be developed in learning to spell may conflict with those which are emphasized in learning to read. Reading calls for recognition of the printed symbol form of words as they stand before the eyes on a printed page or writing board; words are dealt with as units of the whole thought which is the sentence. Spelling calls for selecting and assembling the proper letter units to form a word and fitting them together in the proper order. While reading calls for decoding, it is also concerned with attention to building the meaning of word units, and this requires that children develop rhythmic eye movement and increasingly broad eye span. Spelling, if emphasized too much and too early, is thought by some to conflict with the establishment of these habits.

In the second grade, where many children begin writing in earnest, they need generous help with spelling so that they can write what they want to say and not have to modify meaning and decrease interest in order to stay within the very limited bounds of known spelling. Help can be given in a variety of ways. The teacher may tell a child outright how to spell a word or write it for him on the chalkboard or a scrap of paper. She may begin the writing period by helping the children to make a list on the chalkboard of the words they may need for the writing task they are considering. Or there may be lists of words available on sheets, in large booklets or a card file, to which children can turn for the help they need. Picture dictionaries are valuable at this point also. In many English schools, teacher-made lists with words clearly written in half-inch manuscript writing, are placed in folders labeled "Food Words," "Home Words," "Animals," "Travel," "Holidays," and the like, and suspended from the chalkrail or hung at convenient points about the room. One frequently sees children searching the lists for words they need in their writing. Teachers in schools using a language approach to reading have found ingenious ways to supply children with spelling.

Older children need to be taught to use increasingly mature means of self-help. The word lists and glossaries in the spelling textbooks and other study materials and the dictionary take on value as the child is helped to use them skillfully and economically. All children should be taught to proofread their writing for spelling errors and to take pride in correcting and polishing their work until it is clear and free from errors.

Experience in composing and writing is essential to the learning of spelling. The more use a child makes in his writing of the words he is learning to spell, the more quickly he achieves mastery. The child who is interested in writing gives himself more practice and pays more attention to spelling than does the child who rarely writes and then only under compulsion. The more closely the writing the child does in school resembles the writing he does or sees others do in life outside the school, the more quickly and securely he masters the words he needs to use.

Children learn early in their work with spelling that illegible handwriting and inaccurately formed letters may be interpreted as incorrect spelling. Legible handwriting, together with correct spelling, help to insure accurate interpretation of meaning by the reader.

■ *Spelling and the content subjects*—The writing the children do in their study of the content areas tends to motivate and to reinforce their learning of spelling. They may take notes in connection with their reading or on trips they make. They may record the questions to which they wish to find answers and the results of their independent research. They may write to various sources for material or plan in writing for the interviews they consider important for their study. Each child may report his findings in writing and add it to the cumulative record the group is preparing. They may organize all their material at the end of their study and prepare a permanent record of it. All such experience encourages children to give careful attention to the spelling of the key words in their reading and the words they need for their writing. It gives them practice in self-help through referring to the dictionary and other books and materials. Writing up science experiments helps them to understand the need for accuracy, not only in spelling but in choice of words to carry precise meanings.

It is essential that teachers and children give thought to spelling in each new area of content. A great deal of progress in spelling can take place apart from spelling lessons. Making lists of new vocabulary and recording in individual spelling notebooks all the words that should be mastered, helps to fix in mind both the spelling and the obligation to master it. Obviously, not all the words used in a study need be included in the lists for mastery. Able spellers will learn more words than less able spellers. Children will turn to reference lists for some words while other, more frequently needed and more commonly used words will be actually learned.

Junior high school, high school, and college teachers have an obligation to be concerned with the spellings needed in their areas of work. If children in the elementary school learn the common words of English that are needed as the threads that are woven into sentences in any area of content, then older young people are free to spend their energies on the specific words that are peculiar to the areas they are studying, whether they be words dealing with chemistry, physics, economics, psychology, or any other area.

□ A BASIC SPELLING VOCABULARY

In the days when schools used Webster's blue-backed speller children learned to spell great numbers of words for which they had no possible use. Spelling was thought of as mental discipline and the actual usefulness of the words was of little importance. A great deal of time and effort was expended on spelling for its own sake. But in those days children learned little or nothing of the material considered so important today in the realms of social studies, health, science, and literature. As new emphases crept into the curriculum, the time devoted to spelling had to be curtailed. Each element in the curriculum had to be weighed in the scale of practical value in the lives of children and adults. Many words in the earlier spelling lists were found to be of little use and the total number of words set out to be mastered was greatly decreased. As it became obvious that spelling lists must be shortened, it became necessary to discover which words were the most important for everyone to know and how many it was practical to work on in the elementary school, so that time spent in learning spelling might result in maximum gains for the meeting of practical writing needs.

■ *What words and how many?*—Many studies are available which provide evidence regarding the words most frequently used by adults in many vocations and in all types of writing. There are several studies of words children use in their own writing. A number of the studies in both categories are listed in the bibliography at the end of the chapter.

Probably the most important studies of words used in adult writing were those of Ayres, Thorndike, and Horn. In 1915 Ayres published a list of 1000 words used in literary writings and adult correspondence (1). In 1920, Thorndike published his list of 10,000 most frequently used words derived from samples of textbook, literary and other published materials. In 1931 this list was extended to 20,000 words through analysis of additional material and in 1944 Thorndike and Lorge extended the list to 30,000 words (31, 32, 33). The *Teacher's Word Book* has been widely used by publishers and writers in the construction of textbooks. In 1926 Horn made a study of the writing of people in business and in a variety of types of occupations, tabulating 5,000,000 running words in all and compiling some 36,000 different words from the total (22).

The studies of Ayres, Thorndike, and Horn provided the basis for many later and less extensive studies of adult writing vocabulary. The most important point to come from these studies was the revelation that a relatively small number of words and their repetitions—not over 3,000—accounted for more than 95 per cent of the total number of running words tabulated.

The most important study of the writing vocabulary of children is probably that of Rinsland (26). His study, published in 1945, tabulated more than 6,000,000 running words in children's writing of all types. He gathered together over 100,000 papers, grades 1 to 8, from 416 cities all over the United States. The material included children's independent informal writing, in school and out, as well as their assigned theme writing: Rinsland's published word list contains a total of 14,571 words, all of which appeared three or more times at some level. The study is referred to in the chapter on vocabulary.

Fitzgerald has contributed "A Basic Life Spelling Vocabulary" consisting of 2,650 words compiled from a number of child and adult writing vocabularies (13). These words and their repetitions comprise 93.54 per cent of the more than 6,000,000 running words of the Rinsland list. Fitzgerald considers the mastery of these words fundamental to writing for life. He believes that this writing vocabulary can be mastered by most children by the end of the sixth grade.

Most spelling books today contain not more than 4,000 words in their basic lists. Some of the books provide supplementary lists for the use of able spellers who can go beyond the class.

Horn has called attention in several of his writings to the fact that little is to be gained by teaching large numbers of words. He has found that 2,000 words and their repetitions make up 95.05 per cent of the running words in adult writing; 3,000 words constitute 96.9 per cent; 4,000 words 97.8 per cent; and 10,000 words 99.4 per cent. The gain in teaching additional words diminishes rapidly with each additional 1,000 words and raises doubt as to the value of teaching more than 3,000 or 4,000 words (21).

Folger tabulated the frequency of word usage in the Rinsland vocabulary list (16). He found that 10 words comprise about 25 per cent of all the words in children's written material, 25 words more than 36 per cent, 100 words over 60 per cent, 500 words over 82 per cent, 1,000 words over 89 per cent, and 2,000 words over 95 per cent. There is no study of the words children *might* use in writing if they knew how to spell them.

Ten thousand words seems a fair estimate of the average person's lifetime writing needs. If children in the elementary school can master 2,000 to 2,500 basic words, learn how to build other words from them, and learn to use a dictionary efficiently, they will be able to meet all their spelling needs. They will have the techniques for adding the specialized vocabulary they need later on for all their vocational and social purposes and for any advanced intellectual pursuits into which they may go. The smaller list of words appears completely adequate if the major emphasis in teaching spelling is placed on the primary objective – that of helping each child to develop an effective method of learning spelling. Children who are given rich and stimulating experiences in all phases of the language arts, who enjoy reading and read widely in all sorts of material, who enjoy writing and strive to express their ideas in clear and vivid manner will have little difficulty in acquiring all the spelling they need for the carrying on of all of their interests. Emphasis on methods of self-help throughout the period of learning spelling will encourage children to set high standards for themselves.

■ *Grade placement of words* – In spite of all the research that has been done there is amazingly little agreement among writers of spelling textbooks both as to which words should be included in the spelling lists for the elementary school and as to grade placement of the selected words. Betts compared the lists in 17 spellers published between 1934 and 1940 and also 8 spellers published after 1940 (2, 3). Only about 500 words were agreed upon by all writers of spelling texts, and overlapping from book to book amounts to only about 25 per cent. Beyond the first 2,000 words there is little agreement and still less agreement on the grade placement of the words.

In spite of the fact that a word is studied in an assigned list, it may not be mastered at that grade level unless it receives considerable practice in actual use. It is not uncommon to find children in the upper grades laboring to learn words of several syllables—words for which they have little or no use—while they are still misspelling the simple words they need frequently but have had no help with since the earlier grades. The overlap of textbook lists from grade to grade is too slight to bring about permanent learning of many of the words on the lists.

Uniform spelling lists for all children ignore the obvious differences that exist in learning capacity and need. Children differ greatly in the rate and ease with which they learn and also in the words they need at any given time. A child who enjoys writing, writes easily, and has much to say will need many more words than the child who has little to say and finds it difficult to write that little. A child's linguistic maturity and his personal needs and interests, rather than his grade level, should determine the words he is expected to study.

The most important criterion for the selection of words at any level is the frequency with which the words are needed in writing. The more frequently a word is needed, the more practice it receives and the sooner it is learned. Conversely, once a child has learned to spell a word he tends to find more uses for it than he did before he learned it. The more words he can spell the easier writing becomes and the more a child tends to write.

Research indicates a considerable overlap between the writing vocabularies of adults and of children. But there are some words children have occasion to write which adults rarely use and many words which adults use fairly commonly for which children find no need (7, 13). Words such as *from, when, about, letter,* and *remember* are used frequently by both children and adults. Children have occasion to use in school such words as *spelling, geography, arithmetic,* and their writing includes words like *doll, grandpa, valentine, Hallowe'en, sled,* and *turkey*—words which adults rarely write. Adults, on the other hand, use frequently in their writing such words as *approval, memorandum, merchandise, credit, purchased,* and the like. There is no real answer to the question of how much time and effort should be put into the learning of words children use frequently but which have little use in adult writing, and how much time and attention should be given to words children rarely use but which are important in adult writing. It would seem that helping the child to learn what he needs now and helping him develop techniques for learning later the words he finds he needs is the most acceptable plan. Many schools utilize the plan of teaching at each grade level those words children have need for at that level, and of checking against the research lists to be sure that all the most important words, those that rank high in frequency in research lists, are learned as thoroughly as possible during the elementary school years.

☐ METHODS OF TEACHING SPELLING

Two basic methods of teaching spelling are in use in the schools of this country. Probably the majority of elementary schools use a spelling textbook or workbook, studying a prescribed list of words each week and utilizing the method of learning set up in the textbook. Other schools draw their word lists for class and individual spelling from the actual writing needs of the children at the time, so that there is a maximum of carry-over into the children's writing experience. Thus the practical value of correct spelling is held constantly before the minds of the children as they concentrate on learning the spelling they need to use in their immediate writing.

Some schools combine the two methods. Teachers guide children in keeping their own individual word lists of needed words and words learned and provide help in the learning of them. They also utilize a textbook list to be sure that the common basic words of English are learned progressively, so that by the end of the sixth grade or the eighth grade the child has command of a basic core of spelling which is not only useful as he goes along but will be equally, or increasingly useful in adult life. Unfortunately, there are still all too many teachers, using word lists from either or both sources, who merely *assign* spelling, expect children to study it independently, and then test them on their success in their unguided study without any real *teaching* of spelling at all. There are also teachers who have children record in their notebooks the words they need to learn but provide neither time nor guidance for the learning, expecting the children to assume full responsibility for it.

■ *Beginning steps in spelling*—A child's early writing experience in the first grade begins with dictating for the teacher to write, not with doing the writing himself. His attention is centered on the ideas he wants to express and composing sentences which carry those ideas. The teacher furnishes both the writing and the necessary spelling. The child becomes aware of letters as elements which make up words as he watches the words appear on the chalkboard or on paper under the teacher's hand.

In any area of teaching, it is psychologically sound to introduce a skill in situations which make its use and value clear long before the learner is called upon to master the skill himself. This is true of reading, writing, and dictionary and reference work of all sorts as well as of *spelling.* In this period of initial introduction, some children will learn to spell a number of words. If a story the children are composing uses the word *we* in several sentences, the teacher may say, "Help me spell the word *we.* We use it so many times in this story." Or, "*Thanksgiving* is a very long word, isn't it! Let's say all the letters as I write it. You watch this word in the first sentence so you can remind me what letter to use next." Or, "Here are two words almost alike. This word says '*play*' and this one says '*playing.*' I had to put an *ing* on the end of it."

Certain words for which there is recurring need may be consciously and carefully learned. Perhaps the children need the words *dear* and *mother* for the greeting for the notes they take home on various occasions. Or they need the words *With love,* for the closing of the notes, or *First Grade* for the group signature. The teacher may begin work on techniques for learning by saying to the children "Look at the word carefully. Say it. Think how it looks, which letter is first, and next, and next. Write it on your paper. Now look up here and see if you have it just right. Try it again until you can write it easily." Systematic attention to spelling begins in the second grade in most schools but a foundation for it can be laid in the first grade. Some children will learn to spell a number of words and be well on the way with techniques for learning spelling.

■ *Attitude and motivation*—As in so many other areas of learning, the battle is half won when the learner reaches the point of wanting to learn and assumes some responsibility for his learning. Teachers talk of developing in children a "spelling conscience"—a real concern for spelling and the desire to see to it that the words they write are correctly spelled. Certainly, the interest a child takes in spelling will determine the standard he sets for himself and the effort he will put forth to achieve it. Throughout their entire school experience, children need to be helped to see that what one writes for others to read paints a picture of himself. Material that is incorrectly spelled and carelessly written mirrors a careless, inconsiderate person who is not concerned about the impression he makes and does not care how much time and thought others must spend in trying to decipher his meaning. A correctly spelled, carefully produced piece of writing will be thought of as mirroring a considerate person whose self-respect demands that he live up to a high standard. As they grow older, children need to be helped to see that poor spelling can carry its own penalty in adult life in failure to obtain opportunities and may even, in some fields, result in the loss of one's job.

Writing for real purposes helps to develop pride in good writing. Children need to see value in the things they write and feel personal satisfaction in work well done. They need also the encouragement and motivation that comes with recognition on the part of others that the child has met a high standard. This means that in much of their writing they need to learn to do a rough draft, correct and polish it, then turn out a final product of which they can be proud.

Young children who are beginning to write independently should feel free to ask for help with spelling whenever they need it. They need to be encouraged to write whatever they want to say and to turn to the teacher or to easily used word lists for any spellings they need. While their spelling vocabularies are still small, any effort to stay within the realm of words they have learned to spell is very frustrating and discouraging and results at best in dull, uninteresting writing.

Most children enjoy assuming some responsibility for their learning. They will copy words into their spelling notebooks for study without being told to do it. Some of them will add words that are more difficult than any the teacher asks them to learn. If children help to set their own goals and are given freedom and responsibility in meeting them, they find satisfaction in growing. If the things they write are of value because they serve real purposes, children learn to take pride in correct spelling and to proofread their writing to catch any errors that need correction.

Mutual helpfulness is better motivation for correct spelling than is competition. If children are encouraged to help each other and even to work together when that is profitable, they develop high standards and real concern for good spelling.

■ *Time allotment for spelling*—Research findings are in agreement that 75 minutes per week is adequate time for work on spelling and perhaps even less is necessary (21). Whether children work individually on their own spelling needs or as a class on a class list, there must be time for studying spelling under teacher guidance. Any learning situation which requires strict attention and thoughtful practice calls for short periods of intensive concentration pointed toward clearly understood goals. Short periods of intensive work achieve better results than longer periods which permit dawdling and mind wandering. Children should learn to think of spelling study periods as periods for sharpening their learning techniques as well as periods for mastering specific words. They should strive to attain effective techniques which will bring results with economy of time and effort.

■ *Steps in learning to spell a word*—The most fortunate people, from the point of view of spelling, are those who can store away a mental image of a word and recall it at will. But not all adults remember spelling in the same way. One person, asked to spell a word, can instantly recall a clear visual image of it; another says the letters to himself; one says the syllables to himself, noting the sound pattern; another writes the word and looks at it to see if it looks right to him; still another person does not trust his memory at all but goes to look for the word in a dictionary. Children, too, have differing degrees of sensory awareness and differ greatly in their ability to put away an image of a word which can be recalled at will. Because of this fact all methods of teaching children to spell must emphasize as many sensory approaches as possible but with special emphasis on visual learning, since it is a visual image which is most valuable in proofreading and detecting errors in spelling. Dolch, Fitzgerald, Horn and others agree that a multiple sense approach is important, that vision, hearing, speech, and writing should all be used in learning to spell (9, 14, 21). Fitzgerald lists five steps which should be taken in learning to spell a word: (1) meaning and pronunciation; (2) imagery—seeing and saying the word, syllable by syllable, and spelling it; (3) recall–closing eyes, spelling, checking for correctness; (4) writing the word and checking for correctness; (5) mastery–writing and checking or repeating the entire process until the word is learned (14).

Some authorities are convinced that the unit for observation and study in spelling should be the whole word or the syllable, not the letter. In writing the word *committee* or *interested*, children should be taught to think and write it syllable by syllable, rather than by separate letters (21, 24).

In any group there will be a wide range of individual differences in ease of learning spelling and in various types of needs. Children who learn spelling easily will not long continue to use all the steps in the spelling method they are taught. They will discover which elements are of most worth to them and will minimize or cease to use the others. One child may find it satisfactory to look at the words carefully and write each one once or twice. Another child may find it necessary to say the sequence of syllables aloud as he writes them. An occasional child will find it profitable to say aloud the sequence of letters several times as he looks at the word, then say the sequence to himself as he writes it. This is a long, slow process but it is better to achieve slowly than not to achieve at all. Children for whom spelling is difficult will need a great deal of guidance and encouragement in finding what adaptations of method are best for them and what reinforcement they need to attain mastery. Every child's interest in spelling is greatly increased when he learns a method of study that achieves success regardless of how laborious the method may prove to be.

■ *Spelling rules*–Authorities disagree regarding the value of teaching spelling rules. Horn recommends the teaching of only those rules that apply to a large number of words and have few exceptions among commonly used words (21). All rules should be "discovered" by the children as their attention is called to basic principles which operate in groups of known words. Rules for dealing with silent *e* when adding a suffix, rules for plurals, for *ei* and *ie* are helpful. The facts that *q* is commonly followed by *u* and that proper nouns and most adjectives formed from proper nouns should begin with capital letters are both worth teaching since they involve few exceptions. Certainly no rule should be taught unless it covers a sufficient number of words to pay for the effort of learning it, and then only if children are mature enough to see the points at which it applies.

☐ UTILIZING SYMBOLS-SOUND CORRESPONDENCES

What phonics should be taught, when, and how has been a matter of public concern as well as of concern to educators for more than a hundred years. Most of the research studies deal with phonics in the program of learning to read rather than with phonics as an aid to spelling. Authorities in both England and the United States have called attention to the limitations of phonics from the point of view of spelling more often, perhaps, than they have called attention to its values. Duncan, in a book called "Backwardness in Reading" and published in England, says,

> Because patterns of words are remembered as visual images, pupils who have made the approach to reading through "wholes" . . . have tended to spell well. Probably a phonic approach to reading is responsible for much poor spelling, partly because the natural habit of observing words as wholes has been disturbed and partly because such a high proportion of common words in our language are not phonic (10, pp. 41-42).

More evidence is needed on the extent to which phonics is useful in spelling and the generalization which can be applied in spelling the common words of English that children need to learn. Once children have learned the consonant sounds and the long and short vowel sounds there are many words they can spell by the sound of the letters. They can build words about known elements such as *and*, *in*, and *ing*. They can spell longer words compounded of small ones which they know – *into*, *visit*, *without*, *grandfather* and the like.

On the other hand, most of children's misspellings when they write letters and stories without adult guidance are phonic spellings. The child who wrote "ankshus" for "anxious" and the one whose effort to spell "initiated" resulted in "anisheated" were doing a perfect job in the light of their phonic background. The child spells the word as it sounds to him without regard to the idiosyncrasies of conventional spelling. Over-reliance on phonics is detrimental in spelling the English language, though phonics is obviously helpful at many points.

Schonell, another English writer and researcher, advocates

that spelling material be grouped in small units according to some rational plan (28, pp. 15-16). He suggests grouping:

(a) words which have similar auditory and visual elements: *power, shower, tower*

(b) words of similar visual, but slightly dissimilar auditory elements: *stove, glove, prove*

(c) a combination of grouping according to both common elements and context: *needle, thimble; button, cotton*

(d) grouping according to a common silent letter:

knee, kneel, knock, knob
comb, crumb, thumb, climb

The value of grouping lies in the fact that the child has experience with common letter combinations which he applies, at first consciously and later unconsciously, to new words of similar structure. Schonell advocates, also, that homonyms not be taught together but that each be grouped with other words of similar sound and spelling, as: *there, where, here.*

□ A NEW DEVELOPMENT

Major impetus for changing the teaching of spelling comes from the work of Paul and Jean Hanna of Stanford University and their co-workers, Hodges and Rudorf. The Hannas put 17,000 English words, including all of Thorndike's list of 10,000 most commonly used words and some "far out," infrequently used words, through intricate IBM processing for structure. The findings indicate that English spelling is far more regular in its patterning than is commonly believed. They have studied also the options that exist in English for the spelling of a given phoneme or morpheme. The single sound or phoneme *a* may be spelled in the 14 ways listed earlier. The frequently used /sh/ sound can be spelled *sh, ci,* or *ti;* the /f/ sound can also be spelled *ph* or *gh.* A summary of the Hanna study concludes that

> . . . the orthography reflects the structure of the oral language on which it is based. It suggests that regularities exist in the relationship between phonological elements in the oral language and their graphemic representations in the orthography, and that a pedagogical method based upon aural-oral cues to spelling may well prove to be more efficient and powerful than present

> methods which rely primarily upon visual and hand learning approaches (21, pp. 864-65).

Boord arranged the word lists in five series of spelling textbooks according to spelling pattern. There is clear evidence from his work as well as that of the Hannas that time might be saved in the teaching of spelling by grouping many of the common words according to pattern.

Teachers who are interested in such an approach to spelling need not wait for new textbooks. The wordlists in present texts could be grouped according to pattern. When children encounter one word which exemplifies a pattern, the teacher could help them build a list of others which they can now spell by giving attention to the pattern. The sense of power which children might thus gain would provide motivation for further work with the schemes of symbol-sound correspondences which operate in English spelling.

□ USING THE DICTIONARY

Learning to use the dictionary is an essential part of learning to spell. Picture dictionaries and the simple files or lists of related words that primary teachers use introduce children to alphabetizing. Middle grade children need to be taught how to help themselves through the use of the dictionary and should be taught to use it efficiently and with economy of effort. They should be taught to think of the dictionary as their final authoritative resource in spelling. They will need help for a long time as they learn to use it, however. They cannot look up the spelling of the word *cinnamon,* which was mentioned before, without help with the first letters, since the syllable *cin* could as easily be spelled *cyn, sin,* or *syn.* They need help to interpret the pronunciation key and to select the spelling that fits their meaning. The use of the dictionary cannot be learned in one grade. There is work for all teachers to do from first grade through high school. Children should learn that there are many dictionaries, both general and specialized. Their reference should not be to *the* dictionary but to a dictionary, recognizing the kind of service that each dictionary is designed to render.

■ *Helping children who find spelling difficult*—Everyone is aware of the fact that some children encounter serious difficulty in learning to spell. Fernald, Fitzgerald, Hildreth, and Horn, among others, give suggestions for diagnosing spelling difficulties and remedying them (12, 14, 20, 21). All children who have difficulty in learning to spell need help with building clear-cut images of words. Every child should be taught to employ all the sensory channels in learning spelling. Visual, auditory, speech-motor, and hand-motor impressions need to be interwoven for most children in order to fix an image of the word that can be recalled automatically. Children who have serious difficulty may need more emphasis on auditory imagery or more interweaving of auditory and motor impressions of the word. Fernald recommended tracing the word with the fingers on a large copy to develop a feeling and motion pattern to reinforce the auditory and visual impressions (10). The teacher's task is patient, trial-and-error experimentation with the child who is seriously disabled until she finds what elements of method are most fruitful of results. Emphasis, for such children, must be placed at all times on their accomplishment, however small that may be, not upon their failures. A discouraged, disheartened child finds it difficult to learn. An optimistic child can be endlessly patient in struggling for results if he has helpful and optimistic guidance.

☐ EVALUATION IN SPELLING

Parents, businessmen, and other adults in the community are continually evaluating the school's spelling achievement. Falk quotes the Superintendent of Schools of Madison, Wisconsin, in 1900 as saying:

> A criticism with which we are all familiar, and which usually goes unchallenged, is that our schools fail to make good spellers. It is undeniably true that there is a great deal of bad spelling in our schools. . . . Poor spelling, however, is not a weakness that is confined to the present generation. . . . Letters and notes from parents lead one to doubt seriously the efficiency of the methods of teaching spelling in the past (11, p. 243).

The same criticisms can be voiced today with equal justification.

Evaluation of spelling is tied up with evaluation of the total growth of a child—his attitude toward himself, his confidence in his ability to learn, his interest in writing, and his concept of the importance of spelling. Children who do well in spelling tend to be children who do well in all aspects of language learning. Poor achievement in spelling is usually associated with a low level of achievement in other aspects of language learning.

Teaching and evaluating operate together. As the teacher helps children learn to spell she analyzes their problems and studies their needs for help with sensory perception and means of associating and remembering. She observes a child's responses to the techniques she is utilizing and plans next steps on the basis of those responses. Assigning, allowing time for study, and testing is not teaching spelling. Teaching is working with children, helping them develop even better methods of study, and analyzing and evaluating both one's own methods and the children's achievement.

The best measure of spelling achievement is the quality of spelling a child does when his mind is focused on the content he is expressing and the spelling flows onto the page without conscious effort on his part. Good spelling indicates that the mental images are clear and accurate and that the child can reproduce them unconsciously. Poor spelling indicates a lack of clear images and the consequent inability to select the right letters and arrange them in the right order to produce the word.

Teacher-made tests can be used to measure the spelling that all children have in common. It is difficult to test when the work is highly individualized and each child is working on his own separate list. Some of the teacher-made tests may be tests composed of lists of words. Some of the tests will be dictated paragraphs containing the words the child has been learning.

Standardized tests have a place in the evaluation program (24). Most children learn some spelling without direct teaching, so a standardized test compared with a test on the words a child has actually studied will give some indication of the power the child is gaining in spelling.

No educational program can make satisfactory progress unless the teacher knows in what direction she is moving and has her goals clearly in mind. Most schools set up their goals in the form of anticipated outcomes which they strive to achieve at specified points along the way. It is clearly recognized by everyone that not all children will achieve the outcomes suggested and that some children will surpass them. But the outcomes the teacher strives to achieve chart the path along which her work will move. When the teacher knows where a child stands at the moment in his development of a skill, she can then decide what his next step should be and guide him in taking it.

The following list of outcomes taken from "Using Language," a supplementary curriculum guide for the elementary schools of Wilmington, Delaware, provides a sample of the kind of guidance teachers like to have (34).

Desirable Outcomes of an Effective Spelling Program
Expectancies at the End of the Fourth Grade

By the end of the fourth grade in school, a child, to the extent of his ability, should be able to:

- Use an effective plan for studying spelling words with the teacher's guidance
- Make greater use of word-analysis techniques to improve his spelling
- Develop the habit of checking his written work for spelling errors and correcting them
- Keep a list of words which seem difficult
- Begin to use glossaries, encyclopedias, and simplified dictionaries
- Be able to arrange words in alphabetical order through the first and second letters
- Open the dictionary at the estimated location of the desired word
- Use guide words in a dictionary
- Divide words into syllables
- Select the meaning that best fits a word as it is used in a sentence
- Recognize the diacritical markings of long and short vowels
- Recognize and build compound words and derive the meanings of such words from their component parts
- Use and spell contractions such as *I'll, I'm, it's, haven't, won't*, and *can't*
- Spell certain irregular plurals and certain words doubling the last consonant

Helpful also, may be the points offered by Furness as the psychological determinants of spelling success:

1. Ability to spell seems to be contingent upon two processes – recognition and reproduction.

2. Imagery appears to be involved in spelling but teachers and psychologists are still uncertain of its role.
3. Relationship between intelligence and spelling ability is much lower than that found between intelligence and most other school subjects.
4. There is an emotional factor involved in spelling difficulty. The older the child, the more difficulties and discouragements encountered, but these old attitudes can be replaced with new ones.
5. Indifference, carelessness, and distaste for intellectual drudgery are major factors in poor spelling, especially with the student with a high I. Q.
6. To be a good speller, an individual must first develop a "spelling conscience."
7. "The skillful management of incentives is unquestionably more important than techniques of instruction" (17, p. 71).

Perhaps the realization that there is some dependable sense in English spelling would help to counteract the indifference and distaste many bright children feel for the drudgery of learning spelling as it is now taught. A few bits of action research by teachers here and there seems to indicate that children can become excited over spelling when their attention is called to its logical patterning and the reasons for what is illogical or irregular. The recognition of French, Spanish and other vocabulary borrowings and the retention of borrowed spelling adds interest and zest to learning rather than indifference and dislike.

■ *Spelling*—The sole purpose of spelling is to make possible communication through writing. The more opportunities children have for writing things that are important to them the more value they see in spelling and the more readily they learn it. The teacher's task is to provide opportunities, motivation, and guidance so that each child can develop an effective method of learning spelling that will meet his needs throughout life and to help him learn as many as he can of the common words of English that will form the foundation for his later learning and make possible any form of expression that he needs or wishes to use.

☐ SELECTED REFERENCES ☐

1. Ayres, Leonard P., *Measurement of Ability in Spelling.* New York: Russell Sage Foundation, 1915.
2. Betts, Emmett A., *Spelling Vocabulary Study.* New York: American Book Co., 1940.
3. ———, *Second Spelling Vocabulary Study.* New York: American Book Co., 1949.
4. Boord, Robert O., *Application of the Alphabetic Principle of the English Language in the Presentation of Spelling Vocabularies of Five Widely Used Spelling Series.* Doctoral Dissertation. Bloomington: Indiana University, 1966.
5. Boyer, Harvey Kinsey, "Why You Can't Spell." *Saturday Review,* October 2, 1954.
6. Breed, Frederick S., *How to Teach Spelling.* Danville, N. Y.: F. A. Owen Publishing Co., 1930.
7. Cutforth, John A., *English in the Primary School.* Oxford, England: Basil Blackwell, 1954.
8. Dale, Edgar, and Razik, Taher, *Bibliography of Vocabulary Studies,* Fourth Edition. Columbus: The Ohio State University, 1964.
9. Dolch, Edward, *Better Spelling.* Champaign, Ill.: The Garrard Press, 1942.
10. Duncan, John, *Backwardness in Reading: Remedies and Prevention.* London: George G. Harrap and Co., Ltd., 1953.
11. Falk, Ethel Mabie, "Interpretation of the Language Arts Program to the Parents and Community." *Teaching Language in the Elementary School.* Forty-third Yearbook, Part II, Chicago: National Society for the Study of Education, 1944, pp. 241-251.
12. Fernald, Grace, *Remedial Techniques in the Basic Skills.* New York: McGraw-Hill Book Co., Inc., 1943.
13. Fitzgerald, James A., *A Basic Life Spelling Vocabulary.* Milwaukee: The Bruce Publishing Company, 1951.
14. ———, *The Teaching of Spelling.* Milwaukee: The Bruce Publishing Company, 1951.
15. Fries, Charles C., *Linguistics and Reading.* New York: Holt, Rinehart and Winston, Inc., 1963.
16. Folger, S., "The Case for a Basic Written Vocabulary." *Elementary School Journal,* 1951, 51:254-265.
17. Furness, Edna L., "Psychological Determinants of Spelling Success." *Education,* December 1958, 79:234-239.
18. Gates, Arthur L., *A List of Spelling Difficulties in 3876 Words.* New York: Bureau of Publications, Teachers College, Columbia University, 1937.

19. Hanna, Paul R., and Jean S., *Phoneme-Grapheme Correspondences as Cues to Spelling Improvement.* Washington, D. C.: U. S. Office of Education, 1966. 1716 pp.
20. Hanna, Paul R., and Jean S. "Applications of Linguistics and Psychological Cues to the Spelling Course of Study." *Elementary English.* 42:753-59. November, 1965.
21. Hanna, Paul R., and Jean S., Richard E. Hodges, E. Hugh Rudorf, "A Summary: Linguistic Cues for Spelling Improvement." *Elementary English.* 44:862-865. December, 1967.
22. Hildreth, Gertrude, *Teaching Spelling.* New York: Henry Holt and Company, 1955.
23. Horn, Ernest, "Spelling." *Encyclopedia of Educational Research.* (Bibliography of 215 items.) Edited by Walter S. Monroe. New York: The Macmillan Company, 1950, pp. 1247-1264.
24. ———, *A Basic Writing Vocabulary.* University of Iowa Monographs in Education, First Series, No. 4. Iowa City, Iowa: University of Iowa, 1926.
25. Johnson, Eleanor M., "Two Key Factors in Spelling Success." *Education,* January, 1956, 76:271-74.
26. National Council of Teachers of English: The Commission on the English Curriculum, "Writing," *Language Arts for Today's Children.* New York: Appleton-Century-Crofts, Inc., 1954, pp. 206-260.
27. Pei, Mario, *All About Language.* Philadelphia: J. B. Lippincott Company, 1954.
28. Rinsland, Henry D., *A Basic Vocabulary of Elementary School Children.* New York: The Macmillan Company, 1945.
29. Russell, David H., "A Diagnostic Study of Spelling Readiness." *Journal of Educational Research,* December 1943, 37:276-283.
30. Schonell, Fred J., *Essentials in Teaching and Testing Spelling.* London: Macmillan and Co. Ltd., 1955.
31. Shane, Harold G., and Mulry, June Grant, *Improving Language Arts Instruction Through Research.* Washington, D. C.: Association for Supervision and Curriculum Development, National Education Association, 1963, pp. 68-86.
32. Strickland, Ruth G., *The Contribution of Structural Linguistics to the Teaching of Reading, Writing, and Grammar in the Elementary School.* Bulletin of the School of Education. Bloomington: Indiana University, January 1964.
33. Thorndike, Edward L., *The Teacher's Word Book.* New York: Bureau of Publications, Teachers College, Columbia University, 1921.
34. ———, *A Teacher's Word Book of the Twenty Thousand Words*

Most Frequently and Widely Used in General Reading for Children and Young People. New York: Bureau of Publications, Teachers College, Columbia University, 1932.

35. Thorndike, Edward L., and Lorge, Irving, *The Teacher's Word Book of 30,000 Words.* New York: Bureau of Publications, Teachers College, Columbia University, 1944.

36. Wilmington Public Schools, Division of Elementary Education, *Using Language.* Wilmington, Del.: Wilmington Public Schools, 1955, pp. 131-139.

Stories
Poetry
and
Books

Vicars Bell, in *On Learning the English Tongue*, says, "If there is any activity of the teacher which has upon the child an influence more subtle and more enduring than this of story-telling, I do not know of it. For it does not seem to me untrue to say that the child's philosophical background is formed and painted by the stories in which he lives" (11, p. 101).

Because he believes this to be true, Bell, the headmaster of a small school in England ". . . spends an hour every week telling stories in my infant's room – a giant among mommets – so that from their earliest days in my school they may begin to share my love of our tongue." He admits that a real reason for the time he spends in preparation and story-telling is "because I enjoy it."

We teach English to our children in all of the subjects of the curriculum, but most of the English we use is business English – work-a-day English designed to do the business in hand. Outside of school, the mass media and the common intercommunications of daily life are the full-time diet of most children. If the children are ever to know the artistic and creative possibilities of their language, they must learn to know them through literature. Here in literature is the language at its best. A story, play or poem attains the rank of literature not because of its content but because of the way the content is set forth in language.

In this swift-paced, highly stimulating mid-century period, vicarious experience plays an enormously important role in the lives of both adults and children. Radio, motion picture, television, and the printed page furnish a constant barrage of stimulation of one sort and another to which people react. Motion pictures, television, and even radio demand less of the individual in the way of interpretation and the supplying of background than does a printed page. The sensory appeal of these forms and the added dimensions in which material appears help to make the impressions vivid and lasting. The interests and needs of the times have brought forth new forms in printed materials also and some of these are very popular with all ages of people.

It would be difficult to find any individual, child or adult, who does not like stories and pictures. The tremendous popularity of the comics makes it clear that interest in this form of second-hand experience is very strong, especially during the later elementary school years. The interest of adults in picture magazines and in magazine fiction and mystery stories is a characteristic of our time. Interests may change with age but the desire for experience remains strong throughout life.

Children's eagerness for experience is a never-ending source of interest and amazement to adults. Given any sort of opportunity, children want to do everything, pry into everything, and know about everything that comes their way. To the child who is developing wholesomely and normally, life is full of countless possibilities for experience and adventure—both the first-hand adventure offered by real experience and the vicarious adventure which comes through listening, observing, and reading.

☐ STORYTELLING

Children have always loved stories. In an earlier period they listened with the adults in the great hall of the castle to the tales of the wandering storyteller. His coming meant news of happenings in the world outside as well as tales of tribal heroes, legends of adventure, and fanciful tales. He was teacher as well as entertainer. He taught history, religion, morals and lofty ideals. He kept alive the traditions of the clan and passed on his knowledge of customs and religious beliefs. He preserved the tales of the ancient bards and added flavor in his own way.

Stories have been used the world over to teach as well as to entertain. Whether the stories dealt with Ulysses or the gods on Mount Olympus, with Charlemagne or the Crusades, with the adventures and myths of the Norsemen or with King Arthur or Robin Hood depended upon the area in which they were told, but in all stories right was triumphant and wrong overthrown (8, p. 8). Many primitive tribes, such as the American Indians, entrusted to their elders and sages the task of passing on the standards, ideals, and aspirations of the tribe as well as its history and much of its practical wisdom. This was done through stories of heroism, folk tales, and legends. In Japan, until very recently, the traveling storyteller who tramped or rode into a community on his bicycle, clacking his bamboo sticks together, could always be sure of a rapt audience when he opened his collection of pictures and began his storytelling. Most of the stories were folk tales and history stories, but in later years a few became instruments for direct teaching of health and sanitation and of current social problems.

Listening to stories has been a part of the education of the young in home and community down to the present time. Parents have passed on to their children some of their own experiences and the wisdom they have accumulated from them. Mothers and grandmothers have told the children myths, folk tales, and Bible stories as well as stories from their own experience. Storytelling was an important part of life in many a pioneer home. Today, many public libraries provide a weekly hour for storytelling, and camp leaders and recreation directors include time for storytelling in their programs. Since storytelling has no place in the life in many homes, the school, library, Sunday School, and recreation programs have assumed responsibility for it.

Storytelling is one of the oldest of the arts and one which laid the foundation for the literature and culture of many peoples. Stories that were told again and again were improved, cut and polished down to essential elements and high luster by many storytellers. Thus folk tales, myths, and fables became art forms. The storyteller was actor, preacher, and creative artist. Children sense the perfection of form in "The House That Jack Built," "The Three Billy-Goats Gruff," "The Old Woman and Her Pig," and other accumulative tales. A few modern story writers have used the pattern successfully, but not all have done it well. Among the best examples are Wanda Gág's *Millions of Cats* and Marjorie Flack's *Ask Mr. Bear.*

Storytelling deserves a larger place in home and school than it occupies today. It provides warm, person contact and meeting of minds about a common interest which helps to draw adults and children closer together. Reading stories to children has value but it lacks the personal contact of storytelling.

Many teachers are afraid of storytelling because they have had no training for it. Storytelling does not call for histrionics; the teacher need not be highly trained or have experience in dramatics. He needs only to feel the mood of the story and let himself go in his telling of it so that the child may identify himself with the story. The teacher who is willing to work on storytelling as an art will find in it a delightful opportunity for personal growth as well as a professional and social asset.

Storytelling is valuable at all age levels but is particularly important in teaching younger children. Keen enjoyment of stories begins in the preschool period. A set time for storytelling, while valuable, is not as valuable as telling an appropriate story while children are carrying through an experience, or when the experience is just over. Stories fit into many times and places and stories which the teacher "has in her head" are ready for use on any occasion. The youngest children in the nursery school like improvised stories of themselves and their experiences. Kindergarten age children enjoy particularly the simple accumulative folk tales and more modern stories of similar pattern and complexity. For older children, storytelling is not only interesting in itself but it improves the quality of the children's own expression and leads to interest in reading. Telling an occasional story from Hans Andersen or from Howard Pyle's *The Wonder Clock*, or *Pepper and Salt*, leads the children to read those stories they have enjoyed most and move on to other stories. Stories are used also to fit the areas the children are studying – the American Indian and people of other countries and other times. Folk tales of a people show how they lived, what they thought and did, and what they considered important. The fear of cold is shown in the Russian tales, the fear of wild beasts and of heat in those from India, the dependence on rice in Japan; the superstitions and the concerns of people all show in their folk stories (8, p. 18).

Every storyteller develops ways of his own of learning and telling stories. For most stories, reading them carefully for characters, plot, sequence of events, and general development, and the planning of a good beginning and good ending is quite sufficient. Some stories are told in language which in itself is so appropriate and so beautiful that the story is marred if it is not learned as it is. "The Elephant's Child" in the *Just So Stories* is enjoyed for its beauty of language. "In the High and Far-Off Times, O Best Beloved," is as important to the story as the description of "the great grey-green greasy Limpopo River, all set about with fever trees." Children not only enjoy but pick up and repeat refrains, gems of conversation, and apt and beautiful descriptions. The quality of the use of language is reflected in their own creative expression.

☐ READING ALOUD

Children of all ages can listen to and enjoy stories that they cannot read for themselves, at least not with equal satisfaction. Their listening and comprehension level goes on ahead of their ability to decipher the material on the printed page, and their comprehension of spoken language is more advanced than their comprehension of what they can read independently. This is due in part to the complexity of sentence structure used in the books rather than to problems of word recognition. It is due also to the fact that the ideas presented are partially lost when the reader must concentrate also upon words and sentence form. For the upper primary child, figuring out the words of "The Elephant's Child" or reading the sentences of *Winnie-the-Pooh* requires so much power that little is left over for interpreting and appreciating the beauty and humor of the selections. Many children cannot read the stories at all, though they can enjoy them thoroughly. The beauty of these sentences from Kate Seredy's *White Stag* is missed by the middle grade child when he reads them himself. "Night fell, softly spreading its wings of silence over the sleeping camp. Sentry-fires glowed for a while then closed their eyes and only the stars, vigilant sentinels of the night, kept watch over the earth."[1] The pictures are painted not only by the words but by the way in which they have been strung together like a strand of jewels.

Listening to stories and other material beyond the children's reading level should have a real and legitimate place in all elementary grade classrooms. The material selected for listening should be carefully chosen to add to appreciation, understanding, or knowledge—something which the children cannot as readily gain for themselves. Good oral reading by the teacher has value in itself, as a model for the children's own reading and an aid to interpretation. The material chosen for that reading should have quality and significance for the children. It is not necessary to read aloud material of poor quality which the children bring to school to share. If the contributor needs encouragement to add to his interest in books and reading, his material can be recognized; he can be asked to show his favorite pictures or tell a brief episode from the material. Then he should be asked to take it home again, since it does not appear to fit the class need at the moment. It is often wiser to risk temporary disappointment for an individual than to subject the whole class to a valueless experience with trashy or unsuitable material.

Some of the material read aloud by the teacher will be selected mainly for content: to add information and to provide material

[1] Kate Seredy. *The White Stag*. Viking Press, Inc., 1937, p. 90.

for interpretation and use in work with social studies and science interests. At times, this can be contributed by a capable reader in the class, but often the teacher will find it valuable to present it herself. This is apt to be material for discussion, so that the teacher pauses at appropriate points to help the children interpret the meaning, form associations, and tie it into the total pattern of evolving concepts.

Much that is read aloud should be chosen for its literary quality, to introduce children to an art form. Reading aloud Kenneth Grahame's *The Wind in the Willows* is to give them at once a materpiece of English prose and a heart-warming experience. The warm friendliness of the characters of the story impresses children. Toad and his three animal friends recognize each other's limitations, overlook mistakes, and accept each other with sympathetic understanding, and never reject a friend. Reading the book aloud, a chapter at a time as it was told to Mouse, is the best way to introduce the book to children. Not all of them like it but most of them do, and if they do they want to own it and reread it later on (3).

Reading aloud to children enhances rather than decreases their interest in independent reading. When the motion pictures began to portray some of the classics, many people feared that the books would no longer be read. Experience proved that the sales for a classic mounted appreciably when the classic appeared at a local theater. When children have listened to a story that they would find difficult for independent reading, have savored its style, and have woven together the thought pattern of the story, they can then take it up and read it with sufficient ease to bring real satisfaction. Previous acquaintance with it causes the events of the story to fall into place and the pictures it paints to march in comparatively effortless procession before their eyes. Thus the reading of the story takes on added pleasure and gives the child a sense of growth and power since he can now read this more difficult material. The listening has given him not only the melody but some of the overtones, and these continue to sing in his mind as he reads.

Concurrently with the reading, if the story is a long one, or following it, children are drawn into discussion of the content of the story and, if they are ready for it, the style in which the story is written. Children are encouraged to catch the overtones, read between the lines, and dig for deeper-than-surface meaning. A first grade may then develop a group story of its own, or individual stories based on or suggested by the story they have enjoyed. A fourth grade may look into the origin of some of the words that made the story interesting. Following the story of *Robin Hood* by Howard Pyle, one sixth grade translated into modern English some of the expressions of Robin Hood's day, such as, "Now, seest thou Robin Hood amongst the ten?"; "By my troth, I did reckon full roundly that that knave, Robin Hood, would be at the game today"; and " 'And is it thou that has brought such doleful news'? said Robin to the lass." There is no end to the activities that ingenious teachers devise to strengthen and deepen the values found in listening.

All this is preparation, of course, for a variety of kinds of writing. Children learn to write through study of what good writers have written but study it without loss of appreciation and interest. The stories may be used also as springboards for discussion of words and how they operate in sentences. Attention is given to the way in which an author creates or stimulates response in his listeners and what words do to people.

☐ THE NEBRASKA LITERATURE PROJECT

Under Project English of the United States Office of Education, extensive research at the University of Nebraska has resulted in the development of a program which is centered in the study of literature, often literature read aloud, and which includes work in language and composition integral to such study (36, p. vii). The materials for the curriculum program consist of seventy units for the grade levels one through six and two packets of ancillary materials: *Poetry for the Elementary Grades* and *Language Explorations for the Elementary Grades*. The units suggested for the elementary grades "endeavor to arrange literary works in an articulated sequence designed to develop the concepts essential to the literature program in a spiral fashion" (36, p. viii). The stories selected were considered by teacher committees to be works of substantial literary merit. The core of the program is a collection of literary works which represent the categories or genres found in literature for children: folk, fanciful, animal, adventure, myth, fable, other lands and people, historical, and biography. They are selected for each grade to fit the level of maturity and understanding of the children. There are alternate suggestions to be

ELEMENTARY SCHOOL UNITS

Grade	FOLK	FANCIFUL	ANIMAL	ADVENTURE
1	Little Red Hen Three Billy-Goats Gruff The Gingerbread Boy	Little Black Sambo Peter Rabbit Where the Wild Things Are	Millions of Cats The Elephant's Child Ferdinand How the Rhinoceros Got His Skin	Little Tim and the Brave Sea Captain The Little Island
2	Little Red Riding Hood Story of the Three Pigs Story of the Three Bears	And to Think That I Saw It on Mulberry Street	Blaze and the Forest Fire How Whale Got His Throat The Beginning of the Armadillos The Cat That Walked by Himself	The 500 Hats of Bartholomew Cubbins The Bears on Hemlock Mountain
3	Sleeping Beauty Cinderella or the Little Glass Slipper Mother Holle	The Five Chinese Brothers Madeline Madeline's Rescue	The Blind Colt How the Camel Got His Hump How the Leopard Got His Spots The Sing-Song of Old Man Kangaroo	Winnie-the-Pooh Mr. Popper's Penguins
4	Febold Feboldson	Charlotte's Web	Brighty of the Grand Canyon	Homer Price
5	Tall Tale America Rapunzel The Woodcutter's Child The Three Languages	The Snow Queen The Lion, the Witch, and the Wardrobe	King of the Wind	The Merry Adventures of Robin Hood Island of the Blue Dolphins
6	The Seven Voyages of Sinbad	Alice in Wonderland and Through the Looking Glass A Wrinkle in Time	Big Red	The Adventures of Tom Sawyer

"Language Explorations for the Elementary Grades," *A Curriculum for English*. Lincoln: University of Nebraska Press, 1967, pp. xi and xii.

Grade	MYTH	FABLE	OTHER LANDS AND PEOPLE	HISTORICAL FICTION	BIOGRAPHY
1	The Story of the First Butterflies The Story of the First Woodpecker	The Dog and the Shadow The Town Mouse and The Country Mouse	A Pair of Red Clogs		They Were Strong and Good George Washington
2	The Golden Touch	The Hare and the Tortoise The Ant and the Grass-hopper	Crow Boy	Caroline and Her Kettle Named Maud	Ride on the Wind
3	Daedalus and Icarus Clytie Narcissus	Chanticleer and the Fox The Musicians of Bremen	The Red Balloon	The Courage of Sarah Noble	Christopher Columbus and His Brothers
4	Hiawatha's Fasting Theseus and the Minotaur Arachne Phaeton and the Chariot of The Sun	Jacobs: The Fables of Aesop	A Brother for the Orphelines	Little House on the Prairie The Matchlock Gun	Willa
5	Ceres and Proserpine Atalanta's Race Jason The Labors of Hercules	Bidpai Fables Jataka Tales	The Door in the Wall	Children of the Covered Wagon This Dear Bought Land	Leif the Lucky Dr. George Washington Carver, Scientist
6	The Children of Odin The Hobbit	The Wind in the Willows	Hans Brinker Secret of the Andes	The Book of King Arthur and his Noble Knights	Cartier Sails the St. Lawrence

CORRELATIVE UNITS: "You Come Too"—Poetry of Robert Frost—Grade 6; *Poetry for the Elementary Grades; Language Explorations for Elementary Grades.*

drawn upon if the teacher does not care for the core suggestion or considers it unsuitable for her group.

The units, which were developed in several summer session workshops by invited groups of teachers, contain a wealth of background information for the teacher. These materials are not intended for transmission to the children. They are built on the assumption that a teacher will teach more effectively if she understands something of the literary nature of the stories and their place in the curriculum.

☐ ENJOYING POETRY

Young children can enjoy poetry only through listening. Saying or reading poetry to children should continue all through the elementary school years. Poetry was originally composed for saying and for enjoyment through the ear.

Children like poetry first for its *singing quality:* for its rhyme, rhythm, and all that goes into the melody of verse. Good reading of poetry should bring out its singing quality clearly. Audiences have delighted in hearing Robert Frost, Carl Sandburg, Robert Tristram Coffin, and others read their own poems because each brought out the singing quality of his creations in his own special way. Appreciation of a poem is greatly enhanced through the experience of savoring this quality with the interesting creator of it.

Arbuthnot places the *story element* next in the list of elements which children enjoy in poetry (3, p. 164). "Jack and Jill" and "Hickory, Dickory, Dock" have this element and so does Browning's "The Pied Piper." Many modern poems for children have it too, from Milne's "The King's Breakfast" to the Benéts' "Johnny Appleseed." The story may be a tiny episode or a full-length ballad but there must be some story element present in much of children's poetry.

Children like the *sensory content* of poetry. They like to *see, hear, feel, taste,* and *smell* through the stimulation of words. There are many poems that have special sensory appeal. In Eleanor Farjeon's "Mrs. Peck-Pigeon" children can see and hear the little round head "bob-bob-bob" as it pecks for bread. Children like to make their hands or bodies gallop as the horseman does in Stevenson's "Windy Nights" and they like to use Vachel Lindsay's "The Potatoes' Dance" as a stepping rhythm. In Mary Austin's "The Sandhill Crane" the children can both see and feel the mood and the tempo of the crane as it goes "slowly, solemnly stalking." They can feel the rhythm of the waves as they hear Masefield's "Sea-Fever."

Nonsense poems and humorous ones should be given a place, along with the more serious poems. Young children always enjoy Edward Lear's "A Nonsense Alphabet." Milne's "Hoppity" intrigues both with its humor and with its rhythmic action and sensory appeal. "The King's Breakfast" starts sensibly enough but becomes entirely daft with its hero whimpering, sulking, bouncing, and sliding down the banisters. Mary Jane's attitude toward rice pudding in the poem of that name and the word play of "Sneezles" strike a responsive chord on the basis of content and also delight in the pictures they present and in the intriguing play with words. Walter de la Mare's "Miss T." is amusing and Ffrida Wolfe's "Choosing Shoes" causes every child to nod feelingly because he has felt just the same way. People of all ages chuckle over Laura E. Richards' "Eletelephony." Older children like the humor of Eleanor Farjeon's "Hannibal Crossed the Alps." Their understanding of the strengths and inconsistencies of the early New England colonists is enhanced through enjoyment of the humor of "Pilgrims and Puritans" in *A Book of Americans* by Stephen and Rosemary Benét. This book is filled with amusing sense and rollicking nonsense which no American child should be allowed to miss (3).

There is a vast wealth of poetry to choose from. It is available in the original volumes by individual authors, and also in a number of good anthologies. Several useful volumes should be available to every teacher so that poetry can be found to fit many types of moods, interests, and occasions. There are poems for gay moods and dreamy or solemn ones. The gay whirl of Dorothy Baruch's "Merry-Go-Round" fits at one time and the dreamy thoughtfulness of A. A. Milne's "Halfway Down" fits at another time.

Poetry fits into many periods of the day and into many types and subjects of study. There are poems that deal with weather and the changing seasons, and others that fit into studies of animal life, astronomy, and the geography and history of places and people. Certainly no study of astronomy would be complete without such poems as Lindsay's "The Moon's the North Wind's Cooky," De la Mare's "Silver," and Macdonald's "The Wind and the Moon." Poems can be tucked into odd minutes of the day. While the class is waiting a moment for the music teacher to come or waiting to join the lunch line in the cafeteria there may be time to tuck in a poem or two. It adds to the enjoyment of the moment and gives children a sense of power to find that they know some of their favorite poems without the book.

In addition to fitting into any situation where they will add to the pleasure and richness of experience, poems should have a place in the regular story period. Children enjoy listening to new poems chosen by the teacher and calling for old favorites that they want to hear again. Children are no longer required to memorize certain selected poems, as they were a generation ago. Instead, the teacher rereads the poems children like and encourages them to enter into the repetition if they care to do so. They may supply at first the repetitive parts or the refrain; later, many of the children will be found repeating the entire poem with the teacher. It may be that no two children can repeat the same poems at the end of the year but each child has learned or partially learned the ones he likes best. Taste in poetry is an individual matter. To try to force all children to learn the same poems would be to dull the edge of interest for many children and make some of them actually dislike poetry. In one school, there is an occasional poetry program in the assembly room, with each grade contributing some of the poems it likes best. These are read, recited, dramatized, interpreted rhythmically or through choral speaking, as the children choose. In another school, the sixth grade group builds its own poetry anthology each year. Children select the poems they like best and these are arranged in a mimeographed volume which the group uses and enjoys; then a copy is saved for the next year's group.

Poetry must be read well if children are to learn to like it. Arbuthnot suggests that teachers really work on the matter of good reading, beginning perhaps with Mother Goose, then studying and reading aloud many types of poems in order to learn to interpret them with imagination and delicate precision (3). She suggests that the teacher read a poem silently to become familiar with the words, mood, and tempo of the poem. If, in so doing, the teacher finds that she has memorized the poem, that is the final triumph. A teacher who knows by heart a large number of poems has a valuable resource to draw upon to enrich the experience of her group.

Poems should not be used as reading exercises; in fact, many good reading textbooks no longer include much poetry. Reading poetry is more difficult than reading prose. Often a child loses the whole thought and significance of a poem because he cannot read it in such a manner that it makes sense and he can really understand and interpret it. Yet the meaning is quite clear to him if he listens to the teacher's reading of the poem. Being required to read poetry tends to decrease interest and build bad reading habits, while listening to poetry is, for most children, a pleasant and satisfying experience. It is appreciation and enjoyment that is important at elementary school age.

☐ CHORAL READING

Choral reading of poetry has come into favor in the schools within comparatively recent years. Teachers who have developed it with their children are enthusiastic about its values and if the poetry is well selected, children find keen enjoyment in it. They enjoy being active participants in deciding how a poem shall be read and in testing and evaluating the effectiveness of their decisions. Choral reading can be used to improve voice quality, articulation, enunciation, and the rhythm and flow of speech. Inattentive children are swept into the experience by the enthusiasm of others. Timid children lose themselves in the group and experience the same enjoyment as does the adult who, though he would never sing alone, enters lustily into community singing. Aggressive children and exhibitionists learn to submerge themselves in the group and cooperate wholeheartedly. Children who have never really liked poetry find that they enjoy participating in the group reading.

Choral reading with younger children should be simple and informal. The teacher reads a poem and if the children like it, it is reread several times. If the poem has a refrain, the children love to say it while the teacher reads the stanza. "Hickory, Dickory, Dock" is fun read this way, and Mary Louise Allen's "The Mitten Song."

Children enjoy the discovery that a poem can mark time for walking, skipping or galloping, just as music can. "Hippety Hop to the Barber Shop" suggests a high, free skip with arms swinging loosely, "Ride a Cock Horse to Banbury Cross" can be used for a spirited gallop, and "To Market, to Market to Buy a Fat Pig" for a jigging skip. It is probably better to let a few children at a time interpret the poem so that they can hear the voices of the choir recite the verses.

Older children who have had no experience with choral reading can begin with "The Grand Old Duke of York" or with Stevenson's "Windy Nights" or the Norwegian verse "Huskyhi" in Rose Fyleman's delightful translation. If there are boys in the group who are convinced that they do not care for poetry, "The Pirate Don Dirk of Dowdee," "Jonathan Bing" or Laura Richards' "Antonio" will probably catch their interest.

All verse speaking at first should be done in unison so that children learn to think and speak as a group with light, clear voices and perfect rhythm. When children can speak well in unison they are ready to be grouped in choirs. Children, as well as the teacher, can listen for the higher and lower voices or the lighter and heavier voices in the group. Children will need to be helped to realize that one type of voice is not better than another, only different, and that the differences can be utilized for pleasing effects in their reading. Grouping is made tentatively and voices shifted until the best blends have been attained. It is good ear training for the children to do as much of this as they can. Often teachers start with two choirs, later subdivide to form a third.

A number of poems can be read by two choirs—"Hickory, Dickory, Dock" is one of the easiest ones, and Stevenson's "The Wind" or Eugene Field's, "Why Do Bells for Christmas Ring" can be used in this way. The dialogue type of poem is usually liked. A. A. Milne's, "Puppy and I" and "The King's Breakfast" are good examples.

There are many poems which permit the use of solo voices with the choirs. Vachel Lindsay's, "The Potatoes' Dance" and "The Mysterious Cat" are good for this. Upper grade children can prepare literary selections from the Bible—some of the parables and Psalm 24 and Psalm 103. These can be done very effectively in an upper-grade class.

The teacher will serve as leader at first, to mark the tempo and rhythm exactly and to keep the group together. Later, children can take turns leading. The children should be encouraged from the beginning to react to the poem and to suggest ways of interpreting it. If the teacher does all of the thinking and makes all of the decisions, much of the value is lost.

The values of choral reading lie in the growth which takes place in the children. Occasionally, a group may polish a selection to present at a Parent-Teachers Association meeting or for some other purpose, but for the most part, the values lie, not in the polishing but in the thinking and interpreting, the trying out and evaluating. When the children are satisfied with a production, it is time to move on to another poem. All interpretation of poetry should be sincere and natural, and above all, it should be enjoyed.

□ BOOKS AND MORE BOOKS

Speaking of the books produced for children in the United States, Paul Hazard, member of the French Academy, said in his delightful little book, *Books, Children, and Men,*

> Explorers set forth from America to all the countries in the world to bring back new story material. Artists, designers, engravers, painters from all the countries in the world arrive in America, invited to decorate the pages of children's books. The elite of the country, that long-suffering elite which rebels against any diminution of the spirit, surrounds the coming generation with a solicitude probably unequaled anywhere as a treasury of hope (25, p. 87).

Books for children pour from the presses in great numbers each year. Artists, writers, and editors are cooperating to provide children with a great variety of content and with illustrations which rival in beauty anything available for adults. There are good books and poor books in the lot, just as is true of the output for adults. There are books with unreliable and trashy content and tawdry illustrations as well as thoroughly reliable and significant books with content that is accurate and illustrations of high artistic quality.

Adults who use and enjoy books find in them a source of comfort, inspiration, and information which adds greatly to the richness of living. Books cannot serve as a substitute for living but they can illuminate life and highlight its values and significance. Books can serve as refuge and release when life is difficult; the temporary relaxing of tensions makes it possible to see problems in perspective and helps with gathering the strength and poise that are necessary to work through them. Inspiration gained from the thoughts and experience of others helps to create the insights and attitudes that smooth the way or make it possible to go on philosophically. Books are resources for leisure and for periods when rest and refreshment are the major need. Information is there to enrich and further the established interests and to open up new ones. Children's needs are similar to those of adults and they can learn to use and value books for similar purposes.

Children need physical and material security but they are also reaching out for social and spiritual security. Through wise guidance, the books they read can illumine life so that they see it more clearly and come to understand it. Reading can contribute to growth in information, in insight, and in understanding of the physical world and man as he reacts to it and to his fellows. Books can help the child to see the relationships which exist between man and environment and between man and man. Children need a great deal of reading which helps them understand people, how they respond under a variety of circumstances, and why they respond as they do.

The emphasis upon the study of child development and social groupings which has occupied the thinking of teachers in recent years has caused them to be increasingly aware of the social and emotional problems which confront children. Children have a great variety of personal problems with which they need help and guidance (5). Reading may prove valuable therapy for some children and some types of problems. Introducing a child to a book in which a character faces and solves a similar problem may help the child to understand his own problem better and to face it with courage and optimism. The teacher who knows children's books can put material in the way of a child so that he is not required to bring his problem out into the open but may, in a measure, relieve his own anxieties, fears, and tensions and in so doing gain an added sense of power and confidence. Marguerite de Angeli's book *Bright April* will help many children who face the difficult fact of being colored. Doris Gates' *Blue Willow* can bring hope to an underprivileged child. *The Good Master* or *Caddie Woodlawn* may help a child to accept his role and enter into it without rebellion or resentment. Children who are spared such problems themselves may find in the books understanding of the feelings and needs of other children in the group. *The Hundred Dresses* will fill this need for many children.

Stories of home and family life are popular with children of all ages. The desire for economic security is strong and children enjoy stories in which greater material security is attained. But the longing for emotional security may be even deeper and stronger. Though the family in a story may be poor and struggling to meet family needs, if there is love and loyalty among its members the book holds satisfaction for a child (3, p. 3). Children experience a sense of warmth and well-being in reading the stories of the Ingalls family by Laura Ingalls Wilder. No matter what the danger the family faces, the life inside the cabin is safe and happy. The love and fortitude are always there, along with Pa's gay ballads and the sound of his fiddle. The fortunate child whose home life is secure and happy may learn to see significance in experiences he might otherwise take for granted. The child who has not experienced such happiness in his own home may identify himself with the book family and gain some vicarious satisfaction as well as insight into what family life might be.

Children develop maturity through the facing and solving of real problems that suit their stage of development. They develop also through the experience that comes to them in reading. That is the reason some of the current juvenile delinquency is attributed to unwholesome experience with comics, television, and motion pictures. Through wise guidance in reading, children develop maturity of thinking and absorb some of the ideals and aspirations they find portrayed in their books. Quality of taste, wholesomeness of interests, and maturity of thinking and reaction are the products of good reading.

Some of the books that appear from time to time will be short-lived because they lack the quality and appeal to sustain them. Other books not only fit adult standards but children take them into their hearts on first contact. There are many children's books that fit into specific types of learning situations: books dealing with science, such as those of Zim, Bronson, Webber, and Schneider; geography and history designed to appeal to children, such as Pyne's *Little Geography of the United States* and Foster's *Abraham Lincoln's World*. All of Laura Ingalls Wilder's books fit here too, since they make pioneer life and the westward movement come alive for children. These are books that expand, enrich, and deepen children's thinking. April learned to accept her color and win respect and friendship through her own attitudes; Hannah, in *Thee, Hannah!* learned what it meant to be a Quaker; Johnny Tremain had rich and stirring experiences in Boston during pre-Revolutionary times in spite of a maimed hand. Heroes and heroines who accept handicaps, misunderstanding, and defeat courageously, yet achieve in spite of them, help children with the difficult task of maturing, of growing up socially and emotionally.

Among children's books there are many that will live. One might wish that every child by the age of six could have experience with a good edition of *Mother Goose*, with *Peter Rabbit*, *Millions of Cats*, *Angus and the Ducks*, and *In My Mother's House*. By eight years they should know *The Poppy Seed Cakes*, *Little Pear*, *Winnie-the-Pooh*, and the *Just So Stories*. By ten they will be enriched by experience with *The Moffats*, *The Good Master*, *Little House in the Big Woods*, and *Homer Price*. A little later they will appreciate *Hidden Treasure of Glaston*, *Tree of Freedom*, *Johnny Tremain*, and *Island of the Blue Dolphins*.

The problem nowadays is not one of finding enough books to satisfy children's needs and interests. It is a problem of selection of the best that are available for various purposes. One criterion for selection stands out clearly. A book is good for children only when they truly enjoy it. Conversely, a book is poor for them if they do not enjoy it even though adults rate it high and feel that the children should like it. Their own interests, needs, and tastes, in the last analysis, form the basis for selection. Arbuthnot calls attention to the fact that children's needs are at first intensly and narrowly personal (3, p. 2). The broadening of needs corresponds to the rate of socialization of the child; the child needs both personal happiness and social approval. To keep a balance between the two is a difficult task and book experience may help the child at both points.

☐ LIBRARIES FOR CHILDREN

"Here is an innovation that does honor to the sensibility of a people, and it is an American innovation: the libraries for children." Hazard describes them as light and gay rooms where children feel perfectly at ease, free to come and go, to hunt for a book in the catalogue, find it on the shelves and curl up in a chair or on a window seat to plunge into the reading of it (25). Watching underprivileged children in the libraries of big cities, one knows that these rooms are indeed a refuge from the masses of humanity and the constant clatter and confusion of the streets and the places the children call home. Here is a kind

of leisure that delights them—these peaceful libraries peopled with books. And the books are not just "school books" designed to teach facts, but books of all sorts which enable them to get out of their own tight little skins and try on life as others live it.

More and more new elementary schools are being built about a central library to which children can go for books at any time. A considerable amount of federal money is going into stocking them. The development of interest in individualized reading is opening the way for more and more children to have some opportunity to select for themselves the books they want to read. Children know what they like in books. Teachers guide subtly or directly as need arises but children are allowed the privilege of being individuals and developing their own tastes and interests.

☐ INDIVIDUALIZED READING

The nation-wide growth of interest in individualized or personalized reading is providing many children with access to increasing quantities of books and breaking some of the bonds of basic reading systems. The first requisite for any such program is quantities of good books of all kinds on many topics and at many reading levels. Schools which previously limited children to little besides basic reading textbooks are beginning to use at least a portion of the time devoted to reading for self-selection of books and independent reading at the child's own best pace.

An integral part of any individualized reading program is time for the teacher to confer with each child individually. This makes it possible for the teacher to discuss with the child the book he is reading, to deepen his comprehension and sharpen his interest in further reading as well as to check on his growth in reading skills. The teacher's record of the child's selections and his progress makes it possible for her to guide his selection of material as well as his use of it.

In her little bulletin on *How to Teach Reading With Children's Books*, Veatch makes many suggestions for a personalized use of reading materials (48). She also suggests ways of securing quantities of books beyond just the school plan of requisitioning. Children, given the opportunity, will find ways to help with the acquisition of books, both through their own efforts and through the stimulation of parental interest.

The scheme used by Bell, in England, to stimulate interest in books could be used by any classroom teacher, administrator or librarian (11). He visits each classroom occasionally armed with books with markers protruding. His children say when he enters, "O goody! Tasters today!" He reads snatches from each book–a humorous incident, a beautiful description, an exciting episode, or the build-up of a bit of mystery–then leaves the books for the children to read if they care to. And always, as might be expected, everyone wants them and there is need for signing up and taking turns so that each child may have opportunity to read those he is interested in.

With Bell's scheme as with any other for individualizing reading, there must be opportunities for children to share their findings and enjoyment with the group. Sharing may be verbal reporting, advertising the book, dramatizing a portion of it, talking from illustrations made by the reader, panel discussions by several who have read the book, a debate on points made in the book, or any one of the many possibilities that ingenious teachers and children may devise.

☐ THE EVER-PRESENT COMICS

The consuming interest children show in the comics grows in part out of the fact that this is a swift-paced, stimulating time and comics bring them stories with swift action and vivid experience. These are all in colorful form so that the mind has far less work to do in filling in background and forming mental pictures than if the story were told only in words. In spite of the fact that this is a stimulating period in which to live, the lives of children are less eventful than they were in a simpler period. Careful parents hedge their children about with restrictions and safeguards. Even if they did not, there is not much of excitement or adventure that is either possible or socially permissible for children. Movies, radio, the comics, and now television provide vicariously much of the action, adventure, and excitement that children crave.

A children's book committee of the Child Study Association reported the results of a study of comics which they completed in 1943 (19). The committee found it difficult to classify the types of subject matter found in the comic magazines because of overlapping. They utilized the following rough categories: adventure, fantastic adventure, war, crime and detective, real stories and biography, jungle adventure, animal cartoons, fun and humor, love interest, and retold classics. Adventure, in one form or another, is found in most of the comics. That is something that children look for in all books and stories. Fantastic adventure plays a large part in many comics. Superman, Batman and other favorite characters have qualities that resemble those of fairy tale characters, yet the stories in which they are presented deal with current, everyday life. This background of today's world appeals to children who are increasingly aware of the forces, good and bad, which operate in their environment.

Children find fascination in stories dealing with the avenging of wrongs and the punishment of evil doers. This is their own fantasy pattern, as one can tell from their play as well as from the books they like. Fantastic adventure stories seem to satisfy much the same emotional need as the traditional fairy tales: escape and wish fulfillment. For many children they may provide emotional release for feelings of aggression and frustration.

Comic books, so called, are actually picture stories and are neither better nor worse than the material they present. It is probably a fair estimate that approximately seventy per cent of the comics exploit sex, horror, crime, and abnormalities. At the present time, it is probable that not more than twenty per cent of the comic books contain anything funny. About ten per cent are informative, dealing with classics, Bible stories, science, and social science themes. The language in the comic books varies widely in quality and kind. Some stories are told in simple, straightforward language; others employ an elaborate, self-conscious vocabulary. Gangsters and tough characters use tough language, the vernacular of the streets. In many instances, the hero's English is correct in grammar and diction and in every way above reproach. Children enjoy silly language and language that is not "refined"; they often turn sensible language into silly forms for their own amusement. They ape expressions that catch their fancy, but this is probably a legitimate form of enjoyment and a passing one. There is also a wide range of quality in the drawing and color used in the comics, but they do represent the kind of drawing children themselves tend to do, with action and masses of color predominating. Children can be helped to recognize good and poor quality in this area as well as in content and style of language. Children like "thrillers" and they want something funny but they can learn to prefer material of acceptable quality and to reject the more objectionable material.

Psychiatric opinion, as reported by Frank, differs considerably with regard to the effect of "chills and thrills in radio, movies, and comics" on children (17). The same difference of opinion relates to television. One psychiatrist emphasizes positive values for children, stating that the experience with activity, motility, and movement in which their heroes overcome time and space gives children a sense of release rather than fear. A second, on the other hand, is convinced that the very repetition of "biff and bang" themes day after day causes children to feel that conflict and aggression are too permissible. She is convinced that "thriller" comics make aggression too easy and too colorful and that, if they actually were safety valves as some people maintain, nightmares following them would not be reported so frequently. A third psychiatrist is reported as differentiating between types of readers of comics. He holds that moderate readers use the comics for identification with heroes but that, when they come to realize that the hero's perfection is unrealistic and unattainable, their own development weans them away from the comics. Excessive readers express a different attitude. To them, the hero symbolizes a deity or savior to whom they delegate all responsibility. This attitude appears with relation to television as well, as was the case with the kindergarten age boy who insisted, when he heard the Easter story of the crucifixion of Jesus, that it could not possibly have happened had Hopalong Cassidy been there. The attitude of these children prevents the development of a mature outlook on the material of the comics.

Attempts to ban the comics are never successful, whether resorted to by parents, schools, or communities. A thriving bootleg business is the inevitable result and far more devastating to the development of sound judgment and mature standards than a permissive atmosphere, guidance in selection, and the sharing and discussing of content with adults. Some librarians and teachers have insisted that the reading of comics is not a serious problem if children also read and enjoy better books. Guidance can lead a child from the jungle and animal comics to Kipling's *Jungle Books* and from adventure comics to adventure stories of higher quality. To offer a child a classic in place of a comic may not result in acceptance, but there are many intermediate steps (13). The enthusiasm of children for better books, when those books are easily available and fit the children's interests, makes it clear that they would read many books of higher quality if these were ready at hand. The problem of both home and school, as well as the community through its children's library, is to make better books as readily obtainable as are the comics.

The graphic, rapid moving, easily interpreted medium used in the comics is basically a good technique for some purposes and one that will continue to be used. Perhaps it is a form that educators should have laid hold on first and turned into a valuable teaching tool. This form is of such intense interest to children, that it could very well be utilized more and more. There is evidence that the technique could be used very successfully in the teaching of the social studies to enable children to picture historical scenes and distant places and thus form clearer and more lasting mental images and concepts (39). Roth is convinced that comic books must be defended by people who recognize their advantages "until the reserves come up"—until child psychologists, curriculum experts, and others adapt the technique to helping children learn. There are hopeful instances of such cases.

☐ SELECTED REFERENCES ☐

1. Adams, Bess Porter, *About Books and Children.* New York: Henry Holt and Co., 1953.
2. American Council on Education, *Reading Ladders for Human Relations.* Staff of the Intergroup Education Project in Cooperating Schools. Washington, D. C.: The Council, 1965.
3. Arbuthnot, May Hill, *Children and Books.* Chicago: Scott, Foresman and Co., 1957.
4. ———, *Children's Books Too Good to Miss.* Cleveland: Western Reserve University Press, 1948.
5. Association for Childhood Education International, *Helping Children Solve Their Problems.* Washington, D. C.: The Association, 1950.
6. ———, *Literature With Children.* Washington, D. C.: The Association, 1961.
7. ———, *Knowing When Children Are Ready to Learn.* Washington, D.C.: The Association, 1947.
8. ———, *Storytelling.* Washington, D. C.: The Association, 1942.
9. ———, *This Is Reading.* Washington, D. C.: The Association, 1949.

10. Barbe, Walter B., *Educator's Guide to Personalized Reading Instruction.* Englewood Cliffs: Prentice-Hall, Inc., 1961.
11. Bell, Vicars, *On Learning the English Tongue.* London: Faber and Faber, 1953.
12. Betzner, Jean, *Exploring Literature with Children.* Practical Suggestions for Teaching, No. 7. New York: Bureau of Publications, Teachers College, Columbia University, 1943.
13. Carr, Constance, "Substitutes for the Comics." *Elementary English* 28:194-200; 276-285.
14. Duff, Annis, *The Bequest of Wings.* New York: The Viking Press, Inc., 1944.
15. Eaton, Anne Thaxter, *Reading with Children.* New York: The Viking Press, Inc., 1940.
16. ———, *Treasure for the Taking.* New York: The Viking Press, Inc., 1946.
17. Frank, Josette, "Chills and Thrills in Radio, Movies and Comics." *Child Study* 25:42-46, 48, Spring, 1948.
18. ———, *Your Child's Reading Today.* Garden City, New York: Doubleday and Co., Inc., 1954.
19. Frank, Josette, and Straus, Mrs. H. G., *"Looking at the Comics."* Child Study 20:112-118, Spring, 1943.
20. Gans, Roma, *Guiding Children's Reading through Experiences.* Practical Suggestions for Teaching, No. 3. New York: Bureau of Publications, Teachers College, Columbia University, 1941.
21. ———, *Reading Is Fun.* New York: Bureau of Publications, Teachers College, Columbia University, 1949.
22. Gesell, Arnold, and Ilg, Frances L., *The Child from Five to Ten.* New York: Harper and Brothers, 1946.
23. Gesell, Arnold; Ilg, Frances L.; and Ames, Louise B., *Youth: The Years from Ten to Sixteen.* New York: Harper and Brothers, 1956.
24. Gray, William S., *Reading in an Age of Mass Communication. New York: Appleton-Century-Crofts, Inc., 1949.*
25. Hazard, Paul, *Books, Children and Men.* Boston: The Horn Book, Inc., 1944.
26. Huber, Miriam Blanton, Ed., *Story and Verse for Children* (Rev. Ed.). New York: The Macmillan Co., 1955.
27. Huck, Charlotte S., and Young, Doris A., *Children's Literature in the Elementary School.* New York: Holt, Rinehart and Winston, 1967.
28. Johnson, Edna; Scott, Carrie E.; and Sickels, Evelyn R. (Comps.), *Anthology of Children's Literature* (2nd Ed.). Boston: Houghton Mifflin Co., 1960.
29. La Brant, Lou, "Personal Factors Influencing Reading." *Reading in an Age of Mass Communication.* William S. Gray (Ed.).

New York: Appleton-Century-Crofts, Inc., 1949, Chap. III, pp. 39-57.

30. Larrick, Nancy, *A Parent's Guide to Children's Reading*. Garden City: Doubleday & Company, Inc., 1958.
31. ———, *A Teacher's Guide to Children's Books*. Columbus: Charles E. Merrill Books, Inc., 1960.
32. Meigs, Cornelia L., and others, *A Critical History of Children's Literature*. New York: The Macmillan Co., 1953.
33. Miel, Alice, Ed., *Individualizing Reading Practices*. New York: Bureau of Publications, Teachers College, Columbia University, 1958.
34. National Council of Teachers of English, *Adventuring with Books*. Champaign, Ill.: The Council, (revised periodically).
35. ———, *We Build Together* (Rev. Ed.). Charlemae Rollins, Chairman, Champaign, Ill.; The Council, 1968.
36. The Nebraska Curriculum Development Center, *A Curriculum for English: Language Explorations for the Elementary Grades*. Lincoln: University of Nebraska Press, 1966. A Curriculum for English–Grades 1 to 6.
37. Pickard, P. M. (Ed.), *British Comics: An Appraisal*. London: Comics Campaign Council (undated).
38. Rasmussen, Carrie, *Choral Speaking for Speech Improvement*. New York: The Ronald Press, 1949.
39. Rosenblatt, Louise M., "The Enriching Values in Reading." *Reading in an Age of Mass Communication*. William S. Gray (Ed.) New York: Appleton-Century-Crofts, Inc., 1949, Chap. II, pp. 10-32.
40. Roth, John M., "In Defense of Comic Books." *School Executive* 68:48-50, Sept., 1948.
41. Russell, David H., "Contributions of Research in Bibliotherapy to the Language Arts Program." *School Review* LVIII (1950), 335-342.
42. Sawyer, Ruth, *The Way of the Storyteller*. New York: The Viking Press, Inc., 1942.
43. Smith, Dora V., *Fifty Years of Children's Books*. Champaign, Ill.: National Council of Teachers of English, 1963.
44. Smith, Lillian H., *The Unreluctant Years*. Chicago: American Library Association, 1953.
45. Smith, Nila Banton, Chairman, *Development of Taste in Literature*. Champaign, Illinois: National Council of Teachers of English, 1963.
46. Tooze, Ruth, *Storytelling*. Englewood Cliffs, N. J.: Prentice-Hall, Inc., 1959.
47. ———, *Your Children Want to Read*. Englewood Cliffs, N. J.: Prentice-Hall, Inc., 1957.

48. Veatch, Jeannette, *How to Teach Reading With Children's Books.* New York: Bureau of Publications, Teachers College, Columbia University, 1964.
49. ———, *Individualizing Your Reading Program.* New York: G. P. Putnam's Sons, 1959.
50. White, Dorothy, *Books Before Five.* New Zealand Council for Educational Research. Auckland, New Zealand: Whitcombe and Tombs, Ltd., 1954.
51. Wisconsin English Language Arts Curriculum Project, *Teaching Literature in Wisconsin.* Madison: Department of Public Instruction, 1967.

Drama-tic interpre-tation

Dramatic play is an integral part of living for the young child; it is as natural and spontaneous as the child himself. During his second year the child likes to demonstrate what each of the animals in his picture book says. He enjoys simple finger plays with easy motion and words he understands and can say. During the third year, dramatic play takes on many forms. The child may be a dog racing and barking, a hostess serving make-believe tea, a mother making a birthday cake of moist sand, or a father going to work in the morning. The play is not entirely realistic because time is not a problem to the child at this age. If Father returns from work before the family has finished breakfast no one is disturbed.

Dramatic play is make-believe in which a child relives familiar experiences and explores new ones (20). When he plays doctor, Sunday School, store, or house he demonstrates his interpretation of his experience. In his dramatic play he "tries on life" through playing Daddy, the policeman, or Grandmother and gaining some concept of how it feels to be someone else. Since dramatic play has no plot and no required sequence, it can begin anywhere and end anywhere. The play may be solitary play, as in the case of the three-year-old who makes cakes in the sand and serves them at a party. It may be the solitary play of the ten-year-old who snatches a stick out of the can of trash he is carrying to the alley, strikes a pose, and runs his sword through an imaginary foe. At times there is a parallel type of play, as when children on wheel toys on the playground carry on similar plays with little or no interaction. As the child grows older and has more contacts with children it becomes group play and may take on a very complex social organization. Dramatic play is especially important in the lives of four- to seven-year-olds, though it continues in somewhat different forms well beyond these ages.

A four-year-old spends a great deal of time in dramatic play of many sorts. He may have an imaginary companion if no real one is available. The child himself slips in and out of a role with great ease. He may be a zooming airplane with arms outstretched as wings, banking and swooping; suddenly he stops to ask a question that occurs to him, then zooms off again. The child plays almost anything he has seen in adult life which catches his interest: doctor, storekeeper, train—animate or inanimate, it does not matter.

Mothers have found that dramatizing a new situation with a child before he goes into it results in acceptance of the new situation and confidence in it. One mother tried dramatizing the preliminary steps to a tonsillectomy and the child came out of the ether saying, "It was just like you said it would be." Another mother told of preparing her little daughter for a trip alone on the train by dramatizing the whole procedure. Playing through an experience may give the child a clearer picture of what to expect and helps him to interpret the real experience when it comes.

☐ DRAMATIC PLAY OF SCHOOL AGE CHILDREN

Kindergarten children are keenly interested in dramatic play. A very important unit in the kindergarten is the playhouse corner, with its equipment for washing and ironing, cleaning, cooking, carrying on family life, giving parties, and telephoning to the store or to friends. Large blocks are built into houses, hangars, fire stations, stores, and boats; while smaller blocks are combined with wooden boats, trains, animals, and people for farm, transportation, or any other sort of play. It is far more accurate and realistic play than that of younger children, though boys and girls of five play any part that interests them, regardless of sex, and imagination still helps tremendously with properties. Ray left his play and came to his kindergarten teacher one day in March asking what he could use for a Christmas tree. While the teacher turned the matter over in her mind without bringing up a solution, Ray said, "Oh! I know," picked up the toy ironing board, turned it over so that the crossed legs stood in the air, and went off to decorate it with odds and ends for the family Christmas day that was being played in the playhouse. Play may need guidance at a number of points, although basically it is the children's own and is carried on without adult interference. In one situation several cowboy suits appeared after the Christmas holidays; the boys snatched up long blocks and were preparing for a shooting fray when the teacher casually remarked that the blocks would make good guitars and soon the boys were enthusiastically strumming and singing "Home on the Range," as they sat on their block horses and watched their cattle.

More and more first grades are being supplied with equipment for housekeeping play and with blocks and wooden toys so that children can continue their advances in dramatic play.

Doll play is at its height at age six, though many boys are turning their interest to transportation, community activities, and even to the beginning of enthusiasm for "space travel." Dramatic play occupies a great deal of the free time of children both indoors and on the playground. For this age as well as for kindergarten, outdoor equipment should include well-sanded and painted packing boxes, kegs, sawhorses, boards with cleats to prevent splitting, and short lengths of ladder. With such inexpensive equipment the children can devise many types of play; the interest and the ingenious variations are never exhausted.

Many teachers have found that a costume box adds to the fun of dramatic play and frequently suggests the play itself. For the younger children, gay hats, gloves, purses, and other odds and ends of castoff apparel provide endless pleasure and are used for many purposes. Older children find many uses for a few gay cambric skirts and pairs of trousers, a bodice or other bits of peasant costume, and strips of material that can be twisted and draped in a variety of ways.

Excursions and studies of many sorts often lead to dramatic play, either spontaneously or through encouragement from the teacher. Interest in boats led a first grade group in a harbor city to build boats of scraps of wood, put wrapping paper on the floor and calcimine it blue, then set up an elaborate harbor play, complete with docks, bridges, and lighthouses. Tugs guided ships into the docks, lighthouse tenders carried supplies, and log rafts were towed to the lumber mills. A wide vocabulary was brought into the play and used with great accuracy. Even the most timid child found a role that he could play enthusiastically. Reproducing on the floor a farm, a market, a harbor, an airport, or any other large area the children are interested in, provides the first step in the understanding of mapping and charting, the reducing of a large space to a small one without losing its important elements. Dramatizing an episode or carrying on more extended plays helps children to organize their thinking, clarify meanings, see relationships, fix new vocabulary, and enter in imagination into the life they are reproducing. All of it leads to deeper understandings and broader sympathies.

Interest in dramatic play appears among older children, but it begins to take on different forms and the content differs with age and maturity. Biber, in an intensive study of a group of seven-year-olds, found girls carrying on various types of family-life play on the playroof on occasion, but the boys entered into it very rarely (6). There was little play of family life on the part of mixed groups. Both boys and girls entered into exciting war play with many wounded being carried or assisted from the scene of battle. It was highly exciting play with much rushing about, exceedingly dramatic portrayal of the wounded, doctors, and hospitals, but action appeared more to be desired than consistency. Throughout the year it was clear that girls clung to free, spontaneous dramatic play after the boys had largely abandoned it.

Children of eight and nine very readily turn the material they are studying into dramatic play, as they do the ideas they gain from radio, the movies, and television. A fourth grade group, climbing a steep trail in the park, arrived at a colossal statue of an Indian at the top of the trail a moment ahead of their teacher and were busily dramatizing an Indian council meeting when the teacher arrived. They solemnly decided that they must move westward because the white men were crowding them out of their territory. When the decision had been made, they started soberly down the trail again. The same group later lived for most of a day as true a reproduction of the life of the Lenni-Lenape Indians as they could construct from their reading. A part of the day—building the wigwam, cooking dinner with hot stones and over the coals of their fire—was carefully planned ahead, but much of the conversational interplay and many of the activities and overtones were spontaneous dramatic play. They were so thoroughly saturated with the lore of the period and people that their improvisations flowed freely and naturally.

War interests resulted in a great deal of dramatic play by eight- to twelve-year-olds. A helmeted figure in a child-size camouflage suit might dart from behind any ambush on playground, lawn, or street. "Cops and robbers" were forgotten for the duration of the war and GI's, sailors, marines, aviators, and the enemy took their place in the realistic play of children.

Older children reproduce in play form some of the things they are studying or are interested in, but from the fourth grade on, the planning and organizing they do make theirs more nearly "a play" than just spontaneous dramatic play (14). A fifth grade group which had had a week of camping experience dramatized camp life for another grade. Junior and senior high school pupils put on a school election at the time of a national presidential election. These dramatizations do grow out of social situations but they lack the unplanned spontaneity of dramatic play. When older children are planning and producing an original play, their first attempts may be in the nature of dramatic play, but as they organize and refine their thinking they shape it into fairly definite form.

In spontaneous dramatic play, a child *is* the character he is portraying, for the time at least. In dramatization, the acting of a prepared story or play, a child consciously accepts a role and the obligation to interpret it.

☐ DRAMATIZATION IN THE PRIMARY SCHOOL

In the nursery school, dramatization is found in the finger plays the children delight in playing over and over again. At first the teacher supplies the words but later the children join in as they scoot the train up and down the track, toot the trumpet, and pound the hammer with their hands as accompaniment to the words. In rhythmic play, they imitate rabbits, elephants, ducks, fairies, or snowflakes or do whatever the music moves them to do. Occasionally a small group becomes interested in playing a Mother Goose rhyme but unless the inspiration comes from the children they show little interest in it.

Kindergarten children enjoy playing stories. At this age "the play's the thing." They need very little in the way of stage setting or properties. Imagination can fill all the gaps and provide what is needed. The fact that the three chairs Goldilocks tries are all alike and the beds are each made of two more chairs does not cause the children any concern. The Three Billy-Goats Gruff can "tromp" across a low table top or the floor; if there is a place for the troll that is all that matters. Auntie Katushka's fine feather bed can be pure imagination but the children may want something for a gate to swing on and something for a picnic basket. There need be no costumes, though a few odds and ends from a costume box may add to the pleasure and illusion. If the children feel the need for ears for Peter Rabbit, paper ears pasted on a headband satisfy them completely.

Foster and Headley list the following rhymes and stories as types which lend themselves to dramatization (10, p. 210):

Nursery rhymes—Jack and Jill; Jack Be Nimble; Little Miss Muffet; Hickory, Dickory, Dock; and Little Jack Horner.

Stories—The Three Billy-Goats Gruff; Little Duckling Tries His Voice; The Three Bears; The Story of Dobbin; The Three Goats; The Little Wooden Farmer; Whiffy McMann; The Poppy Seed Cakes; and One Little Indian Boy.

Children in the first grade will enjoy some of the same material. They will want to dramatize a number of the old folk tales which have simple plot and an interesting amount of repetition. "The Three Little Pigs," "The Old Woman and Her Pig," "The Gingerbread Boy," and others of that type will be favorites with most children. Some of the modern stories lend themselves to dramatization equally well.

Most of the playing will be done just for the pleasure it affords and with no audience other than the group itself. On occasion, the group may become interested in playing a story for the kindergarten or in repeating for their mothers one that they have liked especially well.

Stories for dramatizing must fit the interests and the maturity of the group. Children should be allowed to select the stories they like, because they can interpret only those characters and actions which they can enter into with pleasure and understanding. Short stories appeal most if they have clear-cut action and dialogue which either follows a simple pattern as, "Little Pig, little Pig, let me come in!" or "You can't catch me! I'm the Gingerbread Man!" or can be made up in original form by each child who plays.

Second grade children enjoy playing longer stories which have more complex action and more of essential dialogue. Old folk tales are still popular choices. "The Lad Who Went to the North Wind," "The Bremen Town Musicians," "Cinderella," and "The Sleeping Beauty" are stories some groups will tackle enthusiastically. The complexity of the story which can be dramatized depends upon the maturity of the group. If the dramatization of stories is a group interest, the children will be forever watching for stories to play. "Rumpelstiltskin" becomes a favorite with slightly older children, as do stories from Kipling's *Jungle Books* and Howard Pyle's *Pepper and Salt* and *The Wonder Clock*. Stories such as these are highly pleasing to eight- and nine-year-olds. They can turn the story into a workable sequence of action. They may give careful attention to the actual speeches of the characters, but more often they present their own original interpretation of the feelings and attitudes which the characters portray. An eight-year-old boy interpreted Rumpelstiltskin in a manner similar to a witch in "Macbeth" and the children accepted it as just right.

No school experience gives a child a better opportunity to be creative than does playmaking. A child who is thinking independently and portraying his thought and his emotional reaction with sincerity and confidence is having a creative experience. The teacher does not expect to make actors of children but she does try to help every child to respect his own thoughts and feelings and to stand before the group with ideas that are his own.

Children of primary grade age care little more for costumes and properties than do younger children. If they have seen the plays produced by older children they may wish to imitate to some degree, but they will put on many plays of their own making in the classroom with only the odds and ends they can find about the room. If they wish to share the play with an audience of mothers or a neighboring class, they may concoct something which will suggest the essential properties to others. They may also wish to "dress up" in odds and ends from the costume box or to make something which suggests the parts they are playing. A gilt-paper crown makes a queen, a piece of cheesecloth fastened to wrists and shoulders will do for a butterfly or a fairy, a headband with antennae or pink and white ears serves for a bee or a rabbit. A postman may need a letter bag and a policeman may need a cap, but the child rarely feels the need for real disguises.

Learning lines and parroting them forth at the proper points makes children stiff and self-conscious. Getting the "feel" of a part, and a clear concept of the contribution a character is expected to make to the whole, makes it possible for them to coin their own lines as naturally as they talk among themselves. The character talks as the child himself talks and it fits the need perfectly. Often there are real surprises as children develop a play. A first grade put together a favorite poem and some of the rhythmic interpretations they had enjoyed in dramatizing Rose Fyleman's "Fairies." The "fairies at the bottom of our garden" played and danced as only fairies can. One of them remarked, "Look out, there's a bee in that flower." Another answered, "It won't hurt you if you don't bother it. Mr. Dack says so!" Neither the mothers in the audience nor the children saw anything incongruous in tucking in a little nature knowledge furnished by the school gardener.

Dramatizations on the primary school level spring from the children's experience, their social studies interests, stories they have read or listened to, poems that suggest action, or just the children's own original fantasy. The material is not written into a play. It is worked through to the children's satisfaction and they pass on to the next interest. Younger children rarely live with a play long enough to polish and perfect it, though they may wish to play it enough times to permit the individual members of the group to play the parts they wish to play. The values lie in the creative thinking, the planning, and the doing. Repeating to add polish frequently serves only to flatten the whole experience and deprive it of the freshness of thinking and response that is the chief charm in the work of young children. When repetition destroys the fun of playing, the values are gone. Any further repetition falls clearly into the area of diminishing returns.

☐ PLAYMAKING FOR OLDER CHILDREN

Older children as well as younger ones draw much of their material for plays from their own experience. Social studies interests, stories of all sorts, ballads, and other sources may be drawn upon. One of the best ways to understand other cultures and civilizations is to dramatize them. Re-enacting the life of an earlier period—the ancient Greeks and their Olympic games, life in China as Marco Polo found it, or the coming of the Spaniards to Mexico—gives children a clearer concept of the period. Dramatizing a story of France, Japan, or India today may help to create respect for those peoples and some further understanding of the problems with which they deal. Study is necessary to build background for the play. An individual character may require not only studying books but also making the acquaintance of people who come from the area or are steeped in the lore of the period. A great deal of study and thinking may be necessary in order to give the proper flavor and atmosphere to a play.

Building their own plays has far greater value than selecting a ready-made play and producing it. Not only will the background building and the creation of plot and sequence have educative value but the play will actually be better produced.

Children can do well only what they can put themselves into with loss of identity or the submerging of self. This is not possible until the play or the role has become a part of the child. Obviously, participation in the creation of the play helps to make this possible.

Plays for children from nine to twelve years of age are more elaborate in most instances than those of younger children. Often boys and girls of these ages appear to need the help of more properties and more costuming to lose their identity in a part. Imagination no longer supplies all the essential elements and the children are more aware of consistency of details. Often they work long and hard to make their portrayal of time, place, and characters clear to an audience.

Middle grade children do a good deal of dramatizing with no audience except each other, but they enjoy putting on an occasional production that is more finished. For this, they plan the sequence of events with care and give a great deal of thought to portrayal of characters. They may have to find a Chinese laundryman or a French immigrant, if there is one in the community, and engage him in conversation, not only to learn something of his ideas and attitudes but also to catch his form of speech. They will put a great deal of time and effort into the making of simple properties and costumes and perhaps a simple backdrop or something to tack on the wall as suggestive background. If a costume box is available, they can often create from basic garments something that will fit their need.

With these children as with younger ones, the best productions are those for which no lines are written. Each character assumes responsibility for portraying an understood role and fits his own words to his concept of the character and his part in the total action. The reason for this is quite clear. If the child has thought through his part well enough to portray it, he can respond naturally in that part. A child who has memorized lines and cues and forgets what he is supposed to say is powerless until he receives help. The child who is living the part and speaking naturally in it will come forth with something that fits the situation because his confidence rests in ideas, not in set patterns of words.

□ MEETING THE NEEDS OF INDIVIDUALS

Work with dramatization and playmaking can help individual children with their problems in many different ways. The timid child can be guided into participation through a variety of means. If he feels that he cannot play one of the characters he may be willing to help arrange the setting, to announce the play, to usher in the guests, or render some other simple service. After a time he may be willing to assume a minor role in the acting itself, particularly if he does not need to talk. Occasionally a bit of crude costuming will help him to forget himself. Elizabeth, a highly creative but very withdrawn fourth grade child, consistently refused to participate in spontaneous classroom dramatizations. One day when a number of children were absent, those who remained at school became very insistent that she help them so they could go on with their play. Elizabeth ran to the coat cupboard, came back with her brown coat thrown over her head and her arms partly in the sleeves, and became the tiger the children needed. The fierceness of her growls was loudly applauded by the children. Having finally broken through her reserve and gained the children's approval, she participated as a matter of course in later dramatizations.

Occasionally a child who does well with dramatic interpretation insists on carrying major roles at all times. Since the purpose of such work is to develop all children, not to feature those who are gifted, the gifted child (and at times his parents) has to be helped to see the value in all types of participation.

The child whose speech is slovenly and inaccurate will often work hard to make his speech acceptable to an audience and make it carry his contribution to the play. Playmaking may serve as motivation for improved speech for all children.

Participation in a play calls for careful thought for timing and attention to the sequence of events. A child who fails to live up to the obligation of his part may throw the entire play into confusion. A thoughtless child and one whose thinking is muddled may be motivated to improve the quality of his thinking through concern for the group enterprise. The practice he receives in consistent, sequential thinking should make him a little clearer as to how to proceed in other areas of thinking.

☐ PRACTICE IN DEMOCRATIC PROCEDURES

Playmaking calls for democratic interaction. The planning, the trying out of various parts, and the free expression of ideas are all essential to the whole enterprise. Through guidance, children can learn to assume responsibility for co-operation in the working out of plans and for the sharing of ideas. Learning to listen courteously to other people's ideas and to weigh them against one's own is important learning for every child. Trying out ideas, then standing back to look at and evaluate them impersonally, helps a child to grow in maturity of attitude and behavior. Evaluation by the group and by individuals is inherent in the whole process of playmaking. Individuals learn to give up personal desires when they conflict with those of the group and learn to subordinate individual self-interest to group interest.

In preparation for a play, each child may choose the role he wishes to play. The play may be tried throughout with several casts or new characters may be chosen for each logical subdivision. No player is supposed to volunteer for a second turn until everyone has had his turn to play. If the play is to be produced before an audience, the children may select the final cast by any criteria they choose to set up. Children usually see very clearly the need for giving everyone his fair turn at something he wants to do.

☐ UNDERSTANDING HUMAN BEHAVIOR AND MOTIVATION

Drama, especially for older children, involves people and their behavior and emotions. In playing a part a child steps out of himself, his own personality, and into the personality of someone else. He is freed from his own limitations and inhibitions; he may do whatever the part he is playing calls for. Often a large portion of the preparation of a play is consideration of character. "If the man is like this, what will he do?" Playing a fine character and responding through him to noble emotions may help the child himself to stretch upward and may help to fix in him some high ideals. On the other hand, a character who is not admirable stands out in the play for what he is. The child can see him against the entire plot of the play and its interaction. Playing such a part may strengthen the child's dislike for such a person.

Stories children dramatize often deal with ethical questions. Helping the children to sense the values involved is an important part of the teacher's responsibility. If she succeeds in opening the children's eyes to see more clearly what is worthy and what is cheap, she is giving them something of lasting value (21, p. 245). Spiritual and moral values can be made to stand out clearly without preaching. They are inherent in the situations being portrayed as well as in the experience of working together toward a common goal.

☐ PUPPETS AND MARIONETTES

Serving as the players themselves is usually the children's favorite way of carrying out dramatic interpretation. There are other ways that can be used for certain purposes and to add variety to experience. Puppets of a number of kinds can be used with younger children while older children, particularly those of junior high and high school ages, may develop skilled performance with marionettes.

Puppets made with bottles and used to push around on a table, helped to loosen up a group of very timid first grade children of foreign background. They played the story of "The Three Bears" using a quart milk bottle for Father Bear, a pint bottle for Mother Bear, a half pint bottle for Baby Bear, and a pop bottle for Goldilocks. The bottles were wrapped with colored cambric, brown for the bears, and a ball of newspaper covered with cambric formed the head. Children who were not yet ready to play the parts themselves would push the bottles about on the table and talk for the characters with great confidence. The fact that the child was in full view of the audience appeared not to trouble him at all.

Upper primary and intermediate grade groups sometimes use hand puppets made of paper bags or scraps of fabric. Some children learn to manipulate them and talk for them without difficulty. Other groups have tried stick puppets, the character created in color by the child, then thumbtacked to a stick for use above a table top or in a box theater.

Mature fifth and sixth grade children as well as young people in high school may find great pleasure in creating marionettes. Usually, the heads are made of clay, plaster, or just of papier-mâché made with newspaper strips and paste. If children are mature enough to create their own marionettes and to manipulate them by strings they can produce plays which are very popular with child audiences. Choice of subject matter for the plays may be limited by the medium, but children show great ingenuity in their interpretation.

☐ PANTOMIME AND SHADOW PLAYS

Pantomime is a serviceable medium at many points. Some

children who are self-conscious and timid will act a part which requires no talking before they will take a speaking part. They can enter into dramatic activity a step at a time but cannot do it all at once.

There are some types of dramatic material for which pantomime is best. Many schools use it for the portrayal of the Christmas Story. The reverent attitudes of the children testify to the depth of feeling and understanding they put into the playing.

Shadow plays are fun, especially for older children. They learn to think in terms of line and balance, action and grouping. The medium requires them to give attention to clear portrayal of mood and action through use of the body, since they cannot supplement action with words. Shadow plays are used less frequently than other acting, but they have a place in the total program.

☐ THE CHILDREN'S THEATER

The movement for a Children's Theater is creating interest in a number of communities. Children are being given opportunity to join groups of players under skilled leadership and to put on plays for their own and the community's pleasure. They are reading good literature and learning to turn it into plays. They are catching the spirit of other times and places and learning to re-enact it. The whole Children's Theater movement is one in which parents and teachers should be greatly interested. It provides children with wholesome and highly educational out-of-school experience. The leadership that is going into the movement is of high quality. Many a community could well afford to divert some of the funds now going into the apprehension and care of juvenile delinquency into the constructive, character-building values that are being woven into the Children's Theater movement.

☐ THE CHILD AS DOER, NOT ABSORBER

Radio, movies, and television threaten to make of our children passive, "do-less" absorbers who are content to be forever on the receiving end of entertainment. Children of earlier periods were their own entertainers. They put on circuses and shows of their own creation in their back yards and attics and charged a penny or some pins for admission. It took a great deal of ingenuity and family or neighborhood planning to make the show come off. Children made tickets, rigged up sheets or blankets on clotheslines for curtains, concocted costumes, and planned sequences of activity. It required an immense amount of thought and creative effort as well as real skill in working together for a common end. They found ways to include all who wished to participate and took care of the working out of democratic processes themselves.

Now one finds little of this sort of activity in homes and neighborhoods. The children are sitting in the moving picture theater looking and listening or facing a television instrument as many as three and a half hours a day soaking up what they see and hear. They are no longer the doers and creators. While the modern media undoubtedly have brought educational values, they have deprived children of other very important values. Children need many experiences in thinking, planning, carrying through plans, and evaluating outcomes. They need to use their own creative minds and develop them through use. What children plan and carry through, with or without adult guidance, is something suited to their level of development and meaningful to them. The mass media bring them ideas and stimulation but often of an unwholesome and unsuitable sort. People who are interested in the development of children need to give thought to this phase of their development and put forth some effort to bring it about.

Summer camps, organized playground programs, and community centers tend to spend some time on dramatics but could afford to spend more. The interest is there if it is stimulated and guided. Many groups respond as did one fourth grade. The children kept begging for more time for play acting so the teacher suggested that they give some thought to play preparation during their playground periods. For days, knots of children worked at various points on the playground organizing and trying out plays. When each group was ready, it announced its need for time to present its offering. In some instances the teacher had been called on for suggestions, or material from the costume box had been requested, but often the final production was as much a surprise to the teacher as to the other children in the audience.

A child who has developed vital creative interests is rarely a child who carries on antisocial activities or who gets into trouble for lack of guidance. More school and community effort in building wholesome, constructively valuable interests would cut down materially on juvenile delinquency and minimize the possibility of mental breakdown as well as build lifetime values in attitudes, habits, and real mental power.

☐ SELECTED REFERENCES ☐

1. Adams, Fay, *Educating America's Children.* New York: Ronald Press Co., 1946. Chap. XIV, pp. 468-484.
2. Arbuthnot, May Hill, *Children and Books* (Rev. Ed.). Chicago: Scott, Foresman and Co., 1957.
3. Association for Childhood Education International, *Literature With Children.* Washington, D. C.: Association for Childhood Education International, 1961.
4. ———, *Creative Dramatics.* Washington, D. C.: Association for Childhood Education International, 1961.
5. Betzner, Jean, *Exploring Literature with Children.* Practical Suggestions for Teaching, No. 7. New York: Bureau of Publications, Teachers College, Columbia University, 1943.
6. Biber, Barbara; Murphy, Lois B.; Woodcock, Louise P.; and Black, Irma S., *Child Life in School: A Study of a Seven-Year-Old Group.* New York: E. P. Dutton and Co., Inc., 1942.
7. Broening, Angela M., and others, *Conducting Experiences in English.* National Council of Teachers of English. English Monograph No. 8. New York: D. Appleton-Century Co., Inc., 1939.
8. Burger, Isabel B., *Creative Play Acting.* New York: A. S. Barnes and Co., Inc., 1950.
9. Durland, Frances Caldwell, *Creative Dramatics for Children.* Yellow Springs, Ohio: The Antioch Press, 1952.
10. Foster, Josephine C., and Headley, Neith E., *Education in the Kindergarten* (2nd Ed.). New York: American Book Co., 1948.
11. Hartman, Gertrude, and Shumaker, Ann (Eds.), *Creative Expression* (2nd Ed.). Milwaukee: E. M. Hale & Co., 1939.
12. Hatfield, W. Wilbur (Ed.), *An Experience Curriculum in English.* National Council of Teachers of English. English Monograph No. 4. New York: D. Appleton-Century Co., Inc., 1935.
13. Lease, Ruth, and Siks, Geraldine Brian, *Creative Dramatics in Home, School and Community.* New York: Harper and Brothers, 1952.
14. Lee, J. Murray, and Lee, Dorris May, *The Child and His Curriculum* (3rd Ed.). New York: Appleton-Century-Crofts, Inc., 1960.

15. Lewis, George L., and Burkart, Ann K., "Creative Dramatics: A Selective Bibliography." *Elementary English* 39:91-100, February, 1962.
16. Pinto, Vivian De Sola (Ed.), *The Teaching of English in Schools: A Symposium.* London: Macmillan and Co., Ltd., 1946.
17. Siks, Geraldine B., *Creative Dramatics: An Art for Children.* New York: Harper and Brothers, 1958.
18. Strickland, Ruth G., *Guide for Teaching Grades I and II.* Boston: D. C. Heath and Co., 1962.
19. Tooze, Ruth, *Storytelling.* Englewood Cliffs, N. J.: Prentice-Hall, Inc., 1959.
20. United States Office of Education, *Creative Drama: Drama With and For Children; Children's Theater.* Bulletin No. 30. Washington, D. C.: Superintendent of Documents, United States Office of Education, 1960.
21. Ward, Winifred, *Playmaking with Children, from Kindergarten to High School.* New York: D. Appleton-Century Co., Inc., 1947.

Foreign Languages

in the elementary school

American interest in foreign languages burgeoned during the 1950's. Parker, in *The National Interest and Foreign Languages* offers this explanation: "Two facts and one man are largely responsible for this trend. The first fact is a growing awareness that, because of America's present role in the world, more American children need to acquire cultures, preferably through the medium of a foreign language. The second fact is a growing awareness of something long known to educators in other countries: young children learn to speak foreign languages more easily, and with more accurate accent, than do older children or grownups (5, pp. 18-19).

The man credited with the upsurge of interest is Dr. Earl J. McGrath, U. S. Commissioner of Education in 1952, who vigorously advocated foreign language study in the elementary school and who passed on his interest to both educators and laymen.

Considerable encouragement for the movement came from a Canadian neurologist who strongly advocated the study of foreign language in the preadolescent period. He declared that the physiological development of the "organ of the mind causes it to specialize in the learning of language before the ages of 10 to 14. After that, gradually, inevitably, it seems to become rigid, slow, less receptive." He and other neurologists and psychologists condemned the tendency of schools to begin most of their teaching of foreign languages at later ages, "long after a boy or girl has lost full capacity for language learning" (5).

All who deal with young children are aware of their enjoyment of language and the effort they put forth to master their mother tongue. They have freshly acquired skills for learning by ear the sound and syntax patterns of language. Educators and linguists agree that foreign language for young children should be oral language with very gradual introduction to the written language after the oral language is fairly well learned.

☐ FOREIGN LANGUAGE IN THE ELEMENTARY SCHOOL

The elementary school faces a number of problems with relation to the addition of foreign language to the curriculum. In the first place, the curriculum is crowded with subjects, each of which has been added to meet public demands. The question of how much time to devote to foreign language and how to fit it into the day poses knotty problems.

The second question is, who shall teach it? Gesell and Ilg of Yale recommend that the second language, at least for young children, be taught by a special teacher, not the regular classroom teacher for psychological reasons, since children sometimes react unfavorably to talk they do not easily understand from someone with whom they have close interpersonal relations.

Since the major value in an early start with a foreign language lies in the fact that younger children learn to speak it more easily and accurately than do older ones, it is incumbent upon the school to see to it that the teacher's speech is as perfect as possible. There seems little justification for an early beginning if it contains any elements which must be undone or redone later on. Consequently, at present, it is particularly difficult to find teachers who are highly proficient in the language and have enough knowledge of child psychology to be successful teachers.

Because of the shortage of teachers for elementary children and perhaps also because of the factor of cost, a large number of schools are using televised language programs. This may have the advantage that the teacher is an expert who makes careful preparation for each lesson. It has the disadvantage that, unless the classroom teacher finds ways to relate the program to some of the rest of the children's work, it is completely divorced from everything else in the children's learning experience. A major value should be close relationship between this program and the social studies.

From the beginning of the movement for teaching foreign languages in the elementary school (FLES, as it is commonly called) the interest of parents and the public has been most significant. But a good beginning is of little value unless it is followed through consistently. Linguists are interested in the program because of their experience that it takes a number of years to master a language even with consistent opportunity and application. All too often, schools have started enthusiastically with elementary classes but have failed to carry on the work consistently for an eight to ten year period. It is the long sequence which is the great value of the FLES idea. Lacking this, it is disappointing to children, parents, and teachers alike.

☐ VARIATIONS IN PLANS AND CURRICULUM

Schools differ in their methods of handling foreign language programs. In the early 1950's most programs were voluntary. Only those children attended the classes whose parents chose to send them. In some schools, particularly in Cleveland as early as 1921, the program was planned as a part of a major work program for gifted children. With the advent of television teaching, entire elementary school classes participated in the program at the grade levels at which it was offered.

There is variation, too, in the age level at which the program is started. A few schools, particularly laboratory schools, have begun the teaching of a foreign language in the kindergarten. The favored starting point in many schools is Grade 3, after children have made a sound beginning in reading and writing their own language. At any rate, neurologists and educators appear to be in some agreement that superior performance can be anticipated at ages 8, 9, and 10 (6).

The question of time within the school is a controversial one. Advocates of the program insist that utilizing 15 to 20 minutes a day for foreign language does no harm to the rest of the school's program. Many teachers feel, however, that the day is scarcely long enough to do the other work required of elementary school children. Further research is needed to determine when and how much time should be devoted to FLES.

Linguists appear less concerned with which language children shall learn than that they learn a second language. In many schools, the choice of language is made by the parents and the school cooperatively. In other schools, the choice of language depends upon the availability of a qualified teacher or of a satisfactory television or radio course.

In the early days of the FLES program, each teacher created his own course of study. While this had the merit of being tailored (at least theoretically) to meet the needs of the group being taught, it often left much to be desired in terms of sequential grading and techniques for mastery. Now, considerable help is available to the teacher. The Modern Language Association[1] has utilized the help of authorities in the fields of linguistics, cultural anthropology, child psychology, elementary education and foreign language teaching to create materials

[1] Modern Language Association of America, 4 Washington Place, New York, New York 10003.

for the teaching of several languages in the elementary school (3, p. 16).

☐ ENTHUSIASM TEMPERED WITH CAUTION

According to Parker, the official position of the Modern Language Association on FLES after three years of studying a variety of reports on the movement, was this:

> The movement deserves the support of parents and educational administrators because: (1) it recognizes the evidence concerning the process of language learning, introducing study of a second language to children at an age when they are naturally curious about language, when they have fewest inhibitions, and when they imitate most easily new sounds and sound patterns; (2) it recognizes the fact that the greatest natural barriers to international understanding are the unreasoning reactions to "foreign-ness" which are often acquired in childhood but which may be offset by experiences with foreign speech and behavior; and (3) it recognizes the fact that real proficiency in the use of a foreign language requires progressive learning over an extended period.
>
> It is our further judgment that the public should be warned against faddish aspects of this movement. No new venture in American education can long prosper without the wholehearted support of parents, teachers, and educational administrators in a given community. Proponents of foreign language study in the elementary schools should not, therefore, initiate programs until (1) a majority of the parents concerned approve at least an experimental program, and (2) local school boards and administrators are convinced that necessary preparations have been made. Necessary preparations include: (1) recruitment of an adequate number of interested teachers who have both skill in guiding children and the necessary language qualifications, (2) availability of material appropriate to each age level, with new approaches and a carefully planned syllabus for each grade, and (3) adequate provisions for appraisal.
>
> The success of existing programs thus initiated, prepared for, and appraised convinces us of the urgent need of providing, for children who have the ability and desire, the opportunity for continuous progress in language study into and through junior and senior high school (7, p. 22).

While a great deal has been written about the teaching of foreign languages, especially during the last few years, doubts remain regarding a number of points (1). Carroll of Harvard, surveying the research on the subject, came in 1960 to the following conclusions:

1. There is some solid basis for the belief that young children can acquire good pronunciation more rapidly and easily than adults do under normal conditions.
2. Evidence appears to support the conclusion that *time* spent learning a foreign language is more crucial than *age* as such.
3. One can find reports of successful foreign language teaching at every grade level. Some researchers have recommended grades 3 or 4 as the best starting level.
4. It is probably a mistake to select children for foreign language on the basis of intelligence test scores or on the basis of reading skill. The best presently available method is a short trial period of language learning.
5. Evidence is lacking as to whether pupils who study foreign language in the elementary school have an advantage when studying language in high school and college.
6. There are no research reports of any adverse effect of FLES on progress in other school subjects.
7. There is no *one* method of teaching foreign language that should be emphasized. Foreign language instruction should always be introduced in its spoken form followed later by the written form.

Further studies will be needed, particularly longitudinal ones. Perhaps some of these will come from California where, beginning in 1965, every school system must offer foreign language instruction in grades 6 through 12. Because of the number of people of Spanish background in California, this is almost always a program of Spanish.

One such longitudinal study is now under way. The philosophy behind the French model sequences being planned for the Washington State Foreign-Language Program appear particularly promising in their tying together of culture and language. Nostrand postulates that

> . . . if we draw into this sequence all the essential *experience* of the culture and social structure that can be given the most efficiently through the culture's language, then the time required for a modest, active competence in the language can be justified

> as a means toward cross-cultural understanding and toward the learner's increased capability to contribute toward a good society. The essential *knowledge about* the nature of cultures and societies would meanwhile be given partly in parallel sequences of the language arts and social studies; but the foreign-language sequence would apply that general knowledge, elaborate the descriptive knowledge of the foreign culture, and compare that system with the learner's mother culture (6).

Children in the early grades will be learning songs, verses, and proverbs that are also enjoyed by children in the target culture. All children are impressed with the sound of a well-known folk tale told in a foreign language. Through films and dramatization they can learn greetings, forms of courtesy, and the like. The need at the earliest level is to "acquire a 'feeling' for the language and for what it expresses, along with correct pronunciation, intonation and syntax." From third or fourth through sixth grade situational dialogues are to be learned and acted out. Through these and especially through films and tapes, children can become aware of how the children who use the target language in their own culture "act toward adults, how close the people stand to one another in conversing, what their facial expressions and tone of voice mean, and so on." The program carries on through twelfth grade a "co-ordinate system" of language acquisition and cultural understanding.

Many more studies of the kind represented by this five-year study are needed.

☐ CHOICE OF LANGUAGE

If the community contains a group who speak a foreign language, that language is clearly the best choice for the elementary school. If the children who speak that language in their homes need special help with English, that could well be given while the other children learn the language that is foreign to them. Appreciation of each other and each others' culture will grow with growth in language under such circumstances and add greatly to the values for both groups.

☐ TEACHING ENGLISH TO SPEAKERS OF OTHER LANGUAGES

The number of children in the schools of the United States who speak a language other than English as their mother tongue is increasing, not just in California and Florida but in many cities throughout the country. Statistics in California indicate that most of the children who come from foreign-language-speaking homes are of Mexican origin, but increasing numbers are coming from European countries, Germany, Holland, and Portugal particularly. Approximately one child in ten in the kindergartens of California has a Spanish surname, and the proportion of those who do not speak English as their native language is increasing (5, p. 33). Certainly the same is true of parts of Florida and of New York City, Chicago, and other large cities. The Cuban migration into Florida and the Puerto Rican migration into New York City are so large as to create serious problems in the elementary schools. Children enter schools at all times in the year because many families move from place to place in search of employment.

Both California and Florida have instituted special classes for children who do not know English – classes of not more than fifteen which meet daily for at least a half hour. The audio-lingual approach is used with emphasis on increasing facility in the use of oral English. Language loyalty compounds the school's problem. A primary grade teacher once asked feelingly, "How can we make these children practice their English instead of using only Spanish outside the school?" Actually, there is no way to force it, even if one wished to. The child's security is entirely bound up with people who speak the home language. Sometimes failure to use English amounts almost to a rejection of the culture outside the home as well as the language.

Children who speak a foreign language must be helped to recognize the respect in which the school holds their home language. If the school has a foreign language program in which English-speaking children are learning Spanish while Spanish-speaking children are learning English, emphasis on the value of bilingualism rather than monolingualism can pervade the work. In any case, teachers can find many ways to underscore their respect for the child's home language and culture. They can have the child sing a favorite song, tell a story, or recite some verses for the rest of the class, teach the class to count in the foreign language, to use greetings in it, or to note the contribution of that culture to the local one. Teachers are obligated to be mindful of the needs and feelings of these children and to use every opportunity to build them up.

Increasingly, new materials are being made available to help with teaching English as a second language. The National Council of Teachers of English, the Modern Language Association of America, and the Center for Applied Linguistics are all sources to which teachers can turn for help and materials.[2] Miami and Dade County, Florida have created some paperback reading materials[3] that are culture-free for teaching the Cuban children to read. These may prove useful in other school systems for children who face the problem of learning to speak, read, and write English when they enter our schools.

☐ GENERALLY ACCEPTED PRINCIPLES OF LANGUAGE LEARNING

The sounds of the language should receive priority and these should be learned in authentic expressions and sentences, spoken always with the intonation and rhythm used by native speakers of the language.

Children should learn the "system" of the new language and how it operates. This includes the sound system, the grammatical arrangements, and the vocabulary needed for communication. Vocabulary should be presented in such manner that meaning is clear. Patterns should be introduced and practiced until they become automatic. The model children are to imitate should be presented clearly, at normal speed and with normal intonation.

Classroom activities should include dialogues, interchanges, descriptions and comments which involve two or more children at a time. New material should be introduced a little at a time and practiced in a variety of ways by individuals and the group. Simple games may be devised to hold the interest of the children through many repetitions. The emphasis should be on language in actual use. Rules of grammar have little value at this early stage. Any generalizations regarding usage should grow out of many examples.

Teacher-pupil communication should be in the target language. English should be used sparingly and only for necessary explanations regarding form and meaning.

[2] National Council of Teachers of English, 508 South Sixth Street, Champaign, Illinois 61820; Modern Language Association of America, 4 Washington Place, New York, New York 10001; Center for Applied Linguistics, 1755 Massachusetts Avenue, N.W., Washington, D. C. 20036.

[3] D. C. Heath and Company.

☐ SELECTED REFERENCES ☐

1. Carroll, John B., "Foreign Languages for Children." *National Elementary Principal,* May, 1960, 39:12-15.
2. ———, "Wanted: A Research Basis for Educational Policy on Foreign Language Teaching." *Harvard Educational Review,* Spring, 1960, 30:128-140; No. 2.
3. Eriksson, Marguerite; Forest, Ilse; and Mulhouse, Ruth, *Foreign Languages in the Elementary School.* Englewood Cliffs, New Jersey: Prentice-Hall, Inc., 1964.
4. Hughes, Marie M., and Sanchez, George I., *Learning a New Language.* Bulletin 101, Washington, D. C.: Association for Childhood Education International, 1958.
5. Nance, Afton Dill, "Teaching English to Speakers of Other Languages." *On Teaching English to Speakers of Other Languages,* Carol J. Kreider, Editor. Champaign, Illinois, National Council of Teachers of English, 1966.
6. Nostrand, Howard Lee, "The Foreign Culture in a Model Foreign Language Sequence." *The Florida FL Reporter.* Fall, 1967. Vol. 5, No. 3, pp. 11-12.
7. Parker, William Riley, *The National Interest and Foreign Languages.* Third Edition, Department of State Publication 7324, Washington, D. C.: Superintendent of Documents, U. S. Government Printing Office, 1962.
8. Rojas, Pauline, "The Miami Experience in Bilingual Education." *On Teaching English to Speakers of Other Languages.* Carol J. Kreider, Editor. Champaign, Illinois, National Council of Teachers of English, 1966.
9. Shane, Harold G., and Mulry, June Grant, *Improving Language Arts Instruction Through Research.* Washington, D. C.: Association for Supervision and Curriculum Development, National Education Association, 1963, pp. 125-129.
10. Walsh, Donald D., "The FL Program in 1963." *PMLA,* May 1964, p. 26.

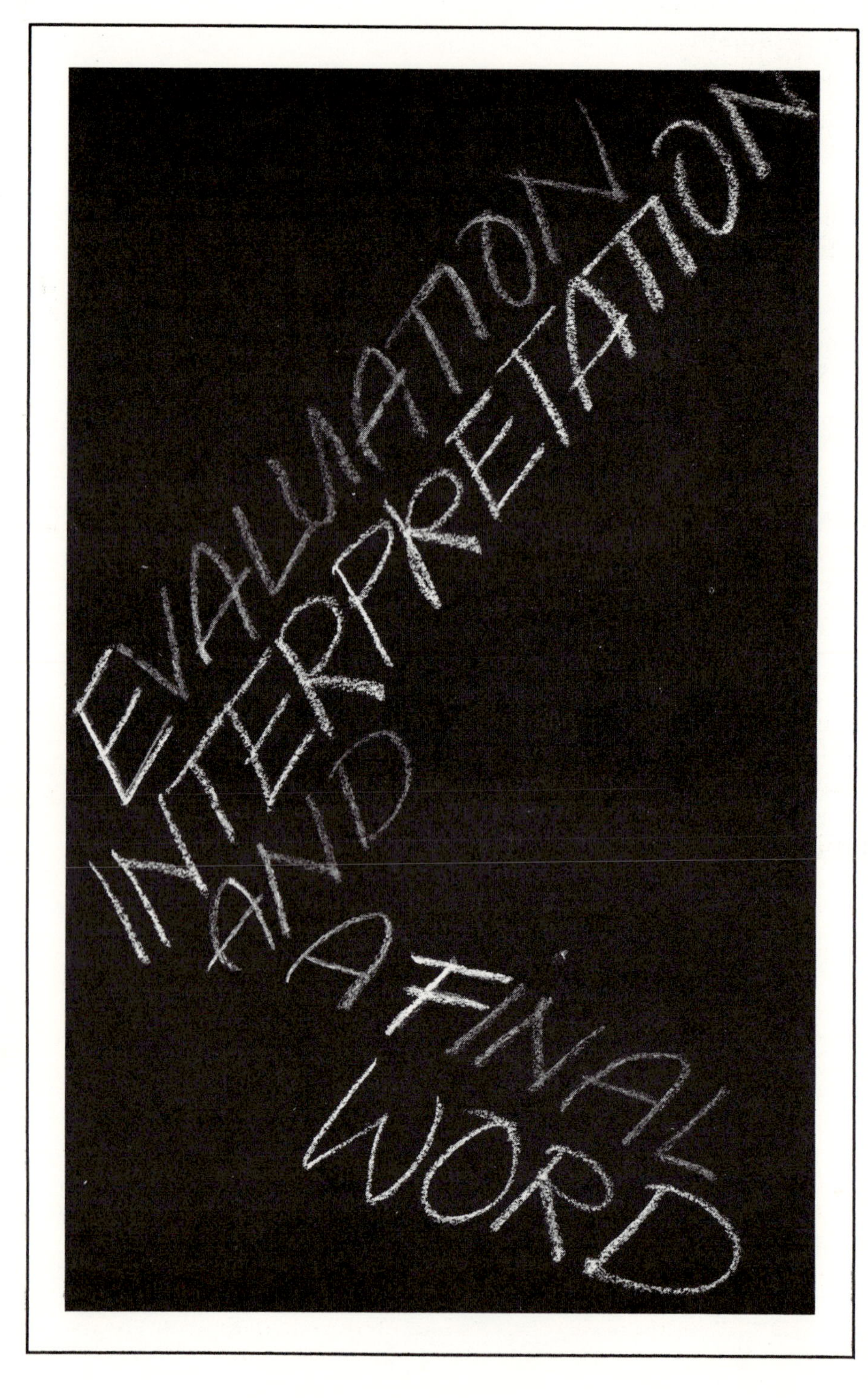
EVALUATION
INTERPRETATION
AND
A FINAL
WORD

Carl Sandburg once wrote, "All my life I have been trying to learn to read, to see and hear, and to write."[1] Speaking of his five years of work on his first novel, he continues, ". . . I [am] still traveling, still a seeker. I should like to think that as I go on writing there will be sentences truly alive, with verbs quivering, with nouns giving color and echoes. It could be, in the grace of God, I shall live to be eighty-nine, as did Hokusai [the great Japanese artist], and speaking my farewell to earthly scenes, I might paraphrase: 'If God had let me live five years longer I should have been a writer.'"

It can be exciting and challenging to children as well as adults to realize that there is no end point in the development of one's use of language. If children are to be led to recognize this, the school must understand and build on the keen interest in language that the young child possesses and the amazing skill he developed from two to five as he learned his language. Teachers need to remind themselves many times of a point that Chukovsky remarks on over and over. "It seems to me," he says, "that, beginning with the age of two, every child becomes for a short period of time a linguistic genius. Later, beginning with the age of five or six, this talent begins to fade. There is no trace left in the eight-year-old of this creativity with words. . . ." He reasons that the child has by this time fully mastered the basic principles of his native language and that the need for creativity has passed. However, he admits that, "If his [the child's] former talent for word invention and construction had not abandoned him, he would, even by the age of ten, eclipse any of us with his suppleness and brilliance of speech" (2).

It is true that the child's need to contrive words of his own to express his meaning has passed because his vocabulary has grown and he handles his grammar with ease. But are these the only reasons for the child's loss of creativity in his use of language? Could it also be true that the school's teaching of reading and writing has kept the child at a low level of language usage while he learned to recognize and reproduce in graphic symbols the commonest of known words without giving him parallel opportunity to use his language at its best and to enjoy making it even better? Has the teacher put her seal of approval on conformity to convention and on the commonplace without any evidence of interest in colorful, vivid, and uniquely personal ways of saying things?

[1] Carl Sandburg, *Complete Poems*. Harcourt, Brace and Co., Inc., 1950, Preface.

The British and Americans at the Anglo-American Seminar in Dartmouth were much impressed by Sybil Marshall, who had taught children in England.

> She protested against the traditional discipline that has called for silence in the classroom and premature emphasis on mistakes. She dwelt on the rich possibilities in the child's own exploration of language, his interest in words, his pleasure in using more of them. To illustrate, she told of a child who was stamping around the room strumming a toy guitar like a Beatle, singing a lyric of his own composing—"maximum capacity, maximum capacity!" The teacher's job is to supply the children plentifully with stories, poems, jingles, songs, and pictures, let them begin selecting for themselves, create an atmosphere of freedom and pleasure in which they continually use words, and take care neither to separate reading, writing, and talking nor isolate English from the other arts (8, p. 42).

Since English is the only subject required throughout the span of public education, it is plain that it should have some kind of continuous, cumulative development from preschool to the end of high school corresponding to the fact that children are growing up. Yet when one searches for this continuity he finds vast disorder and no clear guiding principle. At the Anglo-American Seminar basic differences between the British and American delegations were evident from the beginning, the British inclining to look for the principle of order in the psychological development of the child, while the Americans looked more to subject matter or objective principles of knowledge (9, p. 39). As a matter of fact, what made it possible for the two delegations to understand each other was that, while the two were moving in different directions so that they seemed to have passed in mid-Atlantic, each had experienced some contact with the other's point of view—the British moving toward what had in this country in the nineteen-twenties been called progressive education and the Americans toward the kind of program most Americans picture in their minds when they think of British education. But what was taught in the British schools was strictly English, fundamental work with reading, writing, talking, and listening and learning to use language better. The delegates took pains to make clear that the freedom they wanted for children was not self-indulgence or license "but a way of stimulating them to use their own heads and work more wholeheartedly" (9, p. 44). And the children do work independently with amazing self-control and dependability. Teachers this writer observed were forever saying to children as they completed a task, "Very good. Carry on!" and the children did carry on with purposefulness and independence.

☐ THE RESPONSIBILITY OF THE ELEMENTARY SCHOOL

The schools have always assumed responsibility for the development of language, though the methods, materials, and emphases have changed greatly from time to time. Research has added new knowledge of the way the human mind develops. Case studies have impressed upon teachers and leaders the close relationship between language and all aspects of mental, emotional, and social development. Increased understanding of group processes from the intimate social group to the national and international level has served to emphasize the significance of language in all forms of group interaction. The tremendous increase in the sum total of human knowledge which has come about in recent years has made the significance of vicarious learning stand out clearly. The increased demands which modern life makes on the individual has made ability to communicate outstandingly important.

During the early part of the century elementary schools were silent schools. The teacher who could boast of a room in which one could "hear a pin drop" was proud of her "discipline." Each child worked separately and silently. It was illegal for children to speak to each other even in a whisper. Written communication by means of notes brought dire consequences in many classrooms. "Language" was a "subject" which occupied its little niche in each day's program. Even here there was no real communication; lessons were formal and teacher directed. Children were called on for brief oral or written compositions on subjects which meant little or nothing to them, or they studied letter writing or grammar completely divorced from actual use. Only a few years ago some young student teachers visited a first grade in a large city school system to observe work in the language arts. The children sat rigidly in their seats with hands folded on the desks while the teacher showed them two colored pictures cut from magazines. To lead them to accept her standards, the teacher said, "One of these pictures is for the little boy who does not talk today. The other picture is for the little girl who does not talk today." Later in the morning the teacher attempted to demonstrate for the students a language lesson in which the children were to tell two or three complete sentences each about some pet at home or in the neighborhood. The results of her efforts were discouraging. The children could not learn the lesson emphasized in the presentation of the pictures at one moment and speak freely and spontaneously the next. It is not possible to turn on and off the spigots of a child's thinking at will.

Standards have changed greatly since such procedures received public sanction. Radio, motion pictures, and television emphasize the importance of good speech. The group processes of discussing, planning, and working together which are being utilized more and more in our way of living call for ability to think and respond quickly and well in situations which call for the meeting of minds. The complexity of life and the demands of most vocations make all of the language arts essential for day by day living. These social forces and many others have made educators aware of the fact that all aspects of growth and experience are interrelated. It is no longer possible to think in terms of isolated skills to be taught by meaningless repetition. The language arts are a part of all experience of whatever kind.

Language is so deeply rooted in the whole of human behavior that it is difficult to estimate all its functions clearly. Someone recently remarked on television that 75 percent of an individual's earning power is dependent on his ability to speak and listen. What further proportion of his earning power might depend on his ability to read and write is interesting to conjecture. Any list of goals toward which the school directs its language arts program serves as goals for the entire educational program. Since communication and experience are the means to education and neither functions without language, then language goals and educational goals are one and the same.

☐ DESIRABLE OUTCOMES OF A LANGUAGE ARTS PROGRAM

These are the basic outcomes for which the elementary school strives in its teaching of children:

1. Appreciation of language and recognition of its significance in their own lives as well as its power in human relationships

2. A wholesome self-image which makes possible comfortable interaction with people and experiences
3. Understandings and techniques for effective participation in group life
4. Sensitivity to the feelings, needs, and contributions of others and a sense of social responsibility
5. Effective habits of work and recognition of personal responsibility for achievement
6. Growing intellectual curiosity together with intellectual initiative to follow through to satisfying ends
7. Discriminating and intelligent use of mass media of communication
8. A personal sense of values and maturing moral perception
9. Growing appreciation and enjoyment of worthy personal interests
10. An enlarging concept of and allegiance to the basic values and processes of democratic living both for their own immediate society and for the whole world

Since the elementary schools work with nearly all the children of all the people they have greater opportunity for achieving these outcomes on a wide scale than has any other level of the educational ladder. It requires skill and insight to understand today's children and their needs, and elementary teachers are forever striving to attain the insight and resourcefulness to do a more effective and constructive job.

☐ EVALUATING INDIVIDUAL GROWTH

The language of an individual is in a very real sense the mirror of his personality. A child's spontaneity in the use of language is an indication of his feeling of security. The spontaneity, fluency, and control he shows in his speech indicate quite clearly how well his growth is progressing. The ease of his weaning from the security of home and mother and his adjustment to the life of the school determine his attitude toward the school and the quality of his learning. His speech reflects the normality of the weaning process. The well-adjusted child uses speech freely and with confidence.

Studying the language growth of an individual child is really studying the child as a whole. This cannot be done through pencil and paper tests, either of the standardized variety or teacher-made ones. The most that tests can show is response to arbitrarily selected items of knowledge or skill, and that is usually based largely on memory. Many a child can fill in blanks properly, then misuse the same items in practical situations. He has learned what responses to make in the pencil-and-paper-test situation but not the responses to make in the real life situations. The two are not the same. Studying the child's growth in language means studying his behavior in all types of situations.

Sensibly handled *sociometric studies* reveal a child's place in the social group and the acceptability of his behavior to other children. This knowledge, to be of value, must be followed by intensive study of the child's behavior to learn what attracts or repels other children and why they respond as they do. All behavior which a child manifests is caused by experiences and attitudes which operate in the life of that child. One child may be silent and withdrawn because he has had little experience with children and is so sheltered and dominated by his mother that he has no techniques for participating with other children in play or work experience. Another child may be unacceptable to other children because his experience has caused him to use language aggressively and unpleasantly in order to gain his way or to hold his own with other people. Perhaps a speech defect, poor or different clothing, a foreign accent, or different home standards and demands cause him to be isolated from the group. Not until the teacher is fairly clear as to the cause of the child's problems can she give him the guidance and help he needs.

Anecdotal records, kept in any one of a variety of ways, help the teacher to study a child's development and his learning problems. Some teachers keep a loose-leaf notebook with an index tab for each child. When an incident occurs which is significant, the teacher jots down just enough at the time to recall it, possibly only a word or two, then places a marker in the page so that she can complete the brief sketch of the incident when she has more time after school. Other teachers jot notes on slips and put them into a file or individual envelopes. Any method of recording which carries the greatest values for the time spent is clearly the best method for the teacher to use. The accumulation of incidents and expressions paint a picture of a child which might escape a teacher or be warped out of proper proportions by the teacher's own emotional response to the child.

Elementary school teachers need to become expert in conducting *conferences with parents.* Often a few minutes with a parent sheds a great deal of light on a child's problems. Perhaps the parent explains some of the child's background of physical development or of home or play group experience and aids the teacher in interpreting the child's responses. Sometimes the parent's own attitude toward the child appears as a part of the cause of the child's difficulties. There are many instances in which it is practically impossible to diagnose the problems a child presents without recourse to the home. There are few problems of a serious nature which can be solved without parent-teacher co-operation.

Keeping a file of children's written work also helps with study of individual growth. Children like to put away in large folders, portfolios, or envelopes, samples of their practical and creative writing. Often a child will bring to the teacher something he has written and compare it with his earlier work, saying happily, "Look! This is the way I wrote last fall. Don't you think I am doing lots better now?" or "This is the best report in my folder. I want to show it to my mother the next time she comes to school so she can see how much better I'm doing." Children evaluate their own growth quite frankly and accurately when they are encouraged to do so. The evaluation which follows was written by a fifth grade pupil of the Indiana University Laboratory School.

A STORY ABOUT MYSELF

I am ten almost eleven years old and I am getting on pretty well. I am usually on time for school but sometimes I just barely make it. I have been late about three or four times this year. The reason I am late is that I usually ride with my girl friend in fourth grade and sometimes we don't go till 8:25.

Some children I like and some I don't like. Most of my friends are in other grades. I try to be friendly with those I don't like but I really wish they'd either make friends or leave me alone. I try not to be selfish but I think I am a little bit. At home I find myself asking for the biggest and most of things. I am going to try harder.

There are some subjects which I am not interested in. I try to pay attention but sometimes it's hard. I mean to try harder on this too. The subjects I am most interested in are spelling, reading, and interest groups.

I am a pretty good student in arithmetic, spelling, reading, and music. I think I am good in arithmetic because I usually get all the problems right and they are very easy for me. Though it is not my favorite subject arithmetic is quite interesting to me except when the problems are too easy. I think I could do harder fraction problems and I would like to learn how to add and subtract unlike fractions.

I think I do well in spelling because I usually get all the words right. When I have had no time to study I miss about three or four.

I have always been pretty good in reading because I learned to read when I was five years old. I like to read very much.

I think I sing pretty well in music and co-operate pretty well too. I enjoy singing a lot but I would rather sing in the music room than our room because I like to sing better when I sing with the piano.

I think I need to improve on Social Studies and studies where we have discussions. I try to pay attention and I usually succeed but sometimes it's hard.

Joan

Experience in self-evaluation helps to build pride in achievement and confidence that there can be more achievement. *Confidence is memory of past successes.* The child who sees himself growing and finds satisfaction in that growth is confident that he can press on to ever higher goals.

☐ LANGUAGE AND INTELLIGENT BEHAVIOR

The one true aristocracy in the English-speaking world is the aristocracy of brains, of thinking, and language expresses and reflects thinking (9). The training of the higher mental processes should be a part of the language arts program from kindergarten through college. The mental and linguistic life of the child should be a steady upward progression if education means anything at all. The development of language is in itself the development of mentality. One might say that intelligence is merely the soil in which the language function grows. The concept of intelligence is meaningless except when expressed in terms of intelligent behavior.

If children are to develop the ability to think and to behave intelligently they must have experiences which are planned toward this end. Language cannot be substituted *for* experience in concrete situations but it should be used *in* all types of concrete situations. Any use of oral or written symbols, no matter how abstract, should be connected with experience in a gapless chain, every link of which has its meaning clearly established by reference to experience. It is doubtful whether any but the brightest and most mature of elementary school children are capable of entertaining ideas which are completely divorced from their usual concrete settings or of recognizing the application of those ideas in unfamiliar settings. This capacity belongs to the mature mind. When children are faced with the task of formulating ideas through the medium of language alone and from an inadequate background of experience their ideas are inevitably vague and inaccurate. If they then go on from year to year fashioning new ideas from the unsatisfactory ideas of the year before, little real intellectual development can take place. Language cannot mirror reality for children. Talking or reading about a flight in an airplane cannot give the child the experience of the flight; the flight is so much more than anything that can be said or written about it. More attention to the real significance of the content children are studying would do much to offset verbalism and prevent the inadequate and erroneous ideas children so frequently form.

Behavior and understanding are closely related. Clear ideas are the outgrowth of opportunity to think through and talk experiences. Thorough understanding of the facts and implications of one's behavior tends to result in reasoned choices and sensible behavior. The human being, even in his less mature stages, is a rational individual. He is interested in seeing things as they are, in accepting cause and effect relationships which he can understand, and in acting constructively. Learning to think and reason brings with it a sense of power which adds greatly to the child's security in a complex and confusing world.

□ EVALUATING THE LANGUAGE ARTS PROGRAM

Evaluation is an integral part of the language arts program; it is not an activity engaged in periodically to check on learning. The efficiency of teaching and learning in any school may be roughly gauged by the extent to which language growth keeps pace with practical skill and experience.

The test of anyone's use of language, be he adult or child, lies in the answer to the question, Does the language meet the needs of the individual and fit satisfactorily into the social setting in which he operates? If in addition to being adequate, the use of language can be stimulating, interesting, and pleasantly original and creative, so much the better. Adequacy of speech for the elementary school means the level of informal, everyday speech used by respected people, the accepted use of the term "colloquial." Adequacy of written language calls for reasonable conformity to accepted patterns of practical writing so that others may read and understand with ease.

During the course of a year there will be many occasions when the teacher and children will pause to evaluate their language growth. A child or the teacher may call attention to the efficiency with which business has been transacted in a planning session. "Did you notice how rapidly we took care of plans today? Let's think what made this a good planning period." "Yes, we stayed right on the track and many people gave us good ideas. We listened to each other so carefully that there was no repeating and we could think quickly. Now we know just what we are going to do and have plenty of time to carry out our plans." Or there may be evaluation of progress reports made by the children. The teacher turns the group's attention from what is being reported to the way the reports are being given. She asks, "Now that we have listened to several reports, let's see what suggestions we can make for good reporting. What do people need to know? How can we tell it to them clearly and without taking too much time for talking?" "Suppose we list the good points you have made. First, we need to be reminded of the problem you are working on. Next, we need to know just how much you have accomplished. And last, we need to know what you plan to do to complete your work. If you need our help, explain your difficulty or ask your questions clearly. Clear thinking saves time and helps us to understand just where we are in our work." There will be times when the group will list definite standards on chart or chalk board and check their performance against their standards. They may analyze what makes good oral reading, or what one should try to keep in mind in contributing to discussion or in writing a business letter. The procedure is always a positive one. Children are not made to feel that they have failed or that they are completely satisfactory but that every wise person has goals on ahead toward which he is striving. Children can learn to analyze their own strengths and weaknesses in a thoroughly objective manner and without feelings of guilt, embarrassment or unwholesome inflation of ego.

Emphasis on individual needs and individual growth helps children to see that all people have strength that can be drawn upon as well as weakness that needs to be built up. They learn to respect and like people for what they are and to take genuine interest in their achievements. Children who are themselves guided in this manner are quick to note the improvement in others and are spontaneous and generous in their approval of it. Genuine friendly interest in each other's growth provides incentive for further growth because children value the opinions of their peers.

Growth and improvement in the use of language is more dependent on inner motivation and desire to improve than it is on actual teaching. If a child who comes from a home in which he has learned poor usage is quite satisfied with that usage and feels no personal need to improve it, there is little that the teacher can do. True, he may learn enough to give the right answers when they are called for but he goes from the classroom straight to the playground and uses the forms he is accustomed to accepting. If the child sees value in improving and wishes to do so, he may leave the elementary school with language of appreciably higher quality than that of his home or neighborhood. Since individual motivation is so vital to progress, the real test of a good language arts program lies in the quality of inspiration it affords the child for his own self-improvement.

The purpose of any good evaluation program in the elementary school is to find what each child has achieved and what he needs help with. Rating of children is not the school's function but rather the development of children. Rating, as it has been used in the schools, has often been devastating, tearing children down rather than building them up. A good evaluation program centers its attention upon constructive guidance at all times.

Children are encouraged to keep a list of the books they have read so that the teacher may guide their reading. Conversation while the book is being recorded is usually all that is necessary to judge the quality of comprehension the child has brought to his reading of it. Reading is evaluated in a variety of ways but in the end quality which serves the individual's needs and meets the needs of the social situation is satisfactory quality. Handwriting, spelling, usage, vocabulary, even dramatic interpretation are evaluated co-operatively by the teacher and the individual or group concerned, and always in terms of the purpose, the effort and attitude the individual displays, and the growth needs that are manifested. Evaluation and guidance go together at all times.

□ INTERPRETING THE SCHOOL'S EFFORTS TO PARENTS

Many parents are bewildered and confused by the changes that have taken place in the teaching of the language arts in the elementary schools. They remember schools in which there were daily drill periods in penmanship, assigned lessons and tests in spelling, and daily periods for phonics, word drill, and reading from readers. They recognize the need for language skills and fear that their children may not develop them. Whenever one hears of an outburst of parental criticism of the schools it is usually based on the "failure of the schools to teach the three R's."

A part of the problem is revealed in the response made by a mature teacher to such criticism. She said, "When I graduated from high school more than thirty years ago there were twenty-one of us in the graduating class. The population of the little town I lived in has not changed greatly since that time. This year there are more than one hundred young people in the high school graduating class. I am sure that among that group are twenty-one who read, write, and spell as well as we did when we graduated." That part of the answer is very important. Elementary schools have assumed the obligation of helping each child to attain the highest possible level of linguistic performance of which he is capable. Children who present learning problems are studied, their problems diagnosed, and guidance is planned to meet their needs. In a good modern school no child is allowed to fall by the wayside and be left out of the learning program because he differs from the majority in his needs. In a democratic society every individual child is considered worthy of the best that can be done for him.

Additional numbers and wide range in ability and need are not the only reasons for the changes that have been taking place in educational philosophy and in teaching procedures, nor do they constitute the most important reasons. The basic factor in the changes that have taken place is the fact that more is known about how children grow and develop than was known even a few years ago. Studies have been made also of the language needs of adults in day by day living so that school people have clearer concepts of what children ought to learn in the elementary school as well as how they can best learn it.

Changes in educational practice are not the result of the whims of leaders who sit at college desks thinking of new and different things to do. Schools and educational programs belong to and exist for parents and their children. School people are the designated agents who carry out the school's function. There would be no teachers, supervisors, administrators, nor colleges for teacher education if there were no children and youth who needed to be served. All of those positions exist because young people need to be helped to get ready for active participation in adult society. The primary job of education is that done by teachers with children. All other workers in the educational group are employed to facilitate this basic service.

It is the task of educational leaders to be forever studying society and its needs. They have studied problems of juvenile delinquency and have come to realize that the great proportion of delinquents tend to be young people who did not like school and who felt that the schools were not giving them what they wanted and needed. A child who feels secure in the knowledge that he has a real place at school, and that others care about his progress is not apt to become delinquent. If the work children do at school seems real and vital to them because it fits into their out-of-school as well as in-school experience, they are eager for more of it. Children like to feel that they are growing in ways that seem important to them. A program of educational experience that is geared to their needs and that provides really valuable and life-centered experience will always catch and hold their interest.

Leaders have looked also at the crowded mental hospitals of our country and have learned from the psychologists and psychiatrists that most cases of maladjustment can be traced back to the early home and school experience of children. They have learned that the best insurance known for wholesome mental stability is a happy, well-adjusted childhood. They have learned too, that children are happy and that they work hard and fruitfully when their experiences are meaningful and vital to them and adjusted to their background, their ability, and their present needs. Children lack the maturity to think in terms of long-deferred goals. That ability comes only with maturity. Everyone who has watched children work to achieve ends that are important to them—learning to ride a bicycle, making a model airplane, building a playhouse, putting on a circus—knows that children are not unwilling to work. But the work must have meaning to them now, as they do it. Children are sensible and reasonable persons; they want what they do to make sense and they want to perceive its values *now*, not when they are grown.

Teachers and all others in the educational family need to give a great deal of thought and attention to helping parents understand the changes taking place in schools and the reasons for them. No one can interpret to others what he does not himself clearly understand and appreciate. This fact places on all who work with and for children the obligation to study the changes going on in life outside the school. They need to study the research and the educational literature which offers new knowledge and guidance in adjusting to changing needs.

Many teachers have given careful thought to ways of working with parents and helping them to understand the program of the school, and have devised highly satisfactory methods for home and school co-operation. Some teachers, especially of kindergarten and first grade children, are holding individual conferences with the parents of each child before school opens, becoming acquainted with the parent, learning something of the background and the interests of the child, and inviting the parent to come to school frequently to observe and participate. Introductory conferences are valuable to both parent and teacher and form a good basis for later co-operation.

Teachers have found it worthwhile to invite the parents to visit school, a few at a time, at least once during each semester. Notes are sent home in September telling of the plan and encouraging the parents to visit at other times as well, because the school welcomes their interest. The notes which bear the special invitation for a half day of visitation are signed by the children and each child takes great interest in seeing to it that his mother accepts the invitation or arranges to join a later group if the time set is not convenient. On the day of visitation, the mother may come to school in the afternoon with the child. The program for the session is just the regular work which would be going on were the parents not there, except that some morning activities may be transferred to afternoon if the children wish to do so. When the session is over, upper grade boys and girls take care of any children who must wait at school for their mothers. An older child brings in a teapot of hot water with tea bags and wafers and the teacher and the mothers arrange for tea very informally and begin their discussion in thoroughly relaxed and friendly manner over their teacups. The teacher explains the purpose and values she sees in what the children have been doing and how it all fits into the total program. Parents are encouraged to talk freely and to question or challenge as they wish, but to think of the program for the group as a whole as well as for their own individual child.

Conferences which take the place of written reports to the home offer opportunity to explain the work of each child and to interpret it to the parent. Many teachers feel that such conferences have great value to them as well as to the parents. Rating and comparing children achieves little that is of value and is often devastating in its effect on children. Conferences with parents center attention on the individual child, his strengths, his interests, his needs, and the ways in which home and school can work together for his best good. There are no rigid grade standards. Parents are helped to see that learning is a continuous process which goes on throughout life.

The home, the school, the church, the community and all of society are the child's teachers. The number of hours per year that the school works with the child is small indeed compared with the total in which he is influenced by other educative forces. Conferences between parent and teacher help to analyze the influences operating on the child both in school and out, and to plan constructively for the child's welfare. Moreover, these conferences help to weld the school and the home in better relationships.

It is exciting and challenging to realize that there is no end point in the development of the language arts. It is the school's task to sharpen the child's interest, to develop functional skills which he knows how to use effectively in the many types of situations which he encounters in day by day living, and to motivate him to be "a traveler and a seeker," seeking to do what he does not only adequately but artistically as well.

The basic impulses of man have been described as two in number, *the possessive impulse* and *the creative impulse*. The possessive impulse tends to concern itself with the acquisition of material things and with power over others, and is a source of conflict and disharmony among men. This impulse is responsible for the hidden poverty of our lives, outwardly rich but starved within. The creative impulse, which is concerned with making and doing, gives direction and meaning to our activities and transforms life into an art (7). Akin to that impulse and probably a part of it, though it appears to be lacking in many people, is the desire to acquire knowledge and skill to build up oneself and to enlarge and refine one's method of thinking and operating, both for self and for others.

The framework of our system of education has been fashioned by the society which it serves. The virtues and the deficiencies of that society have been accepted on equal terms. Some think of our schools as fostering the possessive impulse to the exclusion of the impulse to be creative. ". . . the American child breathes with the American air the ambition to acquire and hold his share of the good things of the earth" (7). The creative impulse is present in the child also but it needs opportunity, encouragement, and guidance for growth.

Since schooling occupies so little of a lifetime and all the rest of his growth one must achieve under his own power, perhaps the greatest service a teacher can render a child is to build up his self-respect, his sense of obligation to himself, and his sense of inner power to achieve. This may be what was in the mind of Jesus when he gave his followers the injunction, "Thou shalt love thy neighbor as thyself." The person who holds himself to a high standard usually does it for the sake of others as well as for himself. The social implication is not lacking and the creative possibility is there also.

This mid-century period is a period of transition. Many things that make up life are in flux. Not only are maps being changed, national boundaries erased, old cultures and forms of government dissolved, but whole peoples are faced with basic changes in their patterns of behavior, ideals, and standards of morality. If teachers could give to children some experience with the artist's way of working, some desire to go beyond what is practical and essential to security and prosperity, perhaps that experience would be the most valuable preparation for the drama of living. Classrooms should not be made into factories for pouring knowledge and skills into children as into rows of empty cups. Classrooms should be made into workshops and studios where children seek creatively and co-operatively for experience and learning. Perhaps such an approach would help to solve some of the social ills of this period. This generation of children must rebuild and reshape much that is crumbling and out of order in the world, and the schools must prepare them for that rebuilding. Little that appears solid and immovable can be depended upon to remain so. Children must be taught how to learn and grow, how to stretch on tiptoe to higher achievement, greater satisfactions, more worthy goals.

☐ SELECTED REFERENCES ☐

1. Bodmer, Frederick, *The Loom of Language.* (Lancelot Hogben, Ed.). New York: W. W. Norton & Co., Inc., 1944.
2. Chukovsky, Kornei, *From Two to Five.* Berkeley: University of California Press, 1963.
3. Dixon, John, *Growth Through English.* Reading, England: National Association for the Teaching of English, 1967.
4. D'Evelyn, Katherine E., *Individual Parent-Teacher Conferences.* New York: Bureau of Publications, Teachers College, Columbia University, 1945.
5. Hayakawa, S.I., *Language in Action.* New York: Harcourt Brace & Company, Inc., 1941.
6. Frazier, Alexander, editor, *New Directions in Elementary English.* Champaign, Illinois: National Council of Teachers of English, 1967.
7. Hudnut, Joseph, *Architecture and the Spirit of Man.* Cambridge: Harvard University Press, 1949.
8. Marshall, Sybil, *An Experiment in Education.* Cambridge, England: The University Press, 1966.
9. Muller, Herbert, *The Uses of English.* New York: Holt, Rinehart and Winston, Inc., 1967.
10. Whitehead, Frank, *The Disappearing Dais: A Study of the Principles and Practice of English Teaching.* London: Chatto and Windus, 1966.

INDEX

Appropriate selected references may be found at the end of each chapter.

Abstract concepts, introducing, 169
Abstract language, 25-26
Abstract words, 237
Acceptance, within group, 147
Accuracy, 146; in spelling, 392
Active participation, in dramatic play, 460-462
Activities, transitions among, 117
Adaptation, by teacher, 203
Adjectives, 25, 374
Adjustment: to physical handicaps, 220-223; to school, 144
Adolescent, 42; self-understanding, 176
Adult pressures, 59
Adult wisdom, absorption of, 96
Adverbs, 25, 374
Age, and teaching reading, 255
Aggression, 108
Alphabet: Initial Teaching, 264-265; learning of, 258
American English, 8-9
Anagrams, 172
Analytical listening, 132-133
Anecdotal records, 480
Anger response, 40
Anglo-American Seminar, 476
Appreciation, development of, 39-42
Appreciative listening, 132-133
Aptitude, 49-50
Article, 375
Articulation, 153; differences in, 53; spelling and, 394-395
Assertions, 30
Association, 22; preschool, 76; responses of, 23
Attention: listening and, 129, 135, 137; obtaining, through questions, 30
Attention span, 109, 115, 135, 137
Attentive listening, 132-133
Attitudes, 20-21; abstractions of, 26; development of, 39-42
Atmosphere, influence of, 62-63
Audience, use of, and speech improvement, 205
Audio-visual aids, 137
Auditory acuity, 131
Awareness: interaction and, 27-28; of others, 37

Baby talk, 51
Basal reading programs, 260-262
Bedtime soliloquies, 78
Beginning reading, 260
Behavior, 20-21; language and, 482-483
Bibliographies, 338
Bilingualism, 55-58, 223-225; in elementary school, 464-473
Biography, 36
Block play, 113
Book lists, 296-297
Books, 418-445; criteria for selecting, 436; interest in, 111; types and variety, 288-289, 433-436
Brain damage, 222
British spellings, 388-392
Broadcasting, 197-198
Business letters, 327, 332-334

Cause and effect thinking, 36-37
Children's Theater, 460
Choral reading, 211, 431-433
Church, influence of, 65
Classification: of objects, 34; of things, 33
Classroom: emotional and social climate, 314; informal setting, 144-145, 177
Classroom library, 292
Cleft palate, 97
Club interests, 174
Collective monologue, 27
Colloquial speech, 363
Comic books, 439-442; banning of, 441; categories of, 439; influence of, 66; interpreting, 442; quality of, 440
Commands, 30

Communication, 1; ability in, 13; child's, 21; direct, 327; early forms of, 74; interest in, 172; oral, 3, 28–30; other than oral, 20–21; by signs, 3; by spoken language, 170–171; types of, 30; verbal, 3, 28–30
Community, influence of, 64–66; as language laboratory, 64–65
Community agencies, 65–66
Comparison, concepts of, 33
Compensation training, 221
Comprehension, 89
Concepts: growth of, 34–35; of language, 11
Concrete language, 25–26
Conditioning, preschool, 76
Conferences, parent-teacher, 481–489
Confusion, 22
Congratulations, letters of, 335
Connotations, 31
Consonant sounds, 268; articulating, 154; initial, 394
Content area: newness of, 24; spelling and, 398–399
Conversation, 28–30, 149; carrying on, 30; defined, 136; face-to-face, 192; infant's, 75; informal, 190–192; kindergarten, 117
Copying: advantages in, 334; dictation and, 307–308
Costumes, in dramatic play, 450–454
Courtesy, 31, 158; learning, 107; in letter writing, 335; in speaking, 360
Creative expression, 313–314; climate for, 314–315; forms of, 316–317
Creative impulses, 489
Creative thought, 24, 152
Creative writing, 316, 343–345; elementary grades, 351; primary grades, 351; practical writing and, 351
Criticism, 30
Crosby, Muriel, 296
Crying, 72–73
Culturally deprived, 212–214; Head Start and, 49; oral language, 146; home, effect of, on, 122
Culturally disadvantaged, reading follow-up program, 275–276
Cursive writing, 310, 380

Deafness, 217–218, 220
Defective speech, 216–220
Democratic procedures, 457–458
Derision, 30
Descriptive qualities, abstraction of, 26
Determiner, 375
Development, kindergarten and, 118
Deviation, of language development, 206
Dialectologist, 13
Dialects, 14, 143, 157, 203, 367; Negro, 212; regional, 376–377
Diaries, 316
Dictation: copying, 303, 307–308; in language program, 306; teacher's role in, 304–307; written language and, 302
Diction, 382–383
Dictionary, 248, 292; introduction to, 388; use of, 410–411; teaching, 14
Direct communications, 327
Direct teaching, 20–21
Directions, giving and following, 196
Disagreement, 28
Discipline, classroom, 476, 477
Discussion, 150, 192–194
Dispute, 28
Distinguishing, ability in, 34
Doll play, 450
Dramatic interpretation, 446–463
Dramatic play, 90, 113, 116, 457; active/passive participation, 460–462; behavior and motivation, 458–459; costumes, 450, 454; elementary school, 455–456; individual needs, 456–457; kindergarten, 448–452; learning roles, 454–455; preparing for, 448; preschool child, 109; primary school, 452–455; problem solving through, 456–457; speech correction, 459; speech response, 106
Dropouts, 17, 18

Early readers, 258–259
Ease, child at, 144–145, 314
Eclectic method, in reading, 274–275
Educational practice, changes in, 487
Egocentric speech, 78–79
Elementary school: dramatic play, 455–456; foreign language in, 464–473; language arts in, 12–14, 42–44; responsibility of, 477–478;

Emotional tensions, 97
Emotions, 39
Encouragement, of physically handicapped, 222
England, reading, teaching of, 276–278; spelling differences, 388-392
English language, American version, 8-9; contemporary, 4-5; history of, 5-8; a major language, 8
English (British) spellings, 388-392; patterns in, 390-392
Enjoyment, reading for, 289
Enunciation, 155; spelling and, 394-395
Environment: influence of, 62-63; interest in, 119; language development and, 123-124; language growth and, 177-179; poor, handicap of, 210-212
Ethical questions, dramatizing, 458–459
Ethical standards, acceptance of, 175-176
Evaluation program, purpose of, 485
Experiences, 21-23, 88-93; enriching, 123; expression of, 317-321; firsthand, 22, 62-53, 216; lack of, a handicap, 210-212; linking, 111; with other children, learning through, 113-116; richness and breadth of, 315, 325; self-centered outlook and, 26-27; sharing, 190-192; with things, learning through, 111-113; understanding and, 22; vicarious, 22-23, 62-63, 419; written language and, 350-352
Explaining, 151
Explanation, letters of, 335
Exploration, in kindergarten, 112–113
Expression, 152; of experiences, 317-321; imaginative, 313; individual modes of, 32; poetic, 319, 345-350; as therapy, 313; thought and, 24; written, 300 intermediate grades, 324-325; primary grades, 321-322
Eye dominance, and speech defects, 218

Face-to-face conversation, 192
Facial expressions, 19-20
Family influence, 50-52
Fantasy, preschool, 94
Feeling, 20-21, 39
Files, of child's work, 481
Finger painting, 112
Finger plays, 92
Firsthand experience, 22, 62-63; mentally retarded, 216
First words, 76-78
FLES, 466, 467, 469, 470
Foreign language, 223-225; choice of, 470; conclusions drawn from, 468-469; curriculum, 467-468; elementary school, 464-473; enthusiasm for, 468-470; plans, variation in, 467-468; preadolescent study, 465; principles of learning, 472; teaching of, 466; use of, in the home, 55-58
Foreign language speaking pupils, teaching English to, 470-472
Forms, writing up, 327

Generalizations, concept of, 25
Generative grammar, 371-372
Gestures, 19-20, 74, 108
Gifted children, talking age, 48
Grammar, 357-385; contemporary usage, 358-362; defined, 358; generative, 371-372; improving, 362-363; inherent interest in, 372-373; meanings of, 369-370; new approach, 370-371; terminology of, 374-375;
Grammarian, 14
Grammatical errors, correcting, 65
Grammatical form, differences in, 32
Grammatical usage, 156, 358-369; improving, 362-369; kindergarten, 110-111; sympathetic help needed, 211
Graphic symbols, 2
Group: acceptance by, 147; changes within, 115; specialized language of, 174
Group discussion, 193-194
Group dramatization, 211
Group play, 109, 113
Group processes, understanding, 193
Grouping, in spelling, 408-409, 410
Growth: kindergarten, 118; in written language, 350-352
Growth index, talkativeness as, 87
Growth measurement, 87-90
Guidance, 104-105, 122; through reading, 293; in reading material, 283, 286-288; verbal, 104-105

Hand dominance, and speech defects, 218
Handwriting, 377–381; drill in, 380–381; legibility in, 378; individuality in, 378. *See also* Penmanship
Hard of hearing, 58, 217–218, 220
Harelip, 97
Head Start program, 49, 122–123, 212; following up, 145–146
Health, and language development, 97
Hearing, and articulation, 154
Hearing loss, 58, 217–218, 220. *See also* Deafness
Hero worship, 42
History, early interest in, 36
Home, language in, 122–123
Home atmosphere, 54
Home influence, 50–52
Human affairs, interest in, 175
Human behavior, drama and, 458–459
Human relationships, language in, 13, 37–39

Ideals: abstractions of, 26; development of, 39–42
Ideas, newness of, 24
Identity, loss of, 38
Illiterates, 17, 18
Illusion, and reality, 36
Imaginative expression, 313–314
Imaginative writing, 316
Impulses: possessive, 489; creative, 489–490
Independence, growth of, 41; through written language, 303
Independent writing, 306–307, 308–311, 312–313, 405
Indirect teaching, 20
Individual activities, 116
Individual differences, 120–122, 202–228; in reading, 270–271
Individual needs, 456–457, 485
Individual problems, diagnosing, 272
Individual reading, 438–439; program, 286–288
Infants: first words, 76–78; speech development, 72–73
Inflections, 74, 75
Informal conversation, 190–192
Informality, schoolroom, 144–145, 177
Information, authoritative, need for, 116; seeking of, through questions, 30
Ingrowth stage, of speaking, 79
Initial consonant sounds, 394
Initial Teaching Alphabet, 264–265
Inner resources, 314
Inoffensive language, 173
Inquisitiveness, 420
Integrative behavior, 61
Intellectual equipment, child's, 48
Intelligence, and language growth, 96
Intelligence level, and speech defects, 217
Intelligence quotient, raising, 145
Intelligible language, 153
Interaction, 28; among small children, 103; awareness and, 27–28; democratic, 457; mature, 30; nursery school, 109
Interests: developing, 174–176; expanding, 116; written language and, 350–352
Intermediate school: goals, in written expression, 352–353; oral language in, 166–201
Intonations, 74, 75, 157
Introducing people, 197
Introversion, reading habit and, 282

Jargon, 77, 107, 108; infant, 75
Juncture, and meaning, 12

Kindergarten: conversation in, 117; dramatic play, 448–452; five-year-old in, 110–111; individual differences, 120–122; language in, 117–120; language development, 103–125; language experience, 120; reading in, 259–260; writing in, 302
Knowledge, resources for, 292

Language: abstract/concrete, 25–26; arbitrary nature of, 11–12; behavior and, 482–483; changes in, 9, 244–246; continuing program, 188–189; defined, 3; ease in use of, 144, 146–147; functions of, 18–19, 42–44; growth of, 244–246, 484; human relationships and, 31; improvement of, 485; informal, 179–180; intelligible, 153; interest

Language *(cont.)*
in, 174–175; intermediate school, 167–201; learning of, basic equipment, 47–50; originality, 161; place of, 42–44; science of, 17; significance of, 1–2, 4; social aspects, 31–32; social significance, 4; social studies and, 180–181; substandard, improving, 375–376; sound structure, 10; teaching, opportunities for, 181–183; thought and, 23–25
Language ability, intermediate school, 174–176, 177
Language arts: development of, 43; elementary school, 12–13; formalized teaching, 167–168; interrelationships, 63–64
Language arts program: evaluation, 483–486; results sought for, 478–479
Language development, 43, 47–69; community influences, 64–66; deviation in, 206; ease and confidence in, 143–144; home and, 122–123; imitation and, 106; kindergarten, 103–125; mental development and, 71; nursery school, 103–125; preschool, 71–98; reading and, 257–258; responsibility for, 477–478; school and, 59–64; science and, 175, 181; social studies and, 183–186; stimulation of challenge in, 179; rise of language, 148
Language experience, kindergarten, 120
Language experience approach, 266–268
Language function, 127
Language growth, 47–69, 244–246; environment and, 177–179; evaluating, 477–482, 484; stimulating, 105–106
Language inventions, 83–84
Language needs, individual differences, 202–228
Language requirements, analyzing, 171
Language response, 158
Language skills: developing, 189–199; social studies in, 183–186; science program and, 186–187
Language usage: before and after school, 179–180; levels of, 230
Lateral dominance, 218–219
Learning: child's responsibility, 405; through experience, 111–113, 113–116
Learning role, 292
Left-handedness, 218–219
Legibility, in handwriting, 378
Letter sounds, difficulty with, 108
Letters: drafts of, 334, 336; writing of, 330–336. *See also* Business letters, Personal letters
Lexicographer, 14
Library: children's, 436–438; influence of, 65
Library experience, 292
Linguistic approach, to reading, 263
Linguistic aptitude, 96
Linguistic etiquette, 369
Linguistic geographer, 13
Linguistic historian, 13
Linguistic maturity, 402
Linguistically gifted child, 206–209
Linguistically handicapped, 49
Linguistics, 13
Lip reading, 220
Lisping, 217
Listening, 126–141, 146; attention and, 135; evaluating, 138–139; guide to, 128; importance of, 171–172; improving, 138; kinds of, 130–133; possible dangers, 198; preschool experience, 134–135; primary school, 142–165; process of, 256; to radio, 197–198; responses to, 131; stages of, 130–133; television and, 139–140, 197–198; types of, 131
Listening ability, 131, 133–134, 136–138
Listening habits, 135
Listening problems, 135–136
Listening readiness, 133
Listening skills, 189–190
Literature, 289, 425–428; child's interest in, 315
Localisms, 154
Logical memory, 79
Logical reasoning, 27

Malformations, physiological defects, 218
Manuscript writing, 310, 378–380
Marginal listening, 132–133
Marginal vocabulary, 231, 232, 235

Marionettes, 459
Mass media: influence of, 66; oral reading and, 167
Mathematical thinking, 187
Maturity, through reading, 435
Meaning: conveying, 12; sound patterns, 129; of words, 26
Meaning-bearing words, 129
Memory, in speech, 79
Mental capacity, listening and, 131
Mental deficiency, 50
Mental development, 71, 90; language and, 17–45; in nursery school, 104
Mental growth, 112
Mental operations, developing, 79
Mentally retarded, 215–216
Microfiche, 3
Microfilm, 3
Migrant population, 214–215
Minutes, club meeting, 327
Mnemonic aids, 79
Monologue, collective, 93; two-year-old, 78–80
Mother-child relationships, 50–52
Mother language, 1
Motivation, 51–52; and drama, 458–459; preschool, 76; of slow learner, 216
Movement, restrictions on, 221
Muscular restrictions, 221
Muscles, speech, 72
Music, 117

Naming activity, 86
Nebraska Literature Project, 315, 425–428
Negativism, 58
Negro, culturally deprived, 212–214
Negro dialect, 212
New English, 13
New math, 188
Newspapers, school, 339
Non-English-speaking students, teaching English to, 470–472
Nonsentences, 372
Noun phrase, 375
Nouns: use of, 25
preschool, 85
Number concepts, 34–35
Number sense, 185
Nursery rhymes, dramatizing, 453
Nursery school: individual differences, 120–122; language in, 116–117; language development, 103–125; preschool child in, 107–110; writing in, 301

Objects, properties of, 33
Observation, 146
Offensive language, 172–174
Omnibus words, 34
Ongoing interest, 148
Only child, language of, 52–53
Oracy, 162
Oral expression, 24
Oral language, 62, 149; of culturally deprived, 146; development of, 189; forms of, 161; growth in, 163; importance of, 167; in intermediate school, 166–201; mass media and, 167; primacy of, 198–199; spelling and, 394–395; writing and, 63–64, 162, 169
Oral reading, 205, 422–425; primary grades, 269–270
Oral reports, 196–197
Orientation, to things, 32–35
Original stories, making up, 118
Originality, 161
Orthography, 2
Outlining, need for, 196

Pantomime, 459–460
Paragraphing, 360
Parental affection, need for, 96
Parents: interpreting school to, 486–491; school visits by, 488; teacher's conference, 489
Parts of speech, preschool use of, 85–86
Parliamentary procedure, 194–195
Passivity, in dramatic play, 460–462
Peer groups, influence of, 61–62
Peer relationships, 41, 113–116
Penmanship, 310, 377–381. *See also* Handwriting
Perception, in spelling, 394
Personal letters, 316, 317, 327, 332, 334–336
Personality: analyzing, 38–39; speech and, 364
Personality development, 50–59; speech and, 97–98
Personality problems: reading and, 59; speech defects and, 219–220
Perspective, in listening, 129
Phoneme syllable, 391
Phonics, 262–263; spelling and, 408–409

Phonology, principles of, 82
Physical equipment, child's, 47–48
Physically handicapped, 220–223; language development and, 96–97
Picture books, 92, 110
Picture dictionaries, 248
Pictures, interest in, 108
Pitch, and meaning, 12
Pitman, Sir James, 264
Planning, 150
Play materials, speech response, 106
Play writing, 316
Playground program, 461
Plurals, forming, 82
Poetic expression, 319, 345–350
Poetry, 307, 311, 316, 317–321, 418–445; adaptability, 429–430; choral reading, 431–432; enjoyment of, 428–431; forms of, 346; humorous, 429; natural language, 94; nonsense, 429; preschool child and, 110; reading, 430–431; samples, 311–312; sensory content, 428; singing quality, 428; story element, 428; tempo and rhythm, 432; in unison, 432
Possessive impulse, 489
Potential vocabulary, 231–232, 235
Preadolescents: foreign-language study, 462; growth in, 41; self-understanding, 176; vocabulary growth, 62
Precocious child, 207–208
Preschool years: language development in, 71–98; listening experiences, 134; nursery school, 107–110; vocabulary, 84–86, 237–239
Pressure, freedom from, 315
Primary grades: creative writing, 351; dramatic play, 452–455; listening in, 142–145; oral reading in, 269–270; speaking in, 142–165; story writing, 321
Printing, preschool child, 110. *See also* Manuscript writing
Problem solving, 151; through dramatic play, 456–457
Pronouns, 37; child's use of, 81, 86
Pronunciation, 155; dialectical, 376; differences in, 32; difficulty with, 108; spelling and, 388–390
Provincialisms, 154
Psycholinguists, 71
Publicity, writing, 328
Puerto Rican students, 225; dialect, 212; teaching English to, 470–472
Punctuation, 305, 360, 381–382; in letter writing, 333
Punishment, effect of, 54–55
Puppets, 459

Quantitative concept, learning, 112
Quarreling, 28
Questioning, 33
Questions: asking/answering, 195–196; as attention getters, 30

Radio, 175; effect of, 93; listening to, 197–198
Reading, 146; achievement, 293–294; acuteness in, 284–286; advanced stages, 291–292; age and, 255, 258–259, 295; background for, 257–258; beginning, teaching of, 260; breadth in, 289–291; culturally disadvantaged and, 275; development of, 189; eclectic method, 274–275; for enjoyment, 289; follow-up program, 275–276; grouping for, 170–271; guidance through, 293; importance of, 284; independent, 271; individual, 286–288, 438–439; individual differences, 270–271; language development and, 257–258; language experience approach, 266–268; learning by reading, 271–274; learning, start of, 119; linguistic approach, 263; maturity through, 435; phonics and, 262–263; poetry and, 430–431; primary grade methods, 293–294; process of, 256; speech and, 162; spelling and, 395–396; as taught in England, 276–278; teaching of, 255–279, 280–297; textbook, 271, 288–289; transition period, 283–284; vocal growth and, 285–286; word recognition and, 118, 268–269; written language and, 305. *See also* Oral reading
Reading ability, development of, 280–297; sharpening, 284–286
Reading developmental program, 282
Reading material: guidance in, 283, 286–288; selecting, 290
Reading problems, diagnosing, 294–295

Reading program: ideal, 272; individual, 286, 288
Reading readiness, 119, 260–262
Reading vocabulary, 169
Reality, and illusion, 36
Record keeping, 327, 337–338
Regional dialects, 376–377
Relationships: pupil-pupil, 147; teacher-pupil, 147
Repetition, in teaching infants, 76
Reporting, 151
Reports, 316; writing of, 338–340
Reproductive thought, 24
Responses, reaction to, 28
Rhyme, 317
Rhythm, in reading poetry, 432
Right-handedness, 218–219
Run-on sentences, 373

School: influence of, 62–63; responsibility for language, 9–10
School publications, 339
Science, and language development, 175, 181
Science program, language and, 186–187
Scientific thinking, 37
Second language, 223–225; in elementary grades, 464–473; in the home, 55–58
Secret languages, 41, 172
Security: and language spontaneity, 87; spontaneity and, 89
Security needs, 434
Self-awareness, 37
Self-centeredness, 26–27
Self-confidence, 38
Self-consciousness, 38
Semanticist, 14
Semantics, 243–244
Sensory experience, 111–112
Sentence sense, 305
Sentence structure, 169, 360; preschool, 87–90
Sentences: complete, 86; dramatizing words, 374; expanding, 373–374; growth, in using, 87–88; nonsentences, 372; run-on, 373; subject of, 374; three- and four-word, 107; transforming, 375; types of, 371–372
Sentiment, developing, 40
Sex differences, 53
Shadow plays, 459–460
Sharing period, 149
Siblings, language of, 52–53
Silence, as protective medium, 105–106
Singing tones, 75
Skills: social, 197; speaking/listening, 189–190
Slang, 4, 41, 62, 172–174, 383
Slow learner, motivation for, 216
Slow starter, 209–210
Social activities, preschool, 111
Social awareness, 41
Social behavior, 31
Social contacts, 94
Social development, 109, 115; preschool, 93–96; in nursery school, 134
Social forms, 159
Social interaction, 28, 31; preschool, 104
Social notes, 327
Social problems: interest in, 175; linguistically gifted, 207
Social reaction, stimulating, 106
Social sense, 37
Social skills, 197
Social studies: interrelationships, 180–181; language and, 180–181; language skills and, 183–186
Social understanding, 197
Socialized speech, 27–28
Socioeconomic status, 53–54
Sociometric studies, use of, 480
Solitary play, 109, 115
Sound, reactions to, 129
Sound imitation, 77
Sound patterns: imitating and absorbing, 156–157; recognizing, 129
Sound structure, 10
Sound substitution, 86
Space, concept of, developing, 35–36
Spanish-speaking child, 224–225; dialect, 212; teaching English to, 470–472
Speaking, 146; primary school, 142–165
Speaking skills, development of, 189–199
Speaking vocabulary, 231, 233–234
Speech: clarity in, 153; defective, 216–220; dramatic play and, 457; emotional tones, 60; form of behavior, 72; functions of, 18–19;

Speech *(cont.)*
ideal, 203–204; infant, 73–74, 75; infantile forms, 217; main function, 170; personality and, 364; reading and, 162
Speech defects: causes of, 218; eye and hand dominance, 218; intelligence level and, 219; personality problems and, 219, 220
Speech development: handicaps to, 96–97; personality and, 97–98
Speech deviations, 206
Speech improvement, universality of, 204–205
Speech mechanism, 72–74; defective, 97
Speech patterns, extending, 81
Speech problems, 204
Speech retardation, 210
Spelling, 360, 386–417; *ā* sounds, 388; accuracy in, 392; articulation and, 394–395; attitude, 404–406; basic vocabulary, 399–403; beginning steps, 404; consistency in, 391; content area, 398–399; development, 409–410; dictionary, use of, 410–411; difficulties in, 388–390, 410–411; enunciation and, 394–395; errors in, 408; evaluation in, 411–414; grouping in, 408–409, 410; *-ing*, 391; learning, method in, 392; motivation, 404–406; objectives in, 392; oral language and, 394; perception in, 394; phoneme syllable, 391; phonics and, 408–409; preparation for, 393–394; preschool child, 111; pronunciation and, 388–390; purpose of, 387, 414; reading and, 395–396; regularity in, 409; role of, in school program, 394–399; self-help, 397; silent *g* and *k*, 391; steps in, 406–407; teaching methods, 403–408; time allotment, 406; writing and, 396–398
Spelling achievement, 412
Spelling books, 400–401
Spelling games, 172
Spelling lists, 402
Spelling pattern, 391
Spelling program, 403
Spelling rules, 407–408
Specialized vocabularies, 387
Spoken language. *See* Oral language
Spontaneity, security and, 87
Standards, changing, 478
Status symbols, 2
Stories, 117, 418–445; dramatizing, 453; interest in, 108, 109; original, making up, 118; preschool, 110
Story content, interest in, 174
Story hours, 65
Story telling, 171, 420–422
Story writing, 316
Stress, and meaning, 12
Stuttering, 97
Summer camps, 461
Swearing, 173
Symbol patterns, 3
Symbol-sound correspondence, 36, 408–409
Symbols, and language, 2–4
Syntax, 82; acquisition of, 80–81; mastering, 79; principles of, 82

Talkativeness, growth index, 87
Talking, 149; age for, 51; need for, 105
Teacher: adaptation by, 203; as example-setter, 106–107; influence of, 60–61; parent conferences, 489; personal speech habits, 205; pupil relationships, 137, 314; reading responsibility, 29; written language and, 304–307
Teaching, direct/indirect, 20–21
Telegraphic speech, 80
Telephone, using, 150
Television, 175; effect of, 93; influence of, 66; listening and, 130, 139–140, 197–198
Tempo, in reading poetry, 432
Textbooks: illustrating, 182; learning to read, 271; reading of, 288–289
Thinking, 23–25, 36–37; aloud, 24
Thornton, Evelyn C., 296
Thought: creative/reproductive, 24; language of, 23–25; preschool, 94
Thought process, 94
Time, concept of, developing, 35–36
Time sense, 35
Time words, 35
Twins, language of, 52–53

Unauthorized language, 62, 172–177
Understanding, and experience, 22
Understanding vocabulary, 231–233

Upward Bound Program, 212
Usage: correcting, 365–366; grammatical, defined, 358–359. *See also* Grammatical usage

Verb phrases, 375
Verbal communication, 3
Verbal guidance, 104–105
Verbalism, 182
Verbs, 374
Verse speaking, 432
Vicarious experiences, 22–23, 62–63, 419
Vision, poor, 221
Visual signs, 3
Vocabulary, 229–253; basic spelling, 399–403; development of, 246–250; dramatic words, 374; growth in, 236; infant's, 76; jargon and, 77; learning, 27; marginal, 232; overlapping, 402–403; potential, 232, 371; preschool, 84–86, 229, 237–239; reading, 169; size of, and age levels, 235–237; socioeconomic status and, 54; specialized, 387; types of, 231–235; word selection, 382–383; writing, 400
Vocabulary building, emphasis on, 246
Vocabulary development, 248–250; advanced, 207; problems in, 285
Vocabulary growth: in preadolescence, 62; reading and, 285–286
Vocabulary studies, 239–241
Vocal apparatus, 72–74; quality and pitch, 106–107
Vowel sounds, 268–269

Wider Horizons Programs, 212
Withdrawal, 38
Word choice, 157, 360
Word games, 172
Word lists, 241–243
Word meanings, 172; problems of, 243
Word patterns, and spelling patterns, 391
Word recognition: reading and, 118; preschool, 111
Word recognition skills, 268–269
Word repetition, in teaching infants, 76
Word selection, 382–383; by grade, 401–402
Words: awareness of, 268; coining, 3, 12, 245; confusion in, 22; connotations of, 31; defining, 244; frequency of use, 402–403; grade placement of, 401–403; meaning and, 26; meaning bearing, 129; origins of, 7; play with, 383; relative meanings, 112; sounding, difficulty in, 108; spelling of, learning, 406–407
Writing, 146, 184; creative/practical, 351; developing, 301; early success in, 329; experience in, 350–352; felt pens, use of, 308; growth in, 350–352; interest in, 350–352; kindergarten, 302; language approach, 305; normal development, 302; nursery school, 301; oral language and, 162; orderly sequence, 299; practical/personal, 300; spelling and, 396–398
Writing assignment, "sick sense of failure," 329
Writing standards, 329–330
Writing vocabulary, 231, 234–235
Written expression: goals, intermediate school, 352–353; intermediate grades, 324–355; primary grades, 321–322
Written language, 299–323; awareness of, 107; development of, 189; evaluation, 340–341, 342, 352; experience in, 350–352; first experiences in, 301–302; growth in, 302–304, 350–352; help in, 303, 308–311; independence through, 303; independent, 308–311, 312–313; interest in, 350–352; intermediate grade, ability range, 328–329; oral language and, 63–64, 169; practical forms of, 336–340; reading and, 305; realistic standards, 329–330; situations calling for, 327–328

1 2 3 4 5 6 7 8 9 0